Charlotte M. Yonge

Gavin Budge

Charlotte M Yonge

Religion, Feminism and
Realism in the Victorian Novel

PETER LANG

Oxford · Bern · Berlin · Bruxelles · Frankfurt am Main · New York · Wien

Bibliographic information published by Die Deutsche Bibliothek
Die Deutsche Bibliothek lists this publication in the Deutsche
Nationalbibliografie; detailed bibliographic data is available on
the Internet at ‹http://dnb.ddb.de›.

British Library and Library of Congress Cataloguing-in-Publication Data:
A catalogue record for this book is available from The British Library,
Great Britain, and from The Library of Congress, USA

Cover Image: Charlotte M Yonge, aged about 30. Picture reproduced
with permission from a copy in the possession of Barbara Dennis.

Cover Design: Tracey Brockwell, Peter Lang Ltd

ISBN 978-3-03911-339-2

© Peter Lang AG, International Academic Publishers, Bern 2007
Hochfeldstrasse 32, Postfach 746, CH-3000 Bern 9, Switzerland
info@peterlang.com, www.peterlang.com, www.peterlang.net

Printed in Germany

To my parents, with loving thanks for their support over the years.

Contents

Preface: Yonge and the Realist Canon

Charlotte M. Yonge was one of the best-selling woman writers of the Victorian period, with which her adult life almost exactly corresponded, since she was born in 1823 and died in 1901. Born into a well-off gentry family, and under no financial pressure to write, she nevertheless published some 180 books (for which no comprehensive bibliography has yet been established), as well as single-handedly editing a periodical, the *Monthly Packet*, for forty years. Yonge's extraordinary productiveness reflected her single-minded devotion to writing; she never married, and was reluctant to travel, a lifestyle which is partly explained by the disabling shyness which many of her contemporaries noted in her. In the context of current critical approaches, the fact that her interest in men appears to have been limited to those, who, like John Keble, represented father figures to her, and that she liked to surround herself with a circle of young unmarried women, may seem of more significance than it did to her Victorian contemporaries. Many of Yonge's publications reflect her commitment to the development of popular education through her work as a Sunday School teacher, and in the course of her sixty-year writing career, changes in the nineteenth-century market for fiction led to her novels, like those of Walter Scott, being increasingly categorized as children's literature. Yonge herself, however, described her target audience as 'young ladies', by which she meant unmarried middle-class women between fifteen and twenty-five, and since this corresponded with the demographic aimed at by any mid-Victorian novelist, between the 1850s and the 1870s her novels belonged to the mainstream of development of the Victorian novel and were read with enthusiasm by such eminent Victorians as Tennyson and Kingsley. The present study confines itself to the domestic fiction Yonge produced during this period.

From any short biographical outline, such as the one above, the reader unfamiliar with Yonge's writing might well be tempted to assume that her novels are similar to Ellen Wood's *East Lynne*, the best-selling mid-Victorian weepie whose relentless harping on the remorse of the fallen woman who is its central character, and repetitive assertion of the 'nobility' of her wronged husband, makes it well-nigh irresistible for a modern critic to read the novel 'against the grain' as a subconscious rebellion against a heavy patriarchal Victorian morality. Yonge's novels often have been interpreted in this way, though not always by critics who are actually familiar with her work. Q.D. Leavis, for example, in a scathing review of a 1940s biography of Yonge, describes her as 'a day-dreamer with a writing itch that compensated her for a peculiarly starved life',[1] but the way this characterization repeats the terms of Leavis's earlier study *Fiction and the Reading Public*, which had traced the stultifying effects of the 'substitute living' offered by mass-market fiction back to sensation fiction of the type represented by *East Lynne*, makes it doubtful whether Leavis had bothered to acquire first-hand knowledge of Yonge's work. Similar dismissals of Yonge are to be found in a number of later twentieth-century feminist critics, though often in terms which, as Alethea Hayter comments, show a limited acquaintance with their subject.[2]

If there were indeed no more to Yonge's fiction than Q.D. Leavis's comments imply, the purpose of this full-length critical study of her domestic novels could seem questionable. However, the fact that in *Fiction and the Reading Public* Q.D. Leavis also claims that Charlotte Brontë 'was not master enough of herself to submit her day-dreaming to the discipline of structural organisation',[3] an opinion which very few critics would now endorse, might suggest the need for a reassessment of Yonge's novels parallel to the one which Brontë's work has undergone over the past twenty-five years. It is fair to say, too, that Yonge would have been among the first to condemn the kind of self-indulgent emotionalism represented by *East Lynne*, and that the

---

1   Q.D. Leavis, 'Charlotte Yonge and Christian Discrimination,' *Scrutiny* 12 (1944): 152–3.

2   Alethea Hayter, *Charlotte Yonge* (Plymouth: Northcote House, 1996), 56.

3   Leavis, *Fiction and the Reading Public* (London: Chatto and Windus, 1932), 237.

popularity of her novels is linked to the later Victorian rise of a critique of mass culture, as articulated by Oxford-affiliated writers such as Ruskin and Matthew Arnold, rather than reflecting the newly-literate mass audience to which Ellen Wood appealed.

To appreciate and locate the difference between Yonge and a novelist such as Ellen Wood, it is necessary to understand the cultural implications of Yonge's extremely close relations with Tractarianism, also known as the Oxford Movement (and, later in the century, as Anglo-Catholicism). Yonge's position as a literary protégée of John Keble placed her in the vanguard of Tractarianism, and she remained closely involved with the movement throughout her long literary career, partly owing to family connections such as the Coleridges. If not alert to nineteenth-century doctrinal differences, it is easy for a contemporary reader to confuse Yonge's religious themes, which reflect her novels' Tractarian and High Church settings, with the vague emotional uplift with which Ellen Wood's Evangelical religious rhetoric is chargeable. In assessing Yonge's relationship to mainstream Victorian culture, however, it is worth bearing in mind just what a minority position Tractarianism was when Yonge began writing, in the years following J.H. Newman's scandalous conversion to Roman Catholicism, a period when Tractarian innovations such as surplices and the lighting of candles were regularly followed by prosecutions and mob violence.

Yonge's affiliation to Tractarianism makes her perspective on popular protestant Victorianism that of an outsider, in a way that enables the religious elements of her fiction to take on a critical relationship to Victorian culture which is particularly significant, as this study shows, for her portrayal of the role of women. This critical relationship to the dominant culture extended among the Tractarians to the practice of psychological self-scrutiny which accompanied their extremely controversial revival of the religious institution of confession; in modern terms, one might say that Tractarians such as Yonge engaged in consciousness-raising whose effect was to make them question Victorian social assumptions. Critical readings of Yonge which assume that her work, like *East Lynne*, can safely be read 'against the grain' neglect the critical and psychologically self-aware perspective on Victorian culture for which Yonge is indebted to

Tractarianism. Given the close relationship between popular Evangel-icalism and the publishing industry at the beginning of Yonge's career, it is no exaggeration to say that Yonge's Tractarianism commits her to a critique of the effects of the mass culture which a novel like *East Lynne* represents. In her later novels, when Tractarianism, from being the preserve of an embattled minority, has itself become a mass movement, Yonge's novelistic engagement in this kind of critical perspective is shown by her portrayal of the superficiality which the dissemination even of the beliefs and practices of which she in theory approved had the potential to create.

A formal consequence of this critical perspective to which I draw attention is the way in which Yonge's fiction solicits an active, or 'strong', mode of reading to a far greater degree than most Victorian novels. Explicit narratorial comment, of the kind exemplified by the moralizing authorial interventions of *East Lynne*, is almost entirely absent from Yonge's writing, which relies instead on her striking ability to create lifelike dialogue and on the use of resonant symbolic detail to convey the psychological development of her characters. Although on a first reading this impersonal style of narration often feels disorientating, particularly for a reader less familiar with Yonge's cultural reference points than her original Victorian reader-ship would have been, one of the impressive features of Yonge's writing is her ability silently to coordinate masses of apparently unrelated details so that wider significance becomes apparent in them retrospectively, making her fiction peculiarly rewarding to reread.

The present study seeks to challenge the received critical view of Yonge's domestic novels by placing her fiction in the context of Tractarian aesthetics. Yonge's first encounter with the Tractarian movement during the 1830s, in the form of John Keble, vicar of the parish of Hursley which neighboured her home in Otterbourne, was undoubtedly the formative event of her life. Keble, whose celebrated *Lectures on Poetry* made him one of the foremost literary critics of the day, provided the teenage Yonge not only with religious guidance but with a literary education, and Yonge in turn assumed the role of the child he had never had. Through Keble, Yonge was in touch with some of the leading intellectuals of the mid-Victorian period, men such as J.H. Newman, W.G. Ward and E.B. Pusey, contacts which also helped shape her publishing career. Yonge characterized her own career as a writer as that of a publicist for Tractarian ideas.

Victorian religion is still often stereotyped in present-day literary critical argument as repressive and misogynistic. Following Christine L. Krueger, however, who explores the empowering role played by Evangelical religious discourse in the career of woman novelists such as Gaskell and Eliot,[4] this book argues that Tractarian ideas enabled Yonge to formulate a feminist position which, as expressed in her fiction, questioned or subverted many aspects of Victorian gender ideology. In this respect, her domestic novels represent a continuation of feminist tendencies which are present in the Tractarian movement itself, with its highly controversial establishment of Anglican sisterhoods, and the related promotion of nursing as a career for single middle-class women. One aspect of Yonge's Tractarian subversion of gender ideology to which I draw attention is the surprisingly prominent role which themes of sexual inversion play in her novels.

Although Yonge has been repeatedly characterized as an 'anti-feminist' writer by modern critics, on the basis of her scepticism about whether women should be given the vote, this study suggests that a more nuanced interpretative approach is required. Many Victorians, after all, had reservations about the extension of the franchise per se, and not just the extension of the franchise to women, so that while Yonge's doubts about the benefits of the vote for women are evidence of political conservatism, it is a conservatism that, as in the case of other late nineteenth-century women writers, is not incompatible with feminism. As with other Tractarians such as Keble and Newman, Yonge's political position is perhaps best characterized as one of Carlylean 'Tory Radicalism'.

Making constant reference to Yonge's writing, this study pursues the connection between feminism and Victorian religious discourse beyond the historical and sociological context explored by Christine Krueger into the realm of Tractarian aesthetics, an area which was the

---

4   Christine L. Krueger, *The Reader's Repentance: Women Preachers, Women Writers and Nineteenth-Century Social Discourse* (Chicago: University of Chicago Press, 1992).

subject of pioneering studies by Sussman and Landow in the 1970s,[5] but has been largely neglected in recent criticism. I present this argument over three main sections. Section One, 'Realism, Domestic Ideology and the Tractarian Pyschology of Religion' sets out the theoretical and methodological basis of my study through its extension of existing critical approaches to Tractarian aesthetics. My premise is that the Tractarian reinvigoration of a typological approach to literary interpretation, as practised by Keble and his pupil Isaac Williams, is indebted to the associationist approach to aesthetics which dominated early nineteenth-century British discussion of the subject. The appeal to fundamental intellectual intuitions, not themselves the product of association, on which this form of associationism was based, is reflected in Keble's identification, in the *Lectures on Poetry*, of fundamental theological intuitions underlying the work of pagan poets such as Aeschylus and Lucretius which make possible a Christian and providentialist form of reading which transcends their conscious intentions.

The extension of typological modes of interpretation beyond the Biblical text to the natural world, which Paul Korshin notes as distinctive in the early nineteenth-century revival of typology[6] and which constitutes a defining feature of Tractarian aesthetics, can thus be seen as a providentialist version of associationism, in which all earthly objects ultimately lead to the contemplation of God for the religiously trained mind – a perspective which had been, of course, integral to Hartley's original formulation of an associationist position. Aesthetic and literary critical evaluation consists for Keble and other Tractarians in the identification of *ethos,* or those habitual associative complexes which constitute 'character' in that they are the subject of moral judgement. In Chapter One, I suggest that this Tractarian emphasis on a providentially guaranteed mode of reading, associatively

5   Herbert Sussman, *Fact Into Fiction: Typology in Carlyle, Ruskin, and the Pre-Raphaelite Brotherhood* (Columbus: Ohio State University Press, 1979); George P. Landow, *Victorian Types, Victorian Shadows: Biblical Typology in Victorian Literature, Art and Thought* (London: Routledge and Kegan Paul, 1980).

6   Paul Korshin, *Typologies in England, 1650–1820* (Princeton: Princeton University Press, 1982).

reconstructing the traces of others' characters in writing and, in so doing, forming associatively the reader's own character in a religious direction, allows Tractarian aesthetics to be mapped onto the Victorian realist novel, in a way that is exemplified by Yonge's domestic fiction.

A similar associationist emphasis on the formation of character is shared by leading texts of Victorian domestic ideology, in which 'Woman's mission' is made to consist in the exercise of private 'influence' over other's characters which can indirectly bring about the reform of society. In Chapter Two, I argue that Yonge's fiction represents a synthesis of these Victorian ideas about the role of women with the Tractarian typological understanding of *ethos*, articulating a 'cultural feminism' in which women's achievement of control over themselves is understood as the fulfilment of a providential design for society at large. Within the terms of Yonge's own novelistic aesthetic of the female *bildungsroman*, then, religious and feminist perspectives are integral to her domestic realism, rather than being necessarily in conflict with it, as a number of critics have claimed. The popularity of Yonge's novels throughout the nineteenth century strongly suggests that her religiously inflected understanding of realism was shared by the Victorian public, something which I argue shows the need for a more nuanced critical distinction between realist and naturalist traditions in the nineteenth-century novel.

The religious and providential dimension to Yonge's realism means that character development in her novels is synonymous with religious growth – and also, in the case of her heroines, with a feminist liberation from merely social conventions. In Chapter Three, I identify a model for Yonge's religious realism in J.H. Newman's novel of conversion, *Loss and Gain*, and examine the relationship between the model of character development set out (not altogether successfully) in the novel and the role played by a psychologization of religious belief in his thought more generally.

Newman's appeal to development as the test of authentic religious doctrine invokes typology not only in a religious sense, but also in a scientific or medical sense, as a psychological typology of character in which heretical beliefs are understood as expressions of unhealthy or morbid psychology, and it is this psychological perspective which allows him to identify the heresies of the early Church with the religious positions of his own day, as manifestations of the same underlying mindset. In Chapter Three I suggest that Newman's reaction against the one-dimensional account of human behaviour offered by rationalism, and emphasis on the unconscious dimension of moral life, can be seen as sources for the preoccupation with the unconscious that pervades Yonge's fiction, an interest which extends to questions about her characters' sexual orientation.

Section Two, 'Yonge and the Theory of Fiction: a reading of *The Heir of Redclyffe*', applies this account of a Tractarian mode of realism that is at once typological and character-orientated to an extended reading of Yonge's best-known novel. In Chapter Four, I show that the theme of evidence which informs much of the novel's plot allows a typological interpretation of the clash between the central male characters in which they stand for the conflict between faith and rationalism which is described in Newman's *University Sermons*. At the same time, however, the relationship between typology and the associative development of character in Tractarian aesthetics enables Yonge to unfold typological meaning in tandem with psychological specificity of character in a way which contradicts the widely held modern critical assumption (articulated most influentially by George Levine's *The Realistic Imagination*) that a religious or transcendent significance must necessarily be in conflict with the demands of realism. In Chapter Five, I consider feminist criticisms of one of the central female characters of *The Heir of Redclyffe* in order to show that Yonge's portrayal of this character's moral failure corresponds to a realist and feminist ethic of character development implicit in her novels, rather than representing the inorganic and repressive reassertion of patriarchal standards which critics have claimed. I argue that Yonge's Tractarian conception of development as a revelation of unconsciously held moral intuitions ultimately reflects the intuitionist philosophical position of the Scottish Common Sense philosophers. Modern critical characterizations of nineteenth-century realism, on the other hand, ultimately derive from the assertion of the inductive basis of all knowledge by the intuitionists' great opponent J.S. Mill in *A System of Logic*, a book forming the subject of a lengthy critique by

Newman's disciple W.G. Ward with which Yonge can safely be assumed to have been familiar.

Section Three, 'Tractarianism, Feminism and the Nervous Female Body in Yonge's Domestic Fiction' develops further the case for regarding Yonge's work in terms of a conservative 'cultural feminism'. In Chapter Six, I argue that Yonge's acceptance of Victorian domestic ideology represents a strategic form of feminism, and that her Tractarian emphasis on home as the exemplary site of moral struggle allows her to represent the home as a Utopian space from which the corrupt public sphere can be reformed. As explored in this chapter, such a transvaluation of the domestic is fundamental to Yonge's best-selling novel *The Daisy-Chain*. Chapter Seven identifies affinities between Yonge's depiction of women and the Victorian discourse of mesmerism. In this context, the prominence of the theme of female empowerment through self-control in Yonge's writings reflects a model in which female nervous irritability can be channelled through self-discipline into mesmeric 'influence', a model of female character development which is apparent in many of Yonge's novels.

Yonge's position outside the literary canon inevitably means that my attempt to elaborate a context for the critical reading of her work has wider implications for study of the Victorian novel generally, since the assertion that her work is worth reading must hold up to question some of the criteria by which her novels have been excluded from critical consideration. A recurrent theme of my study is the need to rethink prevailing definitions of Victorian novelistic realism, which, as currently formulated, simply exclude religious (or otherwise transcendental) themes from the terrain of the 'realist novel' altogether. This is not just an issue which affects novelists like Yonge, whose relationship to an explicit set of doctrinal commitments is fairly clear, but, as this study shows, also applies to Charlotte Brontë and even to the work of George Eliot herself, whose tendency to be used 'as a touchstone against which other women writers would be compared and found wanting'[7] has, as Nicola Thompson has argued, done much to exclude other Victorian women novelists from the literary canon.

---

7   Nicola Diane Thompson, 'Responding to the Woman Questions: Rereading Noncanonical Victorian Women Novelists', in Nicola Diane Thompson (ed.),

If, as Christine Krueger has argued,[8] religious discourse in the nineteenth century plays an important role in articulating the position of the woman writer, then a definition of realism which excludes religion must at a stroke exclude most women novelists from the literary canon. Given the important role which irrationalist discourses such as mesmerism played within Victorian culture, and the extent to which, as my study shows, such ideas are integrated within the framework of novels which are usually held up as exemplary of 'realism', then critical definitions of realism which are incapable of accommodating a supernatural dimension begin to look seriously deficient. This is not a new problem in Victorian criticism, as exemplified by such studies such as Eigner's *The Metaphysical Novel in England and America* (1978) and Brooks's *Signs for the Times: Symbolic Realism in the Mid-Victorian World* (1984).

Since my overall aim in this study has been to establish a basis for critical discussion of Yonge's novels, I have avoided any over-elaborated theoretical analysis of the problems of defining literary realism per se. Nevertheless, the nineteenth-century intellectual perspective in which I have situated Yonge's work suggests a number of related avenues by which the theoretical and methodological dilemma posed by nineteenth-century realism might be resolved. At the simplest level, this approach might be summed up by suggesting that criticism of the Victorian novel should take its Romantic, and specifically Wordsworthian, heritage much more seriously. In my account of Yonge's novels, such a Wordsworthian dimension is represented not only by Keble's providentialist reading of Wordsworthian poetics, but also by the use I make of John Foster's account of character development, and by the Wordsworthian dimension that is implicit in the Victorian domestic ideology of such texts as Sarah Ellis's *The Women of England*.

Yonge's own family connections with the Lake poets make in her case the connection between Romantic poetics and realist fiction particularly clear. Yonge's close relationship with Keble can convin-

Victorian Women Writers and the Woman Question (Cambridge: Cambridge University Press, 1999), 8.

8   Krueger, *Reader's Repentance, passim.*

cingly be seen in terms of the pattern of the female literary protégée examined in relation to a preceding generation of women writers by Dennis Low in his recent study, *The Literary Protégées of the Lake Poets*. Low's suggestive remarks about the way in which the multiple allegorical significances embodied in Sara Coleridge's fairytale *Phantasmion* reflect her father's hostility to the kind of one-dimensional allegorizing to be found in Maria Edgeworth[9] resonate with my discussion of Yonge's early realist novel *Abbeychurch*, and are particularly significant in the light of Fouqué's influence on Yonge's major novel, *The Heir of Redclyffe*.

My study suggests that important Victorian religious thinkers such as Keble and Newman articulated what can be described as an existentialist position in terms of the associationist psychology which made such an important contribution to Wordsworth's poetics. This is significant for critical discussion of what constitutes literary realism in the Victorian novel because it suggests that what counts as 'real' might be associatively constructed rather an inevitable experiential given, and so at least partly a *product* of a character's moral choices, an issue I discuss in relation to the treatment of 'unreality' in Yonge's fiction. In some ways, this emphasis on the humanly constructed nature of the real aligns Yonge's novels with the kind of post-structuralist critique of novelistic realism associated with the work of Roland Barthes, and I suggest that, like the demystificatory form of fiction which Barthes envisages, there is a ludic quality to Yonge's writing which encourages the reader to reflect on the very processes by which they are making sense of her fictional world.

At the same time, however, the element of deconstructive play in Yonge's work is circumscribed by what she would have regarded as the enabling constraints of human experience. For Keble, the meaningfulness of the associative play of poetry ultimately derives either from revelation, or from self-evident truths of human consciousness, in a way that reflects the Scottish Common Sense philosophers' intuitionist emphasis on self-evident principles of Common Sense, so that typological forms of significance for Keble are in the last analysis

9   Dennis Low, *The Literary Protégées of the Lake Poets* (Aldershot: Ashgate, 2006), 136–41.

based on a divine ground of reality. That the same is true for Yonge is shown by the emphasis in her novels on the Wordsworthian theme of mental and bodily health which, in the context of the natural theology tradition which was still influential on mid nineteenth-century medical thought, implied a condition of attunement between the individual and the world in which the psycho-physical corresponded typologically to spiritual reality. For Yonge, like Blake in *The Marriage of Heaven and Hell*, 'If the doors of perception were cleansed everything would appear to man as it is: Infinite', and it is the interplay between this redeemed mode of perception and the world of the everyday which her fiction is designed to portray.

Acknowledgements

I would like to express my gratitude to Phil Tew, Steve Barfield, Julia Courtney and Fiona Robertson for commenting on draft chapters, to the Charlotte M. Yonge Fellowship for their friendly interest in my work, and to Roberta Staples of Lady Margaret Hall library and David Latané for facilitating access to issues of the *Monthly Packet*. The early stages of my work on Yonge were greatly helped by Sandra Laythorpe's series of etexts of Yonge's novels, available from Project Gutenberg, and Ellen Jordan's generosity in making the texts of unpublished Yonge letters available to me played a significant role in shaping some of my arguments. I would also like to thank Barbara Dennis for permission to use the photograph of Yonge at thirty which appears on the cover, and for the edition of *The Heir of Redclyffe* in Oxford World's Classics which provided the initial inspiration for this project.

This book was written during a period of research leave funded by the School of English, University of Central England in Birmingham, to which I express my thanks. Chapter Four, and parts of Chapter Five, are based on material originally published as 'Realism and Typology in Charlotte M. Yonge's *The Heir of Redclyffe*' in *Victorian Literature and Culture* 31, no.1 (2003), 193–223, and I would like to thank the editors for permission to reproduce this material here. The love and support of my wife Sue were crucial in enabling me to concentrate uninterruptedly during this book's creation, and no words can express the debt I owe her.

Section One
Realism, Domestic Ideology and the Tractarian Psychology of Religion

Some of the best and most powerful existing critical writing on Yonge argues for a characterization of her as a novelist whose conscious intentions were essentially 'dogmatic' in a way that conflicts with the complexity of moral response inherent in the form of the realist novel, so that her writing either retreats from the demands of realism into the ideological simplicities of romance, or, on a more sympathetic reading, stages a doomed struggle with a typically Victorian morality which it is finally unable to overcome. Such approaches to Yonge assume the essential incoherence of her novelistic mode on the basis of widely accepted, but essentially *a priori* claims about the nature of realism itself. The present study, on the other hand, argues that Yonge was a considerably more self-conscious writer than these approaches assume, and that there is an intellectual and artistic coherence to her approach to realist fiction. This argument involves some analysis of the claims about the nature of novelistic realism invoked by critical characterizations of Yonge as either not essentially a realist novelist at all, or as a realist novelist in spite of herself, and identification of an alternative model for Victorian realist fiction based on nineteenth-century intellectual sources which would have been familiar points of reference in Yonge's Tractarian milieu.

In the following section, I concentrate on setting out the theoretical and methodological background for this alternative perspective on Victorian realism. Yonge, and other writers of what Edwin Eigner has called 'the metaphysical novel',[1] I argue, do not understand realism in the representationalist terms which have dominated twentieth-

---

1   Edwin M. Eigner, *The Metaphysical Novel in England and America: Dickens, Bulwer, Hawthorne, Melville* (Berkeley and Los Angeles: University of California Press, 1978).

century critical discussion of the topic, but conceive of novels in the same terms that the Romantics did of poetry, as, in Shelley's words, 'generals to the bewildered armies of [men's] thoughts'.[2] In other words, for these novelists the realist novel *constitutes* the real from the chaotic mass of the reader's associations, rather than simply *reflecting* a reality which is supposed to lie outside itself. Within the novel too, characters are conceived of as responsible for the reality they inhabit, the associative coherence of which has been shaped by their existential and moral choices, rather than simply reacting to a reality external to themselves. From this perspective, Victorian realism is much closer to what Marshall Brown, in his recent study *The Gothic Text*, has described as gothic fiction's preoccupation with 'the transcendental dimensions of experience'[3] than has usually been assumed. The situation of characters within the Victorian realist novel is also much closer than generally recognized to J.G. Ballard's description of the predicament faced by the postmodern novelist, in which 'the most prudent and effective method of dealing with the world around us is to assume that it is a complete fiction – conversely, the one small node of reality left to us is inside our own heads'.[4]

The Romanticism which I argue informs Yonge's conception of the realist novel, however, escapes postmodernism's nihilistic tendency to ungroundedness by being mediated through a providentialist interpretation of associationism which I trace in the *Lectures on Poetry* of her close friend John Keble, in John Foster's well-known account of autobiography in *Essays in a Series of Letters*, and in the role which the concept of development plays in J.H. Newman's early religious thought. I draw attention to the affinity between this providentialist form of associationism and a Victorian domestic ideology in which the role of woman is conceived as that of constituting the associative centre of the home, a role which I show incorporated the

2   Percy Bysshe Shelley, 'A Defence of Poetry', in Zachary Leader and Michael O'Neill (eds), *The Major Works* (Oxford: Oxford University Press, 2003), 688.

3   Marshall Brown, *The Gothic Text* (Stanford, CA: Stanford University Press, 2005), xiv.

4   J.G. Ballard, 'Introduction to the French Edition of *Crash*', in *Crash* (London: Paladin, 1990), 8.

potential for a critique of Victorian society. This conservative feminist critique blends in Yonge's novels with the Tractarian critique of the dominant Victorian social values of 'rationalism', as formulated by Newman, and I suggest that this critical perspective in Yonge's fiction manifests itself in her novelistic interest in exploring the unconscious, and in her 'queering' of Victorian gender ideology through exploration of the issue of sexual inversion in her fiction.

Chapter One
Reading Charlotte M. Yonge

The Problem of Reading Charlotte M. Yonge Critically

Charlotte M. Yonge is not only outside the established canon of mid-Victorian novelists, but, unlike comparable women writers such as Margaret Oliphant or Mrs Henry Wood, is a figure of whom few present-day readers have even heard. In her own day, however, she was a best-selling and prolific novelist, whose work was regularly compared with Austen and George Eliot. The contrast between Yonge's position in her own day as a highly successful and well-regarded author and her marginal position in modern critical under-standing of Victorian literature poses a challenge for any extended critical study of her work, that of explaining the eclipse of Yonge's critical reputation during the twentieth century. To put it brutally, if Yonge's novels are of a standard to which it is worth devoting much critical attention, then a convincing answer has to be found to the question of why her work isn't better known. As Talia Schaffer has put it, in a recently published article on the problem of interpreting Yonge's work, the literary critic is put into the position of 'fighting to read' Yonge's novels in any critical sense, because of the difficulty of relating them to the modern critical outlook, a point also made by Nicola Thompson when she asks in the preface to a recent essay collection, 'what [...] do you say about a conservative woman novelist like Charlotte Yonge once you've discovered her?'[1]

---

1   Talia Schaffer, 'The Mysterious Magnum Bonum: Fighting to Read Charlotte
     Yonge', Nineteenth-Century Literature 55, no.2 (2000): 244–75, Nicola Diane
     Thompson, 'Responding to the Woman Questions: Rereading Noncanonical
     Victorian Women Novelists', in Nicola Diane Thompson (ed.), *Victorian
     Women Writers and the Woman Question* (Cambridge: Cambridge University
     Press, 1999), 2,

The reputation of Yonge's work has suffered, of course, from the same kind of Modernist-inspired backlash as has affected other Victorian women writers such as Elizabeth Barrett Browning and Christina Rossetti, and it could be argued that a revival of critical interest in her writing is only a matter of time. The fact that such revivals have been most successful in the field of poetry, and have been led by feminist critics, however, indicates a particular theoretical difficulty that confronts the modern critical study of a novelist such as Yonge. Yonge's religious commitment to Tractarianism, the early phase of the Oxford Movement with which she was closely involved through her friendship with John Keble, means that her work as a novelist is resistant to interpretation in terms of a naturalist epistemology. Although there is little overt religious content in her fiction, and a sparing use of coincidence, with events rarely taking place without a natural explanation, her providential plots are orientated around the operation of grace in such a way that unless a supernatural dimension is taken into account it is hard to discern the structure of her novels. The role of religion in Yonge's novels, although unobtrusively presented, is not easily reducible to a vague concern for 'morality' in the way that is typical of most twentieth-century commentary on the Victorian novel: her early novel *The Castle Builders*, for example, combines convincing psychological portraiture of its two ineffectual heroines with a plot that insists on the supernatural influence of partaking in Holy Communion. In these respects, Yonge's fictional mode, though realist, anticipates the Symbolism that Joseph Baker identified in Shorthouse's *John Inglesant*.[2]

As Thomas Vargish has shown, a 'providential aesthetic' is widespread among mid-Victorian novelists.[3] Yonge's Tractarian affiliations, however, led her to a kind of providentialism which stressed a discontinuity between grace and nature modelled on typological interpretation of the Bible, whereas the providentialism of novelists such as Dickens tended to identify grace with nature through the

---

2   Joseph Ellis Baker, *The Novel and the Oxford Movement* (New York: Russell and Russell, 1965), 182–8.

3   See Thomas Vargish, *The Providential Aesthetic in Victorian Fiction* (Charlottesville: Virginia University Press, 1985), *passim*.

Romantic symbol. This intellectual orientation makes her work more resistant to recuperation in terms of philosophically naturalist assumptions which have dominated twentieth-century criticism of the novel. The opposition in Yonge's novels to naturalistic modes of explanation has been recognized in a 1965 article by J.B. Schneewind,[4] whose comment that Yonge's 'Intuitionist morality' results in the 'too easy harmony which makes her work so insipid'[5] suggests the interpretative difficulties this commitment creates for modern critics.

From Yonge's providentialist perspective, it is a matter of faith that life can never pose genuinely conflicting ethical demands,[6] and Schneewind obviously feels that this denial of any objective nature to moral ambiguity renders Yonge unable really to explore questions about moral choice. Schneewind fails to recognize, however, that Yonge's providentialism identifies moral questions with hermeneutic ones, in a way that is reflected in the pervasive, and sometimes disorientating, irony in her fiction. Yonge's characters are not shown as choosing between moral alternatives, because the fundamental moral choice they make lies in how they see the world in which action presents itself.

In order for there to be genuine moral alternatives, a perspective independent of morality would have to be available from which the alternatives could be viewed, and it is the very possibility of this kind of perspective which Yonge and her fellow Tractarians rejected under the name of Rationalism.[7] For Yonge, moral choice is not an epistemological question, but an ontological one, in a way that makes her Tractarian viewpoint akin to a present-day existentialist emphasis on authenticity as constitutive of morality. The difference in moral outlook between Yonge and critics such as Schneewind can be summed up in the words of W.H. Auden's sonnet sequence *The Quest*, whose

4   J.B. Schneewind, 'Moral Problems and Moral Philosophy in the Victorian Period', *Victorian Studies* 9, no. Supplement (September 1965): 40–1.
5   Schneewind, 'Moral Problems and Moral Philosophy', 41.
6   Cf. Anon., 'An Object in Life', *Monthly Packet* 15 (Series 1 1858): 38–9; 'An Object in Life', *Monthly Packet* 15: 490–5.
7   Cf. John Henry Newman, *Newman's University Sermons: Fifteen Sermons Preached Before the University of Oxford 1826–1843*, intro by D.M. MacKinnon and J.D. Holmes (London: SPCK, 1970), 67–72.

emphasis on the relationship between moral choice and personality perhaps reflects Auden's Anglo-Catholic background:

> In theory they were sound on Expectation,
> Had there been situations to be in;
> Unluckily they were their situation:
>
> One should not give a poisoner medicine,
> A conjuror fine apparatus, nor
> A rifle to a melancholic bore.[8]

Like Auden, the Tractarians emphasized that perception of the desirable course of action might be unconsciously determined by personality traits, so that morality might ultimately consist less in the actions taken than in the attempt to become a different kind of person.[9] In a similar way, Yonge's characters *are* their own situations, in that the mental worlds they inhabit are, for practical purposes, made up of the associations which they themselves have chosen. Although Yonge uses realist settings in her novels, their low-key, domestic nature, and the almost entire absence of an explicit narratorial voice, means that we see the nature of the decisions the characters make almost entirely through their own eyes. In the absence of a strongly emphasized perspective independent of the characters, the great theme of Yonge's novels is not one of conflict between equally valid moral choices, but one of self-delusion about the nature of the choices that are being made: a comic vision, rather than a tragic one.

The kind of intuitionist morality Schneewind finds problematic in Yonge's work is no less characteristic of writers such as Elizabeth

---

8   W.H. Auden, 'The Quest', in Edward Mendelson (ed.), *Collected Poems* (London: Faber, 1976), Sonnet 2, ll 8–14.

9   Hurrell Froude warns, for example, that the believer must be on their guard against the possibility that 'any peculiarity of opinion on religious subjects' into which they might fall simply reflects their own 'particular temper' and so constitutes a form of 'self-indulgence' (Richard Hurrell Froude, *Remains of the Late Reverend Richard Hurrell Froude MA, Fellow of Oriel College, Oxford*, 2 vols [London: Rivington, 1838], 2: 182–3). See also E.B. Pusey, *Parochial Sermons*, 3 vols (London: Walter Smith, 1883), 2: 132–42.

Barrett Browning and Christina Rossetti,[10] and arguably underlies the whole Victorian poetess tradition that has recently attracted critical attention.[11] The obviously non-naturalistic form of poetry, however, seems to have made it easier for contemporary critics to accept that literary value in this context might consist in the provocation of sophisticated interpretative strategies on the part of the reader rather than in any supposed degree of approximation to raw experience. Critics of the nineteenth-century novel, however, have been much less ready than critics of poetry to jettison some form of correspondence theory, in which the value of a novel is made to consist in its proximity to the real.

Although the rejection of any appeal to unmediated 'experience' which underlies poststructuralist critical theory[12] might have been expected to put paid to critical arguments which rank novels according to their lack of 'escapism' and closeness to a knowable 'real world', critics such as George Levine have influentially perpetuated these criteria by reinterpreting them in deconstructive terms. For Levine, a novel's integrity is ultimately to be measured by the extent to which its own structures break down in the attempt to present an unrepresentably complex 'reality', so that overly coherent novels can be classified as morally irresponsible 'romance',[13] an argument which conflates themes in George Eliot's writings with the tactics of literary modernism. Despite the deconstructive theoretical gestures, Levine's argument is in the final analysis an empiricist one in the way it appeals to some form of intelligible experience which precedes the intellectual categories by which we attempt to make sense of it; as is shown by Levine's early article on George Eliot and determinism, this

10   Barrett Browning cites the intuitionist philosophers of the Common Sense school Thomas Reid and Dugald Stewart in the footnotes to her early poem 'An Essay on Mind' (Elizabeth Barrett Browning, *Poetical Works*, Frederic G. Kenyon (ed.) [London: Smith, Elder and Co, 1897], 48–9).

11   Cf. Charles LaPorte, 'George Eliot, the Poetess as Prophet', *Victorian Literature and Culture* 31, no.1 (2003): 159–79.

12.   Catherine Belsey, *Critical Practice* (London and New York: Routledge, 1987), 42–7.

13   George Levine, *The Realistic Imagination: English Fiction from Frankenstein to Lady Chatterley* (Chicago: University of Chicago Press, 1981), 15.

philosophical naturalism is derived from J.S. Mill's arguments about induction.[14]

Thomas Vargish has identified similar naturalistic assumptions in the work of distinguished critics of the novel such as Barbara Hardy, who oppose 'dogmatic form' to realism by arguing that in the work of great novelists 'the world [...] breaks or enlarges the scheme and makes the novel more than a treatise or a fable'.[15] As Vargish points out, such criticism 'is not only historically unimaginative but metaphysically hubristic, assuming as it does that the nature of reality has somehow been proved to *be* morally neutral'.[16] Yonge's novels share in a general Tractarian insistence that there can be no neutral way of presenting reality,[17] a position which, as we shall see, is dramatized in *The Heir of Redclyffe*, where Philip's apparently neutral weighing of evidence against Guy is revealed to be motivated by unconscious 'malignity'.[18]

Yonge and the Distinction between Realism and Naturalism

Yonge's refusal of naturalism gives rise to a theoretical difficulty in locating her work within existing critical discussions of realism. The naturalistic philosophical position underlying the arguments of the majority of twentieth-century critics of the Victorian novel has tended to obscure the difference between realism and naturalism in the

14   Levine, 'Determinism and Responsibility in the Works of George Eliot', *Publications of the Modern Language Society of America* 77 (1962): 274–7.

15   Barbara Hardy, *The Appropriate Form: An Essay on the Novel* (London: The Athlone Press, 1964), 82, cited in Vargish, *Providential Aesthetic*, 13.

16   Vargish, *Providential Aesthetic*, 14.

17   Newman, *University Sermons*, 287–90; cf. Yonge's comment on the implications of 'secular education' in *Abbeychurch, or Self Control and Self Conceit* (London and Derby: Burns and Mozley, 1844), 174 (Ch.8)

18   Charlotte M. Yonge, *The Heir of Redclyffe*, Barbara Dennis (ed.) (Oxford: Oxford University Press, 1997), 265 (Ch.20)

nineteenth-century novel, and this has had the effect that novelists such as Yonge, who reject naturalism in the philosophical as well as the novelistic sense of that term, have not been regarded as belonging to the realist canon, despite their work exhibiting all the formal characteristics of realism.[19] From the intuitionist philosophical perspective subscribed to by Yonge along with many other Victorian novelists, however, experience is a product of the mind's interpretative activity, rather than being a raw material on which the mind subsequently works,[20] and this non-empiricist epistemology affects the relationship such writers envisage between the novel and its readership.

Novels in this view do not simply reflect what readers are supposed at some level already to 'know', but to some extent determine what their readers' experience of the world *is to be* through the educative effect exerted by readers' active engagement in the interpretation of the text. They are concerned, that is to say, with what in the language of Victorian criticism would have been called the presentation of the ideal, although the effectiveness and moral influence of this ideal are assumed to depend upon the extent to which it develops out of, and can be seen to be implicit within, everyday experience.[21]

---

19 A similar point could be made about the work of Edward Bulwer-Lytton, another extremely popular nineteenth-century novelist who received little critical attention in the twentieth century.

20 Thomas Reid, *Works*, 7th edn, William Hamilton (ed.) (Edinburgh: Maclachlan and Stewart, 1872), 127–30.

21 The account of the function of the 'impartial spectator' given by Adam Smith in *The Theory of Moral Sentiments*, a very popular and much reprinted work in the early nineteenth century, indicates how this reference of experience to the ideal could be conceptualized within a basically empiricist philosophical framework. For Smith, we arrive at an objective understanding of the moral implications of our actions through imagining the reaction of an impartial spectator (Adam Smith, *Theory of Moral Sentiments*, D.D. Raphael and A.L. Macfie (eds) [Oxford: Oxford University Press, 1976], 134) who, in the last analysis, turns out to be a purely ideal point of reference since, as Smith comments, our moral development consists in constantly refining our conception of this figure so it ceases to correspond with the reactions of any actual person (Smith, *Moral Sentiments*, 247–8). This kind of conception of the ideal underlies the argument

The ideal from this perspective, if truly such, constitutes the real, rather than being in opposition to it, so that the novel becomes 'realist' in a philosophical sense as well as a literary one. This conception of the novel's function underlies Yonge's concern over her moral responsibility as a novelist, who, as she remarked, would have to account to God for every word she had written.[22] Although there have been a number of studies of aspects of the Victorian novel which recognize this non-naturalistic dimension to Victorian literary realism,[23] no critic apart from Schneewind has drawn attention to its underpinnings in the intuitionist philosophy which dominated early and mid-Victorian intellectual life.

The philosophical sense of the term 'realism', according to which the real is that which transcends the world of phenomena rather than being naturalistically reducible to sensory experience, underlies the emphasis on the human potential for 'unreality' which forms a characteristic part of Tractarian discourse. T.S. Eliot's claim that 'humankind / Cannot bear very much reality'[24] is echoed, for example, in the first volume of the series of *Plain Sermons* published by contributors to *Tracts for the Times*, where the fact that 'we only talk and think about [...] [Christianity] as if it were true; we live and act as if it were false, or at least very doubtful'[25] is contrasted with 'the *reality* of religion' which is felt when there is 'danger of death approaching', and which those who have led 'profligate, irreligious lives [...] deaden [...] if possible with a cold heartless insensibility, and rejection of all

presented in Edward Bulwer-Lytton, 'On the Normal Clairvoyance of the Imagination', in *Miscellaneous Prose Works* (London: Bentley, 1868), 27–38.

22 Edward H. Cooper, 'Charlotte Mary Yonge', *Fortnightly Review* 69 (n.s. 1901): 854.

23 E.g. Edwin M. Eigner, *The Metaphysical Novel in England and America: Dickens, Bulwer, Hawthorne, Melville* (Berkeley and Los Angeles: University of California Press, 1978); Barry Qualls, *The Secular Pilgrims of Victorian Fiction: The Novel as Book of Life* (New York: Cambridge University Press, 1982); Vargish, *Providential Aesthetic*.

24 T.S. Eliot, 'Burnt Norton', in *Complete Poems and Plays*, in *Poems and Plays* (London: Faber, 1969), 1: ll 43–4.

25 Anon., *Plain Sermons, by Contributors to the 'Tracts for the Times'* (London: Rivington, 1845), 1: 47.

serious thought; or else with the intoxicating drams of enthusiasm',[26] displacement strategies which are equally 'unreal' from a Tractarian perspective.

Characters in Yonge's fiction frequently feel the unreality of the world around them after someone has died,[27] and Yonge also portrays the agonizing nature of religious doubt as consisting in the all-consuming sense of unreality it produces.[28] One of the most explicit discussions in Yonge's novels of the existential threat posed by unreality takes place in *The Daisy Chain* between the brilliant Oxford student Norman May, and his prospective fiancée:

> 'I suppose everything, our own happiness and all, are given to us to turn into praise,' she said.
>
> 'Yes –' echoed Norman; but as if his thoughts were not quite with hers, or rather in another part of the same subject; then recalling himself, 'Happy such as can do so.'
>
> 'If one only could –' said Meta.
>
> 'You can – don't say otherwise,' exclaimed Norman; 'I know, at least, that you and my father can.'
>
> 'Dr May does so, more than any one I know,' said Meta.
>
> 'Yes,' said Norman again; 'it is his secret of joy. To him, it is never, I am half sick of shadows.'
>
> 'To him they are not shadows, but foretastes,' said Meta. Silence again; and when she spoke, she said, 'I have always thought it must be such a happiness to have power of any kind that can be used in direct service, or actual doing good.'
>
> 'No,' said Norman. 'Whatever becomes a profession, becomes an unreality.'
>
> 'Surely not, in becoming a duty,' said Meta.
>
> 'Not for all,' he answered; 'but where the fabric erected by ourselves, in the sight of the world, is but an outer case, a shell of mere words, blown up for the occasion, strung together as mere language; then, self-convicted, we shrink within the husk, and feel our own worthlessness and hypocrisy.'
>
> 'As one feels in reproving the school children for behaving ill at church?' said Meta.

---

26 Anon., *Plain Sermons*, 1:127–8.
27 E.g. Yonge, *The Young Stepmother, or A Chronicle of Mistakes* (London: Macmillan, 1889), 356 (Ch.26).
28 Cf. Yonge, *The Clever Woman of the Family* (London: Macmillan, 1892), 267–8 (Ch.22).

'You never felt anything approaching to it!' said Norman. 'To know oneself to be such a deception, that everything else seems a delusion too!'

'I don't know whether that is metaphysical,' said Meta, 'but I am sure I don't understand it. One must know oneself to be worse than one knows any one else to be.'

'I could not wish you to understand,' said Norman; and yet he seemed impelled to go on; for, after a hesitating silence, he added, 'When the wanderer in the desert fears that the spring is but a mirage; or when all that is held dear is made hazy or distorted by some enchanter, what do you think are the feelings, Meta?'

'It must be dreadful,' she said, rather bewildered; 'but he may know it is a delusion, if he can but wake. Has he not always a spell, a charm? –'

'What is the spell?' eagerly said Norman, standing still.

'Believe –' said Meta, hardly knowing how she came to choose the words.

'I believe!' he repeated. 'What – when we go beyond the province of reason – human, a thing of sense after all! How often have I so answered. But Meta, when a man has been drawn, in self-sufficient security, to look into a magic mirror, and cannot detach his eyes from the confused, misty scene – where all that had his allegiance appears shattered, overthrown, like a broken image, or at least unable to endure examination, then –'

'Oh, Norman, is that the trial to any one here? I thought old Oxford was the great guardian nurse of truth! I am sure she cannot deal in magic mirrors or such frightful things. Do you know you are talking like a very horrible dream?'

'I believe I am in one,' said Norman.[29]

Yonge suggests that Norman's state of unreality has been caused by his failure to practice the Tractarian doctrine of reserve in his canvassing of arguments against his unprincipled rationalist former schoolmate Harvey Anderson,[30] so that his beliefs have become 'a mere shell of words'. Norman has inadvertently been drawn into decoupling the intellectual validity of his arguments from their moral implications in a way that implicitly assumes that reality is morally neutral: it is this which constitutes the 'magic mirror' of Rationalism in which religious questions remain confined to the dimension of representation, and so become morally powerless. The use of romance allusions here, of course, casts scepticism as an illusory enchantment, a rhetorical figure which goes back to James Beattie and the Common

29   Yonge, *The Daisy Chain, or Aspirations* (London: Macmillan, 1886), 428–9 (Part 2 Ch.9).

30   Ibid., 424 (Part 2 Ch.9).

36

Sense philosophers,[31] with Meta's question 'Has he not always a spell, a charm?' probably intended to allude to the talisman of Faith in Southey's poem *Thalaba* (a favourite poem of Yonge and the Tractarians)[32] whilst the figuring of intellectual search as romance quest recalls Browning's 'Childe Harold to the Dark Tower Came'. As a character, Norman is shown as being particularly liable to the existential danger of rationalist scepticism, because of the 'funny state' caused by nervous irritability to which he has succumbed at various points in the novel;[33] the implication is that by getting drawn into the heat of argument[34] Norman has lost his perception of any reality beyond the sensuous. This also happens to Rachel in *The Clever Woman of the Family*, whose religious crisis is similarly linked by Yonge to a condition that the Victorians would have called 'nervous overstrain', signalled, as in the case of Norman, by an allusion to Tennyson.[35]

Norman succumbs to unreality because of his entanglement with language, and this indicates the paradoxical nature of Yonge's conception of the relationship between fiction and reality. According to her Tractarian beliefs, 'reality' consists in a condition of spiritual and emotional authenticity which language can only betray – hence the need for reserve. Fiction is doubly false, but due to the very overtness of its falsity can perhaps, following a paradoxical logic much invoked

31   Cf. Ernest C. Mossner, 'Beattie's "The Castle of Scepticism": An Unpublished Allegory Against Hume, Voltaire and Hobbes', *Studies in English* 27 (1948): 108–45; Reid, *Works*, 103.
32   Cf. Anon., 'The Story of Thalaba', *Spider Subjects*, March 1874, 6–7 separately paginated insert in *Monthly Packet* (2nd series 1874) vol.17; Christabel Coleridge, *Charlotte Mary Yonge: Her Life and Letters* (London: Macmillan, 1903), 158–61; Yonge, *Heir*, 116 (Ch.8).
33   Yonge, *Daisy Chain*, 340 (Part 2 Ch.9).
34   Ibid., 517–19 (Part 2 Ch.16).
35   Yonge, *Clever Woman*, 267–8 (Ch.22). Rachel's loss of the feeling of personal identity, and hallucination of a 'world of gazing faces' seem modelled on Alfred Tennyson, 'Maud', in T. Herbert Warren (ed.), *Poems and Plays*, rev. Frederick Page (Oxford: Oxford University Press, 1965), Part 2, 5: 1: ll 1–20, 4: 13: 15.

by Roland Barthes,[36] manage to be truer than other kinds of language, in that it lends itself to being understood typologically rather than literally, a view which seems to underlie Yonge's claim in *Womankind* that religious tales and allegories are the hardest things to write.[37] This appeal to a form of language which through its own self-cancellation manages to be indicative of an ineffable truth which it is beyond the capacity of language to represent is one which Yonge shares with nineteenth-century British intuitionist philosophy.[38]

Conservative Feminism and Medical Realism in Yonge

The impossibility of a naturalistic characterization of Yonge's realist fictional world also lies at the root of another theoretical difficulty in locating her work within the terms of modern critical discourse. Yonge was a highly successful professional writer, and through her life-long involvement in schools, and later encouragement of women's colleges, probably did as much as any other single figure in the nineteenth century to promote women's education: it is not unusual in her fiction, for example, for girls to be learning Latin, and sometimes even Greek.[39] Despite these achievements, however, Yonge has often been regarded by modern critics as an antifeminist,[40] largely because of the difficulty of assimilating her work to the tradition of liberal feminism on which most contemporary feminist criticism is based. Yonge's own satires of liberal feminism in *The Clever Woman of the Family* and *The Three Brides* have contributed to this critical

36　Roland Barthes, *Mythologies*, trans. Annette Lavers (London: Vintage, 1993), 135–7.

37　Yonge, 'Womankind', *Monthly Packet* 18 (Series 2 1874): 192.

38　Cf. Dugald Stewart, *Collected Works*, orig pub 1854, 11 vols, William Hamilton (ed.), intro by Knud Haakonssen (Bristol: Thoemmes, 1994), 2: 203–4.

39　E.g. Yonge, *Daisy Chain*, 7 (Part 1 Ch.1); *Abbeychurch*, 28, (Ch.2) in *Abbeychurch / The Castle Builders*, facs. edn (New York and London: Garland Publishing, 1976).

40　Alethea Hayter, *Charlotte Yonge* (Plymouth: Northcote House, 1996), 56.

impression of her as an antifeminist. In *The Three Brides*, however, the narrator comments revealingly on the moral difference between the 'strong-minded' Bessie Duncombe[41] and the young High Church bride who has taken up her ideas:

> There was this difference between Bessie Duncombe and Cecil Charnock Poynsett, that the 'gospel of progress' was to the one the first she had ever really known, and became a reaching forward to a newly-perceived standard of benevolence and nobleness: to the other it was simply retrograding, and that less from conviction than from the spirit of rivalry and opposition.[42]

Yonge implies that Bessie Duncombe's feminism deserves some respect since her 'gospel of progress' represents a stage in her journey towards the true gospel, a point reinforced later on in the novel when she joins members of the Sisterhood of St Faith's in heroic nursing of the victims of the typhoid fever, in an episode which for the Victorian reader would have recalled the real-life involvement of an Anglican Sisterhood in nursing during an epidemic in Plymouth.[43] Yonge's portrayal of Bessie Duncombe indicates that she regarded feminism as potentially identical with true religion in a way which makes her Tractarian opposition to naturalism equivalent to a conservative form of feminism. Women, for Yonge, can only be truly themselves if, like religion, they occupy a position which is unrepresentable in rationalist terms, and this leads Yonge, like many other Victorians, to lay considerable emphasis on women's capacity to exert a rationally unanalysable 'influence'. This non-liberal tradition of feminism, which emphasizes sexual difference, has been described by some recent critics as 'social feminism',[44] or 'cultural feminism'.[45]

---

41 Yonge, *The Three Brides* (London: Macmillan, 1900), 15 (Ch.2).

42 Ibid., 154 (Ch.19).

43 Ibid., 241 (Ch.27); Ethel Romanes, *Charlotte Mary Yonge: An Appreciation* (London: Mowbray, 1908), 54.

44 Beth Sutton-Ramspeck, 'Shot Out of the Canon: Mary Ward and the Claims of Conflicting Feminisms', in Nicola Diane Thompson (ed.), *Victorian Women Writers and the Woman Question* (Cambridge: Cambridge University Press, 1999), 205.

45 Annette R. Federico, '"An 'Old-Fashioned' Young Woman": Marie Corelli and the New Woman', in Nicola Diane Thompson (ed.), *Victorian Women Writers*

As we shall see later in this book, the career of many of Yonge's heroines can be described as a progress from a condition of decentred subjectivity, in which female nervous irritability remains trapped within representation, in passively reacting to a purely sensuous world, towards a condition of moral power in which the achievement of quasi-mesmeric influence imperceptibly brings everything around them into harmony. This model of femininity can also be seen to inform the set-piece debate about the Woman Question slightly later in *The Three Brides*, whose explicitness, as June Sturrock notes, is highly unusual in Yonge's fiction.[46] The debate centres around the issue of political representation for women, of which the American feminist lecturer Mrs Tallboys is an advocate, holding up the partial emancipation of women in the United States as an example. Julius, the clergyman, questions whether 'free friction with the world may not lessen that sweetness and tender innocence and purity that make a man's home an ideal and a sanctuary – his best earthly influence', adding that 'desire of shielding that bloom from the slightest breath of contamination is no small motive for self-restraint, and therefore a great preservative to most men'.[47] This is an argument which Mrs Tallboys dismisses as mere 'sentiment',[48] but is plainly one Yonge herself took seriously, since in *Hopes and Fears* the presence of Phoebe Fulmort and her sisters in the family mansion acts as a restraint upon her dissipated elder brother Mervyn.[49]

Similar arguments against giving women the vote, on the grounds that it would expose them to a 'hardening and roughening process' that would lessen their ability to 'purify the atmosphere wherever they go'[50] can be found in other late nineteenth century

  and the Woman Question (Cambridge: Cambridge University Press, 1999), 242–43.

46 June Sturrock, *'Heaven and Home': Charlotte M Yonge's Domestic Fiction and the Victorian Debate Over Women*, English Literary Studies (Victoria BC: University of Victoria, 1995), 74–80.

47 Yonge, *Three Brides*, 161 (Ch.19).

48 Ibid., 162 (Ch.19).

49 Yonge, *Hopes and Fears, or Scenes from the Life of a Spinster* (London: Macmillan, 1889), 383 (Part 2 Ch.18).

50 Yonge, *Three Brides*, 162 (Ch.19).

writers; in the case of Mrs Humphrey Ward, for example, Beth Sutton-Ramspeck has shown that such arguments do not necessarily reflect an antifeminist position.[51] Although twentieth-century feminist critics, like Mrs Tallboys, have often dismissed such arguments as insubstantial, they testify to an understanding of the role of women which is deeply rooted in nineteenth-century intuitionist thought. The problem with placing women within the system of political representation, Yonge implies, is that it will deprive them of moral power in very much the same way as religious doctrines become inefficacious when analysed in rationalist terms. In this context, Mrs Tallboy's reference to the more emancipated condition of American women seems designed to recall the common nineteenth-century British complaint that American democracy was characterized by coarse standards of behaviour.[52]

Since moral intuitions are essentially unrepresentable by the intellect, women's position outside systems of social representation allows them to mount a privileged claim to such intuitions; in effect, women benefit from a typological relationship to moral intuitions which, as Julius comments, allows them to 'make a man's home an ideal'. Once they occupy a position within political representation, however, as Eliza Lynn Linton comments,[53] women's natural nervous irritability will involve them in an unproductive and embittered partisanship. Yonge suggests this about Mrs Duncombe's political involvement: after she has placed herself within the political process, by proposing a motion to a public meeting, we hear of her 'haranguing' one of the tradesmen to set an example with 'sanatory measures' [sic],[54] and are later told that:

> The opposition made in the town to Mrs Duncombe's sanitary plans, and the contempt with which they had been treated as ladies' fancies, had given a

51 Sutton-Ramspeck, 'Shot Out of the Canon', 204–10.

52 Cf. Charles Dickens, *American Notes and Pictures from Italy* (London: Oxford University Press, 1957), 202–3.

53 Eliza Lynn Linton, 'The Wild Women as Politicians', *Nineteenth Century* 30 (1891): 80–2.

54 Yonge, *Three Brides*, 81 (Ch.11).

positive field of battle, with that admixture of right and wrong on each side which is essential to championship.[55]

Mrs Duncombe's plans for sanitary reform are portrayed as being right in principle, given they are anticipated by the clergyman Julius Charnock Poynsett's suggestions in private to his brother Raymond, who is the local member of parliament,[56] but as having in practice been counter-productive, since, as Raymond notes, 'the irritation it produces must subside before they will hear reason'.[57] In this context, Mrs Duncombe can be seen as a figure who, as June Sturrock comments, is 'a more intelligent and practical version of Rachel Curtis in *The Clever Woman of the Family*',[58] in that her over-enthusiasm makes efforts which in themselves are admirable turn out disastrously.

June Sturrock suggests that Yonge's portrayal of Bessie Duncombe exhibits some incoherence in her conception of the proper social role of women:

> Yonge's treatment of the effects of Mrs. Duncombe's actions seems to imply an unresolved intellectual conflict in regard to women and service. By implication women are too ignorant and incompetent to be involved in public affairs without disaster, and yet they are public-spirited, effective and sympathetic to the need for social action: Mrs. Duncombe is both guilty and not guilty of causing the outbreak of fever.[59]

What Sturrock finds unresolved and conflicting in Yonge's attitudes is, I would suggest, integral to the intuitionist outlook she inherits from Tractarianism, and shares with many other Victorians. Just as J.H. Newman emphasized that the most morally gifted Christians are precisely those who would find it hardest to construct defences of Christianity on an intellectual level,[60] so too Yonge implies that Bessie Duncombe's very nobility of character is what makes her necessarily ineffective in practical terms, since there is an epis-

55   Ibid., 115 (Ch.15).
56   Ibid., 51 (Ch.7).
57   Ibid., 52 (Ch.7).
58   Sturrock, *Heaven and Home*, 83.
59   Ibid., 83–7.
60   Newman, *University Sermons*, 84.

temological discontinuity between moral intuition and reason – a point which is also implicit in Julius's comment that his young curate Herbert Bowater might have managed to pass the examination for his ordination if he had been 'a man of less reality and more superficial quickness'.[61] As Raymond later notes, regretting his own 'truckling to expediency', 'we talked about meddling women, but the truth was that they were shaming us by doing what they could'.[62] Raymond's remark implies that Bessie Duncombe's attempt to improve the drains in Water Lane, even though it is the proximate cause of the typhus that is devastating the town, should be appreciated as a symbolic gesture to which his own practical response has been inadequate. As the 'fast' Miss Moys comments, 'women and parsons [...] are just the same',[63] in that they both must rely on moral grounds, rather than rational ones, in eliciting a response from others, something shown by Julius's disagreement with the dispirited elderly clergyman Mr Fuller over the need to hold a bazaar to raise funds for rebuilding the church, where Mr Fuller's moral failings are indicated by his implied 'sarcasm on faith in aught but £ s. d.'[64]

Yonge's novels, then, are hard to locate within dominant critical paradigms both of realism and of feminism ultimately for the same reason: Yonge's allegiance to an intuitionist position, rather than a philosophically naturalist one, makes the realism and feminism which her novels exhibit incomprehensible without reference to a supernatural dimension of experience. This may make it seem as if Yonge's novels are radically alien to a modern sensibility, but the example of what has been regarded as a paradigmatically 'modern' novel, Flaubert's *Madame Bovary*, suggests that Yonge's fictional mode is less far from the mainstream of novelistic development than it might appear.

As one of Yonge's contemporaries seems to have recognized,[65] there are significant thematic parallels between her fiction and

61   Yonge, *Three Brides*, 229 (Ch.26).
62   Ibid., 222 (Ch.25).
63   Ibid., 162 (Ch.19).
64   Ibid., 51 (Ch.7).
65   Romanes, *Yonge: An Appreciation*, 87–94.

Madame Bovary, a similarity which may help to explain the popularity of her novels in France.[66] As we shall see in a later chapter, Yonge's fiction exhibits that 'medical realism' which Lawrence Rothfield has identified in Flaubert.[67] Both writers deal with nervously irritable heroines (Emma Bovary is described as suffering from nervous ailments on several occasions)[68] who also exert quasi-mesmeric influence over those around them: in her religious phase, for example, Emma is generally recognized as a 'distinguished' woman,[69] and this magnetism becomes if anything stronger in her adulterous phase, anticipating the Decadent theme of the femme fatale.[70] Moreover, in the famous scene where Rodolphe seduces Emma at the agricultural fair, Flaubert's formally innovative blank juxtaposition of the official speeches with Rodolphe's romantic clichés[71] suggests a scepticism both about the meaningfulness of rationalist rhetoric about progress and about the self-serving quality of Byronism to which Yonge could have easily subscribed – Mr Augustus Mill's lecture on Chivalry in *Abbeychurch*,[72] and Philip's fondness for Byron in *The Heir of Redclyffe*[73] are obvious parallels. The moment in Flaubert's novel when the old peasant woman breaks into a 'beatific smile' after being presented with a silver medal, and mutters 'I shall give it to our *curé*, to say some masses for me',[74] and the novel's generally respectful treatment of Catholicism (not to be taken for granted, given the strength of the French tradition of anti-clericalism which Flaubert satirizes) also suggest that spirituality is a viable possibility in Flaubert's fictional world, even if Emma Bovary deceives herself about

66   Barbara Dennis, *Charlotte Yonge (1823-1901), Novelist of the Oxford Movement: A Literature of Victorian Culture and Society* (Lewiston, NY: Edwin Mellen, 1992), 23–8.

67   Lawrence Rothfield, *Vital Signs: Medical Realism in Nineteenth-Century Fiction* (Princeton: Princeton University Press, 1992).

68   Gustave Flaubert, *Madame Bovary*, trans. Geoffrey Wall (Harmondsworth: Penguin, 1992), 53 (Part 1 Ch.9).

69   Ibid., 85 (Part 2 Ch.5).

70   Ibid., 157 (Part 2 Ch.12).

71   Ibid., 113–20 (Part 2 Ch.8).

72   Yonge, *Abbeychurch*, 164–5 (Ch.8).

73   Ibid., *Heir*, 399–400 (Ch.30).

74   Flaubert, *Madame Bovary*,121 (Part 2 Ch.8).

her spiritual life – a form of self-deception which Yonge too portrayed in such characters as Angela Underwood in *The Pillars of the House*.[75] As we have seen is true of Yonge also, Flaubert suggests in the famous passage where he compares language to 'a cracked cauldron on which we knock out tunes for dancing-bears, when we wish to conjure pity from the stars'[76] that there is a fundamental disparity between human moral intuitions and the terms which are available to the intellect to describe them.

In some ways, too, Flaubert's narrative technique is similar to Yonge's, in that the narrative is often focalized through a character, without that character's perspective being intended to be a focus for readerly identification or interpretatively privileged. Flaubert shows us, for example, Emma Bovary inwardly raging at Charles's lack of feeling at the very moment when Charles is turning pale at Hippolyte's cry of agony from the amputation of his foot,[77] suggesting for the attentive reader that she is not only egotistical but not very observant of the feelings of others. Yonge's novels often mount similarly disconcerting switches of perspective, such as when Lucilla in *Hopes and Fears* unexpectedly marries the elderly clergyman 'Mr Pendy',[78] and the reader realizes that her relationship with Robert Fulmort has mostly been reported from Robert's own regretful, but perhaps also rather gloomy and egotistical perspective, or when Alick Keith's misgivings about his sister in *The Clever Woman of the Family* turn out to be entirely justified, in the teeth of all the other characters' disagreement.[79]

75   Yonge, *The Pillars of the House, or Under Wode, Under Rode*, 2 vols (London: Macmillan, 1901), 2: 519–23 (Ch.43).
76   Flaubert, *Madame Bovary*, 154 (Part 2 Ch.12).
77   Ibid., 149 (Part 2 Ch.11).
78   Yonge, *Hopes and Fears*, 491–2 (Part 2 Ch.27).
79   Ibid., 339–42 (Ch.28).

Tractarianism, Psychology and the Active Reader

Whilst it would be perverse to deny that a more definite moral framework is on offer within Yonge's novels than is present in Flaubert's depiction of what the Tractarians would have called 'unreality', the comparison with *Madame Bovary* helps to bring out those critical and ironic elements in Yonge's writing the experience of which is reliant on the reader's willingness to play an active interpretative role, and which have often been neglected by critics who assume that Yonge's religious commitment necessarily implies a dogmatic denial of interpretative freedom to the reader. As a recent paper by Elizabeth Jay has shown, however, the Tractarian milieu within which Yonge moved encouraged an awareness of reading as a self-conscious hermeneutic act rather than the passive reception of an approved 'moral'. Jay draws attention to the prominent role which experiences of reading play within Yonge's novels, and the way these echo what we know of the reading practices of Keble's circle at Hursley, of which Yonge was of course a key member.[80]

As Jay points out, Guy's response to contemporary writing, to which he has not previously been exposed owing to his isolated education, plays an important role in the early part of *The Heir of Redclyffe*. Significantly, Guy and the cripple Charles Edmonstone read Keble's Latin *Lectures on Poetry* together,[81] one of the most sustained and systematic exercises in literary criticism that was produced in nineteenth-century Britain. Jay draws attention to the fact that Tractarianism was very much a minority position within a massively dominant Protestant literary culture, something which helps to explain the priority Keble attached to critical reinterpretation of the Classical tradition, and which forms the context for Yonge's own massively productive elaboration of an Anglo-Catholic literary culture in the form not only of her novels but also her numerous educational works and school textbooks.

---

80   Elisabeth Jay, 'Charlotte Mary Yonge and Tractarian Aesthetics', *Victorian Poetry* 44, no.1 (2006): 43–59.
81   Yonge, *Heir*, 44–6, 58 (Ch.3, Ch.5).

The literary hermeneutic which Keble sets out in the *Lectures on Poetry* anticipates in important respects the kind of active interpretative engagement (or what Harold Bloom has called 'strong reading')[82] which Yonge expects from the readers of her novels. A consequence of Keble's well-known emphasis on poetry as a 'safety-valve' for repressed emotion[83] is his diagnostic stance as a critic, in which reading poetry becomes an exercise in reconstructing the distinctive characteristics of the poet's mind. Keble's critical method is far removed from the excesses of Victorian biographical criticism, however, since he emphasizes that 'a poem is like a picture in which the whole effect is not seldom produced by the most delicate stroke of the brush'.[84] For Keble, any true insight into poetic psychology must grow out of a mastery of verbal detail:

> It may well be [...] that in the general conception of a poem a writer, even of primary rank, is influenced more by his time than by his own predilection. But when we examine single passages, when we scrutinize the similes and imagery, when we subject language and versification to criticism, the true bias of the poet's own mind will again and again come to the surface, whether it be naturally ingrained or the result of long habit: it is from these, when it is seen that there is a real consistency between things important and things trivial, between unexpected illustrations and the careful plan, between random touches and the whole picture, that the most confident inference may be drawn.[85]

Keble envisages a kind of reading which discovers unexpected significances by bringing apparently trivial verbal details into relationship with each other, significantly anticipating the hermeneutic assumptions of much twentieth-century literary criticism. Keble is prepared to admit, in the same way as present-day literary critics, that the process of literary interpretation is interminable; as Keble puts it,

---

82   Harold Bloom, *Agon: Towards a Theory of Revisionism* (New York: Oxford University Press, 1982), 19–26.

83   John Keble, *Keble's Lectures on Poetry, 1832–1841*, 2 vols, trans. Edward Kershaw Francis (Oxford: Clarendon Press, 1912), 1: 55 in Gavin Budge (ed.), *Aesthetics and Religion in Nineteenth-Century Britain*, 6 vols (Bristol: Thoemmes, 2003), Vol.1.

84   Keble, *Lectures on Poetry*, 2: 82.

85   Ibid., 1: 147.

'the problem of the central significance of any poet's writings is too subtle and complex to be proved to demonstration: there will always be room for critics to offer some new probable interpretation'.[86] The practice of 'reading against the grain', in which a textual significance is identified which goes beyond, or even runs counter to, the writer's conscious intentions, and which has been found objectionable in the work of recent literary critics influenced by deconstruction,[87] can also be found in Keble, who argues for example in relation to Lucretius' *De Rerum Naturae* that 'it is quite possible that, while the main argument of a poem avowedly and openly denies that there are gods in heaven above or in the world below, yet, nevertheless, its whole tenor and quality may be on the side of those who love true religion'.[88]

Keble's interest in arriving at an understanding of the poet's mind through a recovery of the pre-conscious or repressed associations revealed by verbal detail[89] brings his interpretative method close to that of modern psychoanalytic critics. Where Keble's assumptions differ from those of most present-day critics, however, is in his ascription of the element in literature which transcends the conscious intention of the writer to a supernatural influence inherent in language. Writers such as Lucretius and Virgil[90] unconsciously anticipate Christianity because, in their pursuit of truth to detail, they are providentially led into religious truth; citing Bishop Butler, Keble argues that: 'when any one has the gift – and this gift has always been deemed the special prerogative of inspired genius – of picking up a thread and clearly and effectively following it through all its windings, there is nothing to prevent his linking the humblest beginnings with the noblest issues'.[91] The view that faithful imitation of Nature will necessarily endow poetry with a typological religious significance also

---

86   Ibid., 2: 224.
87   For a detailed discussion of this critical controversy, see Gavin Budge, 'History and the New Historicism: Symbol and Allegory as Poetics of Criticism', in Philip Smallwood (ed.), *Critical Pasts: Writing Criticism, Writing History* (Lewisburg, PA: Bucknell University Press, 2004), 115–43.
88   Keble, *Lectures on Poetry*, 2: 336.
89   Ibid., 1: 90.
90   Ibid., 412.
91   Ibid., 2: 120–1.

underlies Keble's argument in *Tract 89*, 'On the Mysticism attributed to the Early Fathers of the Church'.[92] Keble's emphasis on the effects of artistic 'truth', manifested in realistic detail, in imparting a quasi-religious or typological significance to works of art, anticipates the writings of Ruskin,[93] who was probably a member of the original Oxford audience to which the *Lectures on Poetry* were delivered; certainly Keble's concluding claim that 'no poet will ever be great who does not constantly spend time and toil in studying the beauty of earth and sky so as to make every detail of the whole bear upon the object of his own love and enthusiasm'[94] has a Ruskinian air.

Keble most clearly sets out the view underlying his techniques of close reading, that providence is at work in the details of language itself, towards the end of his impressive analysis of Aeschylus's theology:

> Beyond all question, Aeschylus held the belief that men's tongues are neither ruled by blind fate nor wanton caprice: but that a higher influence, an influence of mysterious prophetic power, prevails both in the choice of names and in the words which seem to fall from men's lips by mere chance. Therefore, on this ground too, we find him in full accord with revealed truth. For the sacred writers lay it down that among God's people names are mainly bestowed under divine influence, and have a peculiar significance associated with the recipient's disposition, habits, and fortune in life, so that the mere mention of a man's name serves as a token of the presence of a higher Power.[95]

For Keble, like his contemporary Thomas Carlyle, language is in itself prophetic, so that divine order shines through seemingly random expressions for those who can see it; this inherent typological significance to language, for example, is what in such essays as 'The Spirit of the Age' justifies Carlyle's wresting of banal advertising slogans such as 'Morrison's Pill' away from their original context to serve as exemplary manifestations of the complacent rationalist as-

92 Keble, *On the Mysticism Attributed to the Early Fathers of the Church* (Oxford and London: Parker, 1868), 173–4.
93 John Ruskin, *Works*, 39 vols, E.T. Cook and Alexander Wedderburn (eds) (London: Allen, 1903–1912), 2: 60–1.
94 Keble, *Lectures on Poetry*, 2: 483.
95 Ibid., 1: 419.

sumption that there is a quick fix for the human condition.[96] A similarly providentialist view of language underlies the 1850s lectures by Trench that led to the founding of the Oxford English Dictionary. As the first lecture makes clear, a major reason for Trench's advocacy of an etymological dictionary is his assumption that the evolution in significance of key words, such as those for social institutions, will reveal providence at work in the development of society.[97]

Yonge's own extensive scholarship on the etymology of Christian names,[98] drawn upon in the often unusual, and always significant, names given to characters in her novels,[99] reflects Keble's kind of providentialist emphasis on the 'higher influence' embodied in language. This is exemplified in *Hopes and Fears*, in the episode where Bertha Fulmort unconsciously identifies the young English lady who has rescued her from mocking French peasants when she has got lost on an Alpine walk as the sweetheart whose refusal of her brother Mervyn's proposal has been partly responsible for his dissipated ways:

> Bertha, who slept in the same room with Phoebe, awoke her in the morning with the question, 'What do you think is Miss Holmby's name?'
> 'I did not hear it mentioned.'
> 'No, but you ought to guess. Do you not see how names impress their own individuality? You need not laugh; I know they do: – could you possibly have been called Augusta, and did not Katherine quite pervade Miss Fennimore?'
> 'Well, according to your theory, what is her name?'
> 'It is either Eleanor or Cecily.'
> 'Indeed!' cried Phoebe; 'what put that into your head?'
> 'Her expression – no, her entire *Wesen*. Something homely, simple, a little old-fashioned, and yet refined.'
> 'It is odd,' said Phoebe, pausing.
> 'What is odd?'

96 Thomas Carlyle, *Past and Present* (London: Oxford University Press, 1909), 23; cf. John Holloway, *The Victorian Sage: Studies in Argument* (New York: Archon Books, 1953), 37.

97 Richard Chevenix Trench, *On the Study of Words and English Past and Present* (London and Toronto: Dent and Dutton, n.d.), 17–22.

98 Hayter, *Yonge*, 46.

99 e.g. Yonge, *Abbeychurch*, 49, 201 (Ch.3, Ch.10).

'You have explained the likeness I could not make out. I once saw a photograph of a Cecily, with exactly the character you mention. It was that of which she reminded me.' [...]

All the time the likeness to that photograph continued to haunt Phoebe's mind, as she continued to discover more resemblances, and to decide that if such were impressed by the Christian name, Bertha was a little witch to detect it.[100]

Within the world of Yonge's novels, Bertha's ability correctly to divine Cecily's Christian name on the basis of her 'Wesen' (or 'being') is not mere coincidence, but reflects the way in which, as Yonge comments earlier, 'the glacier system was a happy exchange for her *ego*'.[101] As Bertha's liability to stammer[102] indicates, she suffers from temperamentally irritable nerves which at an earlier point in the novel, when she is portrayed as coming under the influence of the excessive subjectivity of German Idealist philosophy,[103] have led to her pathetic attempt to elope with one of her brother's dissolute friends.[104] Bertha's recovery after the breakdown to which this has led is manifested by the redirection of her interests outside the self (hinted at by Yonge's reference to the 'glacier system') and her mysterious intuition of Cecily's name represents an aspect of this greater attunement to the external world. As we shall see in a later chapter, Bertha's development from a condition of disabling nervous irritability to a position of occult power (identifiable with the common Victorian invocation of mesmeric female 'influence') reflects a common trajectory for Yonge's female characters.

The similarity between Keble's and Yonge's providentialist attitudes to linguistic detail extends to the claim that 'the wanton and scoffing tongues and idle chatter of mere men' can legitimately be regarded as 'the utterance of a benevolent deity mysteriously showing us the true path of life by the voice and means of unconscious, or perhaps even hostile, witnesses' which Keble uses to justify his

---

100 Yonge, *Hopes and Fears*, 446–7 (Part 2 Ch.24).
101 Ibid., 439 (Part 2 Ch.24).
102 Ibid., 443 (Part 2 Ch.24).
103 Ibid., 366 (Part 2 Ch.17).
104 Ibid., 408–14 (Part 2 Ch.21).

recuperatory reading of Lucretius.[105] As is shown by the example of Miss Moys's comment in *The Three Brides* that 'women and parsons [...] are just the same'[106] to which I referred earlier, apparently throwaway remarks by characters can often be seen to carry deeper thematic significance, particularly in the context of the word games which frequently appear in Yonge's novels.[107] The thematic weight which Miss Moys's remark bears is especially significant in this respect, because Miss Moys's later action in running off with a groom[108] in imitation of the sensation novel *Aurora Floyd*[109] definitely puts her beyond the moral pale (even her name is probably intended to convey excessive egoism), so that she counts as one of Keble's 'hostile witnesses' whose language testifies to the truth in spite of herself.

Keble's providentialist hermeneutic represents a useful model for literary critical interpretation of Yonge's novels, not only because Keble was an important personal influence on Yonge, but also because Keble emphasizes that literary value consists in *ethos*, that is to say the consistent development of character, as opposed to *pathos*, or the sudden excitement of passionate feelings.[110] Keble in fact anticipates William Aytoun's and Charles Kingsley's 1850s critique of the contemporary 'spasmodic' Romantic poetry modelled on Shelley and Byron,[111] which emphasized moments of passion, and which was closely allied to the fictional mode of the 'sensation novel' of the 1850s and 1860s.[112] The closeness of Yonge's writing to this mid-nineteenth-century return to a 'classicism' romantically defined

---

105   Keble, *Lectures on Poetry*, 2: 349.
106   Yonge, *Three Brides*, 162 (Ch.19).
107   E.g. Yonge, *Heir*, 40–1 (Ch.4).
108   Yonge, *Three Brides*, 287 (Ch.33).
109   Ibid., 194 (Ch.22).
110   Keble, *Lectures on Poetry*, 1: 88.
111   Ibid., 1: 91.
112   Mark A. Weinstein, *William Edmondstoune Aytoun and the Spasmodic Controversy* (New Haven and London: Yale University Press, 1968), 107–8; J.I. Fradin, 'The Novels of Edward Bulwer-Lytton', University Microfilms, Ann Arbor, Michigan, facs. edn, 1973 Doctoral Dissertation Series, publication no.19,238 (Columbia University, 1956), 140–6.

as consisting in the restraint of feeling[113] is shown by Flora's allusion in *The Daisy Chain*, after she has seen the error of her ways, to Taylor's poetic drama *Philip van Artevelde*,[114] which was frequently held up in mid nineteenth-century criticism as representing the opposite pole to spasmodic poetry;[115] Yonge also uses a quotation from this source as a chapter heading in *Heartsease*.[116] The 'passionate verses of Shelley and Byron'[117] which in *Hopes and Fears* fall from the 'dying lips' of Edna, the schoolmistress who has eloped into a clandestine marriage, are of course intended by Yonge to make a point about the potential harmfulness of exposure to this kind of poetry, particularly for members of the lower classes who, as an article in the *Monthly Packet* makes clear, were regarded as more likely to be lacking in self-control in any case.[118]

This appeal to 'ethos', as an underlying unity of character that can be perceived behind a multiplicity of details, has been identified by many critics as characteristic of Tractarianism.[119] It features, for example, in the preface by Newman and Keble to Hurrell Froude's *Remains*, which justifies the controversial publication of Froude's private papers and journal on the grounds that 'his opinions had a wonderful degree of consistency and mutual bearing; they depended on each other as one whole' despite 'the off-hand unpremeditated way in which they seemed to dart out of him, like sparks from a luminous body', proving that he had 'a mind entirely possessed with the subject; glowing as it were through and through'.[120] The remark quoted in one of Froude's letters, that 'R. thinks biography the best means of in-

---

113 Matthew Arnold, 'Preface to Poems (1853)', in *The Nostalgia for Classicism* (Ann Arbor: University of Michigan, 1960), 5–6, *Complete Prose Works*, 10 vols (Ann Arbor: University of Michigan Press, 1960–1974).

114 Yonge, *Daisy Chain*, 656 (Part 2 Ch.26).

115 Weinstein, *Aytoun and the Spasmodic Controversy*, 74, 177–82.

116 Yonge, *Heartsease, or the Brother's Wife* (London: Macmillan, 1891), 421 (Part 3 Ch.13).

117 Yonge, *Hopes and Fears*, 280 (Part 2 Ch.12)

118 Anon., 'Life Among the Factories', *Monthly Packet* 21 (Series 1 1861): 107–8.

119 Stephen Thomas, *Newman and Heresy: The Anglican Years* (Cambridge: Cambridge University Press, 1991), 25–6, fn 36.

120 Froude, *Remains*, 1: xx.

fusing principles against the reader's will',[121] also seems to reflect the Tractarian conception of ethos as a rationally inexplicable moral intuition which is provoked in the mind by encounter with character in action rather than through any kind of theorizing.

Yonge's portrayal in *Hopes and Fears* of the rationalist governess Miss Fennimore's conversion can be seen to invoke this Tractarian appeal to ethos. Miss Fennimore is convinced not by hearing the clergyman Robert Fulmort preach, but by the 'sermon in brick and stone'[122] represented by his action in devoting his share of the family fortune accumulated through gin palaces[123] to the building and endowment of a slum church (a plot element for which there were many real-life precedents).[124] As Miss Fennimore comments, 'when I mark what I can only call a supernatural influence on an individual character, I view it as an evidence in favour of the system that produced it';[125] ultimately, the kind of consistent transcendence of merely self-orientated perspectives which makes it possible to discern ethos testifies to a divine moral influence from outside the self, and this is as true of individual character as it is of poetry as Keble conceives it.

Character and Irony in Yonge's Fiction

The appeal to ethos which underlies Keble's poetic theory can help us understand the narrative mode of Yonge's fiction, over which literary critics have radically disagreed. Many critics have identified Yonge's greatest strength as a novelist as consisting in her remarkable ability to create living characters. In the lengthy and flattering 1854 review of *Heartsease* and *The Heir of Redclyffe* in *Fraser's* that marked her

121 Ibid., 1: 321.
122 Yonge, *Hopes and Fears*, 342.
123 Ibid., 46, 126.
124 Romanes, *Yonge: An Appreciation*, 87–94
125 Yonge, *Hopes and Fears*, 364.

literary breakthrough, the author (probably Charles Kingsley)[126] commented that Yonge 'in common with Miss Austin [...] is chiefly remarkable for truthful delineations of character',[127] a point echoed in a posthumous 1905 retrospective of her work in the *Edinburgh Review*, which notes her 'astonishing power of creating individuals'.[128] Commenting on one of Yonge's most enduringly popular novels, Georgina Battiscombe memorably sums up the way in which the psychological appeal of Yonge's characterization transcends the deliberate plainness of her prose style:

> But how describe the May family, how explain magic to those who have never fallen under its spell? The true addict has read *The Daisy Chain* not once but a hundred times; every word is dear and familiar, a text as sacrosanct as Holy Writ. Outsiders will read the story with interest, even with appreciation, and then sit down to compare it with *Little Women*. 'Yes,' cries the enthusiast, the initiate, 'Miss Alcott is a better writer than Miss Yonge, and *Little Women* a real work of art. But I don't want works of art; I want Ethel and dear Dr. May.' This attitude is indefensible and not a little crazy, only to be understood by those who are also struck down by the May madness.[129]

Q.D. Leavis, however, in a 1944 review of Battiscombe's book in *Scrutiny*, finds Yonge's art as a novelist fundamentally vitiated by 'the ignorant idealization projected by an inhuman theory'.[130] For Leavis, Yonge, as 'a day-dreamer with a writing itch that compensated her for a peculiarly starved life'[131] made her Anglicanism 'a substitute for living, so we see her selecting the anti-Life elements in Chris-

---

126 The article is not attributed in the *Wellesley Index to Victorian Periodicals*, but the enthusiasm of Kingsley (a regular contributor to *Fraser's*) is described in Margaret Mare and Alicia C. Percival, *Victorian Best-Seller: The World of Charlotte M. Yonge* (London: Harrap, 1947), 143–6.

127 Anon., Review of *Heartsease; or, The Brother's Wife*, *Fraser's Magazine* 50 (1854): 490.

128 Anon., 'The Novels of Miss Yonge', *Edinburgh Review* 102 (1905): 358.

129 Georgina Battiscombe, *Charlotte Mary Yonge: The Story of an Uneventful Life* (London: Constable, 1944), 96.

130 Q.D. Leavis, 'Charlotte Yonge and Christian Discrimination', *Scrutiny* 12 (1944): 153.

131 Ibid., 152–3.

tianity for stress and idealization'.[132] Yonge, Leavis claims, 'was incapable of perceiving that moral theory may require revision or reinterpretation in the light of experience or in consequence of a change in the sensibility of a society', so that 'in her fictions moral lesson is deduced from theory as mechanically as in a Sunday-School story of the last century'.[133] Quoting Henry James's remark that 'the essence of moral energy is to survey the whole field', Leavis suggests that 'Miss Yonge is so timid and inexperienced morally that [...] religious small-change is handed us on every possible occasion.'[134]

Leavis appears to have been unaware that James once praised Yonge as a 'genius',[135] and the strikingly negative terms in which she characterizes Yonge's writing form part of a wider argument designed to show that 'the novelist, unlike the theologian, works in terms of concrete particularity'.[136] It is plain, however, that she disputes the critical consensus as to the living quality of Yonge's characters, regarding her fiction as mechanical in applying a fixed moral schema which does not allow for personal or social development. As we have seen Thomas Vargish note, the critical and cultural assumptions displayed here by Leavis, according to which commitment to a definite religious doctrine is incompatible with the truth to life which a realist novelist should exhibit, are intrinsically hostile to any kind of providentialist perspective, and it would seem fair to say that these assumptions have been responsible for Yonge's almost entire erasure from the canon of Victorian novelists. Yonge's reputation, I would argue, has suffered more from the prevalence of such assumptions than writers such as Charlotte Brontë and Dickens, whose work Vargish examines, because of the very consistency and depth of her providentialism, which informs even apparently trivial details of characterization.

132   Ibid., 153.
133   Ibid., 155.
134   Ibid., 154.
135   Elizabeth K. Helsinger, Robin Lauterbach Sheets and William Veeder, *The Woman Question: Society and Literature in Britain and America, 1837–1883*, 3 vols (New York: Garland, 1983), 3: 52.
136   Leavis, 'Yonge and Christian Discrimination', 160.

Leavis's appeal to 'Life' as a source of critical and social values is arguably vulnerable to appropriation by dominant social interests in a way which could amount to an unthinking endorsement of the status quo. Yonge's critical relationship to the values of Victorian society, on the other hand, is shown by the sense of existential angst which is an ever-present undercurrent in the world she depicts, where the wealthy characters are constantly haunted with a sense of purpose-lessness. In *Hopes and Fears*, for example, Phoebe is struck, visiting her brother Robert Fulmort in his rooms in the slum of Whittingtonia, by 'the absence of the undefined restlessness that had for years been habitual to both brothers, and which had lately so increased on Mervyn, that there was relief in watching a face free from it',[137] an *ennui* which it is later suggested Mervyn's dissipated habits, which end by threatening his health, are an unsuccessful attempt to drive away. As many articles in the *Monthly Packet* suggest,[138] the problems posed by boredom were even worse for the young women who were Yonge's principal audience, for whom choosing 'Life' in the way Leavis so glibly recommends was equivalent to surrendering themselves body and soul to the incessant demands of society and family, a threat which is often depicted in Yonge's novels.[139] As Barbey d'Aurévilly tellingly remarked in a review of *Against Nature*, the existential alternative presented by Huysmans's Decadent novel was between 'the foot of the Cross, or the barrel of a gun', a stark moral choice which also informs Yonge's Tractarian outlook.[140]

In a recent article on *Magnum Bonum*, Talia Schaffer attempts to integrate these wildly divergent critical responses through a decon-

---

137   Yonge, *Hopes and Fears*, 255.
138   Cf. Anon., 'An Object in Life', *Monthly Packet* 15 (Series 1 1858): 270–1; Anon., 'Grandmamma. "My Life, and What Shall I Do with It?"', *Monthly Packet* 21 (Series 1 1861): 422; 'Grandmother, "Correspondence"', *Monthly Packet* 24 (Series 1 1862): 441–2.
139   E.g. Yonge's description of Flora's hectic married life in *Daisy Chain*, 561 (Part 2 Ch.19) which it is later implied has brought about the death of her baby (*Daisy Chain*, 577–8, Part 2 Ch.20).
140   J.-K. Huysmans, 'Préface Ecrite Vingt Ans Après le Roman', in *À Rebours* (Paris: Bibliothèque-Charpentier, 1925), xxiv; cf. Pusey, *Parochial Sermons*, 3: 430–2.

structive interpretation of Yonge's narrative strategies. As Schaffer sees it, the interpretative dilemma for modern literary critics is that 'if we read Yonge's narratives against the grain as a realist author, we misrepresent her central motive; yet if we read her as a pious peda-gogue (as she would prefer), we can find nothing to say'.[141] Citing Catherine Sandbach-Dahlström's comment that 'at an imaginative level Charlotte Yonge, as implied author, has access to patterns of thought and feeling that do not accord with the ideology she sets out to preach',[142] Schaffer follows D.A. Miller in arguing that Yonge's novels fulful a Foucauldian disciplinary function, in that they 'depict dissidence for the purpose of subduing it'.[143] Schaffer suggests that the 'Magnum Bonum' of the novel's title, a medical discovery the need for whose secrecy drives the plot and whose nature is never explained, can be seen as representing ideology itself, which 'works best when seen least'.[144]

Schaffer offers a detailed and persuasive reading of *Magnum Bonum* as a novel about the workings of ideology. She focuses in particular on Yonge's portrayal of the 'witty, brilliant, mischievous'[145] Jock's religious conversion, following the episode in which his recklessness leads to himself and his younger brother coming close to death from exposure after they are stranded on a moraine in the Swiss Alps. Schaffer notes that the description of Jock at this point as 'silent, lame, pale, thin, leaning on his stick, his eyes dim with tears'[146] is indicative of the way in which 'physical weakness usually correlates to holiness'[147] in Yonge's fiction, suggesting that 'we can [...] read this change as an objective correlative to the crippling effects of Jock's new faith, which inhibits his ability to see clearly or move at will'.[148]

---

141 Schaffer, 'Mysterious Magnum Bonum', 245.
142 Ibid., 244.
143 Ibid., 247.
144 Ibid., 257.
145 Ibid., 259.
146 Ibid., 262.
147 Ibid.
148 Ibid.

Schaffer's interpretation of the effects of religious faith on Jock, developing Sandbach-Dahlström's somewhat similar argument that the frequency with which cripples appear in Yonge's fiction is an unconscious expression of her frustration,[149] essentially restates Leavis's claim that Yonge is the promoter of an 'anti-Life' ideology. Schaffer extends this argument by drawing attention to the close relationship between the secret of 'Magnum Bonum' and sexuality in Yonge's portrayal of Janet Brownlow, noting that Janet first finds the description in her dead father's secret notebook at 'age fourteen; thus it coincides with menstruation and the onset of adult sexuality'.[150] Yonge implies that Janet's illicit discovery leads to her developing a 'strange leaden weight of reserve, and shame in that long reserve',[151] in terms which as Schaffer points out carry sexual overtones.[152] Schaffer also draws attention to what for a modern reader seem fairly obvious hints of lesbian sexuality in Yonge's description of Janet's friendship with 'an artist in a small way, who had transmogrified her name of Jane into Juanita or Nita, wore a crop, short petticoats, and was odd',[153] with whom she lives in Zürich while studying to become a doctor so that she can pursue her father's discovery.[154]

Although Schaffer confines her argument to *Magnum Bonum*, the points she makes could easily be extended to other novels by Yonge. In *The Three Brides*, for example, the 'muscular Christian'[155] Herbert Bowater's repentance of his over-involvement in cricket at the

149   Catherine Sandbach-Dahlström, *Be Good Sweet Maid: Charlotte Yonge's Domestic Fictior A Study in Dogmatic Purpose and Fictional Form* (Stockholm: Almqvist & Wicksel, 1984), 171–6.
150   Schaffer, 'Mysterious Magnum Bonum', 267.
151   Quoted in Schaffer, 'Mysterious Magnum Bonum', 267; Charlotte M. Yonge, *Magnum Bonum, or Mother Carey's Brood*, 3 vols (London: Macmillan, 1879), 182 (Ch.10; edition is through-numbered across volumes).
152   Cf. Ellis Hanson's argument that in late nineteenth-century Decadent discourse, 'shame' is virtually a synonym for male homosexuality, Ellis Hanson, *Decadence and Catholicism* (Cambridge, MA: Harvard University Press, 1997), 10–13.
153   Quoted in Schaffer, 'Mysterious Magnum Bonum', 265; Yonge, *Magnum Bonum*, 146 (Ch.9).
154   Schaffer, 'Mysterious Magnum Bonum', 265–8.
155   Yonge, *Three Brides*, 46 (Ch.6).

expense of preparation for ordination is accompanied by a deterioration in his general state of health which is so marked that 'the lean, pale, anxious man' is unrecognizable from 'the round-faced, rosy, overgrown boy of a year ago'.[156] The sexual ambiguity Schaffer identifies in Yonge's characterization of Janet Brownlow also has numerous parallels in other novels: in *The Young Stepmother*, for instance, Sophy Gilbert is described as having a 'hoarse boy's voice',[157] and Lucilla's emotionally intense friendship with Horatia Charteris is marked by the adoption of 'little masculine affectations'[158] in their dress.

Schaffer, I would argue, correctly identifies in *Magnum Bonum* the themes of health, sexuality and the 'acceptable sort of feminist self-assertion'[159] represented by Janet's mother Caroline Brownlow, but misinterprets their significance because she underestimates Yonge's self-consciousness as an author, as Sandbach-Dahlström also does. Schaffer convincingly describes the shifting significance of the 'Magnum Bonum' throughout the novel, which as she notes 'mutates from discovery to forbidden knowledge to medicine to experiment, depending on which person's traits it has to confirm at each moment'.[160] Her description of this as an 'incoherence on the plot level',[161] however, and her conclusion that the novel's anticlimactic ending, in which the supposedly secret scientific discovery turns out to have been made independently a few years ago, can be read as exemplifying 'the need to be as skeptical as possible when this thick ideological cover starts stifling [...] Yonge's novels'[162] both imply that Yonge as an author is unaware of the deconstructive sliding of the signifier over the signified which Schaffer has identified in the 'Magnum Bonum' theme. Yonge can thus be represented by Schaffer

156   Ibid., 326 (Ch.37).
157   Yonge, *Young Stepmother*, 42 (Ch.4).
158   Yonge, *Hopes and Fears*, 134 (Part 2 Ch.3).
159   Schaffer, 'Mysterious Magnum Bonum', 258.
160   Ibid., 249.
161   Ibid.
162   Ibid., 275.

as a humorless ideologue whose 'semi-religious icon [...] of middle-class conformism'[163] has been seen through by the postmodern critic.

The unwarranted assumption of critical superiority in Schaffer's reading of Yonge seems not dissimilar to 'Mr Augustus Mills's eloquent lecture' on Chivalry, in which Anne Merton 'heard the words "barbarous institution," fifteen times repeated, and "civilized and enlightened age," at least twenty-three times'.[164] Schaffer fails to note, for example, Yonge's dramatization of the shifting senses of 'Magnum Bonum' in the novel by the obviously playful reference to the 'magnum bonum' variety of pear which startles Caroline at an early stage in the novel,[165] or the way in which the sermon which leads to Jock's conversion can be read as echoing the 'Magnum Bonum' of the novel in its comparison of 'man's search for the One Great Good' to the alchemist's quest for 'one great arcanum', concluding that 'it is the love of Christ that truly turneth all things into fine gold'[166] – an unconscious allusion that both Janet and her mother are described as picking up on.[167]

This ludic quality in Yonge's text is also reflected in the surely deliberate anticlimax, which seems comparable to the last line of Lewis Carroll's parody of the quest-romance, *The Hunting of the Snark*, 'For the Snark *was* a Boojum, you see.'[168] If the true 'Magnum Bonum' is the love of Christ, as is implied by the narrative prominence given to the sermon, then the fictional 'Magnum Bonum' of the novel must inevitably turn out to be a red herring, since otherwise the novel would be suggesting that there is some alternative. The varied aspects in which the fictional 'Magnum Bonum' appears to characters in the novel thus does not manifest simple 'incoherence on the plot level', as Schaffer claims, but dramatizes the characters' own capacities for deceiving themselves. What is disorienting about Yonge's fictional technique here, as in other novels, is that no character, not

163 Ibid.
164 Yonge, *Abbeychurch*, 164 (Ch.8).
165 Yonge, *Magnum Bonum*, 178 (Ch.10).
166 Ibid., 480–1 (Ch.24).
167 Ibid., 482 (Ch.24).
168 Lewis Carroll, 'The Hunting of the Snark', in *Complete Works*, intro by Alexander Woollcott (London: Nonesuch Press, 1939), Fit the Eighth, l 36.

even Caroline Brownlow, has a privileged perspective on the nature of the 'Magnum Bonum', which Yonge expects her readers to work out for themselves.

A similar objection can be made to the assumption underlying Schaffer's deconstructive reading, that Yonge's treatment of health and sexuality is an unconscious projection of her own frustrations. As later chapters in this book will show, significant aspects of Yonge's characterization reflect medical ideas that were current in the nineteenth century. Yonge's characters can certainly be read diagnostically, as Shaffer suggests, but this is because Yonge herself intended her characters to be interpreted this way, not because they are unconscious self-revelations.

The appeal of Schaffer and Leavis to a vitalistic ideology of 'Life' as a source of critical value restates criticisms of Tractarianism that were current in the nineteenth century.[169] At the same time, these critics assume that Yonge's novels promote 'middle-class conformism',[170] ignoring the fact that the 'Church views' which Yonge saw it as her task to promote[171] remained very much the values of a small and embattled group throughout Yonge's lifetime.[172] Schaffer's and Leavis's appeal to a reality of the 'natural' (represented in their criticism by health and unrepressed sexuality), in relation to which they find Yonge's fiction wanting, arguably represents a form of that Paleyan tradition of natural theology from which the Tractarians dissented, in the process incurring Victorian suspicions that by the promotion of sisterhoods, and encouragement of the suspect practice of auricular confession, they were engaged in a systematic project to undermine the authority of the family.[173] It is to this Tractarian critique of the naturalistic tendencies of modernity, and the associated anti-naturalistic poetic of the real which underlies Yonge's fiction, that we shall now turn.

---

169 John Maynard, *Victorian Discourses on Sexuality and Religion* (Cambridge: Cambridge University Press, 1993), 88–9.
170 Schaffer, 'Mysterious Magnum Bonum', 275.
171 Dennis, *Yonge*, 122–7.
172 John Shelton Reed, *Glorious Battle: The Cultural Politics of Victorian Anglo-Catholicism* (Nashville and London: Vanderbilt University Press, 1996), 226–8.
173 Ibid., 193–207.

Chapter Two
Feminism and Yonge's Christian Aesthetic

Narrative and Ideology

Many of the theoretical problems Yonge's novels have posed for modern critics are summed up in the anxiety expressed by the British experimental novelist B.S. Johnson that 'telling stories is telling lies'.[1] As we saw in the last chapter, critics of the novel such as Barbara Hardy and George Levine share the reluctance of E.M. Forster to find anything of value in novelistic plot, as famously expressed in his grudging acknowledgement, 'Yes, oh dear yes, the novel tells a story.'[2] For such critics, consistently with Modernist emphasis on the essential formlessness of reality, the value of a novel is to be located in the extent to which, consciously or unconsciously, it dislocates or ruptures the constraints of plot, since the attempt to impose intellectual order on the chaos of reality, however humanly necessary it may be, is *ipso facto* untruthful. Ultimately, such a critical outlook stems from the perspectivism of Nietzsche, for whom human consciousness was fundamentally 'mendacious'.[3]

Talia Schaffer offers a more sophisticated version of this view when, invoking Peter Brooks's argument that in the nineteenth-century novel 'deviance is the very condition for life to be "narratable"' since 'the state of normality is devoid of interest, energy, and the possibility for narration', she concludes that 'a Yonge novel stops

1   cf. A.S. Byatt and Ignês Sodré, *Imaginary Characters: Six Conversations About Women Writers*, Rebecca Swift (ed.) (London: Chatto and Windus, 1995), 232.

2   E.M. Forster, *Aspects of the Novel* (Harmondsworth: Penguin, 1962), 33–4.

3   Friedrich Nietzsche, 'On Truth and Falsehood in Their Extramoral Sense', in *Early Greek Philosophy and Other Essays*, trans. Maximilian A Mügge (London and Edinburgh: Foulis, 1911), 173–4.

because it has finally overcome its story'.[4] Schaffer suggests that the plots of Yonge's novels aspire to a condition of terminal stasis in which the status quo has become unchallengeable, and so are essentially untruthful and 'ideological' in their failure to acknowledge the moral complexities of 'life'.

This liberal humanist view of the novel begs the question of the standpoint from which such comparisons between fiction and 'life' are to be made since, as many theorists of ideology have pointed out, critical characterizations of an author's ideology must themselves be counted as ideological interventions.[5] Quite apart from this theoretical issue, however, the picture of Yonge underlying Schaffer's reading, as a writer whose recourse to realistic detail inadvertently punctured her own ideological fantasies, seriously misrepresents Yonge's work. Though argued at greater length, Schaffer's view of Yonge credits her with little more self-awareness as a writer than Q.D. Leavis's description of her as 'a day-dreamer with a writing itch that compensated her for a peculiarly starved life'.[6]

Schaffer's claim that the novels end in a condition of stasis and ideological rigidity is contradicted, I would suggest, by Yonge's willingness to return to characters who had featured in earlier writings, and by the frequent provisionality of her plots.[7] *The Heir of Redclyffe*, for example, quite unexpectedly kills off the novel's hero more than a hundred pages before the end, significantly revising the conventional marriage plot by extending it to the birth of Amy's child. Yonge was even prepared to contemplate writing a sequel, which it is hard to imagine a novelist such as George Eliot doing.[8]

4   Talia Schaffer, 'The Mysterious Magnum Bonum: Fighting to Read Charlotte Yonge', *Nineteenth-Century Literature* 55, no.2 (2000): 273–4.
5   Cf. Karl Mannheim, *Ideology and Utopia* (1929) in Terry Eagleton, *Ideology*, Longman Critical Reader (London: Longman, 1994), 61; Roland Barthes, *Mythologies*, trans. Annette Lavers (London: Vintage, 1993), 142–8.
6   Q.D. Leavis, 'Charlotte Yonge and Christian Discrimination', *Scrutiny* 12 (1944): 152–3.
7   Alethea Hayter, *Charlotte Yonge* (Plymouth: Northcote House, 1996), 7–12.
8   Christabel Coleridge, *Charlotte Mary Yonge: Her Life and Letters* (London: Macmillan, 1903), 168.

On a biographical level, we have the personal testimony of Miss Anderson Morshead who, when Yonge was already in her seventies, worked with her on a ladies committee, not a context, as Yonge's own portrayal of such committees in *The Daisy Chain* suggests, in which much mental flexibility was usually displayed.[9] Morshead remarks that it was impossible to foretell how Yonge 'would view a thing', and that 'she never was cut and dried'[10] – a level of unpredictability which is impressive indeed, given that Miss Morshead was familiar with Yonge's extensive writings. Yonge's biographer, Christabel Coleridge, makes a similar comment about the suppleness of Yonge's thinking even in an explicitly didactic work, *Conversations on the Catechism*, in which, she notes, 'the doctrines are not given cut and dried in little sentences to be learned by heart as is now the custom'.[11] Yonge's own advice manual, *Womankind*, written when she was in her fifties, dwells at length on the need for older people to recognize that their values and ideals will inevitably be superseded by those of a younger generation,[12] in a way that seems incompatible with the kind of ideological rigidity attributed to her by Schaffer; as several critics have noted, in *Hopes and Fears* this advice is anticipated by the description of the generation gap between the older lady Honora Charlecote (in many ways a self-portrait) and the young Lucilla Sandbrook.[13]

Schaffer's deconstructive reading of Yonge reflects a sense that the vividness and particularity of her characterization must necessarily be at odds with her own stated view of her fiction as 'a sort of instrument for popularising Church views',[14] a critical approach in

---

9   Charlotte M. Yonge, *The Daisy Chain, or Aspirations* (London: Macmillan, 1886), 349–50 (Part 2 Ch.2).

10   Coleridge, *Yonge*, 293–4.

11   Ibid., 186.

12   quoted in Ethel Romanes, *Charlotte Mary Yonge: An Appreciation* (London: Mowbray, 1908), 171–4.

13   Yonge, *Hopes and Fears, or Scenes from the Life of a Spinster* (London: Macmillan, 1889), 484 (Part 2 Ch.27).

14   Barbara Dennis, *Charlotte Yonge (1823–1901), Novelist of the Oxford Movement: A Literature of Victorian Culture and Society* (Lewiston, NY: Edwin Mellen, 1992), 122–7.

whose support might be cited her biographer's comment that Yonge's characters 'took their development into their own hands, and became far too real to serve only one purpose'.[15] Yonge's choice of the word 'instrument', however, suggests that the key to this apparent contradiction between her strongly-held Tractarian beliefs, on the one hand, and the spontaneity of her characters, on the other, lies in the providentialist perspective which informs her writing. Yonge does not merely conceive of her novels as imitating the workings of providence, but as texts whose interpretation itself takes place within a providential economy, in much the same way as Keble had suggested that a providential economy underwrote the texts of ancient poetry so that they did not just mean what their authors intended. Yonge's typically self-effacing response to a presentation that was made to her late in life is significant in this context:

> The worst of all the day was that one felt it so untrue not to be able to say how one fell short of one's books and ideals, and so swallowing it all! There is nothing for it but to believe that all this being so, these writings have been meant to be instruments.[16]

Despite Yonge's firm conviction about the kind of purpose which her fiction served, she was not interested in using it as a vehicle for propaganda, as is implied by Schaffer's comment that she would have preferred to be regarded as a 'pious pedagogue',[17] because this kind of self-willed intention would have forestalled the wider kind of instrumentality in which she thought her fiction participated. If reality itself is providentially motivated, then Yonge's 'Church views' would be best served by the attempt to represent reality, even if it did not fall neatly into cut and dried patterns. As Elizabeth Jay notes, Yonge's tolerance of this kind of messiness and ambiguity despite the religious basis of her fiction is what makes her writing distinctive in comparison to other mid-nineteenth-century religious novelists such as Newman;[18] it is reflected, for example, in the lack of plot resolution

15   Coleridge, *Yonge*, 182–6.
16   Ibid., 304.
17   Schaffer, 'Mysterious Magnum Bonum', 245.
18   Elisabeth Jay, *Faith and Doubt in Victorian Britain* (London, 1986), 2–5, 71.

for the character of Angela Underwood in *The Pillars of the House*, on which June Sturrock comments.[19] Yonge's writing may have benefited in this respect from the influence of Keble, who regarded Newman's departure from the Anglican communion as a morally culpable failure to cope with the existential demands of intellectual uncertainty.[20]

Keble's Conception of 'Ethos': Providentialist Psychology

We noted in the previous chapter that Yonge's attitudes to language and its development correspond to the providentialist hermeneutic employed by Keble in his *Lectures on Poetry*, and in a similar way I would like to suggest that the apparent conflict to which Schaffer responds, between the richness and particularity of Yonge's character-ization and her commitment to 'Church views', can be resolved if we relate Yonge's novels to the concept of 'ethos' shared by Keble and other early Tractarians. As we noted, the Kebelian distinction between 'ethos' and 'pathos' opposes the habitual complex of feeling which constitutes character to sudden and overwhelming emotion, and when the words are defined in this way it would be fair to say that ethos, rather than pathos, is the central concern of Yonge's fiction. The struggle for self-control which preoccupies characters such as Guy in *The Heir of Redclyffe* when he fights off the temptation to call Philip out to a duel,[21] or Albinia in *The Young Stepmother* when she regrets her unguarded outburst in front of one of her step-children,[22] rep-resents an attempt to merge immediate emotional reaction in a con-

19   June Sturrock, *'Heaven and Home': Charlotte M. Yonge's Domestic Fiction and the Victorian Debate Over Women*, English Literary Studies (Victoria, BC: University of Victoria, 1995), 72.

20   John Keble, *Sermons Academical and Occasional* (Oxford and London: Parker and Rivington, 1848), lxvi–lxviii

21   Yonge, *The Heir of Redclyffe*, Barbara Dennis (ed.) (Oxford: Oxford University Press, 1997), 223–7 (Ch.16).

22   Yonge, *The Young Stepmother, or A Chronicle of Mistakes* (London: Mac-millan, 1889), 64 (Ch.6).

sistency of feeling which will enable appropriateness of response. Likewise, serious moral lapses in Yonge's novels are always portrayed in terms of the systematic and habitual perversion of feeling, such as Laura's perseverance in concealing her secret engagement with Philip from her parents in *The Heir of Redclyffe*,[23] or Robert Fulmort's pained realization that the schoolmistress Edna Murrell's action in eloping with Owen Sandbrook is reflected in the 'passionate verses of Shelley and Byron' which fall from her 'dying lips', and which 'must have been conned by heart, and have been the favourite study'.[24]

Keble privileges epic above lyric poetry because while lyric may represent the expression of momentary feeling, the sustained nature of epic must provide indications of those unifying associative trains which constitute character, or ethos, both in poetry and in ordinary life.[25] It is this consistency inherent in character, I would suggest, that from Keble's Tractarian point of view makes it stand in a significant relationship to the workings of divine providence. Keble can interpret pagan poets such as Aeschylus and Virgil as unconsciously anticipating the Christian revelation,[26] because the associative consistency that defines their poetic greatness is for him not only an indication of their personal virtue, but also marks their special participation in the greater consistency of the divine economy that makes it possible to discern the workings of providence in human history. This is not, of course, an attitude which in the 1830s is confined to Keble and the Tractarians; it is implicit, for example, in Carlyle's 'great men' theory of history, in which an overriding consistency of character inde-

23   Yonge, *Heir*, 445–6 (Ch.34).
24   Yonge, *Hopes and Fears*, 280 (Part 2 Ch.12).
25   Although Keble discusses Greek tragedy at length in the *Lectures on Poetry*, he regards it as deriving from epic, John Keble, *Keble's Lectures on Poetry, 1832–1841*, 2 vols, trans. Edward Kershaw Francis (Oxford: Clarendon Press, 1912), 1: 330–1 in Gavin Budge (ed.), *Aesthetics and Religion in Nineteenth-Century Britain*, 6 vols (Bristol: Thoemmes, 2003), Vol.1.
26   Keble, *Lectures on Poetry*, 1: 399–400, 2: 463–4.

pendent of circumstances is made responsible for providentially ordained historical progress.[27]

For Keble, then, character, as manifested in great poetry, stands in what may be defined as a typological relationship to divine Personality, as manifested in the Incarnation: it is indicative of the Christian revelation, but cannot be simply reduced to its terms because, unlike an allegory, it has its own reality. As I discuss in a subsequent chapter, the concept of typology, as employed by Keble and other Tractarians such as Isaac Williams, is in some ways close to the concept of the symbol as defined by Coleridge. Crucially, however, it avoids the potential theological unorthodoxy implied in Coleridge's tendency to pantheism by emphasizing the epistemological gap between material and spiritual worlds in a way which reflects the intuitionist philosophy of the Common Sense School rather than German Idealism. The characteristic Tractarian emphasis on the inadequacy of Reason to comprehend the moral basis of religion, which underlies their hostility to the Paleyan appeal to evidences of Christianity,[28] reflects this intuitionist emphasis on an epistemological gap.

From the typological standpoint defined by Keble, I would argue, there is no necessary conflict, of the kind assumed by critics such as Schaffer, between realist particularity of characterization in Yonge's fiction and her doctrinally-based moral outlook. Characterization in Yonge's novels can be regarded as akin to the attempt to convey 'inscape' in Gerard Manley Hopkins's poetics;[29] the more telling the psychological detail, the more it testifies to the divine economy of which human psychological processes are part. This kind of 'immanent providentialism',[30] in which, as in early Preraphaelite painting, detail is regarded as valuable for its own sake in that its very par-

---

27   Thomas Carlyle, 'Signs of the Times', in *Critical and Miscellaneous Essays*, 7 vols (London: Chapman and Hall, 1872), 2: 246.

28   Peter Benedict Nockles, *The Oxford Movement in Context: Anglican High Churchmanship, 1760–1857* (Cambridge: Cambridge University Press, 1994), 204–5.

29   Gerard Manley Hopkins, *Selected Prose*, Gerald Roberts (ed.) (Oxford: Oxford University Press, 1980), 77.

30   Thomas Vargish, *The Providential Aesthetic in Victorian Fiction* (Charlottesville: Virginia University Press, 1985), 21–6.

ticularity indicates the divinely ordered whole of which it forms part,[31] helps to explain the characteristic absence of a strong narratorial voice in Yonge's fiction. If the purpose of the novel is to train its readers to identify providence at work in the details of reality, then any attempt to forestall the interpretative process by pointing out a moral would be counter-productive.

Just as Keble subjects poetic texts to minute scrutiny in order to identify associative tendencies of which the authors themselves may have been unaware, so too in Yonge's novels unexplained emblematic details often reveal attitudes or psychological tendencies which characters do not wish, or perhaps are unable, to articulate to them-selves, in a technique which anticipates some aspects of Freudian psychoanalysis. This kind of emblematic commentary is to be found even in the early novel *The Two Guardians*, where Gerald's repressed desire that his sister and her governess should get their comeuppance for their bullying insistence on reading one of the shy heroine's letters is conveyed by his 'sketch of a cat pricking her paw by patting a hedgehog rolled up in a ball'.[32] As critics have noted,[33] in *The Heir of Redclyffe* Philip's busybodying tendency to assume he knows better than his cousin Amy, which eventually leads to Guy's death, is in-dicated at the very beginning of the novel by his breaking off the single camelia flower which Amy has cultivated when he officiously insists on carrying the plant over to the window.[34]

Another telling psychological detail in Yonge's characterization of Philip is his insistence on beautiful bindings for his books,[35] which arguably hints at Philip's rather rigid and constricted character through the associations of the word 'hidebound'. The sense of what Freudians would call an anal personality is also conveyed through the contrast Philip sees between 'the scrupulous neatness and fastidious

31   Herbert Sussman, *Fact Into Fiction: Typology in Carlyle, Ruskin, and the Pre-Raphaelite Brotherhood* (Columbus: Ohio State University Press, 1979), xvi–xvii.
32   Yonge, *The Two Guardians, or Home in This World* (London: Masters, 1885), 74 (Ch.5).
33.   E.g. Hayter, *Yonge*, 7–8.
34   Yonge, *Heir*, 4 (Ch.1).
35   Ibid., 55 (Ch.4).

taste'[36] of his own room and Guy's rooms at Oxford, whose very lack of personal touches indicates that Guy leads the 'hidden life' characteristic of all Yonge's spiritual heroes, though not of course in the sense suspected by Philip, who is investigating his unfounded suspicions of Guy's gambling. The narrator's description of the 'hidden life' led by Frank in *The Castle Builders*, as one of the novel's desultory heroines comes to understand it after he has died saving her from drowning, makes the typological dimension of character in Yonge's fiction clear:

> She was in earnest now; her eyes had been opened to perceive that Frank had led a hidden life, that there was something going on within him, of which his outward acts were the tokens; and for the first time she saw that that hidden life was the real one, that she herself, while satisfied with the material world, was living in a dream, and that it was only they who look at the things that are not seen, whose life had any reality.[37]

The plot of *The Castle Builders*, which contrasts Frank's spiritual consistency even in the face of his father's determined opposition to his cherished plan to become a priest with the inconstancy and lack of determination of the rather wishy-washy heroines, is designed to suggest that goodness does not consist in an abstract and uniform piety, exemplified in the novel by the meaningless rote learning of isolated Biblical texts in which the Evangelical-dominated church committee thinks religious education should consist,[38] but in an intensification of personal character. As the references to 'reality' suggest, Yonge regards the typological dimension of her fiction as dependent upon her success in achieving a realist aesthetic: the more living the novelistic character, the more Yonge has managed to convey that sense of personal authenticity which carries within it a relationship to the divine and makes life, as Keats remarked, 'a

---

36   Yonge, 252 (Ch.19).
37   Ibid., *The Castle Builders; or, The Deferred Confirmation* (London: Mozley, 1854), 214–15 (Ch.14) in *Abbeychurch / The Castle Builders*, facs. edn (New York and London: Garland Publishing, 1976).
38   Ibid., 84–5 (Ch.6).

perpetual allegory'.[39] A similar kind of thinking appears to underlie Richard Hurrell Froude's remark that biography is 'the best means of infusing principles against the reader's will'.[40] The idea that moral improvement is about becoming more and more authentically oneself is, as we shall see, often conveyed in Yonge's novels through the acquisition of appropriate gender characteristics, so that characters' moral progress by the end of the novel is indicated by the distance they have travelled from a condition of sexual inversion, in which female characters have hoarse low voices and display unbecoming eccentricities,[41] and male characters are languid and effeminate.[42]

Associationist Psychology in Evangelicalism and Tractarianism

In arguing that the psychological realism of Yonge's novels grows out of her Tractarian beliefs, rather than being at odds with them, I do not mean to suggest that this blend of associationist psychology and religious doctrine is exclusive to the Tractarians. Although a number of distinctive Tractarian emphases, such as the insistence on set forms of prayer[43] or the interest in church architecture and decoration,[44]

39   John Keats, *The Letters of John Keats, 1814–1821*, 2 vols, Hyder Edward Rollins (ed.) (Cambridge, MA: Harvard University Press, 1958), 2: 67.

40   Richard Hurrell Froude, *Remains of the Late Reverend Richard Hurrell Froude MA, Fellow of Oriel College, Oxford*, 2 vols (London: Rivington, 1838), 1: 321.

41   E.g. the 'hoarse boy's voice' belonging to Sophy Kendal in *Young Stepmother*, 42 (Ch.4); Yonge, *Daisy Chain*, 60 (Part 1 Ch.6).

42   Yonge, *The Clever Woman of the Family* (London: Macmillan, 1892), 80 (Part 1 Ch.6); Charlotte M. Yonge, *The Pillars of the House, or Under Wode, Under Rode*, 2 vols (London: Macmillan, 1901), 1: 7 (Ch.1).

43   John Henry Newman, *Parochial Sermons* (London and Oxford: Rivington and Parker, 1835), 1: 309–11.

44   Cf. Richard Frederick Littledale, *Innovations: A Lecture Delivered in the Assembly Rooms, Liverpool, April 23rd 1868* (Oxford and London: Mowbray and Simpkin, Marshall and Co, 1868), 4, 27.

reflect the influence of associationist psychology on the movement's religious thought, the example of the Baptist John Foster's *Essays in a Series of Letters* shows that this associationism should be understood as part of the Tractarians' inheritance from Evangelicalism. Foster's *Essays* was one of the best-selling books of the early nineteenth century, and opens with a lengthy essay 'On a Man's Writing Memoirs of Himself' which articulates a quasi-Wordsworthian sense of 'the endless progress of life' in which 'its past years lose that character of vanity which would seem to belong to a train of fleeting perishing moments, [...] assuming the dignity of commencing eternity.'[45] From Foster's associationist standpoint, the child is indeed 'father of the Man',[46] in a way which leads him to stress the importance of consistency and habit in the formation of a religious character:

> It would be interesting to record, or hear, the history of a character which has received its form, and reached its maturity, under the strongest operations of religion. We do not know that there is a more beneficent or a more direct mode of the divine agency in any part of the creation than that which 'apprehends' a man, as apostolic language expresses it, amidst the unthinking crowd, and leads him into serious reflection, into elevated devotion, into progressive virtue, and finally into a nobler life after death. When he has long been commanded by this influence, he will be happy to look back to its first operations, whether they were mingled in early life almost insensibly with his feelings or came on him with mighty force at some particular time, and in connexion with some assignable and memorable circumstance, which was apparently the instrumental cause. He will trace all the progress of this his better life with grateful acknowledgment to the sacred power which has advanced him to a decisiveness of religious habit that seems to stamp eternity on his character. In the great majority of things, habit is a greater plague than ever affected Egypt; in religious character, it is a grand felicity. The devout man exults in the indications of his being fixed and irretrievable. He feels this confirmed habit as the grasp of the hand of God, which will never let him go. From this advanced state he looks with firmness and joy on futurity, and says, I carry the eternal mark upon me that I belong to God; I am free of the universe; and I am ready to

---

45   John Foster, *Essays, in a Series of Letters* 7th edn, revised (London, 1823), 5.
46   William Wordsworth, 'My Heart Leaps Up When I Behold', in *The Oxford Authors: William Wordsworth*, Stephen Gill (Oxford: Oxford University Press, 1984), 17.

go to any world to which he shall please to transmit me, certain that every where, in height or depth, he will acknowledge me for ever.[47]

Foster, who was regarded by George Eliot as a genius,[48] makes use of associationism to provide a psychological account of the Calvinist concept of 'assurance', in which the believer attains a conviction of their own election: according to Foster, this assurance is the product of a habitual fixity of character, rather than the immediate result of a dramatic conversion experience, an argument whose emphasis on the prolonged nature of conversion is in line with conservative strands in early nineteenth-century Evangelical thought.[49] Tractarians, on the other hand, often turn associationist arguments against what they perceive as Evangelicalism's corrupting emphasis on religious feeling divorced from practice; the early Newman, for example, uses associationist arguments to question the adequacy of deathbed conversion.

Since for Newman 'even supposing a man of unholy life were suffered to enter heaven, *he would not be happy there*; so that it would be no mercy to permit him to enter',[50] the religious life must consist in the deliberate attempt to cultivate 'holiness, or inward separation from the world'.[51] Newman suggests, in an argument that draws on the language of Brunonian medicine,[52] that this state of sanctification cannot consist merely in experiencing religious emotions, because if these are not associatively reinforced by 'depositing your good feelings into your heart itself by making them influence your conduct'[53] then the attempt to perpetuate the 'state of excitement' through the 'potent stimulants' of 'new doctrines' or 'strange teachers' will end up

47   Foster, *Essays*, 67–9.
48   Bruce Haley, *The Healthy Body and Victorian Culture* (Cambridge, MA: Harvard University Press, 1978), 195.
49   Elizabeth Jay, *The Religion of The Heart: Anglican Evangelicalism and The Nineteenth Century Novel* (Oxford: The Clarendon Press, 1979), 60
50   Newman, *Parochial Sermons*, 1: 3.
51   Ibid., 1: 8.
52   Cf. Günter B. Risse, 'Brunonian Therapeutics: New Wine in Old Bottles?' in W.Y. Bynum and Roy Porter (eds) *Brunonianism in Britain and Europe* (*Medical History*, Supplement no.8), (1988), 48.
53   Newman, *Parochial Sermons*, 1: 136.

by exhausting the capacity for such emotions through overstimulation, leading to 'that fearful ultimate state of hard-heartedness [...] when the miserable sinner believes indeed as the devils may, yet not even with the devils' trembling, but sins on without fear'.[54] The truly religious man, on the other hand, has attained through habitual acts of obedience a state where 'our will runs parallel to God's will',[55] so that 'he is moved by God dwelling in him, and needs not but act on instinct'.[56] For Newman, as I have suggested is also the case for Yonge, sanctity consists in the realization of character so that one's will stands in a typological relationship to that of God, rather than in a state of feeling that is different from everyday life.

Despite this doctrinal difference, the fundamental similarity between Foster's associationist account of the nature of religious belief and the Tractarian point of view can be seen in the importance Foster attaches to personal influence:

> In some instances we have been sensible, in a very short time, of a powerful force operating on our opinions, tastes, and habits, and throwing them into a new order. This effect is inevitable, if a young susceptible mind happens to become familiarly acquainted with a person in whom a strongly individual cast of character is sustained and dignified by uncommon mental resources; and it may be found that, generally, the greatest measure of effect has been produced by the influence of a very small number of persons; often of one only, whose extended and interesting mind had more power to surround and assimilate a young and ingenuous being, than the collective influence of a multitude of persons, whose characters were moulded in the manufactory of custom, and sent forth like images of clay of kindred shape and varnish from a pottery.[57]

As Foster elsewhere notes, since everyone is potentially exposed to a variety of conflicting associations which tend to cancel each other out, the development of any marked individual character must depend upon the acquisition of a 'determining principle', which operates by 'attracting and meeting every impression, that is adapted to coalesce

---

54   Ibid., 1: 139.
55   Ibid., 1: 85.
56   Ibid., 1: 87.
57   Foster, *Essays*, 18.

with it and strengthen it'.[58] Foster seems to envisage that anyone in whom such an associative complex is strongly developed will also naturally tend to convey it to others, in that they too will start selectively to assimilate environmental stimuli along similar lines, especially if they are young and impressionable.

This account of the formation of character is remarkably similar to the way Newman describes the effect of 'the hidden saints' who 'rescue the world for centuries to come' by the way in which they have 'impressed an image on the Church'.[59] Newman emphasizes that the power of religious truth lies in 'the consistency of virtue',[60] an argument which implies that it is the capacity of religion to act as an associative centre for the entire personality that comes to outweigh all other impulses, remarking that 'we shall find it difficult to estimate the moral power which a single individual, trained to practise what he teaches, may acquire in his own circle, in the course of years'.[61] For Newman, this is a reason 'to be satisfied with the humblest and most obscure lot', since 'we could scarcely in any situation be direct instruments of good to any besides those who personally know us, who ever must form a small circle',[62] an argument that is relevant not only to the priority which Tractarian clergymen attached to parochial work (when Newman was writing they were likely to be shut out from any preferment within the Church of England),[63] but also to the position of women. As we shall see in a later chapter, this aspect of Tractarianism is reflected in the conservative feminism of Yonge's novels, which frequently centre around the development of an initially weak, or self-conflicting, character into someone who exerts a quasi-mesmeric influence and moral power on those around them.[64] The

---

58   Ibid., 35.
59   John Henry Newman, *Newman's University Sermons: Fifteen Sermons Preached Before the University of Oxford 1826–1843*, intro by D.M. MacKinnon and J.D. Holmes (London: SPCK, 1970), 96–7.
60   Ibid., 93.
61   Ibid., 94.
62   Ibid., 97–8.
63.   Owen Chadwick, *The Mind of The Oxford Movement* (London: Adam and Charles Black, 1960), 34–9.
64   Cf. Romanes, *Yonge: An Appreciation*, 84.

moral importance in Yonge's novels of this kind of associative centre (often, of course, located in the family) is illustrated by the character of Philip in *The Heir of Redclyffe*, whose moral failure in concealing his engagement with Laura, it is implied, is a consequence of the deracination of his home associations by his elder sister's selfish marriage to a wealthy man she does not love.[65]

Nineteenth-Century Cultural Feminism: the Example of Sarah Lewis

The close relationship between the psychologization of religious belief we have found in Foster and Newman and nineteenth-century ideas about the role of women may be illustrated by reference to Sarah Lewis's popular educational tract, *Woman's Mission*, which is generally accepted by critics as representative of the Victorian gender ideology of 'separate spheres', even though it is partly a translation of a work by Aimé Martin, a French disciple of Rousseau.[66] Lewis opposes demands that women should enabled to participate more actively in public life, asking the rhetorical question:

> Would the greatest possible good be procured by bringing her out of her present sphere into the arena of public life, by introducing to our homes and to our hearths the violent dissensions, the hard and rancorous feelings, engendered by political strife?[67]

Lewis argues that, given the increasing absence of men from the home, the needs of society are best served by use of the 'influence' which domestic women are peculiarly fitted to exert,[68] rather than by

---

65 Yonge, *Heir*, 56–7 (Ch.4).
66 Elizabeth K. Helsinger, Robin Lauterbach Sheets and William Veeder, *The Woman Question: Society and Literature in Britain and America, 1837–1883*, 3 vols (New York: Garland, 1983), 1: 5–13.
67 Sarah Lewis, *Woman's Mission* (London: John W. Parker, 1839), 10–11.
68 Ibid., 22.

female attempts to obtain political power, since power is limited in its operation, whilst 'influence has its source in human sympathies, and is boundless in its operation':[69]

> We see that power, while it regulates men's action, cannot reach their opinions. It cannot modify their dispositions nor implant sentiments, nor alter character. All these things are the work of influence. Men frequently resist power, while they yield to influence an unconscious acquiescence.[70]

For Lewis, social relations cannot be based on political power alone because of the superficial nature of such power. Her contrast between 'power' and 'influence' may be compared to the Coleridgean distinction between 'fancy' and 'imagination':[71] power, like fancy, operates on 'fixities and definites',[72] and lacks the ability to transform the subjects it works on, as both influence and imagination do. Lewis suggests that the more effective influence is, the less it is perceived to exert an effect at all, noting that 'indirect influences are much more powerful than direct ones [...] because they act by a sort of moral contagion, and are imbibed by the receiver as they flow from their source, without consciousness on either side'.[73] Given that the context of Lewis's tract is the 1832 Reform Act, her argument that a democratic society can only function on the basis of a consensus whose locus is outside the democratic process can be regarded as an anticipation of Matthew Arnold's response to a later extension of the electoral franchize in *Culture and Anarchy*, except that where Arnold invokes the humanizing effect of 'culture' Lewis invokes the influence of the domestic woman. In modern terms, the issue of how to foster a sense of social cohesion which Lewis is addressing might be described as a question of 'hegemony' in the Gramscian sense.[74] From

69   Ibid., 13.
70   Ibid.
71   S.T. Coleridge, *Biographia Literaria*, 2 vols, James Engell and W. Jackson Bate (eds) (Princeton University Press, 1983), 1: 301–5.
72   Ibid., 1: 305.
73   Lewis, *Woman's Mission*, 93.
74   Antonio Gramsci, *Selections from Cultural Writings*, David Forgacs and Geoffrey Nowell-Smith (eds), trans. William Boelhaver (London: Lawrence and Wishart, 1985), 98.

Lewis's implicitly middle-class perspective, female 'influence' can ensure the continued assertion of middle-class moral authority by preventing young middle-class males from being seduced by pursuits of the aristocracy[75] which threaten to reduce them to the demoralized condition of the urban poor, a social anxiety which can be traced back to Oliver Goldsmith.[76]

Lewis argues that 'even Christianity itself has achieved, and is to achieve, its greatest triumphs, not by express commands or prohibitions, but by a thousand indirect influences, emanating from its spirit rather than its letter',[77] in terms which bring her position very close to that of Newman's *University Sermons*. Like Newman and the other Tractarians, Lewis assigns reason a very secondary role in the formation of religious belief, arguing that 'though intellect may give dignity and vigour to moral sentiments where they do exist, it has no tendency to produce them where they do not' since 'like an unprincipled ally, it is ever ready to aid either party, and to lend energy to bad passions, as well as loftiness to good ones',[78] a distrustful view of the moral influence of unaided reason which echoes Newman's sermon on 'The Usurpations of Reason'.[79] In much the same way as Newman and Foster, Lewis invokes an associationist psychology to explain the non-rational basis of religious belief, commenting that 'principles have their chief source in influences − early influences, above all; and early influences have more power in forming character than institutions or mental cultivation',[80] and emphasizing that 'the importance of early impressions − of *home* impressions − is proved by

---

75   This is a scenario which seems to be implicit in Lewis's remark that 'young men, flushed with the pride of intellect on entering life, are sometimes impatient of control; fathers are often without tact to exercise wholesome authority in such a way as not to wound that pride; the check is then deposited in the mother's hands; *she* will have no want of tact in using it, for it is precisely in that delicate and indescribable application of means to ends, called "tact", that women are proverbially skilled'. Lewis, *Woman's Mission*, 33–4.

76   Oliver Goldsmith, *The Vicar of Wakefield*, in *Miscellaneous Works*, intro by David Masson (London: Macmillan, 1874), 40–1 (Ch.19).

77   Lewis, *Woman's Mission*, 14.

78   Ibid., 18.

79   Newman, *University Sermons*, 54–74.

80   Lewis, *Woman's Mission*, 19.

the extreme difficulty of eradicating them or counteracting them if bad'.[81] As for Newman, true religion for Lewis is communicated above all through personal influence, rather than through reasoning, and from this perspective the role of the domestic woman, like the pastoral care of the parish clergyman, becomes fraught with all the significance of Providence itself. Lewis contrasts, for example, the perspective of a teacher, concerned only the development of a child's intellect, with the perspective of a mother for whom her child is 'an immortal being, whose soul it is her duty to train for immortality',[82] in terms which recall Yonge's depiction in *Hopes and Fears* of the effects of the governess Miss Fennimore's neglect of the moral welfare of her charges, due to her being 'too much absorbed in the studies to look close into the human beings'.[83]

As I will discuss in a later chapter, the kind of domestic ideology represented by Lewis is central to Yonge's novels, a major pre-occupation of which is the moral effects of family life. Feminist critics have often characterized this Victorian domestic ideology as dis-ablingly restrictive for women,[84] but, as I will suggest, in the context of the important analogies between the role of the domestic woman and the role of the saint within Tractarian thought it is possible to see that a religiously inflected version of domestic ideology offered significant opportunities for the critique of a male-dominated society, of which I argue Yonge's writings often availed themselves. Regarded from this perspective, Yonge is not the conservative figure she has often been made to appear,[85] since her involvement in highly controversial developments such as Anglican sisterhoods[86] and auricular confession,[87] often construed by mainstream Victorian opinion as

---

81   Ibid., 30.
82   Ibid., 22.
83   Yonge, *Hopes and Fears*, 107 (Part 2 Ch.2).
84   E.g. Deirdre David, *Intellectual Women and Victorian Patriarchy: Harriet Martineau, Elizabeth Barrett Browning, George Eliot* (Ithaca, NY: Cornell University Press, 1987), x–xi.
85   Hayter, *Yonge*, 56–7.
86   Coleridge, *Yonge*, 237.
87   Ibid., 232–4.

attacks on patriarchal authority within the family,[88] place her in the forefront of the sexual politics of the second half of the nineteenth century.

Victorian domestic ideology harbours the potential for what has been dubbed 'cultural', or 'social' feminism,[89] in a way which can be seen at work even in *Woman's Mission* itself. Lewis draws attention to a version of the Victorian sexual double standard when she comments acidly:

> The regulation of temper, the repression of selfishness, the examination of motive – how seldom do they form any part of the education of boys! The neglect has a most fatal effect on their happiness, and the happiness of all connected with them. We may see it illustrated in that curious popular paradox, which allows a man to be by his unregulated temper the torment of all around him, and yet retain the name of a 'thoroughly good-hearted fellow'.[90]

Lewis notes that a woman who behaved in a similar way would be condemned as a 'vixen', and suggests that a greater degree of maternal involvement in boys' education would better equip them for their eventual role as heads of families; she also adds that in order to exert this kind of influence, women must undertake a continuing programme of self-education.[91] Far from relegating women to political impotence, the 'separate sphere' for women promoted by Lewis offers a utopian space from which patriarchy itself can be feminized, and I will argue that the same can be said for Yonge's Tractarian beliefs.

---

88 John Shelton Reed, *Glorious Battle: The Cultural Politics of Victorian Anglo-Catholicism* (Nashville and London: Vanderbilt University Press, 1996), 193–207.

89 Annette R. Federico, '"An 'Old-Fashioned' Young Woman": Marie Corelli and the New Woman', in Nicola Diane Thompson (ed.), *Victorian Women Writers and the Woman Question* (Cambridge: Cambridge University Press, 1999), 241–6; Beth Sutton-Ramspeck, 'Shot Out of the Canon: Mary Ward and the Claims of Conflicting Feminisms', in Nicola Diane Thompson (ed.), *Victorian Women Writers and the Woman Question* (Cambridge: Cambridge University Press, 1999), 204–10; cf. Alice Echolls, *Daring to be Bad: Radical Feminism in America 1967–1975* (Minneapolis: University of Minnesota Press, 1989), 243–57.

90 Lewis, *Woman's Mission*, 26–7.

91 Ibid., 34.

Lewis's associationist arguments bring her very close to the kind of moral and educative programme that is set out in Yonge's periodical for women, *The Monthly Packet*.[92] Lewis emphasizes that women can only fulfil their proper role of exercising 'influence' by developing a capacity for self-control:

> The qualities which seem more expecially needful in a character which is to influence others are, consistency, simplicity, and benevolence, or love.
>
> By consistency of character, I mean consistency of action with principle, or manner with thought, or *self* with *self*.
>
> The want of this quality is a failing with which our sex is often charged, and justly; but are we to blame? Our hearts are warm, our nerves irritable, and we have seen how little there is, in existing systems of female education, calculated to give wide, lofty, self-devoted principles of action. Without such principles there can be no consistency of conduct; and without consistency of conduct there can be no available moral influence.[93]

Lewis lays such stress on the ability to be consistent, for which the precondition is self-control, because she conceives of the educative effect of 'influence' in similar terms to Foster and Newman, as consisting in the unconscious transmission of associative complexes of thought and behaviour; inconsistency would obviously prevent the formation of such associations. Lewis's reference to the special irritability of women's nerves invokes widely held medical ideas of the period,[94] and implies that women, as the pre-eminent examples of the nineteenth-century 'nervous subject', stand in particular need of the sobering and 'soothing'[95] effects of religion in order to be able to manifest this kind of consistency. As Lewis makes clear, however, the syndrome of nervousness characteristic of women also makes their situation paradigmatic of the condition of modernity:

---

92   E.g. Anon., 'Sunlight in the Clouds', *Monthly Packet* 1 (Series 1 1851): 149–51; Anon., 'Minor Cares', *Monthly Packet* 7 (Series 1 1854): 120–5; Anon., 'Autumn Wanderings', *Monthly Packet* 18 (Series 1 1859): 103.

93   Lewis, *Woman's Mission*, 104.

94   Janet Oppenheim, *'Shattered Nerves': Doctors; Patients and Depression in Victorian England* (New York: Oxford University Press, 1991), 181–7.

95   John Keble, *The Christian Year*, intro by J.C. Shairp (London and New York: Dent and Dutton, 1914), 1.

It is peculiarly desirable, at this particular juncture of time, that this subject be insisted upon. Man, naturally a social and gregarious animal, becomes every day more so. The vast undertakings, the mighty movements of the present day, which can only be carried into operation by the combined energy of many wills, tend to destroy individuality of thought and action, and the consciousness of individual responsibility. The dramatist complains of this fact, as it affects his art, the representation of surface – the moralist has greater cause to complain of it, as affecting the foundation of character.[96]

The levelling tendencies of mass society, of which Lewis here complains, represent the reverse side of the 'moral contagion'[97] of influence; as her contemporary the popular novelist Edward Bulwer-Lytton noted, the spreading of new forms of crime could be regarded as a transmission of exactly the same kind of associative complex (or epidemic monomania)[98] which for Lewis is a guarantor of virtue. Lewis's concerns about the moral effects of social modernity thus anticipate, in ways which make women emblematic of the condition of England as a whole, the anxieties about mass nervous irritability[99] and urbanization[100] underlying the threat felt in the 1850s and 1860s to be represented by the genres of spasmodic poetry[101] and sensation fiction.[102]

At the same time, however, Lewis suggests that women's nervous irritability is a strength as well as a weakness. Not only does

96. Lewis, *Woman's Mission*, 98.
97   Ibid., 93.
98   Edward Bulwer-Lytton, *Night and Morning*, Knebworth edn (London: Routledge, n.d.), 238 (Book 3 Ch.8).
99   Alan Bewell, *Romanticism and Colonial Disease* (Baltimore and London: Johns Hopkins University Press, 1999), 10–13. Cf. Southey's comparison of the effect of popular political discussion to the effect 'which novel-reading produces upon girls', review of *Propositions for ameliorating the Condition of the Poor* etc., by P. Colquhoun, Quarterly Review 8 (1812): 353
100 William Wordsworth, *Prose Works*, 3 vols, W.J.B. Owen and Jane Worthington Smyser (ed.) (Oxford: Clarendon Press, 1974), 129; John Ruskin, *Works*, 39 vols, E.T. Cook and Alexander Wedderburn (ed.) (London: Allen, 1903–1912), 34: 265–70.
101 Mark A. Weinstein, *William Edmondstoune Aytoun and the Spasmodic Controversy* (New Haven and London: Yale University Press, 1968), 153–7.
102 H.L. Mansel, 'Sensation Novels', *Quarterly Review* 113 (April 1863): 481–514.

women's nervous condition make them more aware than men of the need for self-discipline, but it also makes them more capable of influencing children, since 'the flexibility, the love of the marvellous, the power of being occupied by trifles'[103] which are the concomitants of nervous irritability bring women nearer the perspective of the child. As we shall see, a similar emphasis on the conversion of nervous irritability from a moral weakness to a moral strength informs Yonge's depiction of character in her novels, and is particularly important in the development of heroines such as Ethel May in *The Daisy Chain*, and Albinia Kendal in *The Young Stepmother*. Yonge's novels imply that this disciplining of the nerves is of more than merely personal significance: at the close of *The Daisy Chain*, for example, Ethel's development of a capacity for self-control is shown to have been responsible for the building of the church at Cocksmoor, and by extension for reform of the whole Cocksmoor community.[104] In this wider context, Yonge's Tractarianism can be seen as a response to modernity, and the nervous shock which nineteenth-century commentators saw as its accompaniment,[105] a response in which women play a key role.

Women in Lewis's tract could be said to stand in a typological relationship to modernity, and this typological understanding of character constitutes a further important similarity between her perspective and that of Yonge and the Tractarians. Lewis asserts that the individual's reform of the self is an inescapable precondition for wider social reform,[106] in a way that makes individual character stand in for the state of contemporary society. Through their impact on others, the disorganized impulses of an individual's will mime for her the processes of social disorganization,[107] in an identification of individual and society of which Verlaine's famous evocation of the chaotic

103   Lewis, *Woman's Mission*, 22.
104   Yonge, *Daisy Chain*, 631 (Part 2 Ch.24).
105. Cf. Nicholas Daly, 'Railway Novels: Sensation Fiction and the Modernization of the Senses', *English Literary History* 66, no.2 (1999): 461–87.
106   Lewis, *Woman's Mission*, 97.
107   Ibid., 104–7.

sensibility of the Decadent poet, 'I am the Empire at the end of the Decadence',[108] is only a slightly more extreme example.

Lewis proposes a re-evaluation of the implications of Christian doctrine as the remedy for both personal inconsistency and social disfunction; her remark that 'Christianity has too long, and too exclusively, been regarded as a scheme of redemption, and not enough as a scheme of regeneration'[109] takes aim at that emphasis on the Atonement in Evangelical theology which early nineteenth-century religious commentators such as Edward Irving had found responsible for the respectable middle class's pharasaical tendency to disavow its moral responsibility for the problems of the poor.[110] This also represents a parallel with Tractarian calls for religious reform which, as Stephen Prickett has recently shown, originally had a significant social dimension before the movement was put on the defensive by Newman's defection to Roman Catholicism.[111] The shift of theological emphasis for which Lewis calls, from redemption to regeneration, is fundamental to the Tractarians' reinvigoration of the doctrine of Incarnation and the consequent stress they lay on the progressive sanctification of the Christian believer.[112]

Lewis's advocacy of a theology of regeneration represents the same kind of psychologization of religious belief which I earlier commented is characteristic of the Tractarians, since in terms of her argument a greater sense of the personal significance of religious belief is chiefly desirable because it will enable women to develop more consistent characters capable of exerting influence. True religion for Lewis brings about what in modern terms we would call the integration of the personality, so that her cultural feminism implies the same kind of typological understanding of character which we have

---

108   Paul Verlaine, 'Langueur', in *French Symbolist Poetry*, trans. C.F. Macintyre (Berkeley, CA: University of California Press, 1958), 11.
109   Lewis, *Woman's Mission*, 132
110   Edward Irving, *The Doctrine of the Incarnation Opened*, in G. Carlyle (ed.), *Collected Writings* (London: Strahan, 1865), 5: 126–7, 225–7.
111   Stephen Prickett, 'Keble's Creweian Oration of 1839: The Idea of a Christian University', in Kirstie Blair (ed.), *John Keble in Context* (London: Anthem Press, 2003), 19–33.
112   Chadwick, *Mind of The Oxford Movement*, 47–50.

already found in Keble's *Lectures in Poetry*. Lewis can identify the associative consistency which constitutes individual character with a wider social order because such consistency must participate in the divine economy of Providence, consistency being impossible on any other basis. This is a set of assumptions which may be compared to the argument of Oscar Wilde's essay, 'The Soul of Man under Socialism', in which the most perfect individualism turns out to be identical with socialism, with Christ representing at once the ultimate individualist and the ultimate socialist.[113]

The example of Sarah Lewis's *Woman's Mission* indicates how Yonge's realist narrative mode can be understood as an articulation at once of a Tractarian religious position and of a conservative 'cultural feminism'. Yonge's richly particularized portrayal of figures who gain in consistency of character as the novel unfolds enacts a progression from a realism which apparently simply mimics the sensory world to a realism which by the novel's close has become filled with typological significance as the scene of a self-realization on the part of the characters which is also a realization of their relationship to God. For Yonge's heroines, this discovery of the typological dimension of the self is also a process of female self-empowerment, albeit within the parameters of existing social forms.

113   Oscar Wilde, 'The Soul of Man Under Socialism', in *Complete Works*, intro by Vyvyan Holland (London and Glasgow: Collins, 1966), 1080, 1085–6.

Chapter Three
Development as a Theology of Character in Yonge and Newman

Reading and the Formation of Character

The associationist basis of the emphasis on consistency of character which we have seen is common both to Tractarian religious thought and to conservative cultural feminism of the kind represented by Lewis has particular implications for the novel form which help to explain some distinctive characteristics of Yonge's fiction. Unlike most Victorian novelists, Yonge rarely makes use of a narratorial voice to delineate her characters. Typically, her characters are introduced in an unmediated way through scenes in which they are in conversation, with any background being filled in later, again often in conversations: in *The Heir of Redclyffe*, for example, Philip's disappointment with his sister, a key piece of information in understanding his character, is only explained through a conversation between Guy and Mrs Edmonstone about fifty pages into the novel,[1] although Philip himself alludes to it some twenty pages earlier.[2]

The experience of reading a Yonge novel, then, is one of actively piecing together details which gradually become significant of a larger whole, at once the character's personality and, ultimately, the relation of that personality to an intuition of a wider providential order. This helps to explain why Yonge's novels are so unusually rewarding to reread, as any committed reader of her work will testify. Brief episodes such as Philip's breaking of Amy's camelia at the beginning of *The Heir of Redclyffe*,[3] which on a first reading represent merely

1   Charlotte M. Yonge, *The Heir of Redclyffe*, Barbara Dennis (ed.) (Oxford: Oxford University Press, 1997), 56 (Ch.4).
2   Ibid., 35 (Ch.3).
3   Ibid., 4–5 (Ch.1).

incidental realist detail which is quickly forgotten, on a rereading acquire additional emblematic significance.

The near-absence of a narratorial voice in Yonge's fiction means that the reader is forced to attend to their perception of novelistic character as an associative complex which is formed during the progress of the narrative. Paradoxically, Yonge's strategy of telling readers less about her characters through a narratorial voice is responsible for the vividness of her characterization, which persists in the minds of readers long after the complications of her plots have been forgotten. In order to follow a Yonge novel at all, readers have to realize a character through a mental effort of synthesis, an effect which becomes particularly marked in a family saga such as *The Pillars of the House* with its large cast of characters, most of whom have roughly equal significance in the plot. This technique, of course, depends heavily on Yonge's impressive ability to coordinate narrative detail on a large scale and mastery of convincing dialogue.

Yonge's narrative technique requires the reader to re-enact the kind of formation of associative complexes which Foster and Newman find responsible for the development of character, and this helps to explain why, despite the moral purpose Yonge envisaged for her writing, the novels are so free from the explicit didacticism this might lead a modern reader to expect. Within the providentialist outlook Yonge shares with these writers, all kinds of organization are implicitly significant of divine purpose, a presupposition that underlies their characteristically Victorian assumption that possessing 'character' is necessarily a good thing. In Yonge's fictional world, immoral people cannot have strong characters, something which explains why in *The Clever Woman of the Family* both the morally exemplary characters Alex Keith and Ermine Williams can recognize the 'strongminded' heroine Rachel's intrinsic nobility despite her errors,[4] and why Alex shows so much anxiety about his sister Bessie's ability 'to wriggle too smoothly through life'.[5]

---

4   Yonge, *The Clever Woman of the Family* (London: Macmillan, 1892), 52 (Ch.3), 171–2 (Ch.13), 272–3 (Ch.23).
5   Ibid., 182 (Ch.15).

In view of this nineteenth-century emphasis on 'character' as in itself a force for good, Yonge's fictional mode could be regarded as meeting by purely formal means her period's demand that fiction be morally improving, since the very associative process by which her novels are understood is also that by which the virtuous habits which constitute 'character' in the Victorian sense are formed. The reader's experience of reading a Yonge novel might be described as standing in a typological relationship to their experience of life itself, in that the exercise in actively forming mental *gestalts* demanded by the perception of character in Yonge's fiction is designed to train the reader in the active construction of their own life experience. This kind of unremitting self-consciousness about the shape one's life was taking was demanded by Tractarian religious teaching since, as Pusey insisted, any kind of experience could potentially 'minister to heaven or hell'[6] depending on how it was assimilated, and is reflected in what may to a modern reader seem the extreme scrupulosity of Yonge's exemplary characters, such as when Guy in *The Heir of Redclyffe* agonizes about the moral implications of attending a ball.[7] George Eliot's comments about the relief it was after her loss of religious belief simply to be able to enjoy an innocent experience such as sitting on the grass for its own sake, without worrying about any moral implications, show that this consequence of associationist psychology also informed Evangelical attitudes.[8]

From a theological perspective, Yonge's fictional technique could be said to correspond to Tractarian doctrinal emphasis on the Incarnation: the reader has in a sense associatively to incarnate Yonge's characters in the same way as the Christian believer is called in their life to incarnate Christ Himself. The role which character development plays in Yonge's fiction can thus be compared to the crucial place concepts of 'development' occupy in the religious thought of Newman and other Tractarians. As I will suggest, 'devel-

---

6   Owen Chadwick, *The Mind of The Oxford Movement* (London: Adam and Charles Black, 1960), 149–50.
7   Yonge, *Heir*, 139–42 (Ch.10).
8   Elizabeth Jay, *The Religion of The Heart: Anglican Evangelicalism and The Nineteenth Century Novel* (Oxford: The Clarendon Press, 1979), 232–6.

opment' for Newman is not just about the gradual historical unfolding of Christian doctrine and the corporate structures of the Church, but is also about the religious condition of the individual believer, because in terms of associationist psychology social collectivity and the collectivity of the ideas that compose the individual mind are identical. If consistency of individual character is only possible on the basis of a correspondence between that character and the providential order, so too must collective consistency of religious doctrine and ecclesiastical discipline presuppose the kind of divinely ordained status which Newman eventually came to identify with Roman Catholic claims for the infallibility of the Church, a conclusion which, of course, led to his conversion. In this context, the life history of the individual believer and the history of the Church become typologically equivalent in their formation of an established character through selective assimilation of surrounding influences, a point of view which underlies not only Newman's venture into fiction in *Loss and Gain*, and his autobiographical writing in the *Apologia pro Vita Sua*, but also his study of heresy in the *Essay on the Development of Christian Doctrine*.

Association and Incarnation in Newman

The relationship in Newman's thought between associationist psychology and the doctrine of the Incarnation can be seen in his discussion of the Personality of Christ in the *University Sermons*. Newman makes a case for the moral superiority of the Christian conception of a personal God, arguing that while: 'Natural Religion was not without provision for all the deepest and truest religious feelings, yet presenting no tangible history of the Deity, no points of His personal character (if we may so speak without irreverence), it wanted that most efficient incentive to all action, a starting or rallying point.'[9]

9   John Henry Newman, *Newman's University Sermons: Fifteen Sermons Preach-
     ed Before the University of Oxford 1826–1843*, intro by D.M. MacKinnon and
     J.D. Holmes (London: SPCK, 1970), 23.

Newman, in alluding to associationist psychology, extends the argument which eighteenth-century Anglican theologians such as Warburton had made against Deist questioning of the need for revealed religion, that while there might not be anything in the Scriptures which from a strictly rational point of view could not be immediately deduced from Nature, it doesn't follow that the human mind would be capable of making this deduction if unassisted by Revelation.[10] Newman refines this point, however, by invoking an epistemological gap between rational and moral forms of knowledge, which is only be overcome by the non-rational force of association which Christianity makes possible:

> The life of Christ brings together and concentrates truths concerning the chief good and the laws of our being, which wander idle and forlorn over the surface of the moral world, and often appear to diverge from each other.
>
> And hence will follow an important difference in the moral character formed in the Christian school, from that which Natural Religion has a tendency to create. The philosopher aspires towards a divine principle; the Christian, towards a Divine Agent. Now, dedication of our energies to the service of a person is the occasion of the highest and most noble virtues, disinterested attachment, self-devotion, loyalty; habitual humility, moreover, from the knowledge that there must ever be one that is above us. On the other hand, in whatever degree we approximate towards a mere standard of excellence, we do not really advance towards it, but bring it to us; the excellence we venerate becomes part of ourselves – we become a god to ourselves.[11]

Although a philosopher might be able to appreciate the worth of the moral virtues on purely rational grounds, Newman makes the subtle existential point against 'the pantheistic system of the Stoics, the later Pythagoreans, and other philosophers'[12] that an individual's moral development will always be corrupted by self-centredness unless the moral ideal is incarnated in a divine Person. Without a doctrine of original sin from which we require redemption, or, to put it more abstractly, that recognition of the essential externality of mor-

---

10   William Warburton, *The Divine Legation of Moses Demonstrated*, Works (London, 1811), 3: 212–14 in *Collected Works*, facs. edn, 13 vols, intro by Gavin Budge (Bristol: Thoemmes Press, 2005).

11   Newman, *University Sermons*, 27–8.

12   Ibid., 28.

ality to the self which is involved in the 'consciousness of *the not-ourselves that makes for righteousness*',[13] as Matthew Arnold puts it, moral endeavour will inevitably end in self-righteousness, the Luciferian sin of pride or the desire of Adam and Eve to be 'as gods'.[14] Yonge's portrayal of Philip in *The Heir of Redclyffe*, whose mastery of classical learning is pointedly contrasted with Guy's chivalric reading,[15] seems designed to exemplify the confusion of one's own position with a universal standard of morality which Newman suggests is the consequence of a rationalist ethics: with every conscious intention of behaving in an ethically justifiable way, Philip manages morally to corrupt his fiancée Laura and to behave with unconscious 'malignity' towards Guy.[16]

Newman's argument that Christ's life 'brings together and concentrates' otherwise scattered moral truths implies that for the believer Christ acts as an associative centre which strengthens moral feeling, in a way which parallels the description of the effect of the domestic woman on her family we have examined in *Woman's Mission*. Newman's associationist conception of the role of Christ can be compared to the description of the role of poetry to be found in Shelley, who comments in *A Defence of Poetry* that with the breakdown of Graeco-Roman culture: 'the world would have fallen into utter anarchy and darkness, but that there were found poets among the authors of the Christian and chivalric systems of manners and religion, who created forms of opinion and action never before conceived; which, copied into the imaginations of men, became as generals to the bewildered armies of their thoughts'.[17] For Shelley, poetry promotes culture by forming a imaginative nexus which can assimilate and organize the mental associations with which it comes into contact; as Shelley puts it, poetry 'compels us to feel that which we perceive, and

---

13   Matthew Arnold, *Literature and Dogma*, in *Dissent and Dogma*, R.H. Soper (ed.) (Ann Arbor: University of Michigan Press, 1968), 196 in *Complete Prose Works*, 10 vols (Ann Arbor: University of Michigan Press, 1960–1974), Vol.6.
14   Genesis 3:5, King James Version.
15   Yonge, *Heir*, 30, 43–5, 150 (Chs 3, 4, 10).
16   Ibid., 265 (Ch.20).
17   Percy Bysshe Shelley, 'A Defence of Poetry', in Zachary Leader and Michael O'Neill (eds), *The Major Works* (Oxford: Oxford University Press, 2003), 688.

to imagine that which we know'[18] thus bridging the epistemological gap between cognitive rationality and moral intuition.

Shelley, of course, regarded Jesus's teaching as 'instinct with the most vivid poetry',[19] so the difference between Newman's Christology and Shelley's humanist approach to Jesus really comes down to the question of where agency should be located. Just as we have seen Yonge acknowledge that the instrumentality of her writings could not be bounded by her conscious intention, so too Newman, in keeping with Christian orthodoxy, locates the efficacy of Christ in a life which is to be viewed as significant of God's providential care, rather than as Shelley does, simply in Jesus's own words. For Newman, the poetry of Christian doctrine consists in the associative whole of Christ's life, which by transcending the content of what he actually said endows Jesus and his teaching with a typological relationship to the divine. Newman's associationist reading of theology may be compared to Keble's theological poetics in *Tract 89*, where Wordsworthian nature poetry is assimilated to the mystical language of the Church Fathers by invoking the associations we inevitably have with the natural world, which Keble suggests constitute divine authorization for a poetic extension of the references to Nature in the revealed word of the Bible.[20] From this perspective, the language of the Wordsworthian poet, like the incarnate example of Christ, can legitimately be regarded in a typological way, as an emanation of the divine rather than simply the expression of a human individual.

Newman's emphasis on the Personality of Christ as fundamental to a distinctively Christian conception of morality is reflected later in the *University Sermons* in his arguments against Paleyan utilitarianism, a theological position which Newman regards as leading to a Socinian denial of the doctrines of original sin and redemption. Newman questions in particular what he sees as Paley's reduction of the divine moral attributes to the single dimension of benevolence,[21]

---

18   Ibid., 698.
19   Ibid., 688.
20   John Keble, *On the Mysticism Attributed to the Early Fathers of the Church* (Oxford and London: Parker, 1868), 169–70, 173.
21   William Paley, *Works* (London: Allman, 1833), 127.

arguing that there are other independent moral principles such as justice,[22] a disagreement which in a nineteenth-century theological context had obvious implications for the doctrinal status of Christ's Atonement for sin. The Atonement was interpreted in Evangelical theology, with which Newman is in agreement here, as a way of reconciling the conflicting demands of God's justice and His mercy.[23] To abolish the possibility that God's agency is subject to competing moral requirements, as in Newman's view Paley's one-sided emphasis on divine benevolence does, is by implication to undermine the divinity of Christ, and the concept of divine Personality itself, in that it removes the need to attribute any supernatural efficacy to Christ's sacrificial death, which instead becomes merely a tragic accident.

Once our notion of God has been reduced, as in Paleyan theology, to an abstract principle of benevolence, Newman suggests, the perversion of moral intuitions by a perspective centred on self, from which the Personality of Christ was intended to rescue the human mind, becomes inevitable. In the last analysis, true religion can only be based on an existential commitment to a personal relationship with a divine Being who remains permanently located outside the purview of the self:

All persons who are subjects of Revealed Religion, coincide in differing from all who are left under the Dispensation of Nature. Revelation puts us on a trial which exists but obscurely in Natural Religion; the trial of obeying for obedience-sake, or on Faith [...] Here, then, Revelation provides us with an important instrument for chastening and moulding our moral character, over and above the matter of its disclosures. Christians as well as Jews must submit as little children. This being considered, how strange are the notions of the present day concerning the liberty and irresponsibility of the Christian! If the Gospel be a message, as it is, it ever must be more or less what the multitude of self-wise reasoners declare it shall not be, – a law; it must be of the nature of what they call a form, and a bondage; it must, in its degree, bring darkness, instead of flattering them with the promise of immediate illumination; and must enlighten them only in proportion as they first submit to be darkened. This,

22   Newman, *University Sermons*, 105.
23   Boyd Hilton, *The Age of Atonement: The Influence of Evangelicalism on Social and Economic Thought, 1795–1865* (Oxford: Clarendon Press, 1988), 8, 33, 179.

then, if they knew their meaning, is the wish of the so-called philosophical Christians, and men of no party, of the present day; namely, that they should be rid altogether of the shackles of a Revelation: and to this assuredly their efforts are tending and will tend, – to identify the Christian doctrine with their own individual convictions, to sink its supernatural character, and to constitute themselves the prophets, not the recipients, of Divine Truth; creeds and discipline being already in their minds severed from its substance, and being gradually shaken off by them in fact, as the circumstances of the times will allow.[24]

As is indicated by the hostile references to liberal Christian thinkers such as Thomas Arnold, Newman's insistence on personal obedience as a precondition of religious faith implies the conservative ecclesiology which is typical of the Tractarians. What is noteworthy, however, is that Newman argues for the necessity of obedience on associationist grounds. For Newman, the Apostolic practice of consigning 'each particular church to the care of one pastor, or bishop, who was thus made a personal type of Christ mystical, the new and spiritual man; a centre of action and a living witness against all heretical or disorderly proceedings'[25] implies that the moral authority of the Church stems from the way in which bishops, and other ordained clergymen, constitute, like Christ Himself, associative centres in their own persons enabling their flock to bring together moral intuitions which would otherwise remain scattered: as Newman puts it, their function is one of 'concentrating the energies of the Christian body'.[26]

24   Newman, *University Sermons*, 172–3.
25   Ibid., 30.
26   Ibid.

The Critique of Rationalism in Yonge and Newman

The importance assumed by the practice of personal obedience in Tractarian religious thought is reflected within Yonge's fiction by an emphasis on the moral harm done by disobedience which was regarded as excessive even by some nineteenth-century critics.[27] In *The Heir of Redclyffe*, for example, Amy is only saved from falling down a precipice by a 'habit of implicit obedience and confidence'[28] which enables her to have faith in Guy's ability to pull her up from the bush from which she is hanging. A more extended example, which is closer to Newman's critique of religious liberalism, can be found in Yonge's portrayal of Bertha Fulmort in *Hopes and Fears*, on whom the influence of her religiously liberal governess, Miss Fennimore,[29] has the effect of making her reject all authority which she cannot 'evolve' out of her 'individual consciousness',[30] as Bertha puts it in language which significantly echoes German Idealist philosophy,[31] ending in a pathetic attempt to elope with her brother's roguish associate because her self-centred perspective has made her incapable of distinguishing between her own adolescent romantic fantasies and Jack Hastings's self-interested 'speculation to patch up his own fortune'.[32] Yonge's comparison of the relationship between Miss Fennimore and Bertha to that between 'Helvetius [*sic*] and the better class of encyclopaedists' and the Jacobins[33] makes clear the wider social implications of her

27 R.H. Hutton, 'Ethical and Dogmatic Fiction: Miss Yonge', *National Review* 12 (1861): 215.
28 Yonge, *Heir*, 392 (Ch.30).
29 Yonge, *Hopes and Fears, or Scenes from the Life of a Spinster* (London: Macmillan, 1889), 363 (Part 2 Ch.17).
30 Ibid., 366 (Ch.28).
31 Compare the satirically named German governess Miss Ohnglaube ('Miss Without-Belief') in Charlotte M. Yonge, *Heartsease, or the Brother's Wife* (London: Macmillan, 1891), 50–1 (Part 1 Ch.5) and the 'Germanism' of Caroline's prospective fiancé in *The Two Guardians, or Home in This World* (London: Masters, 1885), 147 (Ch.9).
32 Yonge, *Hopes and Fears*, 399 (Part 2 Ch.20).
33 Ibid., 403 (Part 2 Ch.20).

depiction of rationalism's role in sapping the sources of moral authority. Even after Bertha has seen the error of her ways, Yonge implies that the nervous disease resulting from this episode is likely to make her a permanent semi-invalid,[34] a fate which is comparable to that of Laura in *The Heir of Redclyffe*.[35]

The view that authority can only be mediated through personal relationships, and cannot be grounded on rational deduction, which we have found both in Newman and Yonge, reflects a Burkean conservatism. which in Yonge's case was lifelong.[36] Newman's insistence that moral principles are irreducibly plural, and cannot be accounted for solely in terms of benevolence, however, also suggests a more direct relationship between his thought and the British intellectual tradition of Common Sense philosophy which was one of Burke's sources.[37] Thomas Reid, the founder of the Common Sense School, was responsible for one of the most cogent philosophical critiques of Hume before Kant, and Newman is known to have studied his writings;[38] the prominence of references to Hume in the *University Sermons*, who is at one point described as an Antichrist,[39] makes it probable that Newman had this philosophical context for his arguments in mind. Reid's fundamental criticism of Hume, and of the Lockean tradition of which he considered Hume's unremitting scepticism had exposed the absurdity, was that the hypothesis of 'ideas', conceived of as really existing 'pictures in the mind', on which Hume based his philosophical arguments, illegitimately reduced the oper-

---

34   Ibid., 439 (Part 2 Ch.24).
35   Ibid. (Ch.44).
36   Barbara Dennis, *Charlotte Yonge (1823–1901), Novelist of the Oxford Movement: A Literature of Victorian Culture and Society* (Lewiston, NY: Edwin Mellen, 1992), 31–6.
37   Edmund Burke, 'Reflections on the Revolution in France', in *The French Revolution 1790–1794*, Vol.8 of *The Writings and Speeches of Edmund Burke*, 9 vols, L.G. Mitchell and William B. Todd (eds) (Oxford: Clarendon Press, 1989), 138.
38   See Johannes Artz, 'Newman as a Philosopher', *International Philosophical Quarterly* 16 (1976): 263–87.
39   Newman, *University Sermons*, 126.

ations of the mind to a single dimension, the 'comparison of ideas'.[40] Reid proposed an alternative model of the mind, in which an indefinite number of mental principles (called by Reid 'principles of common sense'),[41] which could not be reduced to a common denominator, were responsible for our intuitive knowledge of the external world – a knowledge, of course, the rational justifiability of which had been called into question by Hume's sceptical arguments.

There is a striking parallel between Reid's epistemological pluralism and Newman's insistence on irreconcileable moral principles which is reinforced by the similarity of the terms in which Reid and Newman characterize their opponents: like Reid,[42] Newman argues that scepticism is the result of an 'excessive attachment to system'[43] in which the imagination, by substituting illegitimate hypotheses for solid knowledge,[44] renders the mind impervious to the force of genuine evidence, because of its unsystematic and fragmentary character.[45] For both Newman and Reid, scepticism unfits the mind at once for the attitude of obedience on which religious belief rests and for the patient work of scientific discovery, an equation of religious orthodoxy and scientific method which may be seen writ large in the account of induction by Newman's contemporary, the historian of science William Whewell.[46] Although Newman, as I have commented, stresses the epistemological gap between philosophical rationalism and the moral intuitions of faith, he is able to invoke scientific method in support of his account of the nature of religious belief because he assumes that science deals in causal relationships whose nature is fundamentally unknowable in the same way as the basis of our moral intuitions. In this regard, Newman's thinking seems to reflect the

40 Thomas Reid, *Works*, 7th edn, William Hamilton (ed.) (Edinburgh: Maclachlan and Stewart, 1872), 206.
41 Ibid., 230–4.
42 Ibid., 234–6.
43 Newman, *University Sermons*, 7.
44 Ibid., 68–9.
45 Ibid., 274–5.
46 Cf. Richard Yeo, *Defining Science: William Whewell, Natural Knowledge, and Public Debate in Early Victorian Britain* (Cambridge: Cambridge University Press, 1993), 57, 118.

epistemology of Thomas Brown,[47] a near-contemporary member of the Common Sense school, the championing of whose philosophy by the prominent Evangelical Thomas Chalmers may well have brought him to Newman's attention.[48]

For Newman, the danger of rationalism is that it leads to the adoption of a position which is 'unreal',[49] in the morally loaded sense which we have seen that term took on in Tractarian religious discourse. The rationalist, in choosing to privilege a single mental principle as the basis of their system, allows their imagination to substitute its own creations for the genuine evidence of their moral intuitions, and so runs the risk of ruining their 'religious perceptions'.[50] For Newman, rationalism already constitutes a moral fall, in that its substitution of imagination for evidence leaves us with no defence against temptation. Since 'the world overcomes us, not merely by appealing to our reason, or by exciting our passions, but by imposing on our imagination',[51] those who have already weakened their sense of the difference between imagination and evidence by adopting a system will find that its implicit doctrinal compromise: 'which, when viewed in theory, formed no objection to the truth of the Inspired Word, yet, [...] in the intercourse of life, converts them, more or less, to the service of the "prince of the power of the air, the spirit which now worketh in the children of disobedience"'.[52] Against the seduction of the imagination in which worldliness consists is set God's condescension to human weakness in the Gospel, which 'by affording us, in the Person and history of Christ, a witness of the invisible world, addresses itself to our senses and imagination, after the very manner in which the false doctrines of the world assail us'.[53] Newman identifies the one-sided emphasis on the redemptive power of faith

---

47   Thomas Brown, *Life and Collected Works*, 8 vols, intro by Thomas Dixon (Bristol: Thoemmes Press, 2003), 1: x.

48   Thomas Chalmers, 'Preface to Dr Brown's Lectures on Ethics', in *Lectures on the Philosophy of the Human Mind*, 20th edn (London: Tegg, 1860), xxxiv–xl.

49   Newman, *University Sermons*, 110.

50   Ibid., 68.

51   Ibid., 122.

52   Ibid., 132.

53   Ibid., 121–2.

alone characteristic of the Calvinistic theology of Evangelicalism as an example of the reductive effects of system and its corresponding condition of moral 'unreality':

> A system such as this will of course bring with it full evidence of its truth to such debilitated minds as have already so given way to the imagination that they find themselves unable to resist its impressions as they recur. Nor is there among the theories of the world any more congenial to the sated and remorseful sensualist, who, having lost the command of his will, feels that if he is to be converted, it must be by some sudden and violent excitement [...] It is welcomed by the indolent, who care not for the Scripture warnings of the narrowness of the way of life, provided they can but assure themselves that it is easy to those who are in it; and who readily ascribe the fewness of those who find it, not to the difficulty of connecting faith and works, but to a Divine frugality in the dispensation of the gifts of grace.[54]

The language of debilitation and excitement which Newman employs here invokes the categories of Brunonian medicine,[55] implying that the Calvinist's conviction of Assurance is a kind of mania, in which imaginative impressions take on a force which is independent of reality,[56] and that the associated theological emphasis on sudden conversion satisfies the addictive craving for nervous stimulation to which those are subject who have deadened their nerves through abuse of other 'stimulants', such as alcohol.[57]

The connection Newman makes here between the rationalist adoption of system and addiction, regarded as the overstimulation of one particular faculty of the mind,[58] suggests that he regards system as a kind of perversion of the process of development, in which the mind, rather than changing through assimilation of fresh experiences to its associative centres, starts to circle in a self-reinforcing associative

---

54   Ibid., 147–8.
55   Günter B. Risse, 'Hysteria at the Edinburgh Infirmary: The Construction and Treatment of a Disease 1770–1800', *Medical History* 31 (1988): 48.
56   Cf. Alexander Crichton, *An Inquiry Into the Nature and Origin of Mental Derangement*, 2 vols (London: Cadell and Davies, 1798), 2: 35–9.
57   Cf. Roy Porter, *Doctor of Society: Thomas Beddoes and the Sick Trade in Late-Enlightenment England* (London and New York: Routledge, 1992), 94–9.
58   Crichton, *Mental Derangement*, 2: 29–33.

loop which ultimately exhausts it.[59] This characterization of rationalism as a kind of nervous fever can be seen to underlie Newman's account in the *Essay on the Development of Christian Doctrine* of the nature of heresy, which he emphasizes is always apparently more rational and systematic than Christian orthodoxy.[60] As is shown by the example of Norman's episodes of mental overstrain and related crisis of faith in *The Daisy Chain*, Yonge makes a similar connection between rationalism and nervous illness, and I would like to suggest that this helps to explain some elements of her fictional technique. Despite her commitment to writing fiction which conveys 'Church views',[61] Yonge deliberately avoids the fictional mode popular amongst many mid-nineteenth-century religious novelists, where plot is readily translatable into doctrine,[62] because, I would argue, she regards this kind of subordination of character to an interpretative scheme as symptomatic of exactly the kind of mentally unhealthy and self-regarding rationalism which in her view it is the purpose of fiction to counteract. Yonge's practice in this respect may be contrasted with Newman's own foray into the realist novel in *Loss and Gain*, which critics have agreed in finding unsuccessful.[63] Yonge, I would claim, manages fictionally to embody the concept of development in her fiction more successfully than Newman himself does, in a way that could be regarded as representing an apologia for those Tractarians who, like Keble, decided to remain within the Anglican church rather than converting to Rome.

59 Cf. Erasmus Darwin, *Zoonomia*, facs. edn of 1794–1796 edn, 2 vols (New York: AMS Press, 1974), 1: 86–9. Such an addictive spiral in response to overstimulation is characteristic of Brunonian accounts of disease in general, not just of mental disease.

60 John Henry Newman, *An Essay on the Development of Christian Doctrine*, J.M. Cameron (ed.) (Harmondsworth: Penguin, 1974), 343.

61 Dennis, *Yonge*, 122–7.

62 Joseph Ellis Baker, *The Novel and the Oxford Movement* (New York: Russell and Russell, 1965), 69–72.

63 Jay, *Religion of The Heart*, 2–5.

Yonge's Multidimensional Fictional Technique in *Abbeychurch*: the Departure from Edgworthian Didacticism

One of the fullest expressions of Yonge's views about the relationship between fictional technique and moral purpose is contained in a 1844 letter[64] to a cousin, which remained unpublished until recently, written in response to some reported criticisms of her first novel, *Abbeychurch*, by a Miss Robertson. Yonge defends her novel at length, but the key portion of the letter occurs near the beginning, where Yonge describes 'where I think she and I completely differ in idea and principle':

> I think her, and Anne's notion of a story or moral tale, seems to be that it must in its whole tendency elucidate some one principle, as its one ground of action, and that any thing beyond a little mere decoration is irrelevant, but it seems to me that things in real life hardly ever happen all with that pointed tendency to one thing; those who seek for a salutary lesson, in all that passes around them may find the honey in their flowers infinitely varied, though at the same time each according to their own character, experience, or wants, will make these lessons tend in one certain way; therefore since nature and real life are allowed to be the most instructive things to be found, I thought a story taking in the mixture of events and characters differently acted upon by the same circumstances would be more useful, than one written on the other plan.[65]

As the reference to the genre of the 'moral tale' indicates, a key point of reference in this discussion is the fiction of Maria Edgeworth, whose writing Yonge, who had been brought up by her parents on 'the Edgeworth system',[66] would have known well. Yonge here refuses the schematic quality of such well-known tales for children such as 'Lazy

---

64   Yonge, Letter to Alethea Yonge, 30 September 1844 in Charlotte Mitchell, Ellen Jordan and Helen Schinske (eds) (2007), *The Letters of Charlotte Mary Yonge (1823–1901)*, no.12, <http://hdl.handle.net/10065/337>. I am grateful to Ellen Jordan for making the text of this letter available to me in advance of the online publication of this edition.

65   Yonge, Letter to Alethea Yonge, 30 September 1844, no.12.

66   Christabel Coleridge, *Charlotte Mary Yonge: Her Life and Letters* (London: Macmillan, 1903), 56.

Lawrence', where, as she notes, all the fictional incidents are meant to convey the same moral lesson, a mode of writing which is also, in a lesser degree, characteristic of Edgeworth's novels for adults, such as *Belinda*. Yonge outlines instead a fictional mode in which personal character, rather than an overarching scheme, determines the moral significance of events, in a way which from an aesthetic viewpoint has the advantage of avoiding the monotony inherent in Edgeworth's schematic approach and from a theological viewpoint avoids the danger that over-rigid authorial intentions might end up substituting themselves for the providential lessons of 'nature and real life'. This aspect of Yonge's approach to fiction shows the faulty nature of the kind of argument presented by Q.D. Leavis, and followed by Talia Schaffer, that, in comparison to Edgeworth, Yonge's religious commitment involves a lack of 'any sympathy for and even recognition of the natural sources of healthy life';[67] Edgeworth's rationalism in fact removes her writing further away from realism than does Yonge's religious outlook.

The Paleyan nature of Edgeworth's moral position, shown for example in the hostility she demonstrates towards any form of exaggeration in conversation even when the intent is not to deceive,[68] exposed her to criticisms which may be seen to parallel those which Newman directed at the religious liberalism which was Paley's legacy. In a long review of her writings, John Foster criticized the moral implications of Edgeworth's almost total omission of a religious per-

---

67   Q.D. Leavis, 'Charlotte Yonge and Christian Discrimination', *Scrutiny* 12 (1944): 153.

68   E.g. Maria Edgeworth, *The Parent's Assistant, or Stories for Children* (London: Macmillan, 1897), 70–1, compare Paley, *Works*, 147–8. A similar insistence on the moral indivisibility of truth underlies Guy's correction of Charles's tendency to exaggeration (*Heir*, 60–1 Ch.5), though Yonge and her circle generally attach more value than Edgeworth to the imaginative use of language (cf. Anon., 'School Sketches', *Monthly Packet* 12 [Series 1 1856]: 196, where the sympathetically described imaginative tendencies of an Irish schoolboy are contrasted with the attitudes of a school usher, who regards him as 'telling falsehoods').

spective in her fiction.[69] Even though he has no substantive objections to the content of Edgeworth's moral teaching, as far as it goes,[70] Foster rejects her assumption, corresponding to the liberalism of Newman's opponents, that it is possible to teach morality independently of a religious perspective,[71] since in the absence of this kind of transcendent dimension Edgeworth can only appeal to 'a combination of principles undefined, arbitrary, capricious, and sometimes incompatible'[72] as the source of moral value. Foster draws attention to the way in which this lack of a transcendent reference point empties Edgeworth's position of moral content when she comes to deal with her own class:

> She shows [...] a very great degree of tolerance for the dissipation of the wealthy classes, if it only stop short of utter frivolity or profligacy, and of ruinous expense. All the virtue she demands of them may easily comport with a prodigious quantity of fashion, and folly, and splendour, and profuseness. They may be allowed to whirl in amusements till they are dead sick, and then have recourse to a little sober useful goodness to recover themselves. They are indeed advised to cultivate their minds; but, as it should seem, for the purpose, mainly, of giving dignity to their rank, and zest and sparkle to the conversations of their idle and elegant parties. They are recommended to become the promoters of useful schemes in their neighbourhoods, and the patrons of the poor; but it does not appear that this philanthropy is required to be carried the length of costing any serious percentage of their incomes. The grand and ultimate object of all the intellectual and moral exertions to which our author is trying to coax and prompt them, is confessedly, – self-complacency; and it is evident that, while surrounded incessantly with frivolous and selfish society to compare themselves with, they may assume this self-complacency on the strength of very middling attainments in wisdom and beneficence.[73]

Foster's criticisms of Edgeworth can be seen to be making a very similar argument to the one Newman makes against the rationalist mentality. If conceived abstractly, without reference to a divine

69   John Foster, 'The Morality of Works of Fiction', in J.F. Ryland (ed.), *Critical Essays Contributed to the Eclectic Review*, 2 vols (London: Bohn, 1856), 1: 417–28.
70   Ibid., 421–3.
71   Ibid., 418–21.
72   Ibid., 421–3.
73   Ibid., 423.

Person, morality inevitably degenerates into the 'self-complacency' Foster finds characteristic of Edgeworth's portrayal of the leisured classes. Similar criticisms of 'moral tales' in the Edgeworthian mould, on the grounds that the real lesson taught by such fiction is one of self-conceit, can be found in mid nineteenth-century critics of children's literature,[74] a point which is implicit in Yonge's tale, 'The Six Cushions'.[75]

Although the middle-class focus of Yonge's novels may seem to limit their moral range, placed in the context of these criticisms of Edgeworth's fiction Yonge's often challenging portrayals of a middle class sliding into moral deliquescence for want of self-discipline can be seen to represent social critique of a kind that is absent from Edgeworth's work. Given Newman's and Foster's attacks on the moral complacency inherent in religious liberalism, it can be seen to be no coincidence that such social critique in Yonge's novels goes hand in hand with a critique of the effects of rationalism. This is a context that can be seen to inform even Yonge's first published novel, *Abbeychurch*.

In the letter already quoted, Yonge explains that despite the somewhat Edgeworthian tone of *Abbeychurch*'s subtitle, 'Self Control and Self Conceit', the intended 'moral' of the book is relative to the situations of the characters, rather than one that can be stated abstractly:

A plan or rather two or three plans which I thought might give hints of the dangers of the present race of young ladies I certainly had, and I suppose the two or three make it seem confused. I wished to shew that the over use of good things is an abuse of them, I mean that self control is wanted in love of almost all that is excellent or harmless [...] that self conceit may exist in a thousand different unsuspected forms; as in [...] admiration of what is peculiarly our own, in contempt for the abilities of others, even when we are modest in our estimate of our own abilities or goodness [...] that strict and scrupulous obedience is the only guide which will not lead us astray in some way or other – that people may

74 Anon., 'Children's Literature', in Lance Salway (ed.), *A Peculiar Gift: Nineteenth-Century Writings on Books for Children* (Harmondsworth: Kestrel, 1976), 312, originally published in *Quarterly Review*, 13 (1860), pp.469–500.

75 Cf. Charlotte M. Yonge, 'The Six Cushions', *Monthly Packet* 2 (Series 2 1866): 548.

do right from not the best motive, or spoil their best deeds by their manner of doing them – that those who have the clearest knowledge of right and wrong will without a humble spirit do worse than the meek spirited who have the least knowledge – that a fault is not an equal fault in all.[76]

As the terms in which Yonge frames her discussion make clear, the central problematic of the novel is the self and its relationship to moral judgement, in a way which can be compared to Newman's existential critique of the moral effects of rationalism. Like Newman, Yonge regards 'obedience' as the only remedy against the vicious circle inherent in the self-centred perspective, since this involves a relationship of personal commitment to what is outside the self.

At one level, *Abbeychurch* is a kind of 'condition-of-England' novel.[77] Early on, Yonge describes the effect of the new railway in doubling the population of the town, which has made necessary the construction of the new church around the consecration of which the novel's fairly slight plot centres.[78] As Elizabeth, the heroine of the novel, comments, 'our town consists of the remains of old respectable England, and the beginning of the new great work-shop of all nations, met together in tolerably close companionship'[79] and her sister Helen draws a contrast between the 'beautiful Gothic Church'[80] on which 'neither pains nor expense had been spared'[81] and the frightfulness of the 'gas manufactory and the union poor-house',[82] a comparison which recalls Pugin's 1841 *Contrasts*, where plates of a modern town full of gas works and dissenting chapels, and of a poor-house designed as a Panopticon, are pointedly juxtaposed with their more humane and Catholic medieval equivalents.[83] Since Yonge's own father had a keen

76 Yonge, Letter to Alethea Yonge, 30 September 1844, no.12.
77 Dennis, *Yonge*, 104–8.
78 Yonge, *Abbeychurch, or Self Control and Self Conceit* (London and Derby: Burns and Mozley, 1844), 19–20 (Ch.2) in *Abbeychurch / The Castle Builders*, facs. edn (New York and London: Garland Publishing, 1976).
79 Ibid., 44 (Ch.3).
80 Ibid.
81 Ibid., 47 (Ch.3).
82 Ibid., 48 (Ch.3).
83 A.W. Pugin, 'Contrasts; or, A Parallel Between the Noble Edifices of the Middle Ages and Corresponding Buildings of the Present Day', in Gavin Budge

interest in the visual arts and was closely involved in the construction of the real-life Gothic church on which Yonge's fictional one is based,[84] Yonge was probably well acquainted with Pugin's works, which were one of the few sources available on Gothic design.

Elizabeth, and her sisters Helen and Kate, can be seen to represent different varieties of the 'nervous temperament' that in nineteenth-century medicine was thought to be typical of women. This is particularly noticeable in the case of Elizabeth, who early in the novel is described as 'ardent'[85] and 'impetuous and violent';[86] it is also implied that she is a consumptive,[87] a condition linked in nineteenth-century medical thought to nervous irritability.[88] In her letter, Yonge comments that Elizabeth was 'always intended to be like myself, only worse trained and more useful',[89] a remark whose implications are made clear by Yonge's characterization of her childhood self as 'excitable, shrill-voiced, and with a great capacity of screaming'[90] and mention of the 'nervous fright'[91] from which she used to suffer. As her biographer remarks, 'what she was at fifteen, that she was, with modifications, at fifty',[92] so that Yonge's consistent interest in the nervously irritable woman, and the question of how she might transcend her own condition to become a 'mesmeric' woman who could exert 'influence', which we shall examine in later chapters of this book, must be understood as partly autobiographical. Like Rachel in *The Clever Woman of the Family*, Elizabeth's inherent nobility of character is emphasized,[93] despite her mistakes.

(ed.), *Aesthetics and Religion in Nineteenth-Century Britain*, Vol.4 (Bristol: Thoemmes, 2003), plates are unpaginated. facs. edn of 2nd edn, 1841 (the poorhouse plate first appears in this edition).

84 Coleridge, *Yonge*, 48–54.
85 Yonge, *Abbeychurch*, 10 (Ch.1).
86 Ibid., 13 (Ch.1).
87 Ibid., 16, 40, 53, 77 (Chs 1, 3, 4, 5).
88 Darwin, *Zoonomia*, 1: 354–60.
89 Yonge, Letter to Alethea Yonge, 30 September 1844, no.12.
90 Coleridge, *Yonge*, 82–3.
91 Ibid., 62.
92 Ibid., 120.
93 Yonge, *Abbeychurch*, 14 (Ch.1).

Kate and Helen are less strongly characterized than Elizabeth. Kate is described early on as 'a mere good-natured gossip',[94] but is also classed with Elizabeth as having a tendency to consumption, shown by a 'fixed hectic look',[95] a combination which suggests that her form of nervous irritability, unlike that of Elizabeth, is purely reactive rather than self-directed. This characterization of Kate is also supported by the strongly negative portrayal in Tractarian writing generally of the effects of gossip as 'wasting' the mind,[96] and also by the description of her, in the discussion among the visiting family which concludes the novel, as 'a piece of thistle down [...] drifted about by every wind that blows'.[97]

Helen, in contrast to the overstimulated condition in which her two sisters exist, exhibits all the symptoms of a syndrome of nervous understimulation, as this was understood in nineteenth-century medical thought;[98] early on in the book, she is described as habitually looking 'dismal and fretful',[99] suffers from 'sullen moods'[100] and while on the morning of the church consecration Elizabeth is running 'upstairs and down, here, there and every where', Helen's lack of energy is shown by the fact that all she does is to arrange 'the fruit with much taste'.[101] As Elizabeth remarks, with characteristic exaggeration, 'any one with any experience of Helen's ways, had rather walk ninety miles in the rain, than be at the pains of routing her out of the corner of the sofa to do any thing useful'.[102] Her cousin Anne notes, however, that Helen's recent extended stay with relatives, which has left her discontented with home life, has made her aware of

94   Ibid., 15 (Ch.1).
95   Ibid., 16 (Ch.1).
96   E.B. Pusey, *Parochial Sermons*, 3 vols (London: Walter Smith, 1883), 3: 269–75; Author of 'Gentle Influences', 'Gossip, or, The Domestic Demon', *Monthly Packet* 17 (Series 1 1859): 77–8.
97   Yonge, *Abbeychurch*, 313 (Ch.14).
98   John Brown, *The Works of Dr John Brown*, 3 vols, intro by William Cullen Brown (London: Johnson and Symonds, 1804), 1: 110–16.
99   Yonge, *Abbeychurch*, 16 (Ch.1).
100   Ibid., 211 (Ch.10).
101   Ibid., 63 (Ch.5).
102   Ibid., 127 (Ch.7).

the extent to which she 'used to be indolent and waste [...] [her] senses',[103] and one of the themes of the novel is Helen's attempt to develop a greater strenuousness which will qualify her for her sister's friendship, and Elizabeth's corresponding attempt to stop 'opposing and despising Helen'.[104] The prospect of a developing friendship between Helen and Elizabeth at the novel's close[105] implies that the two sisters will eventually bring each other to a happy medium on the Brunonian continuum of excessive and deficient nervous irritability,[106] a process which in Helen's case has already been set in motion by her stay at Dykelands with Mrs Staunton, whose tendency to sentimental gushing about Helen in her letter[107] suggests that it is the influence of her nervous irritability which is responsible for Helen's improvement from her previously morally inert condition.

Helen is thus shown as learning to struggle with the 'besetting sin' to which she is temperamentally subject, in a way that corresponds to the Tractarian emphasis on religious growth as a process of developing awareness of character flaws of which one had previously been unconscious and bringing them under the control of the will.[108] A similar argument can be made about Elizabeth, who at the end of the novel is shown gazing at the newly consecrated church and realizing 'there is much that is fearfully wrong in me to be corrected, before I can dare to think of the Confirmation'.[109] In Elizabeth's case, however, her besetting sin is rationalism, and this makes her moral struggle exemplary of the wider Tractarian struggle with the implications of modernity.

One of the major incidents of *Abbeychurch* is the visit Elizabeth and Kate make to attend a lecture on the nature of chivalry at the Mechanics' Institute, an organization which their father, the local clergyman, has opposed, on the grounds that its non-denominational

103   Ibid., 121 (Ch.6).
104   Ibid., 252 (Ch.11).
105   Ibid., 293–94 (Ch.13).
106   The Brunonian concept of a continuum of disease is illustrated by Samuel Linch's 'Table of Excitement and Excitability' in Brown, *Works*.
107   Yonge, *Abbeychurch*, 41 (Ch.3).
108   Pusey, *Parochial Sermons*, 2: 132–42.
109   Yonge, *Abbeychurch*, 311 (Ch.14).

nature makes it an example of the 'education-without-religion system'.[110] Later in life Yonge changed her view of the effects of the Mechanics' Institutes, but in this early work the Mechanics' Institute stands for exactly the kind of rationalistic liberalism which we have seen Newman and Foster argue prepared the ground for moral corruption. The sisters' visit is reported in the town's 'wicked Radical newspaper'[111] in order to embarrass their father, whose annoyance at their conduct functions as the moral dénouement of the plot, since the novel accords his judgements authoritative status. As her father recognizes, Elizabeth in fact was ignorant of the prohibition on attending the Mechanics' Institute, having been absent on a visit when it was set up, but the novel suggests that she has been led into this inadvertent moral fall, which she bitterly regrets, through her besetting sin of rationalism.

Before this incident, Elizabeth herself notes that 'although I know and believe as firmly as I do any other important thing, that mere intellect is utterly worthless, I cannot feel it, it bewitches me as beauty does some other people',[112] and she later describes how on waking after the visit she has had in her ears 'like a dream of Papa's voice, reading the Lesson at Church' the words 'It was a tree to be desired to make one wise',[113] an allusion to the story of Adam and Eve.[114] Elizabeth's description of herself as actuated by 'a mad spirit, like what drives wicked men to drinking',[115] implies , in the same way we have seen Newman do, that her tendency to a rationalism that makes 'knowledge and discernment' her 'idol'[116] is a kind of mania or addiction for which her nervous irritability is responsible. The character of Elizabeth can thus be seen to stand in a typological relationship to the social modernity which the novel shows developing in the town of Abbeychurch. Elizabeth, who, as a character comments,

---

110   Ibid., 174 (Ch.8).
111   Ibid., 51 (Ch.3).
112   Ibid., 108 (Ch.6).
113   Ibid., 249–50 (Ch.11).
114   Genesis 3:6, King James Version.
115   Yonge, *Abbeychurch*, 251 (Ch.11).
116   Ibid., 136 (Ch.7).

has 'so much mind',[117] is peculiarly liable to the temptations presented by the nineteenth-century 'march of mind', as embodied in the Mechanics' Institute, an institution that must have been particularly attractive to middle-class women in the early part of the nineteenth century, as is shown by Charlotte Brontë's involvement with it,[118] since there were few other public educational opportunities available. But, just as the Mechanics' Institute has been the venue for lectures by 'Chartists and Socialists',[119] so too many nineteenth-century commentators blamed the 'march of mind', and its accompanying intensification of commercial activity, for what they regarded as record levels of mental illness,[120] of which in their view working-class political radicalism was a symptom.[121] Elizabeth, then, represents the nineteenth-century 'nervous subject',[122] whose addiction to rationalism is in danger of allowing the self to succumb to the nervous shock of modernity[123] in a way which must be counteracted by that 'culture of the feelings'[124] which in *Abbeychurch* is shown to be provided for Elizabeth by the newly constructed Gothic church, as, at the novel's close, her eyes are 'fixed on the bright red cross in the centre window over the Altar' and she recalls the last of her 'old fits of ill temper' on the day the first stone of the church was laid.[125]

117   Ibid., 99 (Ch.5).
118   Sally Shuttleworth, *Charlotte Brontë and Victorian Psychology* (Cambridge: Cambridge University Press, 1996), 26.
119   Yonge, *Abbeychurch*, 182 (Ch.9).
120   Shuttleworth, *Charlotte Brontë and Victorian Psychology*, 46–51.
121   Cf. Janet Oppenheim, *'Shattered Nerves': Doctors; Patients and Depression in Victorian England* (New York: Oxford University Press, 1991), 100–5.
122   Peter Melville Logan, *Nerves and Narratives: A Cultural History of Hysteria in Nineteenth-Century British Prose* (Berkeley: University of California Press, 1997), 1–2.
123   Cf. Nicholas Daly, 'Railway Novels: Sensation Fiction and the Modernization of the Senses', *English Literary History* 66, no.2 (1999): 461–87.
124   John Stuart Mill, *Autobiography and Literary Essays*, J.M. Johnson and Jack Stillinger (eds) (Toronto: University of Toronto Press, 1981), 151 in *Collected Writings*, 38 vols (Toronto: University of Toronto Press, 1969-91), Vol.1.
125   Yonge, *Abbeychurch*, 310–11 (Ch.14).

Religion and the Unconscious in Yonge and Newman

Even in an early Yonge novel such as *Abbeychurch*, one can see that Yonge's narrative technique of 'thick description',[126] in which characters' motivations have to be arrived at by the reader through a process of induction on the basis on a large number of apparently insignificant details, tends to suggest dimensions to behaviour which go beyond either that of which the characters are conscious, or what is apparent to readers on a first reading, and in this respect Elizabeth's seduction by rationalism anticipates the unconscious 'malignity'[127] of Philip in *The Heir of Redclyffe*. This unconscious element in behaviour plays an important role in the account of religious development which Newman sets out in the *University Sermons*. Newman justifies the theological attempt to arrive at collective doctrinal clarification, as opposed to the reductive agnostic equation of religious creeds with 'private opinions' underlying liberalism, on the grounds that there is a 'necessary [...] connexion between inward religious belief and scientific expositions'.[128] He locates this connection in the unconscious:

> As the inward idea of divine truth, such as has been described, passes into explicit form by the activity of our reflective powers, still such an actual delineation is not essential to its genuineness and perfection. A peasant may have such a true impression, yet be unable to give any intelligible account of it, as will easily be understood. But what is remarkable at first sight is this, that there is good reason for saying that the impression made upon the mind need not even be recognized by the parties possessing it. It is no proof that persons are not possessed, because they are not conscious, of an idea. Nothing is of more frequent occurrence, whether in things sensible or intellectual, than the existence of such unperceived impressions. What do we mean when we say, that certain persons do not know themselves, but that they are ruled by views, feelings, prejudices, objects which they do not recognize? [...] What is memory itself, but a vast magazine of such dormant, but present and excitable ideas? Or consider, when persons would trace the history of their own opinions in past

---

126 Clifford Geertz, 'Thick Description: Toward an Interpretive Theory of Culture', in *The Interpretation of Cultures* (London: Hutchinson, 1975), 3–30.
127 Yonge, *Heir*, 265 (Ch.20).
128 Newman, *University Sermons*, 319.

years, how baffled they are in the attempt to fix the date of this or that conviction, their system of thought having been all the while in continual, gradual, tranquil expansion; so that it were as easy to follow the growth of the fruit of the earth, 'first the blade, then the ear, after that the full corn in the ear', as to chronicle changes, which involved no abrupt revolution, or reaction, or fickleness of mind, but have been the birth of an idea, the development, in explicit form, of what was already latent within it. Or, again, critical disquisitions are often written about the idea which this or that poet might have in his mind in certain of his compositions and characters; and we call such analysis the philosophy of poetry, not implying thereby of necessity that the author wrote upon a theory in his actual delineation, or knew what he was doing; but that, in matter of fact, he was possessed, ruled, guided by an unconscious idea.[129]

Newman's example of the peasant echoes Coleridge's discussion of the problem of communicating truth early on in *The Friend*, where Coleridge argues that the 'truth' of beliefs held by peasants, such as the belief in ghosts, should be regarded as a function of the greater truths which such explicitly held beliefs unconsciously symbolize, rather than as being something to be determined by empirical verification;[130] for Newman, employing the concept of inchoate and obscure 'impressions' put forward by Hume,[131] such a belief represents an incoherent or unintelligible expression of a 'true impression'. Coleridgean precedents also lie behind Newman's claim that a person may be 'possessed' by an idea, without being conscious of it, as Elizabeth in *Abbeychurch* and Philip in *The Heir of Redclyffe* are arguably 'possessed' by the idea of rationalism: Newman's language echoes Coleridge's prefatory remark in *On the Constitution of the Church and State* that 'it is the privilege of the few to possess an idea: of the generality of men, it might be more truly affirmed, that they are possessed by it.'.[132] Newman's conception of the way the effects of such an unconsciously held idea become manifested in behaviour is

129   Ibid., 321–2.
130   S.T. Coleridge, *The Friend*, 2 vols, Barbare E. Rooke (ed.) (Princeton: Princeton University Press, 1969), 1: 46–7.
131   David Hume, *A Treatise of Human Nature*, 2nd edn, L.A. Selby-Bigge and P.H. Nidditch (eds) (Oxford: Clarendon Press, 1978), 1–2.
132   Coleridge, *On the Constitution of the Church and State*, John Colmer (ed.) (Princeton: Princeton University Press, 1976), 15.

comparable to the notion of associative centres which we have identified in John Foster's and Sarah Lewis's writing; these New-mano-Coleridgean 'ideas' emerge gradually as a result of being able coherently to assimilate their experiential surroundings to themselves, a developmental narrative which Coleridge, and after him Trench, also apply to language.[133] Newman's reference to the 'philosophy of poetry' alludes to Keble's *Lectures on Poetry* where, as we have seen , Keble argues that the associative coherence which characterizes the work of a great poet must make their poetry expressive of, or stand in a typological relationship to, the 'idea' of the providential economy of Christianity even in cases such as Virgil or Aeschylus where this could not be a conscious intention.

Newman's description of a 'system of thought [...] in gradual, tranquil expansion' anticipates the aims both of his novel *Loss and Gain* and of his autobiography *Apologia pro Vita Sua*, whose narratives attempt to depict the process of conversion to Roman Catholicism as the inevitable consequence of the development of a personal religious commitment. In *Loss and Gain*, for example, the narrator comments after a lengthy conversation between Reding and his friend Carlton:

> It is impossible to stop the growth of the mind. Here was Charles with his thoughts turned away from religious controversy for two years, yet with his religious views progressing, unknown to himself, the whole time. It could not have been otherwise, if he was to live a religious life at all. If he was to worship and obey his Creator, intellectual acts, conclusions, and judgments must accompany that worship and obedience. He might not realise his own belief till questions had been put to him; but then a single discussion with a friend, such as the above with Carlton, would bring out what he really did hold to his own apprehension, would ascertain for him the limits of each opinion as he held it, and the inter-relations of opinion with opinion. He had not yet given names to these opinions, much less had they taken a theological form; nor could they, under his circumstances, be expressed in theological language; but here he was, a young man of twenty-two, professing, in an hour's conversation with a friend,

---

133   Coleridge, *Biographia Literaria*, 2 vols, James Engell and W. Jackson Bate (eds) (Princeton University Press, 1983), 1: 82–3 fn; Richard Chevenix Trench, *On the Study of Words and English Past and Present* (London and Toronto: Dent and Dutton, n.d.), 13–16.

what really were the Catholic doctrines and usages of penance, purgatory, councils of perfection, mortification of self, and clerical celibacy. No wonder that all this annoyed Carlton, though he no more than Charles perceived that all this Catholicism did in fact lie hid under his professions; but he felt, in what Reding put out, the presence of something, as he expressed it, 'very unlike the Church of England', something new and unpleasant to him, and withal something which had a body in it, which had a momentum which could not be passed over as a vague, sudden sound or transitory cloud, but which had much behind it which made itself felt, which struck heavily.[134]

This narratorial intervention is obviously designed to portray Reding as a man who is unconsciously possessed with the 'idea' of Catholicism, even though he is not yet able to articulate its doctrines to himself or others. Reding's individual development as a character is designed to function typologically, standing for the collective development of Christian doctrine as a whole towards its final form in Roman Catholicism. In terms of Newman's novel, of course, the problem is that this passage exists at all: what makes *Loss and Gain* unsatisfactory is that Newman is not a skilled enough novelist, or perhaps does not trust his readers enough, merely to suggest the inevitability of his hero's progress towards Roman Catholicism through significant detail.

In this context, Yonge's ability to embed her Tractarian outlook in the realistic world of her novels without resorting to narratorial explanation can be seen as a significantly more effective form of religious apologia, since the psychological truth of her characterization is thus enabled to indicate the religious truth of Tractarian doctrine as the only basis on which consistent moral goodness is possible. Newman's autobiography, *Apologia pro Vita Sua*, is of course also designed to hold up personal moral consistency as evidence for the truth of the author's Roman Catholic beliefs, in the wake of Kingsley's slur that 'truth, for its own sake, had never been a virtue with the Roman clergy',[135] a particularly damaging suggestion

---

134 John Henry Newman, *Loss and Gain* (London: Burns, 1848), 180–1 (Part 2 Ch.6).

135 Charles Kingsley, *'What, Then, Does Dr Newman Mean?': A Reply to a Pamphlet Lately Published by Dr Newman* (London and Edinburgh: Macmillan, 1864), 5.

in the context of Paleyan moral philosophy.[136] It may be questioned, however, whether Kingsley's clumsiness as a controversialist did not make life easy for Newman as an apologist,[137] since although Newman was generally agreed to have vindicated his personal consistency, the *Apologia* provides no answer to the rather subtler argument made by Keble in the preface to his *University Sermons*, that Newman's desire for religious certainty led to his succumbing to the very thirst for system of which he accuses the rationalists.[138] Newman's reluctance to explore possible unconscious motivations for his actions may be what prompted Oscar Wilde's description of the *Apologia* as a portrait of a 'troubled soul in its progress from darkness to darkness'.[139]

Character and Sexual Inversion in Yonge

Newman's conversion to Roman Catholicism was widely referred to by hostile nineteenth-century commentators as his 'perversion',[140] in a way that indicates how the theory of the unconscious involved in appeals to the notion of development was understood to extend to issues of sexuality, issues of course which were key to the notorious preference for celibacy manifested by Newman, and his fellow 'religious perverts',[141] and to the Tractarian revival of auricular con-

136   Paley, *Works*, 147–8.
137   Brenda Colloms, *Charles Kingsley: The Lion of Eversley* (London: Constable, 1975), 272.
138   John Keble, *Sermons Academical and Occasional* (Oxford and London: Parker and Rivington, 1848), lxvi–lxviii.
139   Oscar Wilde, 'The Critic as Artist', in *Complete Works*, intro by Vyvyan Holland (London and Glasgow: Collins, 1966), 1010.
140   Ellis Hanson, *Decadence and Catholicism* (Cambridge, MA: Harvard University Press, 1997), 263–70.
141   Frederick S. Roden, *Same-Sex Desire in Victorian Religious Culture* (Houndmills: Palgrave Macmillan, 2002), 6. Newman's sister, Harriet Mozley, obliquely censured Newman's declaration of a preference for celibacy (Jay, *Religion of The Heart*, 132–9, fn).

fession and of sisterhoods.[142] The congruence between late nineteenth-century Anglo-Catholicism and a 'queer' sexuality has been explored by several recent critics, and Talia Schaffer has drawn attention to the presence of a proto-lesbian character in Yonge's *Magnum Bonum*, represented by Janet Brownlow.[143] Although Schaffer follows Georgina Battiscombe in claiming that Yonge 'did not know that sex existed',[144] I would like to conclude this chapter by suggesting that the presence of recognizably sexually inverted characters in Yonge's narratives indicates a link between the aesthetic of development we have been exploring and her conception of gender roles.

Theories of sexual inversion were in circulation in Britain from the mid nineteenth century, and, as Jeffrey Weeks notes, were linked to the medical concerns about the effects of masturbation[145] which had been current since the eighteenth century.[146] It is worth noting that Hughes's *Tom Brown's Schooldays*, first published in 1857, a book Yonge could hardly have failed to read given her professional interest in children's literature, contained a fairly explicit reference to the presence of homosexual relationships at Rugby School.[147] The Victorian concept of sexual inversion, of course, was not straightforwardly equivalent to the present-day notion of homosexual identity, since the link with ideas about masturbation implied that a sexually inverted state was to some extent a product of the individual's choices. The issue of sexual inversion in Yonge is thus linked to her wider emphasis on the development of individuals to fulfil the demands of their gender roles, a theme which, as we have already noted, in the

142   John Shelton Reed, *Glorious Battle: The Cultural Politics of Victorian Anglo-Catholicism* (Nashville and London: Vanderbilt University Press, 1996), 193–207.

143   Talia Schaffer, 'The Mysterious Magnum Bonum: Fighting to Read Charlotte Yonge', *Nineteenth-Century Literature* 55, no.2 (2000): 265.

144   Ibid., 266.

145   Jeffrey Weeks, *Coming Out: Homosexual Politics in Britain from the Nineteenth Century to the Present* (London: Quartet Books, 1977), 23–5.

146   Thomas Laqueur, *Solitary Sex: A Cultural History of Masturbation* (New York: Zone Books, 2003), 13–16.

147   Thomas Hughes, *Tom Brown's Schooldays* (London: Gawthorn, n.d.), 140 (Part 2 Ch.2).

case of her female characters is often represented by their transition from a state of nervous irritability to a state of mesmeric influence.

This can be illustrated by the example of Clement Underwood in *The Pillars of the House*, one of Yonge's most clearly sexually inverted characters. Clement is introduced early in the novel with the comment that he 'looked so much as if he ought to have been a girl, that Tina, short for Clementina, was his school name'.[148] After Clement has been sent away to be trained up as a clergyman in Robert Fulmort's London parish, he comes back imbued with a suspiciously extreme Anglo-Catholic ritualism which borders on what Victorians would have called Romanism.[149] It is made clear that Clement is committed to a celibate life,[150] and the emotional satisfaction he finds in same-sex friendships is a recurrent theme.[151]

A discussion with his brother Felix identifies Clement's tendency to priggishness with the lack of a 'manliness' which Clement calls 'the great temptation of this world', although Felix suggests that he is failing to distinguish between 'true and false manliness'.[152] This distinction echoes Thomas Hughes's *The Manliness of Christ*, where Hughes responds to what he regarded as the damaging effects of the label of 'muscular Christianity' that had been attached to his position by stressing that manliness is not mere athleticism, but the moral courage exhibited 'when a man or a woman is called to stand by what approves itself to their consciences as true [...] against all discouragement and opposition from those they love or respect'.[153] In terms of this definition, however, Clement's want of manliness is not unambiguous: although Felix cannot understand the sense of self-abasement which prevents Clement from facing the rest of the family after he has inadvertently been made drunk, Clement's comment that 'if I am alone now, I think I can bring myself to bear up outwardly as you wish' is described as made in a voice from which 'the affected

---

148   Yonge, *The Pillars of the House, or Under Wode, Under Rode*, 2 vols (London: Macmillan, 1901), 1: 7 (Ch.1).
149   Ibid., 1: 141–2 (Ch.8).
150   Ibid., 2: 264 (Ch.34).
151   Ibid., 1: 79, 2: 251, 267 (Chs 5, 34).
152   Ibid., 1: 208 (Ch.12).
153   Thomas Hughes, *The Manliness of Christ* (London: Macmillan, 1894), 37.

tone had vanished',[154] implying the genuineness, and hence the manliness, of Clement's remorse. Likewise, Dr May, who represents a moral arbiter in the novel, notes that young men like Clement, even though they 'may run into what seems queer to us', are like the Arthurian knights who departed from the Round Table for the higher aim of the 'Quest of the Sancgreal',[155] a comparison which Yonge makes in her own person in her advice manual *Womankind*,[156] and which echoes the notion of the 'New Chivalry' as a kind of sublimated homoeroticism which Ellis Hanson notes was employed by homosexual apologists towards the end of the nineteenth century.[157]

During the course of the novel, whilst Clement continues to undertake feminine roles such as nursing the aged Fulbert Underwood,[158] it is emphasized that he also becomes more manly as a result of his work as a vicar in the country parish of Vale Leston. When Clement reluctantly realizes that it is his duty to accept his uncle's patronage, the narrator comments that 'it was curious how this weight of responsibility was extinguishing self-consciousness and making a man of him',[159] and later Clement's progress to manliness is confirmed when it is noted that Robert Fulmort 'never expected to see his tall, docile, self-complacent chorister all the man that the Vicar of Vale Leston Abbas had become'.[160] Crucially, these descriptions link Clement's previous lack of manliness to his self-consciousness, a connection which is also indicated by Robert Fulmort's earlier remark to Felix, relative to Clement's upbringing in the clergy house of St Matthew's, that '*esprit de corps* in so small a place as this is apt to become so concentrated as not to be many removes from egotism'.[161]

Victorian concerns over the effects of masturbation centred around the reinforcement the practice was thought to give to the

---

154 Yonge, *Pillars of the House*, 1: 209 (Ch.12).
155 Ibid., 2: 284 (Ch.35).
156 Ethel Romanes, *Charlotte Mary Yonge: An Appreciation* (London: Mowbray, 1908), 171–4.
157 Hanson, *Decadence*, 213–14.
158 Yonge, *Pillars of the House*, 2: 277 (Ch.35).
159 Ibid., 2: 263 (Ch.34).
160 Ibid., 2: 523 (Ch.43).
161 Ibid., 1: 220 (Ch.13).

imagination, in encouraging a dangerous kind of solipsism: according to nineteenth-century medical thought, the nervous stimulation consequent on masturbation created an associative complex entirely centred on self, whose strength was such that it threatened entirely to detach the mind from reality and render the masturbator insane.[162] The relation between Clement's self-involvement and his lack of manliness suggests the influence of these theories of masturbation: Clement's extreme ritualism for Yonge threatens to be a form of mental masturbation, until his parochial responsibilities impress on him 'the stamp of thought and reality'.[163] A similar argument can be made about sexually inverted female characters in Yonge's novels, such as Clement's sister Angela Underwood, or Horatia Charteris in *Hopes and Fears*: Felix comments on the 'passion for excitement'[164] or nervous stimulation, that has been responsible for Angela's conversion to Evangelicalism, something that can also be seen to be responsible for Horatia's flighty behaviour, and final conversion to the Plymouth Brethen, about which Lucilla comments that 'dissipation, religious or otherwise, old Rashe *must* have'.[165]

Sexual inversion in Yonge's novels exhibits both the dangers and the benefits of the imagination itself, leading either to a self-centred perspective or, alternatively, to a noble commitment to the ideal which exceeds that of which other people are capable: Lucilla, who finally, as the narrator notes, shows herself incapable of 'real aspiration',[166] notes that there was 'something great'[167] in Horatia. Given Yonge's recognition of the disadvantages of her own strong imagination,[168] it may be that the presence of sexually inverted characters in her fiction reflects a self-identification with the category of sexual inversion. Yonge's own slightly regretful remark to Elizabeth Wordsworth, 'self-

---

162   Laqueur, *Solitary Sex*, 210–16.
163   Yonge, *Pillars of the House*, 2: 277 (Ch.35).
164   Ibid., 2: 584 (Ch.46).
165   Yonge, *Hopes and Fears*, 464 (Part 2 Ch.25).
166   Ibid., 521 (Part 2 Ch.29).
167   Ibid., 464 (Part 2 Ch.25).
168   Coleridge, *Yonge*, 62, 126–8.

consciousness is a misfortune, not a fault'[169] certainly seems to point in this direction.

169   Romanes, *Yonge: An Appreciation*, 150.

Section Two
Yonge and the Theory of Fiction: a Reading of *The Heir of Redclyffe*

Charlotte M. Yonge's *The Heir of Redclyffe* stands at the centre of her novelistic *oeuvre*, because not only is it the novel which exhibits the most extended typological patterning to be found in Yonge's work, but is also the novel which incorporates some of Yonge's most sustained reflection on the moral effects of fiction and on the possibility of an authentic feminism. The novel self-reflexively plays out the unresolvable differend between a naturalistic rationalism and an intuitionism which acknowledges the possibility of the transcendent in the persons of its two main characters, Philip Morville and his cousin Guy, whose relationship of what Eve Kosofsky Sedgwick would call homosocial paranoia[1] is indicated by the way in which the novel's title is ultimately found to refer to both characters. The contrast extends to these characters' romantic relationships with the two sisters, Laura and Amy Edmonstone, where the refusal of Philip and Laura to acknowledge any responsibilities beyond their own emotional needs is shown to have a stunting effect on Laura's development as an independent woman, and to the forms of culture which they represent, where the world of imaginative fiction is shown to have been morally sustaining for Guy in a way that the utilitarian logic of Philip has signally failed to be.

The sheer popularity of *The Heir of Redclyffe* in the mid-Victorian period reflects the currency of typological modes of interpretation in Victorian culture generally, and so my account of the novel begins by enlarging the treatment of typological thought beyond the predominantly Tractarian context in which previous chapters have situated it, suggesting that the connection between typology and

---

1   Eve Kosofsky Sedgwick, *Between Men: English Literature and Male Homosocial Desire* (New York: Columbia University Press, 1985).

realism evident in artistic movements such as Preraphaelitism reflects the pervasive influence of the British intuitionist tradition of Common Sense philosophy. The implications of typological significance for the form taken by Yonge's realist fiction are then examined, and it is argued that her use of typology requires a peculiar degree of self-consciousness on Yonge's part about the moral dangers of the excessive subjectivity which the Victorians felt to be inherent in the novel form. In *The Heir of Redclyffe*, it is suggested, Philip represents this excessive subjectivity in a way which reflects Newman's characterization of the effects of rationalism.

The Heir of Redclyffe comments self-reflexively on the moral effects of acknowledging the possibility of transcendence in the way that its own typological mode of realism demands, and this aspect of the novel, I suggest, is intimately linked to the presentation of the effects of the secret engagement between Laura and Philip. I argue against the view of a number of critics that Yonge's portrayal of the permanently blighted nature of Laura's life reflects a heavy-handed and dogmatic moral outlook, suggesting instead that Yonge's purpose is the conservative feminist one of showing how Laura's unquestioning acceptance of Philip's demands for secrecy prevents her attainment of the 'separate sphere' of true womanhood and makes her instead into an *ersatz* man. Philip's discouragement of Laura from reading imaginative literature forms part of the process whereby her independent femininity is corrupted, and I examine the relationship between Yonge's claims for the beneficial moral effect of fiction and Tractarian criticism of J.S. Mill's *A System of Logic*, to which I suggest *The Heir of Redclyffe* represents a contribution.

Chapter Four
Typology and Realism in *The Heir of Redclyffe*

Typology in Victorian Culture

The analysis of Tractarian religious and aesthetic thought presented in the preceding chapters has explored the intimate relationship between a providentialist conception of associationism, which I have identified in the writings of Keble and Newman, and a typological approach to literary interpretation which I have suggested is applicable to Yonge's domestic novels without undertaking an extended reading of her fiction in these terms. The moment has now come to put the interpretative approach which I have been theorizing to the test by applying it to Yonge's best-known novel, *The Heir of Redclyffe*, whose runaway success in 1853 marked Yonge's breakthrough as a writer. First, however, I would like to broaden the scope of my argument by extending the examination of the role played by typological forms of interpretation in Victorian culture beyond the largely Tractarian intellectual milieu with which the previous chapters have dealt. Some appreciation of the wider context in which typological hermeneutics would have been familiar to the Victorian reader is necessary to understand the centrality of *The Heir of Redclyffe* to mid-Victorian culture, and to establish its position in the mainstream of the development of the realist novel.

Historians of the novel such as Ian Watt, following Lukács's pronouncement that 'the novel is the epic of a world without God',[1] have tended to portray the novel form as inescapably committed to a secular view of the world, something which precludes the possibility of typological significance in the realist novel. As should have become apparent from my argument so far, Yonge's novels present

---

1   Ian Watt, *The Rise of the Novel: Studies in Defoe, Richardson, and Fielding* (London: Chatto and Windus, 1957), 84.

something of a problem for this characterization of the novel form, since they possess all the features Watt identifies with what he calls 'formal realism'[2] (to an extent that led Victorian critics to complain about her excessive and undiscriminating realism)[3] but combined with a religious perspective that extends far beyond superficial pieties, informing minute details of plot and characterization. The fact of Yonge's astonishing popularity might also lead us to question the adequacy of the Wattsian secularist characterization of novel form; since *The Heir of Redclyffe* was one of the best-selling novels of the nineteenth century, it must have appealed to an audience which went well beyond Yonge's fellow Tractarians.

An alternative to this rather one-sided presentation of novelistic realism can be found in Edwin M. Eigner's 1978 study, *The Metaphysical Novel in England and America*, which focuses on non-naturalistic kinds of significance in the nineteenth-century novel in a way that makes its preoccupations close to the typological hermeneutic to which I have drawn attention in Yonge. Eigner's description of the techniques of what he identifies as the English and American *Bildungsroman* has many points of contact with Yonge's novelistic techniques; he emphasizes, for instance, the use of paired characters to explore contrasting paths of development which is such a prominent feature of Yonge's treatment of the characters of Guy and Philip in *The Heir of Redclyffe*.[4] Eigner presents his school of 'metaphysical novelists' (centred around the figure of Bulwer-Lytton) as an alternative to the realist tradition, and makes a convincing case for including Dickens, classed by most critics as a realist, among his 'metaphysical novelists', suggesting that even novelists such as Eliot and Hardy switch into a 'metaphysical' mode at points in their otherwise realist novels.[5]

---

2   Ibid., 83–5.
3   R.H. Hutton, 'Ethical and Dogmatic Fiction: Miss Yonge', *National Review* 12 (1861): 214.
4   Edwin M. Eigner, *The Metaphysical Novel in England and America: Dickens, Bulwer, Hawthorne, Melville* (Berkeley and Los Angeles: University of California Press, 1978), 68–84.
5   Ibid., 227.

Chris Brooks develops Eigner's category of the 'metaphysical novel' in his 1984 study *Signs for the Times: Symbolic Realism in the Mid-Victorian World* in which, in the course of a discussion of Carlyle (a Victorian thinker who has recently been shown to have been significantly influenced by Common Sense philosophy)[6] he draws attention to the centrality of typology to an understanding of realism.[7] Brooks's wide-ranging study applies this idea of a typological realist mode (what he calls 'symbolic realism') to painting and architecture as well as the novel. Although my focus here is the typological dimensions of Yonge's realist narrative, I think Brooks's extension of the concept of typology is amply justified by the influence of Common Sense philosophy on nineteenth-century aesthetic thinking in general.[8]

The general currency in mid-Victorian culture of the kind of link I am examining between realism and typology in Yonge can be seen very clearly in Pre-Raphaelite painting, where the realist detail of, for example, Holman Hunt's 'The Light of the World' was given a quite elaborate allegorical explanation by contemporary critics.[9] This understanding of realist detail in a typological light was given theoretical justification by John Ruskin. In *Modern Painters* Ruskin makes it clear that detail in painting is to be valued for its typological relationship to God's work in Creation: pictorial detail reveals a loving attention on the part of the painter which indicates the infinite detail (and infinite loving attention) to be found in Nature.[10]

6   Carlyle's indebtedness to Common Sense philosophy is described in Ralph Jessop, *Carlyle and Scottish Thought* (Houndmills: Macmillan, 1997).

7   Chris Brooks, *Signs for the Times: Symbolic Realism in the Mid-Victorian World* (London: George Allen and Unwin, 1984), 14.

8   Ruskin's writings are an example of the influence of Common Sense philosophy on nineteenth century aesthetics, which has been detailed in a French context by James W. Manns, *Reid and His French Disciples* (Leiden: Brill, 1994).

9   F.G. Stephens, *William Holman Hunt and His Works: A Memoir of the Artist's Life with Description of His Pictures* (London: Nisbet, 1860), 24–31.

10   John Ruskin, *Works*, 39 vols, E.T. Cook and Alexander Wedderburn (eds) (London: Allen, 1903-12), 2: 60–1.

Although modern commentators have tended to separate the Ruskinian interest in landscape from the kind of narrativizing interpretation of pictorial detail which Victorian commentary on 'The Light of the World' exemplifies,[11] in fact these two tendencies are intimately linked in Ruskin's work, and in Victorian culture more generally. Ruskin himself suggested that the hallucinatory vividness of detail in Pre-Raphaelite painting should be regarded a testimony to the moral strenuousness of its practitioners,[12] and shows himself quite capable of narrativizing and moralistic interpretation even of natural details, such as light, in the early books of *Modern Painters*.[13] What connects this narrativization of painting with the theological argument from design underlying much of Ruskin's writing on landscape is the assumption, for which Ruskin is indebted to Common Sense philosophy, that the visible world is a collection of signs whose intelligibility depends fundamentally on the interpretative activity of the perceiver: a picture for Ruskin is not merely a coloured surface, but requires to be made sense of, because the material world is, regarded in itself, a fundamentally unintelligible mass of mere sensations.

In a more popular context, similar tendencies towards a typological interpretation of pictorial realism can be found in the catalogue entries written by the organizers of the 1880s Whitechapel Exhibitions, Samuel and Henrietta Barnett, and their helpers. Though these entries have been dismissed by some modern critics as mere 'moralising', the Barnetts' interest in landscapes shows that their understanding of the moral influence of painting extends beyond simple narrative pictures. The Barnetts', and Ruskin's, preoccupation with the social function of art, makes the connection in their thought

11   Cf. Frances Borzello, 'Pictures for the People', in Ira Bruce Nadel and F.S. Schwarzbach (eds), *Victorian Artists and the City* (New York: Pergamon Press, 1980), 34–6.
12   Ruskin, *Works*, 12: 330–2, 334.
13   Ibid., 4: 77–84.

128

between realism and typology strikingly similar to the concerns of Yonge's religiously inflected domestic realism.[14]

Given the importance of typology in Victorian culture generally, it is striking that existing criticism makes little or no attempt to explain why there was such an upsurge in typological modes of writing in the first half of the nineteenth century. Paul J. Korshin's 1982 study *Typologies in England 1650–1820* makes clear that typology in the context of Biblical interpretation or allusion flourished during much of the eighteenth century, after a lull at the century's beginning, but that the proliferation of 'natural typology', of the kind adumbrated by Wordsworth's use of apocalyptic language in the Simplon Pass episode of *The Prelude*, is a phenomenon specific to the early nineteenth century. As G.B. Tennyson argues in his 1984 essay '"So Careful of the Type?" – Victorian Biblical Typology: Sources and Applications', the ascription in Landow's *Victorian Types, Victorian Shadows* of typology's renewed importance simply to the influence of Evangelicalism is inadequate: the centrality of typological thinking to the Tractarian position shows that it must have a broader cultural source than 'Evangelical sectarianism'. A similar argument might be made about Sussman's *Fact into Figure*, which is even more summary in its discussion of the reasons for typology's renewed popularity in nineteenth century art. Unfortunately, beyond detailing the use the Tractarians made of typology, Tennyson has nothing further to add: he shows that Keble was referring to 'types' in the context of poetic theory as early as 1814, but gives no reason for the sudden surge in intellectual popularity of typological modes of thinking during the early nineteenth century.[15]

One obvious correlative of the renewed interest in typology is the Romantic Movement. Both Tennyson and Hilary Fraser, in her 1986 book *Beauty and Belief: Aesthetics and Religion in Victorian Literature*, make a connection between the role of typology in Tractarian

---

14   See Gavin Budge, 'Poverty and the Picture Gallery: The Whitechapel Exhibitions and the Social Project of Ruskinian Aesthetics', *Visual Culture in Britain* 1, no.2 (2000): 43–56.

15   G.B. Tennyson, '"So Careful of the Type?" – Victorian Biblical Typology: Sources and Applications', *Essays and Studies* 37 (1984): 34.

thought and Coleridge's notion of the symbol. But this again cannot constitute an adequate explanation for the importance typology took on in the early nineteenth century: in 1814, the date of publication of Keble's first essay linking poetry and theological 'types', Coleridge had yet to publish most of the writings for which he is best known today, and what he had published had only achieved extremely limited circulation. One of Landow's major sources for nineteenth century thinking about typology, Thomas Hartwell Horne's *An Introduction to the Critical Study and Knowledge of the Holy Scriptures*, which he describes as 'standard reading for British Divinity students',[16] was first published in 1818, only three years after publication of the *Biographia Literaria*. To suggest that Horne's sympathetic treatment of typological interpretation reflects the influence of Coleridge would be to assume an improbably rapid assimilation of an avant-garde thinker into the theological mainstream.

The typological worldview of the early Victorians, as I hope my previous chapters have suggested, is constituted by a confluence of philosophy, psychology and theology within the thought of the period. This philosophical theology is not the German Idealist influenced Higher Criticism which became important later in the nineteenth century: the orthodox Thomas Hartwell Horne, for example, roundly rejects the demystifying German school of interpretation represented by Bauer and his followers.[17] If one looks at the almost entirely British theological and interpretative sources referenced by Horne, such as Bishop Lowth's *Lectures on the Poetry of the Hebrews*, they belong largely to the second half of the eighteenth century, and it is to writings of this period, and their influence upon the Tractarians, that we must look to find an explanation for the Victorian interest in typology, and the typological strain in Charlotte Yonge's narrative technique.

16   George P. Landow, *Victorian Types, Victorian Shadows: Biblical Typology in Victorian Literature, Art and Thought* (London: Routledge and Kegan Paul, 1980), 22.

17   Thomas Hartwell Horne, *An Introduction to the Critical Study and Knowledge of the Holy Scriptures*, 4th edn (London: Cadell, 1823), 499.

Horne himself offers a justification for the 'spiritual interpretation' of the Biblical text that is typology in the following terms:

> All our ideas are admitted through the medium of the senses, and consequently refer in the first place to external objects: but no sooner are we convinced that we possess an immaterial soul or spirit, than we find occasion for other terms, or, for want of these, another application of the same terms to a different class of objects; and hence arises the necessity of resorting to figurative and spiritual interpretation. Now, the object of revelation being to make known things which 'eye hath not seen nor ear heard, nor have entered into the heart of man to conceive', it seems hardly possible that the human mind should be capable of apprehending them, but through the medium of figurative language or mystical representations.[18]

Horne is arguing that the legitimacy of typological interpretation rests on the same basis as that of any kind of language we use to talk about the immaterial realm of mind. Since all our ideas are material, in that they come to us through the senses, when we want to talk about the mind (which Horne assumes is radically non-material) we are forced to invent metaphorical applications of our ideas in order to convey our meaning. Since the Bible is a divine revelation of that which transcends the material world, typological interpretation of it must be legitimate, since it is only by means of such figurative applications that Revelation could be conveyed in human language at all.

It is no coincidence that Horne here virtually in the same breath justifies typological interpretation along with all metaphorical uses of language (including, of course, poetry). Horne is deftly summarizing over a century of post-Lockean theological debate about the status of Biblical language. Early eighteenth-century freethinkers such as John Toland[19] and William Collins[20] had invoked Locke's hostility towards metaphor in the *Essay Concerning Human Understanding*, in order to argue for the redundancy of Biblical revelation itself. If, as Locke had argued, metaphor cannot convey any meaning which goes beyond the ideas we receive through the senses, then presumably, Toland and

---

18   Horne, *Introduction to Critical Study of the Scriptures*, 496.
19   John Toland, *Christianity not Mysterious* (Dublin: Lilliput Press, 1997), 31–5.
20   Anthony Collins, *A Discourse of the Grounds and Reasons of the Christian Religion* (London, 1724), 91–2.

Collins claim, the Bible cannot be understood to convey any religious truth which is not already available to us through the senses. Collins in particular attacks New Testament typological interpretation of Old Testament prophecy as an intellectually illegitimate and 'mystical' use of language.[21]

Religious orthodoxy, then, is intimately bound up with the defence of the intellectual validity of metaphor, in which Horne engages in the passage I have quoted. In this respect, Horne's argument reflects half a century of Anglican defences of metaphor as producing a kind of knowledge which is not available to the senses, defences which include Lowth's *Lectures on the Poetry of the Hebrews*, Burke's *Philosophical Inquiry into the Origin of our Ideas of the Sublime and Beautiful*, and Butler's *Analogy of Religion*. But this is only half the picture, since these defences of the validity of metaphorical language do not address the Lockean philosophical basis of the freethinkers' advocacy of Natural Religion.

As we have noted, a radical dualism stands behind Horne's defence of typological interpretation. The mind for Horne is essentially 'immaterial', so that language, which derives from the material realm of ideas, can only be made to refer to the mental realm by the tropological interpretation to which the mind subjects it. Furthermore, Horne implies, we can only arrive at a knowledge of the immateriality of the mind through a fundamental spiritual intuition: we can be 'convinced' of this immateriality, but obviously not through the agency of the material world, since this would be a contradiction in terms.

Landow draws attention to the presence of this mind/body dualism in Victorian typological thought generally, but fails to root it in anything specific to the early nineteenth century intellectual context. A more definite philosophical source for the Victorian typological worldview can be found in the intuitionism of the Common Sense

21   Collins, *Reasons of the Christian Religion*, 97–9. Collins uses an indirect manner of presentation, but the argument is implicit in the way he juxtaposes his claim that the evidence for Christianity rests on essentially allegorical interpretations of the Old Testament with a lengthy quote from William Whiston to the effect that such allegorical interpretations of the Old Testament are absurd.

tradition, whose influence in Britain was at its height in the early decades of the nineteenth century.[22]

Typology in Keble

In Yonge's case, the typological dimension of her novelistic realism reflects her close association with Tracctarianism. M.H. Abrams[23] and Stephen Prickett,[24] have suggested that the aesthetic position which her mentor John Keble puts forward in *On the Mysticism which has been Attributed to some Early Fathers of the Church* and in his *Lectures on Poetry*, can be seen as a rewriting of Wordsworth's theory of poetry in religious terms. As I have previously argued, this Tractarian version of Romantic poetics informs Yonge's novels in a way that allows her to combine domestic realism with the transcendent dimension of religious typology.

In Keble's view, the analogies which the Wordsworthian poet finds between Nature and his own mind are ultimately justified because Nature itself is an expression of the Divine Mind. Even though the sympathy between Nature and the mind described by Wordsworth is in itself a kind of fiction, for Keble it can nevertheless be said to be true insofar as the relationship between poet and Nature is regarded in a typological light, as an analogy of the mind's relationship to God. Keble suggests that the metaphorical language used by the Wordsworthian poet about Nature has a claim to be regarded as possessing the status of truth inasmuch as it is founded on the divinely inspired language of Biblical revelation.[25]

22 Landow, *Victorian Types*, 22.
23 M.H. Abrams, *The Mirror and the Lamp: Romantic Theory and the Critical Tradition* (Oxford: Oxford University Press, 1971), 144–8.
24 Stephen Prickett, *Romanticism and Religion: The Tradition of Coleridge and Wordsworth in the Victorian Church* (Cambridge: Cambridge University Press, 1976), 91–119.
25 John Keble, *On the Mysticism Attributed to the Early Fathers of the Church* (Oxford and London: Parker, 1868), 169–70, in Gavin Budge (ed.), *Aesthetics*

Keble is interested in Wordsworth's realist poetic not only for its literary implications, but because he regards it as conveying an actual truth about the nature of the world: that is to say, he is a 'realist' not only in a literary sense, but in a philosophical one. Both Abrams and Prickett, followed by Hilary Fraser, assume that Keble's poetic theory was influenced by Coleridge, but this is to ignore the extent to which Keble deliberately sets himself against the subjectivizing tendency of Coleridgean poetics. As Prickett himself implicitly recognizes, the whole thrust of Keble's poetics is against regarding poetry as the product merely of the poet's individual mind.[26]

The realist philosophical position evident in Keble's poetics reflects the influence of the Common Sense philosophy of Thomas Reid and his pupil Dugald Stewart. One important aspect of Common Sense philosophy was the analogy it claimed between perception and language. Reid and his followers developed Berkeley's claim that the process of perceiving an external world was in important respects like the process of interpreting a language: in both cases, there is no natural relationship of resemblance between the material impression on our senses and what we end up understanding by it. The acoustic vibrations which constitute the material existence of a word are not in any way 'like' the concept it evokes in our minds, and in the same way for Reid and other Common Sense philosophers our physical sensations bear no kind of 'resemblance' to the world of our perceptions (a claim which they regarded as having been conclusively established by Hume's demonstration that it was impossible to justify our natural belief in an external world by a process of rational

and Religion in Nineteenth-Century Britain, 6 vols (Bristol: Thoemmes, 2003), Vol.3.

26   Prickett's recognition that Keble has a (philosophically) 'realist', anti-subjective view of poetry is shown by his comment that Keble's attitude towards Nature is more akin to 'the medieval and early Church's tradition of allegorical correspondences' (Romanticism and Religion, 105), and his comment that Butler's Analogy of Religion reinforced the influence of Wordsworthian poetics on Keble (Romanticism and Religion, 107–6). Keble's realist view of poetry would also seem to lie behind the avoidance of Coleridgean vocabulary which Prickett notes (Romanticism and Religion, 117).

deduction from our sensations).[27] In the view of Reid and his followers, the world was filled with divinely instituted signs which, by a providential dispensation, our minds were enabled intuitively to decipher: all knowledge became for them a form of revelation.[28]

The affinity of this realist philosophical account of perception to the traditional Christian belief in typology was clear to late eighteenth- and early nineteenth-century theologians, and can be seen to underlie Keble's assimilation of Wordsworthian poetics to the Tractarian religious outlook. If all perception is interpretation of a divine language, then, conversely, the metaphorical language of the Bible can be regarded as a mode of perception, possessing a reality which is equal to any evidence of the senses. In this view typology, or use of Biblical metaphor, is not merely a literary game, but a vital reality inherent in our perceptions of the world, and the poetic language of a Wordsworth shares in this divinely guaranteed reality insofar as it is related to Biblical typology. For the Common Sense philosophers, the ability to perceive itself forms part of mental activity, and as such can be improved by practice;[29] the associative relationships which constitute typology in the Tractarian view consequently represent a form of training in the perception of the divine. Keble's realist position is thus utterly antithetical to Coleridgean poetics: for Keble to account for poetry simply in terms of the individual poet's psychology, as Coleridge does, would be to undermine both his theological and epistemological position.[30]

For Keble, God guarantees the special reality of Biblical metaphor in a way which distinguishes them from the normal metaphors of human speech:

27 Thomas Reid, *Works*, 7th edn, William Hamilton (ed.) (Edinburgh: Maclachlan and Stewart, 1872), 127–30.
28 Ibid., 134.
29 Ibid., 174.
30 An example of the use of Common Sense philosophy in an important work of late eighteenth century theology can be found in William Magee's *Discourses and Dissertations on the Scriptural Doctrines of Atonement and Sacrifice*, first published in 1792, which refers to Reid and Stewart in support of its argument from typology (*Discourses and Dissertations on the Scriptural Doctrines of Atonement and Sacrifice* [London: Bohn, 1852], 138).

The Author of Scripture is the Author of Nature. He made His creatures what they are, upholds them in their being modifies it at His will knows all their secret relations, associations, and properties. We know not how much there may be, far beyond mere metaphor and similitude, in His using the name of any one of His creatures, in a translated sense, to shadow out some thing invisible. But thus far we may seem to understand, that the object thus spoken of by Him is so far taken out of the number of ordinary figures of speech and resources of language, and partakes thenceforth of the nature of a Type [...] Let an uninspired poet or theologian be never so ingenious in his comparisons between earthly things and heavenly, we cannot build any thing upon them; there is no particular certainty, much less any sacredness in them: but let the same words come out of the mouth of GOD, and we know that the resemblance was Intended from the beginning and Intended to be noticed and treasured up by us; it is therefore very nearly the case of a Type properly so called.[31]

Keble is concerned in this passage to establish the difference between the divine origin of 'a Scriptural Type' and the human origin of a 'mere illustration or analogy'. What distinguishes the two for Keble is the very fact of the first having appeared in the inspired word of Scripture; this implies 'that the event or observance itself to which we annex the figurative meaning was ordered [...] from the beginning with reference to that meaning'.[32] Keble's view here seems to invoke the doctrine of the literal inspiration of Scripture: God's dual role as Creator of the world and as divine Author of Scripture, means that Scriptural metaphors partake of the reality of the world itself, in a way that merely human metaphors can never do, so that the Type is, in an important sense, identical with Nature.

The crucial nature of the difference in epistemological status between scriptural and non-scriptural 'allusions to the works of nature' is apparent in the way Keble uses to illustrate this difference the key Type of Christian theology, Abraham's sacrifice of Isaac. If we knew of the sacrifice of Isaac only through the non-scriptural author Josephus, Keble argues, Christians might still have chosen to refer to the sacrifice of Isaac 'by way of similitude and comparison' when discussing the Crucifixion, but it would not be possible to regard it as a Type. What underpins the typical status of the sacrifice of Isaac

31   Keble, *On the Mysticism*, 169–71 in Budge, *Aesthetics and Religion*, Vol.3.
32   Ibid., 170.

is the fact that it is recounted in Scripture, so that the comparison to the Crucifixion 'must have been intended in the first sanctioning of the type, being the inevitable result, in all minds that fear GOD, and watch for the signs of His presence'.[33] For Keble, God himself has willed the comparison between the Crucifixion and the sacrifice of Isaac, in that the inclusion of the story of Abraham and Isaac within the inspired text has made it morally inevitable that a pious Christian will discover its resemblance to the Crucifixion. Keble suggests that the use in the inspired text of the Bible of metaphors taken from Nature has, in a similar way, made it morally inevitable that the pious Christian will discover religious significance in Nature, and that it is justifiable to claim that this religious significance is an objective feature of Nature itself, not merely a meaning attached to Nature by the individual consciousness.

As Keble points out, taken to its logical conclusion this typological outlook on the world implies that 'the whole world of sense' potentially possesses spiritual meaning, since the natural Types of Scripture must inevitably become intimately associated with our experience of Nature as a whole, a process which is facilitated by the way in which in Scripture 'so many of the chief visible objects are invested with spiritual meanings'.[34] Religious belief for Keble offers the key to an entire renewal of our perceptions of very much the same kind as Coleridge in the *Biographia Literaria* attributes to the influence of Wordsworth's poetry. For Keble, religious perception of the world is an exercise in defamiliarization, something which is also characteristic of the critical aesthetic of Yonge's novels. Newman's emphasis on the role played by imagination in religious belief helps to suggest why Tractarians such as Yonge attached so much importance to their literary work:

The world really brings no new argument to its aid, – nothing beyond its own assertion. In the very outset Christians allow that its teaching is contrary to Revelation, and not to be taken as authority; nevertheless, afterwards, this mere unargumentative teaching, which, when viewed in theory, formed no objection to the truth of the Inspired Word, yet, when actually heard in the intercourse of

33   Ibid.
34   Ibid., 174.

life, converts them, more or less, to the service of the 'prince of the power of the air, the spirit which now worketh in the children of disobedience.' It assails their *imagination*.[35]

By demonstrating that the narrative mode of literary realism can be successfully employed in the service of religious belief, Yonge may be said to effect a conversion of her readers' imagination which Newman and the Tractarians would regard as potentially more far-reaching than any rational argument.

Typology in *The Heir of Redclyffe*

Although Yonge's novels share Keble's brand of typological realism, I do not want to suggest that this is altogether an unproblematic heritage for Yonge as a novelist; indeed, I think that much of what makes Yonge an interesting writer is her self-conscious struggle with the implications of typological realism for the novelistic represent-ation of experience. Famously, Yonge submitted her novels to Keble for correction.[36] Feminist critics have often interpreted this habit of Yonge's as a gesture of submission to male authority, but from the perspective I have been outlining it might be viewed as indicating some anxiety on Yonge's part about the double-bind inherent in the demands of typological realism in the novel.

Typological realism is problematic for Yonge because of the novel form's basic demand that the novelist create a fictional world, a requirement which threatens to disrupt that direct communication be-tween the mind and God to which intuitionist and typological thinkers appealed. An article in the *Monthly Packet* suggests considerable ambivalence about the moral influence of the novel form. Even novels

35   John Henry Newman, *Newman's University Sermons: Fifteen Sermons Preached Before the University of Oxford 1826–1843*, intro by D.M. Mac-Kinnon and J.D. Holmes (London: SPCK, 1970), 132.

36   Georgina Battiscombe, *Charlotte Mary Yonge: The Story of an Uneventful Life* (London: Constable, 1944), 72.

which are in themselves morally sound, the writer argues, can have a harmful effect on the minds of readers owing to the unreal nature of the worlds they create: novels play upon the feelings which excite us to action without actually providing any scope for that action, and in so doing they tend to weaken our capacity to form virtuous habits. The very unreality of novels enfeebles those divinely implanted intuitions which are our guide to action in the real world, and the only remedy for this, the writer suggests, is to be careful not to read too many novels.[37]

The danger of the novel form is that it encourages an excessive subjectivity which tends to insulate the mind from its native intuitions of the divine reality outside itself. This negative characterization of the inherent tendencies of the novel form is reinforced by a further article published in the *Monthly Packet* a couple of years later, in which novelistic modes of characterization are held responsible for encouraging egotism. The problem with novels, the writer suggests, is that they tend to instil an excessively self-analytical and self-conscious attitude towards our own characters, by promoting a habit of mind in which our own actions are regarded as those of a character in a novel. This mindset is responsible for an isolation from those beneficial moral intuitions naturally prompted by the external world, and hence for 'undisciplined passions' which God must 'tame by chastening and trials'.[38]

These articles indicate that Yonge must have regarded her commitment to typological realism, both as literary style and religious-philosophical position, as demanding a high degree of self-consciousness in her work as a novelist. As her comments on 'sensation fiction' show, Yonge was aware that novelistic realism had a tendency to degenerate into naturalism and sensationalism:[39] from the point of view I have been suggesting Yonge and Keble shared, this is 'unreal' because it implies it is possible to lead lives which have no dimension which transcends the material world. For this reason,

37   B.L.K., 'Imagination', *Monthly Packet* 1 (Series 2 1866): 472–3.
38   Anon., 'Egotism', *Monthly Packet* 5 (Series 2 1868): 517.
39   Charlotte M. Yonge, 'Authorship', in Georgina Battiscombe and Marghanita Laski (eds), *A Chaplet for Charlotte Yonge* (London: Cresset, 1965), 192.

Yonge's own novels, even where they incorporate incident which might find a place in a sensation novel, such as the conviction of an innocent youth for murder in *The Trial*, resolutely downplay such elements in favour of a concentration on 'the trivial round, the common task' (as Keble puts it).[40]

Yonge also seems to have been aware, however, of dangers posed by including typological elements in her fiction. In her novel *The Pillars of the House*, which belongs to a later phase of her career, one of the characters is counselled against looking out for 'types' by a clergyman;[41] it is no coincidence that this character, Geraldine, is consistently described as over-sensitive and imaginative to a degree that endangers her health. For Yonge, then, the kind of imaginative correspondences in which typology deals themselves have the potential to lock readers into a merely subjective (and therefore morally harmful) novelistic world, if these correspondences are ones that are merely fabricated by the author's imagination.

Since both typology and realism, considered in isolation, pose the threat of a morally sapping subjectivity in the novel, the difficulty of the typological realism to which Yonge is committed is how to combine the two. For Yonge, realism must include a transcendent, or typological, dimension in order to avoid the kind of isolated self-consciousness which she sees 'sensation fiction' as promoting, but conversely that typological dimension must be *real*, in the sense that it is recognized as transcending the consciousness of the author. Yonge's fictional style can be seen as an attempt to negotiate the fine line between the potential unreality of self-regarding religious rhetoric, on the one hand, and what she would have regarded as the equally 'unreal' state of mind induced by the mere proliferation of novelistic incident, on the other.[42]

---

40   Keble, 'Morning', in *The Christian Year* (London and New York: Dent and Dutton, 1914), 153.

41   Yonge, *The Pillars of the House, or Under Wode, Under Rode*, 2 vols (London: Macmillan, 1901), 1: 171 (Ch.10).

42   The Tractarians' general suspicion of the potential for 'unreality' in ostentatious religious phraseology is reflected in the doctrine of 'reserve' set out by Isaac Williams in Tracts 80 and 87, 'On Reserve in Communicating Religious Knowledge' (in Budge, *Aesthetics and Religion*, Vol.3).

One of the most obviously typological moments in *The Heir of Redclyffe* is the episode where Guy, the hero of the novel, after having been falsely accused of gambling, strives to keep his hereditarily fierce temper and avoid challenging his accuser, his cousin Philip, to a duel:

> The sun was setting opposite to him, in a flood of gold, – a ruddy ball, surrounded with its pomp of clouds, on the dazzling sweep of horizon. That sight recalled him not only to himself, but to his true and better self; the good angel so close to him for the twenty years of his life, had been driven aloof but for a moment, and now, either that, or a still higher and holier power, made the setting sun bring to his mind, almost to his ear, the words, –
> Let not the sun go down upon your wrath,
> Neither give place to the devil.
> Guy had what some would call a vivid imagination, others a lively faith. He shuddered; then, his elbows on his knees, and his hands clasped over his brow, he sat, bending forward, with his eyes closed, wrought up in a fearful struggle; while it was to him as if he saw the hereditary demon of the Morvilles watching by his side, to take full possession of him as a rightful prey, unless the battle was fought and won before that red orb had passed out of sight. Yes, the besetting fiend of his family – the spirit of defiance and resentment – that was driving him, even now, while realizing its presence, to disregard all thoughts save of the revenge for which he could barter everything – every hope once precious to him.
> It was horror at such wickedness that first checked him, and brought him back to the combat. His was not a temper that was satisfied with half measures. He locked his hands more rigidly together, vowing to compel himself, ere he left the spot, to forgive his enemy – forgive him candidly – forgive him, so as never again to have to say, 'I forgive him!' He did not try to think, for reflection only lashed his sense of the wrong: but, as if there was power in the words alone, he forced his lips to repeat, –
> 'Forgive us our trespasses, as we forgive them that trespass against us.'
> Coldly and hardly were they spoken at first; again he pronounced them, again, again, – each time the tone was softer, each time they came more from the heart. At last the remembrance of greater wrongs and worse revilings came upon him; his eyes filled with tears, the most subduing and healing of all thoughts – that of the great Example – became present to him; the foe was driven back.[43]

43   Yonge, *The Heir of Redclyffe*, Barbara Dennis (ed.) (Oxford: Oxford University Press, 1997), 225–6 (Ch.16).

Yonge's use of free indirect discourse in this passage allows her to blend psychological description of Guy's state of mind with Biblical allusion, in such a way that when Guy begins to think of 'the great Example', Jesus, the reader can hardly fail to recognize that the entire scene Yonge has created is based on the Temptation in the Wilderness – Guy has rushed out into the moorland, is seated in a high place (like the 'pinnacle of the temple') and is resisting 'the hereditary demon of his family' in the same way that Jesus overcame not only Satan, but the hereditary influence of original sin. Having established this parallel between Guy and Christ, Yonge is fairly discreet about employing it, but it is noticeable that Guy's awakening to a new religious life occurs at Christmas, which could be interpreted as a birth of the Christ child within the individual soul, and that his rehabilitation with the Edmonstones, from whom the accusation of gambling has alienated him, occurs at Easter, and so represents a kind of resurrection.

At one level, of course, Yonge's use of typology here could be seen as a development of the Romantic symbol. However, it is important to distinguish between Tractarian typology and some varieties of Romanticism: as Keble's discussion of typology makes clear, one of the essential characteristics of the Type is that it is authorized by the inspired language of Scripture itself. From the Tractarian point of view, this establishes the essential objectivity of typological language, freeing it from the imputation of fancifulness or morbidity.

Typology, then, is the opposite of the 'pathetic fallacy' of which Ruskin accuses Coleridge and other writers.[44] Keble himself, in his *Lectures on Poetry*, plainly regards Wordsworth as an essentially typological writer, and the distinction between a kind of figurative language which projects the writer's feelings onto the external world in a Shelleyan manner, and a kind which respects the objectivity of the external world is central to later nineteenth century discussions of Wordsworth.

Stopford Brooke, for example, in his 1874 book *Theology in the English Poets*, makes a distinction between the essential theological

44   Ruskin, *Works*, 5: 201–20.

soundness of Wordsworth's poetry and the theological unsoundness of Coleridge on precisely these grounds. In Wordsworth's poetry, despite the deep feeling which animates it, the distinction between mind and the world outside it is preserved intact, and this allows for God's moral prompting through natural objects (an example of this in Yonge would be the way in which Guy's response to the beauty of the setting sun allows his 'best self' or 'a still higher and holier power' to bring the Biblical text to mind). By contrast, for Stopford Brooke Coleridge's poetry is essentially morbid because it blurs the distinction between mind and world in a manner which prevents this kind of divine influence from reaching the mind: if the mind is projected onto the external world in what Ruskin calls the 'pathetic fallacy', then the natural world cannot exercise any moral influence, being ignored in favour of the mind's own projections, and for Brooke this is the explanation both for Coleridge's moral weakness and for his unsound religious opinions.[45] Yonge seems to making a very similar point in a later discussion of Byron between Guy and Philip.[46]

The requirements of Tractarian typology, then, constrain Yonge to negotiate a stylistic tightrope in the passage we have just been examining. Although Yonge uses typology to make Guy's moral struggle present to her readers, she must be careful not to allow this psychological dimension to obliterate the external landscape which Guy occupies. This is why, for example, she is very careful to state that it is not the setting sun itself which brings the Biblical text to Guy's mind, but his 'best self' or 'a still higher and holier power' acting *by means of* the sun. This is an important distinction, because if the sun and the Biblical text were allowed to become symbolically fused, the distinction between mind and world would be lost, and the passage would be encouraging a kind of projective religious emotionalism which Yonge elsewhere warns against.[47]

Although Yonge is careful to guard against a Romantic symbolic fusion in this particular passage, from a Tractarian perspective it

---

45   Stopford Brooke, *Theology in the English Poets: Cowper, Coleridge, Wordsworth and Burns* (London and New York: Dent and Dutton, n.d.), 91–3.
46   Yonge, *Heir*, 400 (Ch.30).
47   Ibid., *Castle Builders*, 269–70, 326 (Chs 18, 21).

might be questioned whether the novel as a whole really succeeds in preserving the distinction between religious significance and its sensory embodiment on which the validity and orthodoxy of typology depend. Guy is perhaps too obviously the embodiment of Christ-likeness, and Yonge may have come to feel that the overall effect of *The Heir of Redclyffe* was to encourage that projection of religious emotion onto the external world which we have seen her careful to guard against on a local level. Certainly in the subsequently published novel *The Castle Builders*, which uses a very similar set of plot-elements, the consumptive young clergyman whose nobility of character corresponds to Guy is kept offstage throughout the entire narrative, and the chief representative of true religious values who, in a scene which parallels the shipwreck in *The Heir of Redclyffe*, comes to the rescue of the silly heroines when they are cut off by the sea, is the 'dry' and stand-offish clergyman Mr Brent.[48]

Subjectivity and Typology

Although the Tractarian account of typology and Romantic theories of the symbol may superficially appear quite similar, it would probably not be going too far to say that the whole point of the Type for the Tractarians is that it is *not* the Symbol (understood in a Coleridgean sense, as implying a unity between the mind and Nature), in that it preserves a separation between the objects of the material world and the significance which the mind finds in those objects. For the Tractarians, even Nature is not meaningful in itself, but only insofar as a higher power has attached meanings to natural objects, a point which we have found both in Yonge's description of Guy's resistance to temptation and in Keble's *On the Mysticism which has been Attributed to some Early Fathers of the Church.*

Yonge's attempt to resist the dangers of subjectivity can be seen in her methods of characterization and her treatment of the narratorial

48   Ibid., 189 (Ch.13).

voice. As Sandbach-Dahlström has noted, psychological complexity in Yonge's characterization is always associated with moral failure: good characters in Yonge have no 'psychology'.[49] This does not necessarily mean that Yonge's characterization is always static, but that the narrative focus of her novels tends to shift away from those characters who have successfully come through their moral struggles. This is true, for example of the character of Felix in *The Pillars of the House*, Kate after her spiritual awakening in *The Castle-Builders* and Guy in *The Heir of Redclyffe*.

In view of the anxieties about the moral nature of subjectivity we have seen expressed in the *Monthly Packet*, Yonge's assumption that psychological complexity is morally pernicious becomes explicable. For Yonge, the psychologically complex character is in a state of mind which is cut off from the common, fundamental intuitions of divine reality on which moral health depends; that is to say, they are in a condition which exactly resembles that of the reader of too many novels. The implicit equation in Yonge's work between the morally suspect status of the novel reader and the morbidly self-regarding psychology which makes for an 'interesting' novelistic character is suggested by the echo of the title of her novel *The Castle Builders* in the Monthly Packet writer's comment that the 'loss of energy in the character' occasioned by excessive novel-reading is only outdone by the still more enervating habit of 'building castles in the air':[50] Yonge's characters in that novel drift desultorily from one project to another in a search for 'excitement' which parallels other contemporaries' descriptions of the quest of the reader of 'sensation fiction' for ever more striking novelistic incident.[51]

As a novel-writer, Yonge is in the business of producing what Stanley Fish calls 'self-consuming artefacts', novels which draw attention to the fictional status of their own discourse, with all the moral limitations which for Yonge that fictional status implies. Novelistic

49   Catherine Sandbach-Dahlström, *Be Good Sweet Maid: Charlotte Yonge's Domestic Fictior A Study in Dogmatic Purpose and Fictional Form* (Stockholm: Almqvist & Wicksel, 1984), 42.
50   B.L.K., 'Imagination', 473.
51   H.L. Mansel, 'Sensation Novels', *Quarterly Review* 113 (April 1863): 485–7.

realism *can* only depict the morally failing character, because the unreality of novelistic discourse stands in an analogical relationship to the 'unreality' (or alienation from God-given moral intuitions) of such characters' state of mind: like the novelist, these characters construct for themselves a world which is independent of God. As Sandbach-Dahlström notes, the primary moral fault displayed by characters in Yonge's novels is a condition of 'self-sufficiency', the same independence from the externality of the real which the world of a novel potentially possesses.[52]

Yonge's suspicion of the moral effects of the novel form means that her aim as a novelist is to shock her readers out of an uncritical absorption in her own novelistic discourse, and it is here that the typological element in her narratives becomes important. Because for Yonge this typological symbolism should serve as a means by which her reader are enabled to transcend the purely 'sensational' dimension of novelistic discourse (just as her characters are shown as transcending through intuition the material dimensions of their lives), it is vital that it is never integrated into novelistic discourse by being explicitly commented on. Typology, as an irruption of divine reality into the self-enclosed discourse of the novel, is made in the reader's experience to stand in for the unrepresentable intuitions whereby Yonge's characters transcend the material world.

The Tractarian 'reserve' with which Yonge presents typological elements is responsible for that demotion of the authority of the narratorial voice on which critics of her novels have commented.[53] The narrator of a Charlotte Yonge novel, although not explicitly characterized, is nevertheless not 'omniscient', with the result that characters in the novel, the figure of the author and Yonge's reader are placed on a level in regard to interpretation of events. Yonge's novels thus come to exhibit a curious kind of self-reflexivity in which questions about interpretation debated by characters in the novel are also ones which readers themselves must address, and to which the narratorial voice can offer no answers.

---

52 Sandbach-Dahlström, *Be Good Sweet Maid*, 150.
53 Ibid., 12.

The Relation between Faith and Reason in *The Heir of Redclyffe*

The Heir of Redclyffe provides a privileged site in which to explore the relationship between typology and realism in Yonge's novels generally, because the potential conflict between these modes of apprehending the world is thematized at an explicit level by the plot and reflected in different styles of writing. It has been generally recognized by critics that Yonge's portrayal of the character of Guy, last scion of the accursed ancient family of the Morvilles, is influenced by Romance writing.[54] Philip, Guy's poor cousin, on the other hand, is presented in a much more novelistic and psychologized fashion, as acting under the influence of jealous feelings of which he is himself unaware. [55]

It has also been recognized by critics that Yonge's portrayal of Philip and his inadvertently corrupting influence on his cousin Laura, one of the daughters of the Edmonstone family which provides a substitute home for both him and Guy, is intended as a critique of Utilitarianism.[56] One signal of Philip's identification with utilitarian rationalism is the way he encourages Laura in mathematical studies in order to 'strengthen her mind' so that she will better be able to ex-ercise the self-command necessary to keep their clandestine engage-ment a secret.[57] Philip is also consistently portrayed as engaging in consequentialist moral reasoning, to such an extent that he is liable to attribute quite unrealistic 'ultra-prudential' motives to other char-acters;[58] 'prudence' is a quality repeatedly ascribed to him by other characters and by the narratorial voice.

What has not been noticed by critics, however, is the extent to which the implicit identification of Philip with Utilitarianism informs the entirety of *The Heir of Redclyffe*, down to small details of plot and

54 Yonge, *Heir*, xi–xviii, Sandbach-Dahlström, *Be Good Sweet Maid*, 28–37.
55 Yonge, *Heir*, 267, 469 (Chs 20, 36).
56 Ibid., xviii.
57 Ibid., 153 (Ch.10).
58 Ibid., 259 (Ch.19).

characterization, with the result that the entire novel can be read in typological terms, as a kind of allegory of the doubting nineteenth-century soul's path to faith. The modernity of Philip's novelistic characterization is thus intended to function for readers as a sign of his status as a nineteenth-century Everyman, something recognized by the prominent nineteenth-century Dutch Neocalvinist Abraham Kuyper, who attributed his own conversion to religious orthodoxy from the rationalism of his youth to the recognition of himself in the character of Philip.[59] The Romance elements associated with Guy's character-ization, on the other hand, indicate his moral transcendence of the material world. Late in the book, for example, a painter sees in Guy's expression, as he gazes up at some stained windows, the model he needs for his picture of Sir Galahad, a fairly obvious hint on Yonge's part.[60]

As Sandbach-Dahlström notes, Guy is a Christ figure, a typological correspondence which is established at a fairly early point in the plot. Too easy an identification with Guy, however, is prevented by the difficulty felt by readers in sympathizing with Philip even when he has been forgiven by Guy after the moral breakdown of his repentance, a difficulty which Yonge's own brother registered by declaring that he felt Philip deserved a good kicking.[61] Philip's representative status of course requires such sympathy, but he has been portrayed so consistently by Yonge as a self-absorbed and domineering prig[62] that sympathy is difficult to grant (though the difficulties the Edmonstone family find in forgiving Philip, despite the pleading for him by Guy and his wife Amy, parallel readers' difficulties in this respect).[63]

One of the major plot elements in *The Heir of Redclyffe* also possesses typological significance, in a way that does not appear to

59   Donald N. Petcher, 'What Does It Mean to be Kuyperian?', April 1996, <http://kuyperian.blogspot.com/2004/10/what-does-it-mean-to-be-kuyperian. html> (accessed 13 January 2007).
60   Yonge, *Heir*, 403 (Ch.30).
61   Robert Lee Wolff, *Gains and Losses: Novels of Faith and Doubt in Victorian England* (New York: Garland, 1977), 134, 135.
62   Yonge, *Heir*, 240 (Ch.17).
63   Ibid., 537 (Ch.40).

have registered in previous commentary on the book. Philip's married sister (another female figure whose rationalism Yonge appears to treat as more morally culpable than Philip's), sends word in a letter that she has seen a £30 cheque of Guy's being paid to a notorious member of the gambling fraternity, which she takes as evidence that Guy has succumbed to this hereditary vice of the Morvilles.[64] Guy has in fact written this cheque for his weak-minded and impoverished musician uncle, to get him out of a scrape.[65] Guy in the meantime has requested £1000 from his guardian, Mr Edmondstone, which he intends as a donation to an Anglican sisterhood which is being founded.[66] Philip brings his sister's letter to Mr Edmonstone's attention, and, taken in conjunction with the request for £1000, this suggests that Guy has become habitually addicted to gambling. Guy cannot explain either the cheque (because this would expose his uncle) nor his request for the £1000, because Philip's sister is at the head of a party against Miss Wellwood, the would-be founder of the sisterhood, and would use this against her if she heard of it.[67]

This misunderstanding dominates the rest of the novel's plot, largely because of what is shown to be Philip's all too consistent rationality. Philip spurs his rather woolly-minded uncle on to enquire into the matter, dictating the letter himself, and when Guy writes in answer that he denies on his honour that he has been involved in gambling, although he cannot explain the circumstances on which the suspicion is grounded, it is Philip who will not let his uncle be satisfied with Guy's word. Philip takes it upon himself to go to Oxford to enquire about Guy's behaviour at university, and when he finds no evidence of dissipation on Guy's part will not admit that this strengthens Guy's cause, though Yonge comments that he feels 'like a lawyer whose case is breaking down'.[68]

During Philip's absence abroad, Guy is rehabilitated with the Edmonstones owing to his heroic involvement in a rescue from a

64   Ibid., 201–2 (Ch.14).
65   Ibid., 213–20 (Ch.15).
66   Ibid., 221 (Ch.15).
67   Ibid., 229 (Ch.16).
68   Ibid., 257 (Ch.19).

shipwreck: although as Charles points out, this does not amount to a logical proof of his innocence,[69] it does encourage Mr Edmonstone to meet Guy in London personally, where by a minor coincidence the matter of the cheque is cleared up. Philip, however, will not accept that this clears Guy for the imputation of gambling[70] – after all, there is still the request for £1000 to be accounted for – and refuses to attend Guy's subsequent marriage to his cousin Amy, Laura's sister.[71] Even after Guy has devotedly nursed him back to health, after the fever to which he has succumbed on his travels in Italy, Philip still harbours a doubt of Guy's innocence, though Yonge comments that he 'had rather believe Guy blameless',[72] and he is only finally convinced when Guy, having caught the fever himself, is going through on his deathbed the provisions of his will, which include a bequest to the Anglican sisterhood for which he had requested the £1000.[73]

Philip goes on demanding proof of Guy's innocence long after the other characters have been convinced of the purity of his character, and is consistently associated (along with Laura, who is under his influence) with the language of moral reasoning and calculation. One of the key moments in the characterization of Philip as an exemplar of strong-minded rationality comes when he confronts Guy in his rooms at Oxford:

> Philip had been used to feel men's wills and characters bend and give way beneath his superior force of mind. They might, like Charles, chafe and rage, but his calmness always gave him the ascendant almost without exertion, and few people had ever come into contact with him without a certain submission of will or opinion. With Guy alone it was not so; he had been sensible of it once or twice before; he had no mastery and could no more bend that spirit than a bar of steel. This he could not bear, for it obliged him to be continually making efforts to preserve his own sense of superiority.[74]

69   Ibid., 322 (Ch.24).
70   Ibid., 360–1 (Ch.28).
71   Ibid., 365 (Ch.28).
72   Ibid., 438 (Ch.33).
73   Ibid., 463 (Ch.35).
74   Ibid., 255 (Ch.19).

Philip's consistent and unwavering rationality gives him no advantage over Guy, whose strength springs from the sensitivity with which he responds to his moral intuitions rather than from any brilliance of intellect. At several significant points in the book, Philip's own over-confidence in his intellectual power leads him to overstep the mark where Guy is concerned, and so to forfeit the authority which his mental superiority had gained him. He responds, for instance, to the news of Amy's engagement to Guy (after the circumstances surrounding his cheque to the gambler have come out), with a letter expressing his 'surprise' that Mr Edmonstone has been satisfied with 'so incomplete an explanation of circumstances' and suggesting that Guy be put on a period of probation before he is allowed to marry Amy. Mr Edmonstone finds this a piece of impertinence, and although Guy self-denyingly tries to defend Philip by arguing that there is 'justice and reason' in Philip's letter, the only person who does not find Philip's behaviour inappropriate is Laura (a mark of how much she is under his influence).[75] At a later point in the book, too, when after her marriage Philip condescendingly tries to give Amy advice on how to handle a man of the character he takes Guy to be, she replies 'I think you forget to whom you are speaking', leaving him 'as much taken by surprise as if a dove had flown in his face'. Philip's gaffe is that, in presuming on his intellectual superiority, he has 'forgotten that she was Lady Morville, not the cousin Amy with whom Guy's character might be freely discussed'.[76]

Philip's rationalistic approach to life is thus linked by Yonge with his inability to perceive the true nature of Guy's character and with his tendency to usurp the authority which properly belongs to others (notably Mr Edmonstone). It is possible to read typologically these aspects of what is a very convincingly realist plot, as corresponding to what Yonge would have perceived as an excessive domination of utilitarian reason in nineteenth-century Britain generally. Given the typological equation between Guy and Christ, Philip's insistence on logical proofs of Guy's character, and his inability to respond to the intuitive trust which Guy awakens in those

75   Ibid., 346–51 (Ch.27).
76   Ibid., 407–8 (Ch.30).

who come in contact with him, make him a 'type' of the tendency of misplaced rationalism to weaken the mind's intuitive awareness of the source of religious belief in a personal response to God by demanding inappropriate kinds of evidence for religious belief. Believing in Christ, Yonge seems to be suggesting in *The Heir of Redclyffe*, is like believing in a person: the demand for logical evidence by its very nature must obstruct such a belief, whose essence is trust.

Newman and the Usurpations of Reason

This typological reading of *The Heir of Redclyffe* is made more plausible by the similarity of the relationship in the novel between Faith, in the person of Guy, and Reason, in the person of Philip, to Newman's account of the nature of religious belief in his 1843 *University Sermons*. The influence on Newman of the British intuitionist tradition of Common Sense philosophy, to which I have drawn previously drawn attention, helps to explain this parallel.[77]

Newman argues in his sermon 'The Usurpations of Reason' that 'there is no necessary connexion between the intellectual and moral principles of our nature',[78] claiming, in a phrase which might stand as a summary of the relationship between Guy and Philip, that 'the history of Revelation [...] [is] the triumph of the moral powers of man

---

77   There is evidence in Newman's philosophical notebooks that he read both Thomas Reid and Dugald Stewart, as is shown by Johannes Artz, 'Newman as a Philosopher', *International Philosophical Quarterly* 16 (1976): 263–87. Scottish Common Sense philosophy was an influence in general on the Oriel College 'Noetics', of whom Newman was one; their leading light Edward Copleston refers to Stewart in his *Inquiry into the Doctrines of Necessity and Predestination* (cited in Richard Whately, *Elements of Rhetoric* [Oxford and London: Murray and Parker, 1830], 410–11), and promoted the study of political economy, of which Stewart was a major contemporary representative (A.M.C. Waterman, *Revolution, Economics and Religion: Christian Political Economy, 1798–1833* [Cambridge: Cambridge University Press, 1991], 180–6).

78   Newman, *University Sermons*, 55.

152

over the intellectual, of holiness over ability, far more than of mind over brute force'.[79] One of Newman's principal targets in the sermon is the rationalistic tradition of theology associated with William Paley. Since for Newman reason by its very nature is incapable of making us morally better or more religious, the rationalistic seeking of 'evidences' for Christianity cannot in fact benefit true religion, but can only represent an essentially self-seeking aggrandizement of the authority of Reason itself through an extension of rational modes of enquiry beyond their proper province.[80]

In a gesture which is reminiscent of Reid's and Stewart's philosophical intuitionism, Newman appeals to essentially non-rational intuitions as the true source of religious belief:

> In matter of fact, how many men do we suppose, in a century, out of the whole body of Christians, have been primarily brought to belief, or retained in it, by an intimate and lively perception of the force of what are technically called the Evidences? And why are there so few? Because to the mind already familiar with the truths of Natural Religion, enough of evidence is at once afforded by the mere fact of the present existence of Christianity; which, viewed in its connexion with its principles and upholders and effects, bears on the face of it the signs of a divine ordinance in the very same way in which the visible world attests to its own divine origin; – a more accurate investigation, in which superior talents are brought into play, merely bringing to light an innumerable alternation of arguments, for and against it, which forms indeed an ever-increasing series in its behalf, but still does not get beyond the first suggestion of plain sense and religiously-trained reason; and in fact, perhaps, never comes to a determination. Nay, so alert is the instinctive power of an educated conscience, that by some secret faculty, and without any intelligible reasoning process, it seems to detect moral truth wherever it lies hid, and feels a conviction of its own accuracy which bystanders cannot account for.[81]

For Newman, the true sources of religious evidence are 'the signs of a divine ordinance' which are intuitively apparent to everyone who is in a morally right frame of mind; intellectual ability can never go a step beyond this source of evidence, all it can do is multiply arguments which are in themselves inconclusive. Newman argues in a

79   Ibid., 57.
80   Ibid., 69
81   Ibid., 66.

later sermon, using Christ's ministry to the apostles as an example, that because of the essentially moral nature of religious truth, the medium by which it is spread is not that of rational argument but of personal influence. Newman goes so far as to suggest, in a way which is very relevant to our previous discussion of the 'reserve' and lack of explicit comment which is characteristic of Yonge's use of typology, that it may not be possible really to convey religious truth in language at all:

> Moral truth will be least skilfully defended by those, as such, who are the genuine depositories of it..it cannot be adequately explained and defended in words at all [...] Its views and human language are incommensurable. For, after all, what *is* language but an artificial system adapted for particular purposes, which have been determined by our wants? And here, even at first sight, can we imagine that it has been framed with a view to ideas so refined, so foreign to the whole course of the world, as those which (as Scripture expresses it) 'no man can learn', but the select remnant who are 'redeemed from the earth', and in whose mouth 'is found no guile'? Nor is it this heavenly language alone which is without its intellectual counterpart. Moral character in itself, whether good or bad, as exhibited in thought and conduct, surely cannot be duly represented in words. We may, indeed, by an effort, reduce it in a certain degree to this arbitrary medium; but in its combined dimensions it is as impossible to write and read a man (so to express it), as to give literal depth to a painted tablet.[82]

Newman's argument suggests that the failure of the rationalizing Philip to grasp the nature of Guy's character is essentially the same as the failure of novelistic discourse to convey moral goodness. Goodness cannot be analysed in words, it can only be experienced, so that the reader of *The Heir of Redclyffe* could be regarded as in very much the same position as Philip himself, in being excluded from the perception of Guy's true character by the very necessity of articulating that perception in language. That Yonge agrees with Newman about the personal nature of moral truth is suggested in *The Heir of Redclyffe* by Charles's trust that if Mr Edmonstone can once be brought to meet Guy, Guy's 'personal influence' will convince him of the true nature of his character.[83]

82   Ibid., 84–5.
83   Yonge, *Heir*, 323–4 (Ch.24).

Newman's claim that the true grounds of faith are intuitions that simply cannot be articulated in rational argument is reflected in the inconclusive nature of the only proofs Philip can find of Guy's moral character. The question about Guy's character can stand in a typological relationship to the question of religious faith in Yonge's novel, because, as should be apparent from this brief discussion of Newman, both stand in a similarly incommensurable relationship to the intellectual standards to which rational argument appeals. Philip's tendency to overstep proper bounds of behaviour and lay down the law to other people can also be understood to correspond typologically to the tendency of Reason in the modern age, as Newman sees it, to attempt to aggrandize itself in areas where it is, strictly speaking, incompetent. It is significant that Yonge stresses throughout Guy's comparative lack of intellectual acuteness: unlike Philip, he is no great scholar, and has to struggle to gain admission to Oxford. Guy's inability to defend himself against Philip's accusations reflects Newman's argument in his sermon 'Personal Influence, the Means of Propagating the Truth' that 'the minute intellect of inferior men has its moment of triumph' even over 'some of the most deeply-exercised and variously gifted Christians'.[84]

84   Newman, *University Sermons*, 84.

Chapter Five
Realism, Utilitarianism and the Unconscious in *The Heir of Redclyffe*

Realism and Romance in *The Heir of Redclyffe*

The problem with interpreting Yonge's narrative typologically, as I have done in the previous chapter by identifying the conflict between Philip and Guy as a conflict between utilitarian reason and faith, is that it runs the risk of making Yonge seem unconcerned with realism. In part, this is a problem inherent in the critical interpretation of her novels: Yonge's characteristic emphasis on dialogue, and avoidance of thematizing narratorial interventions, mean that her novels often lack an obvious interpretative centre, so that a critical account, such as the one I have just offered of *The Heir of Redclyffe*, is obliged to schematize precisely because the novels at first reading appear so unschematic, with thematic coherence, as a Victorian critic complained, threatened by a flood of realist detail.[1] The impression that there must be a tension between the typological and realist dimensions of Yonge's narrative, however, is also a product of some fundamental assumptions underlying modern critical accounts of the nature of novelistic realism, and in this chapter I would like to examine arguments that Yonge is not basically a realist writer as a way of suggesting that our notions of 'realism' in the novel need reformulation if we are to arrive at an adequate conception of the narrative mode of writers such as Yonge.[2]

1   R.H. Hutton, 'Ethical and Dogmatic Fiction: Miss Yonge', *National Review* 12 (1861): 214.
2   My own earlier article, 'Realism and Typology in Charlotte M. Yonge's *The Heir of Redclyffe*', *Victorian Literature and Culture* 31, no.1 (2003): 193–223, itself assumes some tension between typological and realist elements in Yonge's fiction (e.g. 'Realism and Typology', 208–9). The present chapter represents a reconsideration of this issue.

One of the most extended critical discussions of a purported tension between Yonge's realist narrative mode and her attempt to imbue the world of her novels with a transcendent religious significance can be found in Catherine Sandbach-Dahlström's 1984 study *Be Good Sweet Maid: Charlotte M. Yonge's Domestic Fiction: A Study in Dogmatic Purpose and Fictional Form.* Sandbach-Dahlström characterizes what she regards as these two poles in Yonge's writing as a conflict between 'realism' and 'romance', an opposition which goes back to Arnold Kettle's Marxist account of the development of the novel as the supplanting of the aristocratic form of the romance by the bourgeois form of the novel.[3] Sandbach-Dahlström, however, follows Northrop Frye in characterizing the romance element of *The Heir of Redclyffe* as embodying cyclical mythic significances which are arguably present in all literature, quoting Gillian Beer to the effect that the history of the novel cannot really be separated from that of the romance in the neat way assumed by Kettle.[4]

Sandbach-Dahlström presents many plausible reasons for regarding *The Heir of Redclyffe* as a romance, including the Gothic elements in the book and the identification of Guy with romance heroes such as Galahad and La Motte Fouqué's Sintram.[5] She finds, however, that a number of aspects of the novel's plot set its 'romance mode' at odds with its 'realist mode' in ways which cannot simply be attributed to the differing perspective of present-day readers,[6] since the novel itself provides 'rational explanations of conduct and common-sense points of view that contract with the Romance pattern and that conflict with the book's dogmatic and didactic purposes'.[7]

One of the principal sites of conflict between realist and romance values identified by Sandbach-Dahlström lies in Yonge's implied attitude toward the authority of parents. She notes a 'difficulty in

3   Arnold Kettle, *An Introduction to the English Novel: Volume One, to George Eliot* (London: Arrow, 1962), 30–8.
4   Catherine Sandbach-Dahlström, *Be Good Sweet Maid: Charlotte Yonge's Domestic Fictior A Study in Dogmatic Purpose and Fictional Form* (Stockholm: Almqvist & Wicksel, 1984), 28.
5   Ibid., 31.
6   Ibid., 29.
7   Ibid., 45.

believing in the way Mr Edmonstone accepts Philip's interpretation of Guy's conduct and bans all further intercourse between Guy and Amy', and particularly in the way Mrs Edmonstone simply acquiesces in the prohibition, given that 'up to this point in the novel [...] she has functioned as the moral authority in the Edmonstone household', and has been Guy's confidante.[8] Sandbach-Dahlström finds a similar difficulty in 'the moral indignation expected over Philip and Laura's secret understanding', noting that 'from the beginning readers have not all shared the narrator's view of the reprehensibility of their conduct' and citing mid-twentieth-century studies by Georgina Battiscombe and Elizabeth Jenkins, as well as a response by Yonge's contemporary R.H. Hutton, the Victorian practitioner of the 'higher journalism'.[9] For Sandbach-Dahlström, these difficulties are symptomatic of moments when 'a narrow didactic purpose informs the work', a view in whose support she enlists Yonge's own later comment, in a response to the 1870s debate over the Woman Question, that 'there is no true success or happiness for any woman who has not learned to efface herself'.[10]

Sandbach-Dahlström remarks that one reason we have 'difficulty in accepting Mrs Edmonstone's conduct [...] is [...] a result of the way the implied author succeeds in arousing a sense of outraged justice in the reader', a position which she identifies with 'Charles Edmonstone's rational view of Guy's banishment'.[11] Since Charles is 'guilty of filial disrespect' in 'arguing vehemently with his father', she finds here again 'an opposition between the implied author's imaginative vision of the injustice of Guy's treatment and didactic purpose which is to teach the duty of children to obey their parents'.[12] Sandbach-Dahlström is right to find that the reader's moral consciousness can be identified with Charles Edmonstone at this point, but what I think is less convincing about the argument she presents is its basic as-

---

8   Ibid., 47–8; e.g. Charlotte M. Yonge, *The Heir of Redclyffe*, Barbara Dennis (ed.) (Oxford: Oxford University Press, 1997), 48–9 (Ch.4).
9   Sandbach-Dahlström, *Be Good Sweet Maid*, 46.
10   Ibid., 48.
11   Ibid.
12   Ibid., 49.

sumption that the reader's moral standards remain static in the course of reading the novel, so that the undoubted moral tension the reader experiences between their knowledge of Guy's innocence and the reasons for Mr Edmonstone's prohibition can only finally be judged as a moral incoherence caused by Yonge's 'didactic' purposes.

Sandbach-Dahlström herself notes a 'move away from the Edmonstone's moral standards' towards the end of *The Heir of Redclyffe*.[13] I would like to expand on this aspect of her argument in order to suggest that many of the apparent tensions between realism and typology (or 'romance') can be resolved if we regard Yonge's fundamental concern as with a process of moral *development* in which the reader's judgements are continually relativized. Sandbach-Dahlström's own example illustrates this feature of Yonge's narrative: the Mrs Edmonstone who represents a source of moral authority at the beginning of the novel, towards the end 'appears chiefly as a nuisance, worrying her daughter constantly with excessive solicitude'.[14]

My claim is that critical interpretations of Yonge have suffered from the assumption, evident in Sandbach-Dahlström, that a clear 'moral' is intended to be drawn from her work. Yonge is a much more sophisticated and self-conscious writer than this interpretative perspective allows, with a narrative technique that can be compared with that of the Henry James who so much admired her writing,[15] or the Lawrence who announced his intention to disrupt the 'old stable *ego* of the character'.[16] Viewed in this context, critical complaints such as those cited by Sandbach-Dahlström, to the effect that Yonge metes out a 'punishment' to Laura that is disproportionate to the fault represented by her secret engagement, misinterpret the purpose of Yonge's narrative, which is not to apportion reward for actions, but merely to describe what she sees as their psychological consequences. Sandbach-Dahlström herself indicates the possibility of this kind of reading

13 Ibid., 51.
14 Ibid.
15 See Elizabeth K. Helsinger, Robin Lauterbach Sheets, and William Veeder, *The Woman Question: Society and Literature in Britain and America, 1837–1883*, 3 vols (New York: Garland, 1983), 3: 52.
16 D.H. Lawrence, letter to Edward Garnett (1914), in D.H. Lawrence, *Selected Literary Criticism*, Anthony Beal (ed.) (London: Heinemann, 1955).

of Yonge when she argues at a slightly later point that 'Philip and Laura's unhappiness at the end of the novel' can be seen 'in realist psychological terms' as 'a plausible consequence of the imperfection of their relationship throughout the novel'.[17] Critical claims about Yonge's purported 'moralism', of the kind Sandbach-Dahlström reports, are based on assumptions about her narrative intentions for which there is little support in Yonge's own writing, which eschews narratorial comment of the kind which is supposed to be typical of the Victorian novel.[18]

It would be foolish to dispute that Yonge regarded her novels as serving a morally educative purpose, but I would suggest that, far from being crudely 'didactic' in the sense of asserting moral judgements that are assumed to be applicable in all circumstances, Yonge's novels are designed to act as occasions for the reader to reflect on the process of interpretation by which they arrive at the moral judgements which they apply to the text. This self-reflexive quality of Yonge's narrative can be illustrated by the example of Charles Edmonstone's reaction to Mr Edmonstone's prohibition of Guy and Amy's meeting. Sandbach-Dahlström, as I have already commented, straightforwardly identifies Charles's viewpoint not only with that of the reader, but also with a 'rational view of Guy's banishment'.[19] But at the point in the novel where Mr Edmonstone makes his prohibition, the reader has no more information about the circumstances which have led to the accusation that Guy has taken to gambling than Charles or Mr Edmonstone do, so that although we may sympathize with Charles's position, the fact that the narrative has for a short while left us in doubt about Guy prevents us from identifying his perspective with a straightforwardly 'rational view', despite Sandbach-Dahlström's claims. Since the nineteenth century regarded gambling as a form of physical addiction[20] to which it has been suggested Guy is hereditarily prone,[21]

17 Sandbach-Dahlström, *Be Good Sweet Maid*, 56.
18 Ibid., 12.
19 Ibid., 48.
20 Cf. the reference to gambling in Charles Mackay, *Extraordinary Popular Delusions and the Madness of Crowds* (1852) (Ware: Wordsworth Editions, 1995), xvi. Mackay's reference to 'excitement' shows that he conceptualizes

it is far from clear that Mr Edmonstone's response is disproportionate, given that he believes the evidence is conclusive. In the equivalent present-day situation, I think it can safely be assumed that most parents would do everything in their power to prevent their daughter going out with a heroin addict.

The identification between Charles Edmonstone's point of view in this situation and that of the reader, to which Sandbach-Dahlström draws attention, far from suggesting that Charles's viewpoint is an inherently reasonable one, can be interpreted as a way of destabilizing the reader's moral judgements. Charles, who is a cripple, is unreliable as a moral guide. As Yonge makes clear at an early point in the narrative, Charles's disability has damaged not only his physical health, but his moral health, since:

> His idle, unoccupied life, and habit of only thinking of things as they concerned his immediate amusement, made him ready to do anything for the sake of opposition to Philip, and enjoy the vague idea of excitement to be derived from anxiety about his father's ward.[22]

This remark is echoed in Yonge's comment that 'Charles [...] found anxiety on Guy's account more exciting, though considerably less agreeable, than he had once expected',[23] just before he argues with his father about Guy's treatment. Though by this point in the novel, we know that Guy has been unjustly accused, Charles is shown as failing to serve Guy's cause because he is led astray by 'the pleasure of galling his cousin',[24] so that the 'fretfulness and ill humour'[25] which are shown as responsible for much of Mr Edmonstone's anger against Guy (whose unguarded opinion of Mr Edmonstone's modest intellectual abilities has been reported by Philip's sister) are seen to be equally characteristic of Charles himself.

gambling within the account of addictive behaviour put forward within Brunonian medical theory.

21   Yonge, *Heir*, 71, 80, 46 (Chs 5, 4).
22   Ibid., 50 (Ch.4).
23   Ibid., 237 (Ch.17).
24   Ibid., 238 (Ch.17).
25   Ibid., 245 (Ch.17).

Charles's lack of effectiveness, however, stems from those very characteristics which he shares with the reader of novels, as that figure was stereotyped in nineteenth-century discussions about the dangers of excessive novel-reading. We learn at an early stage in the novel that, unlike Philip, Charles is an avid reader of novels (Philip remarks on 'the cheap rubbish in which Charlie is nearly walled up there'),[26] something which is symptomatic of the love of 'excitement' which leads him astray when he has to defend Guy. Charles's characteristic tendency to over-dramatize situations (at one point, for example, he parodies a stage-direction, 'Enter Don Philip II, the Duke of Alva, alguazils, corregidors and executioners'[27] in order to cast Philip as the leader of the Spanish Inquisition) reflects a tendency attributed to the excessive novel-reader in an article published in Yonge's journal, the *Monthly Packet*.[28]

Charles's argument with his father, then, parodies that desire of the novel-reader for dramatic confrontation which Sandbach-Dahlström's remarks express, and which is exposed as inadequate in the face of Yonge's moral realism. I will suggest later that a similar argument can be made about Yonge's portrayal of the way in which Laura's and Philip's relationship is poisoned by the secrecy of their engagement. This downbeat and very tough-minded conclusion consciously plays against the conventions of the novel form in such a way as to encourage the reader to reflect on their own assumption that romantic commitment of the kind Laura and Philip have shown to each other should be rewarded, no matter what it costs other people. Readers such as Sandbach-Dahlström and R.H. Hutton, I would claim, have failed Yonge's moral test, or at least refused it.

The assumption we have found in Sandbach-Dahlström that there is a necessary conflict in *The Heir of Redclyffe* between the demands of realism and those of 'romance' (as represented by the typological implications of Laura's disobedience to her father) also underlies George Levine's assertion in *The Realistic Imagination* that 'romance forms' embody 'the secret lust of the spirit to impose itself on the

---

26 Ibid., 30 (Ch.3).
27 Ibid., 227 (Ch.17).
28 Anon., 'Egotism', *Monthly Packet* 5 (Series 2 1868): 517.

world' in way which must be resisted by realism.[29] Levine, like Sandbach-Dahlström, implicitly identifies 'realism' with secular humanism, so that this formulation suggests that realism in the novel can only be achieved by the exclusion of a religious perspective. Whilst we have indeed identified a thematic conflict between 'romance' (in the debased form of the modern 'romantic novel', rather than the medieval romance) and 'realism' in *The Heir of Redclyffe*, it is plain that the definition of 'realism' to which Yonge's narrative implicitly appeals is rather different from that of Levine. Yonge is certainly interested in using realism to expose 'the secret lust of the spirit to impose itself on the world', but as has already been apparent from our discussion of the relationship between Guy and Philip, she identifies this 'secret lust of the spirit' with secular rationalism.

The unsatisfactory nature of Levine's rigid demarcation between realism and 'romance' is suggested by Jennifer Green-Lewis in her 1996 study *Framing the Victorians: Photography and the Culture of Realism*. For Green-Lewis, Levine's attempt to argue that the two are absolutely distinct smacks of 'cultural mythmaking':[30]

> The 'metaphysical novel' [...] may [...] defy its own presumed obsession with 'the why of reality' and shift its attention to the consideration of a 'materialistic world view', because of the necessity of exposing the consequences of that world view, 'so that metaphysics, which the positivists had banned from philosophy, might be restored as a legitimate province for human inquiry'.
>
> In other words, the metaphysical novel, to use Eigner's term, or romance, to use mine, for the sake of disproving realism is as likely to engage with its issues as it is to eschew them. This propensity raises a question that may appear to bring romance closer to the province of realism, for can we really say that a work 'about' realism is distinctively different from a work 'of' realism? Both kinds of works address the same questions, thereby verifying the centrality and significance of the questions.[31]

---

29 George Levine, *The Realistic Imagination: English Fiction from Frankenstein to Lady Chatterley* (Chicago: University of Chicago Press, 1981), 15.
30 Jennifer Green-Lewis, *Framing the Victorians: Photography and the Culture of Realism* (Ithaca: Cornell University Press, 1996), 72.
31 Green-Lewis, *Framing the Victorians*, 32.

I would claim that the religious orientation of Yonge's writing leads her to question the nature of realism in a way that makes her work just as epistemologically self-conscious as any of the writers Levine studies in *The Realistic Imagination*. As Green-Lewis argues, there can be no justification for excluding such metaphysically oriented testing of the limits of realism from the category of realism itself, particularly since Levine wants to include this kind of reflexivity in his definition of realism.

The contrast in the valence of the romance/realism distinction as it is employed in Yonge's novel and in the work of critics such as Levine and Sandbach-Dahlström reveals that some fundamental philosophical issues are in play. These issues, I will later suggest, are explicitly thematized in *The Heir of Redclyffe* by Yonge's emphasis on the remorselessness of Philip's 'logic', which prevents him from accepting any evidence for Guy's innocence long after all the other characters have accepted that the accusation of gambling cannot be justified, and is shown to be responsible for the novel's catastrophe in which Guy dies in nursing Philip back to health.[32] In drawing attention to the role of a certain conception of logic in Philip's downfall, Yonge, I will argue, is responding to the debate over J.S. Mill's major philosophical statement in *A System of Logic*, a debate which was current at the time she was writing the novel. This debate turns around Mill's restatement of the Humean position, that religious questions such as the theological argument from design or the possibility of miracles must be rigorously excluded from the domain of logic, and the fact that critical assessment of *The Heir of Redclyffe*'s 'realism' depends on arguments as to whether or not reason is inherently secular in nature[33] can be regarded as a sign of the novel's implication in this controversy.

Before addressing the wider philosophical ramifications of my claim that Yonge's novels belong to the mainstream of nineteenth-century realism, however, it is necessary to establish Yonge's moral credibility as a realist writer. Levine's assertion that 'romance' em-

32 Yonge, *Heir*, 406–9 (Ch.30).
33 See John Milbank, *Theology and Social Theory* (Oxford: Blackwell, 1990) for detailed exploration of this theoretical issue.

bodies 'the secret lust of the spirit to impose itself on the world'[34] seeks to align his secular humanism with the moral authority he argues is inherent in the novel form itself. For Levine, the formal realism of the novel[35] represents a guarantee that religious claims to transcend materiality will always finally emerge as inauthentic (even in despite of authorial intention) because they will inevitably foreclose ongoing experiential possibility, a view which is implicit in his description of the 'characteristic morality' of Victorian realism as 'a George Eliot-like dissolution of easy moral categories',[36] in which a 'metaphysical sanction' is replaced by a 'humanist sanction'.[37] Sandbach-Dahlström's diagnosis of a tension between the 'didactic' purpose she attributes to Yonge and the formal realism of *The Heir of Redclyffe* reflects Levine's assumption that the moral orientation of the novel form is inherently secular and humanist in nature.

I have been suggesting, however, that Yonge quite consciously exploits the devices of formal realism in the service of the religious perspective that underlies her novels, in a way that precludes her project for the moral education of the reader from being written off as a simple 'didacticism' which is at odds with the inherent tendencies of the novel form. In view of Levine's assumption that any transcendent moral claims put forward in a novel will inevitably end up being dissolved by the implications of novelistic realism itself, the question of how Yonge portrays the ongoing action of experience on her characters becomes of the highest importance in assessing her title to the moral authority of realism. For critics such as Levine and Sandbach-Dahlström, transcendent moral claims of the kind to which Yonge is committed necessarily lead to a falsification or exclusion of experience, something identified by Sandbach-Dahlström in Yonge's treatment of Laura's secret engagement. I should like to suggest, in contrast, that Yonge's religious position is not incompatible with an

---

34   Levine, *Realistic Imagination*, 15.
35   Ian Watt, *The Rise of the Novel: Studies in Defoe, Richardson, and Fielding* (London: Chatto and Windus, 1957), 83–5.
36   Levine, *Realistic Imagination*, 180.
37   Ibid., 11.

engagement in rendering the impact of experience on her characters which fully equals anything to be found in the Victorian novel.

Levine's anti-transcendent characterization of the novel form in *The Realistic Imagination* is anticipated in his 1968 study *The Boundaries of Fiction*, where in the course of a long discussion of J.H. Newman's religious novel *Loss and Gain* he argues that Newman's failure as a novelist is due to his inability 'to accept the challenge of what Morse Peckham calls "disorientation" [...] [which] depends in good measure on the writer's capacity to keep himself open to experience and free of local commitment'.[38] Newman's preoccupation with the religious transcendence of the material world is squarely to blame for the shortcomings of his novel, Levine suggests, because it 'allowed him to reject as "unreal" everything that went on in this world and, if not to distort, at least to exclude much experience'.[39] In Levine's view, Newman's religious commitment isolates him from the mainstream evolution of the nineteenth-century novel, which is centrally concerned with 'finding an adequate authority which might legitimately restrain uncontrolled self-will and yet allow the fullest possible development of self'.[40]

Although Levine doesn't mention Yonge, it is clear that his account of the novel would find her religious commitment, like that of Newman, incompatible with the requirements of novelistic realism. And yet Levine's description of the central problematic of the nineteenth-century novel as the search for a way of curbing 'uncontrolled self-will' which would nevertheless be compatible with 'the fullest possible development of self' is strikingly applicable to the plot of *The Heir of Redclyffe*, which portrays Guy's struggle with the hereditary Morville temper as the means by which he attains the generosity of character of which Philip is incapable. This is brought home towards the end of the novel by an episode in which Guy's widow Amy, while visiting the Morvilles' ancestral home of Redclyffe which Philip has inherited owing to an entail, is unable to recognize the portrait of the

---

38   Levine, *The Boundaries of Fiction: Carlyle, Macaulay, Newman* (Princeton: Princeton University Press, 1968), 195.
39   Ibid., 209.
40   Ibid., 259

wicked Sir Hugh to which Guy had told her he bore so much resemblance, and fetches a portrait of Guy in order to compare the two:

> There proved to be more resemblance than either of them had at first sight credited. The form of the forehead, nose, and short upper lip were identical, so were the sharply-defined black eye-brows, the colour of the eyes; and the way of standing in both had a curious similarity; but the expression was so entirely different, that strict comparison alone proved, that Guy's animated, contemplative, and most winning countenance, was in its original lineaments entirely the same with that of his ancestor. Although Sir Hugh's was then far from unprepossessing, and bore as yet no trace of his unholy passions, it brought to Amabel's mind the shudder with which Guy had mentioned his likeness to that picture, and seemed to show her the nature he had tamed.[41]

The device of contrasting Guy's 'animated, contemplative and most winning countenance' with that of his ancestor Sir Hugh recapitulates the development of Guy's character during the novel, making the characteristically Victorian point that the development of a 'best self' goes hand in hand with the restraint of self.

The assumption of critics such as Levine and Sandbach-Dahlström that a transcendent religious perspective is incompatible with the portrayal of a developing response to experience demanded by novelistic realism is contradicted by the developmental emphasis of *The Heir of Redclyffe*, which has often been described as a *bildungsroman*. However justified may be Levine's criticisms of Newman's failings as a novelist, his claim that Newman's religious perspective is in itself fundamentally incompatible with the realist novel's emphasis on self-development does not seem to take into account the very important role which ideas about 'development' play in Newman's major theological work, the *Essay on the Development of Christian Doctrine*.

I will argue later that an emphasis on development, which we have already seen to be characteristic of the Tractarians in general, is an important point of reference in the debate surrounding Mill's *A System of Logic*, to which I have already suggested *The Heir of Redclyffe* can be seen as a response. In this context, Levine's own

---

41   Yonge, *Heir*, 581 (Ch.43).

interest in Darwin[42] is highly suggestive, since it implies that the concept of 'development' which he uses to find Newman lacking is modelled on Darwin's theory of evolution, with all its associated Humean and Millian empiricist epistemological assumptions. Yonge's appeal, however, is to a concept of 'development' which emphasizes the unconscious dimension of the mind, and this implies that the typological implications of her plotting are not essentially in tension with her mode of novelistic realism, despite the critical claims we have been examining.

Before we turn this wider argument, however, about the intellectual context to which *The Heir of Redclyffe*, and Yonge's work as a novelist generally, belongs, we need to examine in more detail the criticisms of Yonge's treatment of Laura, to which I have already referred. Although the secret engagement is only a subplot in *The Heir of Redclyffe*, it has very important consequences for the novel's ending, since it is the reason why Yonge suggests that Philip and Laura's marriage will not be a happy one. This aspect of *The Heir of Redclyffe* has attracted criticism from early on in the novel's reception, so that we may regard the portrayal of the secret engagement and its consequences as a test case for claims of the sort I am advancing about the moral coherence of Yonge's realist world.

Morality and Character in *The Heir of Redclyffe*

One of the principal difficulties which readers of *The Heir of Redclyffe* have found in the novel is its treatment of the consequences of Laura's secret engagement to Philip.[43] As Laura herself is made to comment towards the end of the book, the result of this act of concealment is that even her own fiancé, who had urged her to conceal

---

42   Cf. George Levine, *Darwin Among the Novelists: Patterns of Science in Victorian Fiction* (Cambridge, MA and London: Harvard University Press, 1988).

43   Sandbach-Dahlström, *Be Good Sweet Maid*, 46.

the engagement in the first place, 'cannot have that honouring, trust-ing, confiding love that [...] he would have had if I had cared first for what became me'.[44] This is a judgement in which Philip seems to concur even when he is blaming himself, saying 'I taught you to take my dictum for law, and abused your trust, and perverted all the best and most precious qualities'.[45] Yonge makes clear that this condition of moral fall is permanent when she comments on the final page that despite their outward prosperity, Philip and Laura led 'a harassed, anxious life with little of repose or relief'.[46]

It is noticeable that Yonge treats Laura's lapse into the utilitarian moral calculation responsible for the decision to conceal the engage-ment much more harshly than she does Philip's, something that makes this conclusion represent something worryingly close to the Victorian sexual double standard. Laura's adoption of an inappropriately ration-alistic approach towards human relationships is particularly proble-matic, Yonge implies, because she is a woman. As her brother Charles puts it, the consequence is that she becomes Philip's 'slave and auto-maton'.[47]

It would be easy to dismiss this conclusion as simply ex-emplifying a rigid Victorian 'moralism'. Even Victorian readers, however, felt that the blighted life Yonge suggests Laura is doomed to lead was a punishment out of all proportion to her actual offence. R.H. Hutton, for example, commented that Yonge's view of Laura's trans-gression was 'extravagant beyond measure [...] entirely the old feudal notion, that in the father resided the right to give or withhold the daughter's hand, and that in giving it herself she committed an act of petty treason', and finds the author guilty of 'that morbid intro-spectiveness which is the worst form of ethical speculation'.[48]

Hutton's objection is clearly directed at the typological dimen-sion of Yonge's fiction which we identified in the previous chapter. From a typological point of view, Laura's final 'harassed' state is

---

44   Yonge, *Heir*, 583 (Ch.43).
45   Ibid., 584 (Ch.43).
46   Ibid., 594 (Ch.44).
47   Ibid., 447 (Ch.34).
48   Hutton, 'Ethical and Dogmatic Fiction', 215–16.

required by the moral 'fall' she has undergone through taking Philip's word as law rather than trusting to her own God-given moral intuitions (even before discovery of the engagement, Laura is described as 'harassed'[49] and out of sorts). Laura, like Eve, has committed the original sin of aspiring to the judgement of good and evil for herself, so that her failure to confide in her father corresponds to an implicitly atheistic lack of trust in God.

Yonge intends us to contrast Laura's mistaken reliance on Philip's rationalizing with her sister Amy's unquestioning dependence on intuition. In a rather melodramatic incident when Guy and Amy are on their honeymoon in the Alps, Amy slips and finds herself hanging onto some brushwood just above a precipice, and when Guy comes to her rescue he demands that she raise one hand so that he can pull her up: although Amy feels 'as if relinquishing her grasp of the tree was certain destruction' her 'habit of implicit confidence and obedience' leads her to comply, and Guy pulls her up 'even while the bush to which she had trusted was detaching itself, almost uprooted by her weight!'[50] As Yonge comments, 'If she had waited a second she would have been lost, but her confidence had been her safety' – an implicit contrast to the lack of confidence Laura has shown in her family's reactions to her relationship with Philip.

Given the clear typological significance of Laura's final state, Hutton's complaints of a lack of proportion between Laura's fault and Yonge's consequent consignment of her to 'a harassed, anxious life' can be linked to the more general objections to the doctrinal basis of Yonge's fiction which he presents in the same review. Contrasting the modern 'speculative age' with the 'medieval Catholic ages' to which he suggests Yonge's Tractarianism is a throwback, he accuses her of mere religious formalism:

> When it became evident that men had the power of getting at reality first-hand, whether in the facts of physical nature, or of intellectual research, or of religious experience, then that chasm began to open between the ecclesiastical and the natural-religious forms of civilisation which has never been understood at all by the ecclesiasticists, and which is even yet but imperfectly understood

49   Yonge, *Heir*, 172 (Ch.12).
50   Ibid., 392 (Ch.30).

by their opponents. The prophecy of the former is, that if we give up the inviolability of the *form*, we lose all certainty of retaining our hold on the *realities* of religion, and must, sooner or later, drift into Atheism in belief, and mere anarchical individualism in society, each man doing what is right in his own eyes.[51]

Hutton suggests that there is a divide in Yonge's fiction between her realism (her 'truthful and inspiriting delineations of life from an affirmative and spiritual point of view') and the shaping of her fiction by typological significance (Yonge's respect for which he characterizes as 'a feeble reverence for damnatory theories and sacerdotal fictions').[52] Hutton's argument can be seen to anticipate the dichotomy between 'realism' and 'romance' which, as we saw in the previous section, underpins twentieth-century claims that the novel is an inherently secular form, since the characteristic which distinguishes 'romance' from 'realism' is its hospitality to typological forms of meaning.

As Catherine Sandbach-Dahlström has pointed out, romance is an important presence in *The Heir of Redclyffe*, with the novel's hero, Guy, who has grown up reading medieval romances, portrayed as embodying their values in many respects.[53] The question of whether the comfortlessness of the life finally allotted to Laura is not disproportionate to her fault in a way which testifies to an incompatibility between the realist and the typological dimensions of the novel, is thus one on which the overall coherence of Yonge's moral vision in *The Heir of Redclyffe* depends. If Laura's bleak final condition is not justified by her behaviour, but simply determined by the application of some preconceived typological scheme, as Hutton suggests, then Yonge's depiction of Guy's redeeming effect on those around him, whose overtones are equally typological, must come under suspicion of being merely sentimental, its emotional effectiveness not earned by Yonge's writing, but illegitimately borrowed from its religious source.

---

51   Hutton, 'Ethical and Dogmatic Fiction', 228.
52   Ibid., 230.
53   Sandbach-Dahlström, *Be Good Sweet Maid*, 31.

I would like to suggest that Hutton's argument for the irreconcileability of typology and realism in Yonge's fiction, an argument which foreshadows modern critical claims about the necessary conflict between 'romance' and 'realism', shows a misconception of the narrative mode which characterizes Yonge's novels. Far from realizing a static typological scheme, as Hutton implies, the characters in Yonge's novels possess typological significance precisely because they are involved in a process of development. What enables characters such as Guy and Laura at once to be morally convincing individuals within the realist context of Yonge's fiction, and to represent typologically moral principles such as chivalry or utilitarian rationalism, is the way in which the notion of 'development' in nineteenth-century British thought applies at once to the individual and society.

It is important to distinguish the concept of 'development', as Yonge and her Tractarian associates conceived of it, from that of 'progress'. Understood within the context of the pre-Darwinian British natural theology tradition, for which species were fixed rather than evolving,[54] the biological metaphor of 'development' referred to an unfolding of the inherent nature of either an individual or an institution, but without any implication that improvement was a necessary result. Hutton, in contrast, does assume that 'development' is equivalent to 'progress', and this helps to explain his frustration with the typological orientation of Yonge's fiction.

Hutton pays tribute to 'the free development of character and action' in Yonge's writing,[55] but objects to the way in which 'the free play of her moral idealism'[56] is restricted by what he describes as a 'whole world of sacred conventionalisms'.[57] Hutton appeals to the notion of development as something which necessarily sets the individual against 'the hierarchical order of society which Miss Yonge

---

54   Cf. Janis McLarren Caldwell, *Literature and Medicine in Nineteenth-Century Britain: From Mary Shelley to George Eliot* (Cambridge: Cambridge University Press, 2004), 53.
55   Hutton, 'Ethical and Dogmatic Fiction', 214.
56   Ibid.
57   Ibid., 215.

has been taught to accept', and laments that 'she has no perception of the fact, that half the beauty and spirit of the noblest institutions of society has sprung from the *free play* of individual excellence'.[58] This complaint suggests that Hutton's perception of a lack of proportion between the minor nature of Laura's fault of filial disobedience and the 'Nemesis' of 'morbid misery'[59] which is entailed upon her as a result springs ultimately from his liberal political and religious position, in which living 'religious intuitions' are regarded as opposed to the dead 'form' of religious establishments.[60]

Hutton appeals to an opposition between the content of individual's intuitions and inert social and religious forms as the basis for his claim that Yonge's fiction is unthinkingly in thrall to 'sacred conventionalisms',[61] and contrasts what he characterizes as her 'morbid introspectiveness'[62] with that 'action of the negative and critical faculties' which is 'vitally essential to the healthy condition of the mind'.[63] Unlike Hutton, however, Yonge does not assume that the development of individual moral intuition implies a progression beyond the religious forms in which it is expressed, regarding it instead as a unfolding or realization of what is already potentially contained within those forms.

This difference in viewpoint is reflected in the contrasting ways Yonge and Hutton employ the characteristically Victorian critical rhetoric of 'health' to describe Laura's development as a character. For Hutton, Yonge's inability to slough off the 'unmoral [...] dogma' of the father's 'right to give or withhold the daughter's hand'[64] results in the 'morbid introspectiveness'[65] of her portrayal of Philip and Laura's final unhappiness. The implication of the language of morbidity which Hutton employs here is that the very incompatibility of this 'feudal' dogma with modern social mores has resulted in its

58   Ibid., 216.
59   Ibid., 215.
60   Ibid., 228.
61   Ibid., 215.
62   Ibid., 216.
63   Ibid., 229.
64   Ibid., 215.
65   Ibid., 216.

assuming an exaggerated role in Yonge's narrative, with the proliferation in the novel of psychologically motivated description of the consequences of its infringement being compared to the inflammation surrounding dead bodily tissue.

Hutton, then, offers a 'symptomatic' reading of the novel, in which Laura's final condition of morbidity is interpreted as testifying to something morbid in Yonge's conception of her character, conflating the psychology of character and author. This symptomatic hermeneutic shows a fundamental misapprehension of Yonge's narrative method, which is concerned to present unhealthily subjective (or 'morbid') states of mind in such a way that the reader is not encouraged sympathetically to participate in them, since to do so would not only propagate such corrupting states of mind, but also imply a kind of Byronic approbation of them.[66] Hutton's misreading of Yonge consists in presupposing a form of sympathetic identification between reader and character which the dramatic and dialogue-based nature of Yonge's narrative technique is designed to avoid.

The difference between Yonge's and Hutton's conceptions of novelistic narrative corresponds to the distinction between typology and the Romantic symbol which I discussed in the previous chapter. Hutton's criticism of the 'morbidity' of Yonge's portrayal of Laura assumes that a novel is characterized by a symbolic fusion of the perspectives of reader, author and the individual character in which all character development should ultimately be seen as having been for the best, because if it be shown as having gone wrong (as in the permanent blight that has fallen upon Laura), the reader's own process of moral development, gone through in the course of reading the novel, will have been thrown off track. Hutton's accusation of 'morbidity' thus ultimately reflects a view of the novel derived from

---

66 Cf. Jean-Philippe Esquirol, *Mental Maladies* (trans. 1845), extract in Sally Shuttleworth and Jenny Bourne Taylor (eds), *Embodied Selves: An Anthology of Psychological Texts 1830–1890* (Oxford: Clarendon Press, 1998), 256 and Edward Bulwer-Lytton, *Night and Morning*, Knebworth edn (London: Routledge, n.d.), 238–9 (Book 3 Ch.8); Adam Smith, *Theory of Moral Sentiments*, D.D. Raphael and A.L. Macfie (ed.) (Oxford: Oxford University Press, 1976), 16.

Walter Scott (an author regarded as eminently 'healthy' by the Victorians), in which narrative construction plays the part of a benevolent Providence.

Yonge's challenge to the novelistic conventions of the mid-Victorian period is striking. In most Yonge novels, characters can, and do, die at any point in the narrative: one of the most harrowing examples is the sudden (and avoidable) death of Flora's baby from opium withdrawal in *The Daisy Chain*,[67] an episode which most Victorian novelists would have omitted, or at least softened, but the death of Guy in *The Heir of Redclyffe* is in its way equally unexpected, since up to that point the novel seems to be heading for a happy ending in which Guy and Philip are reconciled. The apparently arbitrary nature of events such as these in Yonge's novels testifies to a wish to avoid glibly providentialist plotting of the kind which Hutton's hermeneutics of the Romantic symbol seems designed to encourage, in favour of an emphasis on a typological relationship between reader and character in which the capacity for unreflective sympathetic identification is consistently held up to question.

Yonge emphasizes the potential for sympathetic identification to become unhealthy in a dialogue between Laura and Amy towards the end of *The Heir of Redclyffe*, in which Laura confesses her bafflement at the repentant Philip's criticism of the way 'she idolized him in a manner that was neither good for herself nor him'.[68] Amy tries to explain what Philip means, recalling that 'dear Guy [...] kept it always before my eyes from the very first that we were to look to something else besides each other' and comments to Laura that 'if that other is first, it would make you have some other standard of right besides himself; then you would be a stay and help to him.'[69] Laura, however, cannot even envisage that Philip might have anything for which to reproach himself, and the chapter ends on a downbeat note:

> But though her idolatry was complete, it did not seem to give full satisfaction or repose. As to Philip, though his love for her was unchanged, it now and then

67 Yonge, *The Daisy Chain, or Aspirations* (London: Macmillan, 1886), 566–7 (Part 2 Ch.20).
68 Ibid., *Heir*, 553 (Ch.42).
69 Ibid.,

was felt, though not owned by him, that she was not fully a helpmeet, only a 'Self' [...] still reflecting on him his former character, instead of aiding him to a new one.[70]

Amy's emphasis in this dialogue on the way in which 'to look to something else besides each other' provides a 'standard of right' testifies to the ethical dimension of typological understanding for Yonge. Amy is suggesting that human relationships themselves must be regarded from a typological perspective, if they are to preserve that dimension of transcendence in which their ethical character consists. In context, Amy's reticent references to 'that other' can be read as referring to the role Guy plays in *The Heir of Redclyffe* as a Christ-figure, both for her within the world of the novel, and for the novel's reader. As a 'type' of Christ, Guy both is and is not Christ (he is certainly not symbolically fused with Christ). The Christ-*likeness* which both Amy and the novel's reader perceive in Guy works both to provide a transcendent dimension to his moral struggle, and to suggest a perspective from which his 'faults'[71] are evident.

Laura's 'idolatry', on the other hand, indicates a mental identification between her own and Philip's identity. The purely immanent, this-worldly quality of such a Romantic symbolic fusion gives it an immediacy which is the negation of any ethical dimension: the relationship is defined in terms of an imagined collective 'self' which precludes any active engagement with the world outside, an *égoisme à deux*. Within such a relationship, development of character is impossible, because any change diminishes that sympathetic identification of selves on which the relationship is entirely founded. Philip's vague feeling of dissatisfaction with Laura by the end of the novel, which at first can seem rather like ingratitude, reflects a startlingly modern characterization by Yonge of a relationship that is 'stuck'.

In this context, Hutton's complaint that Yonge's description of the blighted life Laura and Philip end up leading is a sop to 'sacred conventionalisms'[72] can be seen to be misguided. Yonge's emphasis on the 'harassed' nature of Laura's final state represents a critique of

---

70   Yonge, *Heir*, 554 (Ch.42).
71   Ibid., 553 (Ch.42).
72   Hutton, 'Ethical and Dogmatic Fiction', 215.

those conventional Victorian ideals of womanhood which would encourage the kind of romantic idolatry that is shown to be not only her moral downfall, but destructive of the very relationship in whose service it is enlisted.

The relationship between Laura and Philip can be compared to the relationship depicted in Robert Browning's 'Porphyria's Lover' (written, of course, around the same time), in which the unhinged narrator strangles Porphyria in order to ensure that she continues to 'worship' him.[73] Although conveyed in a more subdued manner, *The Heir of Redclyffe*'s equivalent to this moment occurs when, after Laura has agreed not to reveal his inadvertent declaration of love to her father, Philip advises her to 'strengthen her mind' by studying algebra:

> Philip, with all his sense, was mystifying himself, because he was departing from right, the only true 'good sense'. His right judgement in all things was becoming obscured, so he talked metaphysical jargon instead of plain practical truth, and thought he was teaching Laura to strengthen her powers of mind, instead of giving way to dreams, when he was only leading her to stifle meditation, and thus securing her complete submission to himself.[74]

Like the narrator of 'Porphyria's Lover', Philip ends up 'stifling' the woman he loves, in that he encourages Laura to substitute the merely logical perspective of algebra for her transcendent moral intuitions. Unbeknownst to himself, Philip's logic is really only a way of asserting his male power over Laura, who has to submit her mind entirely to Philip, because his logic has excluded any standard beyond her worldly experience by which to judge him – and worldly experience is something in which, as a man, he is always going to be her superior. The feminist implication in Yonge's depiction of Laura is that only a recognition of the transcendent dimension in human experience, as represented by typology, can guarantee female independence.

---

73 Robert Browning, 'Porphyria's Lover', in *The Poems*, 2 vols, John Pettigrew and Thomas J. Collins (eds) (Harmondsworth: Penguin, 1981), l 33.
74 Yonge, *Heir*, 153–4 (Ch.10).

I will return later to the Nietzschean will-to-power hinted at in Yonge's emphasis on the remorselessness of Philip's logic.[75] It is necessary, however, to insist on the patronizing quality of Hutton's complaints about the 'morbidity' of Yonge's depiction of Laura, because they express an assumption which has also formed the basis for some recent feminist critiques of her novels[76] that Yonge is unthinkingly in thrall to a patriarchal ideology. Criticisms such as these misintepret Yonge's cultural feminism because they ignore the existentialist orientation of Yonge's moral vision. Laura's conceal-ment of her engagement is portrayed as having such harmful con-sequences for her ultimate happiness, I would suggest, because above all it prevents the development of her character. It is the concept of development, rather than any appeal to what a modern reader might regard as conventional 'Victorian values', which informs the morality of *The Heir of Redclyffe*.

In this respect, one might compare the uncomfortable starkness of Yonge's moral frame of reference to that of another writer of the 1850s, Charles Baudelaire. The facile Enlightenment optimism with which Hutton insists that Yonge's failure to provide a happy ending for Laura is a sign of her psychological 'morbidity' is exactly the kind of attitude which in his essays on Poe Baudelaire argues is responsible for the moral and aesthetic emptiness of the literature of his day.[77] Within the moral economy of Yonge's writing, as within that of Baudelaire, the consequence of an acceptance of free will is the possibility of damnation, and the most powerful testimony to Yonge's essentially feminist outlook is her willingness to embrace this pos-sibility as much in the depiction of her female characters as in that of her male ones.[78]

---

75   E.g. Yonge, *Heir*, 255 (Ch.19).
76   Cf. Talia Schaffer, 'The Mysterious Magnum Bonum: Fighting to Read Char-lotte Yonge', *Nineteenth-Century Literature* 55, no.2 (2000): 244–75.
77   Charles Baudelaire, 'Edgar Allan Poe: His Life and Works', in *Selected Writ-ings on Art and Literature*, trans. P.E. Charvet (Harmondsworth: Penguin, 1992), 192.
78   Compare the ending of *The Clever Woman of the Family*, where after her death Bessie Keith is discovered to have made a mercenary marriage due to her

Hutton's disparagement of the moral consequences Yonge attributes to Laura's secret engagement as an inappropriate revival of the 'old feudal notion' that such an engagement constituted 'an act of petty treason'[79] misses the point because, as in the novel's depiction of Guy's chivalric qualities, what interests Yonge is the moral truth for which the 'old feudal notion' might stand. Philip's rationalistic dispersion of Laura's moral inhibitions is depicted as an act of corruption not because Yonge confuses the convention of asking a father's permission with an absolute moral value, as Hutton implies, but because she regards Laura's unease at her father's not being consulted as significant of this formality's association in Laura's mind with important moral truths.

Yonge's insistence on the danger inherent in simply abrogating a social institution, no matter how trivial it might appear when taken by itself, reflects the kind of thinking behind Coleridge's discussion of the nature of moral truth in *The Friend*. Coleridge makes the point that seemingly innocuous rationalistic arguments against belief in ghosts helped to bring about the popular spread of atheism to which he attributes the moral catastrophe of the French Revolution, because, however much an educated audience might be able to distinguish questions about the nature of ghosts from questions about the nature of religion, in the minds of an ignorant audience this superstition was vitally connected with religious belief itself.[80] From this perspective, no matter how outmoded by nineteenth-century modernity Laura's assumption that her hand ought to be bestowed by her father might actually be, Philip is as guilty of violating Laura's innocence through his rationalistic dismissal of this punctilio as if he had physically seduced her, as Philip himself recognizes towards the end of the novel.[81]

hopeless entanglement in debt (*The Clever Woman of the Family* [London: Macmillan, 1892], 339–42 (Ch.28).

79 Hutton, 'Ethical and Dogmatic Fiction', 215–16.
80 S.T. Coleridge, *The Friend*, 2 vols, Barbare E. Rooke (ed.) (Princeton: Princeton University Press, 1969), 1: 46.
81 Yonge, *Heir*, 584 (Ch.43); cf. Sarah Ellis, *The Women of England: Their Social Duties and Domestic Habits* (London and New York, 1839), 32.

Yonge's typological understanding of Laura's relationship to her father, then, is psychologically sophisticated, in that the typological equivalence of Laura's not very intelligent father to God (which is implied by Yonge's emphasis on Laura's 'idolatry' in setting her relationship with Philip above her relationship with her father)[82] emerges from her depiction of the stultifying effect the concealment of the engagement has on Laura's character, rather than being imposed on the narrative from a pre-determined set of allegorical equivalences, as Hutton's review implies. This aspect of Yonge's narrative technique can be seen as related to the characteristic de-emphasizing of narrative voice in her novels.[83]

Hutton's review fails to note that the 'Nemesis' of 'morbid misery'[84] which he identifies as Laura's fate is never directly described in the novel, but is left for the reader to infer from Yonge's repeated use of words such as 'harassed'. Yonge is careful to avoid narratorial 'omniscience', because this would run the danger of stifling the reader's developing moral insight into the false position into which Laura has placed herself, in exactly the same way as Philip stifles Laura's moral intuition by his overbearing logic. The typological significance of the narrative can only be conveyed by indirection, because for Yonge the hermeneutic activity of the reader is constitutive of typology; if these kinds of significances were baldly stated by an omniscient narrator they would become reified, and hence mere 'sacred conventionalisms'[85] in the way suggested by Hutton, whereas if they arise in the course of reading the novel the reader comes to enact a process of moral development analogous to that which Yonge's characters are described as undergoing. From this perspective Yonge's novelistic technique can be seen as a way of putting into practice the principle of 'reserve' described by Isaac Williams in 'On Reserve in Communicating Religious Knowledge'.[86]

82 Yonge, *Heir*, 554 (Ch.42).
83 Sandbach-Dahlström, *Be Good Sweet Maid*, 12.
84 Hutton, 'Ethical and Dogmatic Fiction', 215
85 Ibid.
86 Isaac Williams, 'On Reserve in Communicating Religious Knowledge', Part One, *Tracts for the Times* 4 (1842): independently paginated and 'On Reserve in Communicating Religious Knowledge', Conclusion, *Tracts for the Times* 5

Yonge in fact satirizes the kind of 'sacred conventionalisms' of which she is accused by Hutton in her novel *The Castle-Builders*, when the two somewhat naïve and silly heroines agree to teach in a school run along non-denominational Evangelical lines, and find that the pupils have been taught to regurgitate a set of disconnected Biblical texts, without understanding anything about the doctrines behind them.[87] Yonge's typically understated point here resembles the argument made at length in Coleridge's *Confessions of an Inquiring Spirit* against the Evangelical doctrine of the plenary inspiration of the Bible, on the grounds that this doctrine denatures the Biblical text by converting the process of human response to the divine embodied in the Bible into an alienating divine ventriloquism.[88] The response of the heroines of *The Castle-Builders* is to teach the children the Catechism, which lands them in hot water with the school authorities, who find this overly denominational.[89]

Hutton, too, objects to Yonge's advocacy of:

The practice that young children should learn by rote creeds and prayers which are admitted to be beyond their understanding in order that the *form of words* may be familiar to them against the time when the meaning thereof shall become apprehensible.[90]

But, as an article in the *Monthly Packet* makes clear, for Yonge the best defence against the kind of reification of religious doctrine which she finds in Evangelicalism lies in the implicit and unstated nature of the commentary on the words of the Bible which is provided by traditional religious formularies.[91] Yonge regards typological signif-

(1843): independently paginated in Gavin Budge (ed.), *Aesthetics and Religion in Nineteenth-Century Britain*, 6 vols (Bristol: Thoemmes, 2003), Vol.3.

87 Yonge, *The Castle Builders; or, The Deferred Confirmation* (London: Mozley, 1854), 84–6 (Ch.6), in Charlotte M. Yonge, *Abbeychurch / The Castle Builders*, facs. edn (New York and London: Garland Publishing, 1976).

88 Coleridge, *Confessions of an Inquiring Spirit*, Harold Bloom (ed.) (New York: Chelsea House, 1983), 51–2.

89 Yonge, *Castle Builders*, 108–9 (Ch.8).

90 Hutton, 'Ethical and Dogmatic Fiction', 217.

91 Yonge, 'Conversations on the Catechism. Conversation XXXIII. The Third Commandment. Reverence', *Monthly Packet* 10 (Series 1 1855): 253–5.

icance as something which can only truly be understood if the mind is unconsciously immersed in it, and for her this applies to interpretation both of the Bible and of fictional narrative.

Hutton's review assumes that Yonge is essentially a *doctrinal*, or 'dogmatic' writer, but this is far from an adequate characterization of her fiction. Yonge is above all interested in the relationship between character and religious *practice*, and because of this she is capable of acknowledging the moral stature of those who occupy religious positions differing from her own, even whilst she implies that such integrity is achieved rather in spite of the tendency of their own doctrines than because of it. An example of this are the unworldly elderly ladies in *The Castle-Builders* who are in charge of the school: despite Yonge's portrayal of the harmful practical effects of their Evangelical doctrines when applied to education, Herbert Somerville, the High Church clergyman who represents the centre of moral authority in the novel, remarks on their personal goodness.[92]

A similar point may be made about the presence of typological significance in Yonge's fiction: these significances are not presented by Yonge as doctrines by which the narrative stands or falls (something which would make her novels into Bunyanesque allegories), but as hermeneutic possibilities, ways in which the reader can interpretatively engage with her texts. Typology is above all an interpretative *practice* for Yonge, so that for an omniscient narrator to dictate a religious 'moral' would in fact be to foreclose the possibility of typology altogether.

Typology for Yonge is integral to a process of development which takes place at a moral level in respect of her characters, and at an interpretative level in respect of her reader's experience of the text, with both, from Yonge's Tractarian perspective, being understood as analogous to the Church's continuing response to divine revelation as represented in the Bible. Yonge's advocacy of doctrinal formulations such as the Catechism being learnt by rote in schools, of which Hutton is so critical, can thus be seen as intimately related to the narrative mode of her novels, since in both cases Yonge's assumption is that the kind of uncritical linguistic absorption which characterizes both rote-

---

92   Yonge, *Castle Builders*, 315 (Ch.21).

learning and the reading of fiction lies at the basis of a process of associative development in which meaning emerges retrospectively as an active interpretative construction of the mind. An example of this process, whereby ritually absorbed signs become converted into lived experience, can be found in *The Castle-Builders*, where the two heroines, who have not bothered to have themselves confirmed, have the significance of the eucharist explained to them by their young friend Frank through analogy with the ringing of the doorbell by a beggar – an allusion, though perhaps an unconscious one on Frank's part, to the ritual of ringing a bell whilst the Host is being consecrated.[93]

What interests Yonge about typology is its potential, through solicitation of active interpretative engagement, to transgress the boundary between the fictional world of her novels and the real lives of her readers, and in this her deployment of typological significance may be compared with Keble's account of typology in 'On the Mysticism attributed to the Early Fathers of the Church', to which we have already referred in the previous chapter. What is striking about Keble's account of typological meaning, as we noted, is his claim that the use of natural imagery in the Bible potentially licenses the attribution of typological significance to the whole world of sense through a process of association.[94] Typology for Keble transgresses the boundaries of the Biblical text, and in so doing establishes a religious culture or, to use one of Keble's favourite words, *ethos*.

When Hutton complains that Yonge is a mere 'ecclesiasticist' who assumes that 'if we give up the inviolability of the *form*, we lose all certainty of retaining our hold on the *realities* of religion',[95] he is invoking a distinction between form and content which is thrown into question by the appeal to a typological perspective. From the point of view of Yonge and Keble, typology is what permits the possibility of a language about God which is not, in theological terms, idolatrous.

93   Ibid., 155 (Ch.11).
94   John Keble, *On the Mysticism Attributed to the Early Fathers of the Church* (Oxford and London: Parker, 1868), 173–4, in Budge, *Aesthetics and Religion*, Vol.3.
95   Hutton, 'Ethical and Dogmatic Fiction', 228.

The distinction between content and form relied on by Hutton breaks down in this context, because to claim that God is the 'content', or even the 'reality', of one's theological language, is already to succumb to idolatry, in that it implies a reification of the notion of God. That very 'conventionalism' about typology to which Hutton objects is what safeguards religious reference from the possibility of idolatry, because it makes evident that any claim about God expressed by means of typology is essentially provisional, subject to further interpretation of the biblical text.

Implicit within Keble's account of the associative nature of typology is a model of religious development both within individuals, through the progressive education of their perceptions, and within the Church as a whole, through the embodiment of typology in doctrinal formulations and religious ritual, a model which John Henry Newman would later articulate at length in his *Essay on the Development of Christian Doctrine*. From this perspective, Laura's idolizing of Philip, and consequent condition of what Hutton describes as 'morbid misery',[96] can be seen as the reverse side of her decision to refuse the typological identification of paternal with divine authority under the rationalistic influence of Philip. Laura's final unhappiness shows that for Yonge, the only alternative to a typological outlook on the world is a condition of idolatry from which the possibility of moral development has been excluded.

Idolatry and Moral Corruption

Yonge's insistence on the consequences of Laura's 'idolatry' of Philip is illuminated by the extended discussion of idolatry which was published in the *Monthly Packet* a couple of years later in 1855, as part of a series of 'Conversations on the Catechism'. The relevance of this mostly theological account of idolatry to the issue of Laura's relationship with Philip is established by a comment near the end of an

96   Ibid., 215.

article on the first commandment by one of the interlocutors that 'when people fall in love they grow like idols to each other', which is seconded by the instructress, who adds that 'lovers do make each other the first object, unless their minds are under proper control, and many varieties of evils thus arise'.[97] In the following article, it is made clear that this is a danger to which women are particularly prone:

> *Miss O.* I think there is one sort of idolatry which is a peculiar danger of women, and, therefore, I had better speak of it here – I mean that of over-reliance upon some one person. It was part of our punishment that woman should cling to man with a sense of her inferiority, and this often leads to the temptation of being blindly led, so fastening our admiration on those we love as to put them, as it were, between us and God.

> *Audrey.* The idolatry of affection.

> *Miss O.* Yes, that is one branch – the other I meant is the temper that enables women to be led captive. I did not so much, at that moment, mean over-love as over-trust. I mean, that we had often rather shape our views of right and wrong, and guide our actions by the counsel of some one we look up to, than by the rule of God's law.

> *Audrey.* But I thought it was right not to be self-reliant, and that we ought to be guided.

> *Miss O.* So we ought, to a certain point – but our guides are but men. There is no safety in giving the *whole* keeping of our consciences to another. Our rule of right and wrong, and our doctrine, must be what Scripture and our own Church teaches us, not merely what an individual, or a few individuals, may say. We must have an external standard.[98]

The description of idolatry here carries an implicitly feminist message – although men may be 'guides', their advice is to be regarded critically in the light of religious teaching, something which Laura has singularly failed to do in the case of Philip.

97 Yonge, 'Conversations on the Catechism: Conversation XXX. The First Commandment', *Monthly Packet* 9 (1st series 1855): 19.
98 Yonge, 'Conversations on the Catechism: Conversation XXXI. The Second Commandment', *Monthly Packet* 9 (Series 1 1855): 181

The discussion of idolatry in these articles, which reflect Yonge's own experience of teaching the catechism in a church school, follows eighteenth-century accounts, such as that of Warburton in *The Divine Legation of Moses*, in attributing idolatry to the corruption of an original revelation through the practice of 'a caste of priests' keeping the 'hidden meaning' of the signs through which this revelation was recorded 'to themselves as a mystery', and so promoting a 'transition into gross idolatry among the common people'.[99] The noteworthy feature of the account of idolatry put forward in these articles, however, is its emphasis on the greater moral blameworthiness of the Israelites for their lapses into idolatry, as opposed to those for whom it was the normal condition.

In response to Helena's comment that the Israelites 'seem to have picked up portions of every heathen worship they could find, and to have followed them all together without any consistency', Audrey suggests that this 'was because to the other nations these heathen rites were shadows of guesses at truth, while to the Israelites they were only unmeaning, profane superstitions', a view which is seconded by Miss O.[100] What is being implied by Yonge here is that pagan beliefs themselves might stand in a typological relationship to Christian truth, a view which underpinned the eighteenth-century Anglican tradition of mythography[101] and which is reflected by the inclusion in the same numbers of the *Monthly Packet* of a series of retellings of stories from Greek mythology which strongly hint at typological significances.[102]

But even though paganism might possess a certain kind of typological validity for those who practise it, Yonge makes clear that the deliberate adoption of pagan beliefs by the Israelites was incompatible with development towards moral truth by the comment that they 'followed them all together without any consistency'. By turning their back on a superior revelation, the Israelites have ignored

99 Ibid., 'Conversations on the Catechism', Conversations on the Catechism XXX. The First Commandment', *MP* 9 (1855): 2.
100 Ibid.
101 Cf. J.B. Bullen (ed.), *The Sun is God* (Clarendon Press: Oxford, 1989).
102 E.g. Anon., 'Mythological Legends: The Legend of Glaucus and Polyidus', *Monthly Packet* 9 (Series 1 1855): 269.

their moral intuitions in a way that those born heathens have not, and consequently lack any moral reference point. A similar point is made later in the article when the religious beliefs of the Romans and the Greeks are compared. The self-conscious adoption of Greek mythology by the Romans is described as an act of self-corruption, because incompatible with the national characteristics of 'the grave, self-devoted, incorruptible race of iron'; the Romans had 'not so much intellect to discover the true lessons under the legends' and so sank into abject idolatry, whereas the Greeks 'looked beyond their mythology, and felt after God' in that they regarded their mythology as indicative of higher moral truths.[103]

The account of idolatry offered in these *Monthly Packet* articles helps to explain why Yonge implies a much harsher moral verdict on Laura than she does on Philip, as we noted at the beginning of this section. Like the Israelites and the ancient Romans, Laura has deliberately corrupted her own moral intuitions. Even if, as Hutton suggests, the 'old feudal notion'[104] of a father's authority had been excessive, and to that extent idolatrous, it would still, like the mythology of the Greeks, have borne a typological relationship to the truth, but for Yonge, Laura's assumption of a right to pick and choose the object of her idolatry is altogether corrupt, in that it implies a secret preference of self (what Yonge often refers to as 'self-sufficiency')[105] which must inevitably be at odds with that ethical relationship to the Other in which moral development consists. As Philip realizes towards the end of the novel, Laura is 'not fully a helpmeet, only a 'Self''.[106]

Philip, on the other hand, even though he was the one who originally advocated concealment of the engagement from Laura's father, has in so doing only acted in accordance with the rationalism which Yonge notes in 'Conversations on the Catechism' is 'the

---

103 Yonge, 'Conversations on the Catechism', 9.
104 Hutton, 'Ethical and Dogmatic Fiction', 215.
105 Sandbach-Dahlström, *Be Good Sweet Maid*, 150.
106 Yonge, *Heir*, 554 (Ch.43).

present snare and temptation of the educated in our own country'.[107] Even though reason is Philip's idol, and consequently tends to warp his judgement in the direction of a disguised selfishness (since 'Self', according to the *Monthly Packet*, is 'at the root of most other idolatries')[108] Yonge suggests that Philip is effectively in the position which 'Conversations on the Catechism' attributes to Socrates, someone whose idolatrous worship only stems from the absence of knowledge of anything better.[109]

At an early point in *The Heir of Redclyffe* we learn that Philip has sacrificed his prospects of a brilliant university career by taking a commission in the army in order to provide for his sisters to continue living in the family home after the death of his father.[110] His act of self-sacrifice has proved in vain, however, since his younger sister has died, and his elder sister, responsible for bringing Philip up after the death of their mother, has married a wealthy doctor who, as Mrs Edmonstone comments to Guy, 'is much older than she is, not her equal in mind or cultivation, and though I hardly like to say so, not at all a religious man.'.[111] In an earlier scene, we see Philip's disappointment with his sister's mercenary behaviour from his comment that visiting the family home makes him think of Tennyson's 'Locksley Hall',[112] a poem which contains a vitriolic description of an unworthy marriage:

> Yet it shall be: thou shalt lower to his level day by day,
> What is fine within thee growing coarse to sympathise with clay.
>
> As the husband is, the wife is: thou art mated with a clown,
> And the grossness of his nature will have weight to drag thee down.[113]

---

107 Yonge, 'Conversations on the Catechism: Conversation XXX. The First Commandment', *MP* 9 (1855): 15.
108 Ibid., 18.
109 Ibid., 9.
110 Yonge, *Heir*, 21–2 (Ch.2).
111 Ibid., 56 (Ch.4).
112 Ibid., 35 (Ch.3).
113 Alfred Tennyson, 'Locksley Hall', in *Poems and Plays*, T. Herbert Warren, rev. Frederick Page (eds) (Oxford: Oxford University Press, 1965), ll 46–50.

Since in the same scene Philip comments that Margaret's husband 'does not know what conversation is', and describes their marital home as a 'tumult of gossip, and novelty, and hardness',[114] the implications of his allusion to 'Locksley Hall' are fairly clear. Mrs Edmonstone suggests that the effect of this 'great disappointment' has been to give him 'a severity, an unwillingness to trust'[115] which in the light of later events can be seen as responsible both for Philip's decision to conceal the engagement between himself and Laura, and for his continued refusal to believe in Guy's innocence.

After this revelation, Guy exclaims 'Oh! it is a cruel thing to find that what one loves is, or has not been, all one thought',[116] and later, after he has been accused of gambling, deliberately visits Philip's family home in order to strengthen his disposition 'to excuse the sternness, severity, and distrust which were an evidence how acutely a warm heart had suffered'.[117] What Yonge is drawing attention to here, in a way that explains the less severe moral judgement implied by the narrative on Philip's concealment of the engagement, is the disruption of Philip's home-life by his sister's selfish marriage, the home-life for which he has of course sacrificed all his prospects. Because his sister has not proved to be 'all he thought', Philip is a man without a moral centre, in that home associations cannot provide for him any kind of moral touchstone. In the circumstances, the novel implies, it is not surprising that Philip over-invests in his relationship with Laura to such an extent that he cannot bear the prospect of being parted from the woman he significantly describes as 'my home; my first, my most precious interest'.[118]

The idolatrous nature of Philip's love for Laura is implied by Yonge's comment that 'he rather sought to preserve Laura as she was than to make her anything more'.[119] By the end of the novel, the implied fixation of Laura and Philip into a condition of co-dependence

114 Yonge, *Heir*, 35 (Ch.3).
115 Ibid., 57 (Ch.4).
116 Ibid.
117 Ibid., 247 (Ch.18).
118 Ibid., 119 (Ch.8).
119 Ibid., 120 (Ch.8).

190

has become, as we have already seen, exactly what is wrong with their relationship. Unlike Laura, however, Philip has not the benefit of uncompromised family relationships by which to judge this romantic involvement. The significance of family structures, the novel seems to suggest, is not only that they represent other loyalties which ought to prevent romantic love from becoming all-consuming, but also that they possess an inherent dynamism which ultimately gives them their typological significance by preventing the kind of unhealthy fixity which characterizes Philip and Laura's relationship and stands between them and God. Philip's lack of understanding of this dynamic dimension of family life lies behind his mistake in inappropriately cautioning Amy about Guy's character after their wedding, showing that 'he had, after a fashion, forgotten that she was Lady Morville, not the cousin Amy with whom Guy's character might be freely discussed'.[120]

Fiction and Moral Truth

The blending of theological and psychological categories apparent in Yonge's suggestion that Laura and Philip have succumbed to idolatry in their love for one another reflects Tractarian religious thought in general. Newman, for example, in his *Essay on the Development of Christian Doctrine*, suggests that one of the distinctive characteristics underlying the bewildering ramification of different forms of heresy is that it is 'self-sufficent' in a way that apparently gives it the advantage over orthodoxy, in that it is 'by its nature, its own master'.[121] Newman's psychological characterization of heresy finds abundant echoes in Yonge's novels, where, as Sandbach-Dahlström has pointed out,[122] the condition of 'self-sufficiency' poses a constant moral threat,

---

120 Ibid., 407–8 (Ch.30).
121 John Henry Newman, *An Essay on the Development of Christian Doctrine*, J.M. Cameron (ed.) (Harmondsworth: Penguin, 1974), 176.
122 Sandbach-Dahlström, *Be Good Sweet Maid*, 150.

a condition of which Philip's own unconscious desire for mastery is exemplary.

In this context, the very active role which Philip takes in promoting suspicion of Guy's gambling[123] could be interpreted as representing typologically the effects of the heretical frame of mind which he has already manifested in persuading Laura to keep their engagement a secret. By concealing the engagement, Philip has already preferred his private judgement to the demands of social institutions[124] in the way deplored by Tractarians as characteristic of Protestantism,[125] a moral and hermeneutic individualism which is arguably reflected in the determination Philip shows to make his own interpretation of the inconclusive evidence against Guy prevail at all costs, and the way his incorrect suppositions about Guy are shown to proliferate in his own mind.[126] Since Philip's behaviour is also obviously motivated by his jealousy of Guy,[127] and by the kind of homosocial panic[128] which Eve Kosofsky Sedgwick has identified in other nineteenth-century novels,[129] psychological and theological understandings of his behaviour mingle. Philip, in his desire for a degree of conclusiveness which the available evidence simply won't afford,[130] might even be regarded as a kind of portrait of Newman himself, whom Keble regarded as having been led astray by a characteristically nineteenth-century lust for certainty[131] in which, as

123 Yonge, *Heir*, 199–209 (Ch.14).
124 Ibid., 120 (Ch.8).
125 John Henry Newman, *Newman's University Sermons: Fifteen Sermons Preached Before the University of Oxford 1826–1843*, intro by D.M. MacKinnon and J.D. Holmes (London: SPCK, 1970), 296–7.
126 Yonge, *Heir*, 406–7 (Ch.30).
127 Ibid., 117, 261 (Chs 8, 19).
128 E.g. Yonge, *Heir*, 255.
129 Eve Kosofsky Sedgwick, *Between Men: English Literature and Male Homosocial Desire* (New York: Columbia University Press, 1985), 92.
130 Yonge, *Heir*, 257 (Ch.19).
131 Keble, *Sermons Academical and Occasional* (Oxford and London: Parker and Rivington, 1848), lxvi–lxviii.

Elizabeth Wordsworth commented to Yonge, his intellect was 'too strong for his *nature*'.[132]

In the character of Philip, the plot of *The Heir of Redclyffe* equates the ability to arrive at a correct interpretation of evidence with a condition of moral integrity in a way that echoes wider mid-nineteenth-century debates surrounding the utilitarianism of John Stuart Mill. Mill's *A System of Logic* privileged the role of experience in forming judgements in a way which many nineteenth-century commentators felt ignored the important role played by intuitions derived from the mind's own intellectual powers, especially in moral questions. In particular, what troubled the Tractarians about Mill's *Logic* was its exclusion of religious or moral experience from any kind of epistemological authority so that the Church became an intellectual and social irrelevance. The plot of *The Heir of Redclyffe* engages with this debate about the role of moral judgement in intellectual life by implying that Philip's moral aberration renders him unable to perceive kinds of evidence which are apparent to other characters. These forms of evidence, Yonge suggests, are exactly those on which depend the moral judgements formed by readers of novels, so that *The Heir of Redclyffe* can be interpreted as a vindication, directed against Mill's sensationalist philosophy, both of the epistemological authority of the novel and, by extension, of the authority of the woman writer, based on that appeal to the evidence of intuition which was characteristic of nineteenth-century philosophy in the tradition of the Scottish Common Sense school.

To understand how the philosophical debate surrounding Mill's *Logic*, about the relationship between experience and intuition in the process of judgement, informs a theory of reading which asserts the intellectual value of fiction, we must turn to the important role which an account of the reading process plays in the influential Evangelical Thomas Chalmers's 1814 *On the Miraculous and Internal Evidences of the Christian Revelation*. Chalmers argues that the morally strenuous Christian believer has access to a form of evidence in the inspired word of the Bible in a way which the non-Christian does not:

---

132 Ethel Romanes, *Charlotte Mary Yonge: An Appreciation* (London: Mowbray, 1908), 152–7.

The man who devotes himself in the spirit of a thorough moral earnestness to the perusal of Scripture, feels a growing homage in his heart to the sanctity and the majesty and the authority which beam upon him from its pages – and in more conspicuous light, and with more commanding effect, the longer that this holy exercise is persevered in. And the question recurs - might not this growing probability grow into a complete and irresistible certainty at the last? [...] It is no condemnation of this evidence, that, only seen by those who have thus reached their way to it, it has not yet come within the observation of others who are behind them, who have not given the same serious and sustained attention to the Bible, or not so much made it the book of their anxious and repeated perusals – nor their right understanding of the book, the subject of their devoutest prayers. It is true, the resulting evidence is of that personal and peculiar quality, which cannot be translated in all its proper force and clearness into the mind of another – yet may it be a good and solid evidence notwithstanding – as much as the ocular evidence for the reality of some isolated spot which I alone have been admitted to see, and which no human eyes but my own have ever beheld. The evidence is not at all weakened by this monopoly.[133]

Chalmers suggests that 'serious and sustained attention to the Bible' develops in the believer an ability intuitively to perceive kinds of moral evidence for its truth, such as 'the sanctity and the majesty and the authority which beam upon him from its pages', which not only remain hidden from the less committed but which can't really be rationally articulated at all. The claims for the significance of the typological linkages to be found in scripture which we have found in Keble could be compared to Chalmers's position, since both thinkers argue that non-rational forms of evidence can legitimately be identified in the Biblical text, forms of evidence which Keble calls 'mystical' or 'poetic'.[134] Chalmers's argument draws upon the account of perception put forward in Scottish Common Sense philosophy, according to which sense-data are not assumed to be immediately intelligible to the mind, as they are in the sensationalist philosophies of Locke and Hume, but require active interpretation by the mind.[135]

133 Thomas Chalmers, *On the Miraculous and Internal Evidences of the Christian Revelation*, 2 vols (Glasgow: Collins, n.d.), 2: 70–1.
134 Keble, *On the Mysticism*, 4.
135 E.g. Thomas Reid, *Works*, 7th edn, William Hamilton (ed.) (Edinburgh: Maclachlan and Stewart, 1872), 135.

Thomas Reid, for example, emphasizes the role played by attention in developing the mind's capacities for perception, something which he argues would not take place if perceptions were merely passively imprinted on the mind, citing the capacity of sailors to spot land from indications which would be invisible to others.[136] For Reid, perception is a process of reading signs which is acquired partly through experience, but which ultimately rests on intuitive forms of knowledge which he calls the 'principles of common sense'.[137]

Chalmers simply inverts this Reidian argument: if perception is a process of reading signs, then for Chalmers the reading of the Biblical text can be legitimately characterized as a form of perception in which religious truth is intuitively revealed to the believer, provided the moral faculties on which perception of such truths depends have been sufficiently exercised. Although Chalmers, as a good Evangelical, confines this argument to the Biblical text as a product of plenary inspiration, from the Tractarian perspective, in which the Bible is not assumed to be immediately intelligible to all believers, but only comprehensible as mediated through the traditions and formularies of the Church,[138] there would be less justification for drawing a rigid distinction between sacred and secular texts in this respect. All forms of reading, and even novels, would contain the potential for the intuitive revelation of moral truth, provided that the reader's moral faculties were in a healthy state of perception, just as for Keble the significance of Biblical typology inevitably spills over into secular forms of poetry.[139]

This kind of understanding of the reading of fiction as a process whereby the reader's intuitive moral perceptions are evoked is apparent in the prominence which references to novel reading assume in *The Heir of Redclyffe*. Soon after Philip's secret avowal of his attachment, Laura is 'made very uncomfortable' by a cousin's dec-

136 Reid, *Works*, 185.
137 Ibid., 230–6.
138 Richard Hurrell Froude, *Remains of the Late Reverend Richard Hurrell Froude MA, Fellow of Oriel College, Oxford*, 2 vols (London: Rivington, 1838), 1: 412–514.
139 Keble, *On the Mysticism*, 173–4.

laration 'that it was positively impossible and unnatural that the *good* heroine of some novel should have concealed her engagement from her parents' and feels she has to find 'many excuses'.[140] For Yonge, it is obvious that the novel (even, as in this case, a bad novel) can excite moral intuitions whose truth can transcend the particular circumstances which the novel presents – the irony in this passage is that the cousin towards the end of the book is encouraged by the example of Laura's secret engagement into considering an elopement with the tutor Philip has officiously recommended.[141]

A similar emphasis on the potential moral and religious value of the novel is also apparent in the reactions of characters to the news of Philip and Laura's clandestine engagement. Amy, for example, comments that Laura's concealment of Philip's attachment to her can be put down to the fact that Philip discouraged her from reading novels and so she was unaware of the full implications of what she was doing.[142] Charles also comments on the strange 'incompatibility of so novelish and imprudent a proceeding with the cautious, thoughtful character of both parties',[143] and Philip and Laura's marriage is repeatedly associated with the dénouement of a novel.[144] The implication is that those who do not read novels are destined to live them out.

This ironic association of Philip and Laura with the kind of impulsive behaviour found in novels forms part of the critique of utilitarian rationalism in *The Heir of Redclyffe*. In much the same way as Newman argues that 'the power of imagination' progressively leads rationalists into less and less rationally justifiable forms of scepticism,[145] Yonge portrays Philip's excessively logical way of thinking as leading him into morally questionable behaviour, and eventually into downright foolishness. In the matter of his clandestine engagement with Laura, Yonge makes clear that Philip reasons himself into

140 Yonge, *Heir*, 174 (Ch.12).
141 Ibid., 365, 578–9 (Chs 28, 43).
142 Ibid., 426 (Ch.32).
143 Ibid., 449 (Ch.34).
144 Ibid., 533, 545, 579 (Chs 40, 41, 43).
145 Newman, *University Sermons*, 67–72.

believing that they are 'doing nothing in an underhand way',[146] and this is also true of his behaviour towards Guy, where his unconscious jealousy and 'malignity' are apparent to other characters,[147] but concealed from Philip himself by his ability to rationalize his own motives. Philip's excessively rationalizing approach to life eventually betrays him into catching the fever, because his quickness in finding ulterior motives for other characters' actions leads him to disregard Amy and Guy's attempts to dissuade him from continuing with his travel plans, on the grounds that 'the whole objection was caused by Guy's dislike to submit to him, and a fit of impatience of which Amy was the victim', an impression which is based on a suspicion 'that his cousin wanted to escape from his surveillance and follow the bent of his inclinations' towards gambling.[148]

Nicola Thompson, in an extensive discussion of Yonge's nineteenth-century critical reception, has drawn attention to the way in which 'critics tend to focus their comments on the effects *The Heir of Redclyffe* has on its readers, rather than on the work's intrinsic literary qualities',[149] a tendency which I would suggest reflects the understanding of fiction as an occasion for the development of moral intuition on the part of its readers which is present in Yonge's novel itself. As Thompson points out, Yonge's nineteenth- and early twentieth-century critics frequently emphasize the power of Yonge's characters to endure in the mind long after the reader has finished the novel in which they appear,[150] and discussions in Yonge's letters reveal that she herself experienced her characters in this way. This aspect of Yonge's novelistic technique suggests that characters in her novels are not merely objects of the reader's moral judgement, but are intended to function as associative centres for moral intuitions that would otherwise remain scattered and fragmentary. In this respect, character in Yonge's novels fulfils the same purpose of moral self-

---

146   Yonge, *Heir*, 271 (Ch.20).
147   Ibid., 265 (Ch.20).
148   Ibid., 406–7 (Ch.30).
149   Nicola Diane Thompson, *Reviewing Sex: Gender and the Reception of Victorian Novels* (Houndmills: Macmillan, 1996), 97.
150   Ibid.

integration which we have seen Newman attribute to the Personality of Christ, and which constitutes the Tractarian rationale for set forms of religious observance. Formally, Yonge's novels may be 'loose, baggy monsters', as Henry James described Victorian fiction,[151] but they achieve coherence by an associative dynamic internal to the development of character, and this makes them, in Umberto Eco's phrase, peculiarly 'open' works,[152] in that the reader is left with associative complexes capable not only of organizing their experience of the text, but of structuring moral response to the world beyond the text.

Yonge's portrayal of the way in which Philip's rationalistic dismissal of fiction is responsible for his own susceptibility to the irrational motive of jealousy reflects an outlook in which, paradoxically, the fictional is potentially more 'real' than the everyday world of fact, in the sense that it is closer to the mind's immaterial moral intuitions. The historian J.A. Froude, writing at a time when he was still under Newman's influence, set out this Tractarian understanding of fiction in an apologia for medieval hagiography:

> The Lives of the Saints are not so much strict biographies, as myths, edifying stories compiled from tradition, and designed not so much to relate facts, as to produce a religious impression on the mind of the hearer. Under the most favourable circumstances, it is scarcely conceivable that uninspired men could write a faithful history of a miraculous life. Even ordinary history, except mere annals, is all more or less fictitious; that is, the facts are related, not as they really happened but as they appeared to the writer; as they happen to illustrate his views or support his prejudices. And if this is so of common facts, how much more so must it be when all the power of the marvellous is thrown in to stimulate the imagination. But to see fully the difficulties under which the writers of these Lives must have laboured, let us observe a few of the ways in which we all, and time for us, treat the common history and incidents of life.
>
> First; We all write Legends. Little as we may be conscious of it, we all of us continually act on the very same principle which made the Lives of Saints such as we find them; only perhaps less poetically.
>
> Who has not observed in himself, in his ordinary dealings with the facts of every-day life, with the sayings and doings of his acquaintance, in short, with

151   Henry James, 'Preface', in *The Tragic Muse* (New York: Scribner's, 1936), x.
152   Umberto Eco, *The Open Work*, intro by David Robey, trans. Anna Cancogni (Cambridge, MA: Harvard University Press, 1989), 3–4.

198

every thing which comes before him as a *fact*, a disposition to forget the real order in which they appear, and re-arrange them according to his theory of how they ought to be? Do we hear of a generous self-denying action, in a short time the real doer and it are forgotten; it has become the property of the noblest person we know; so a jest we relate of the wittiest person, frivolity of the most frivolous, and so on; each particular act we attribute to the person we conceive most likely to have been the author of it. And this does not arise from any wish to leave a false impression scarcely from carelessness; but only because facts refuse to remain bare and isolated in our memory; they will arrange themselves under some law or other; they must illustrate something to us – some character – some principle – or else we forget them. Facts are thus perpetually, so to say, becoming unfixed and rearranged in a more conceptional order.[153]

Froude invokes the principle of development, as Newman had articulated it, in order to explain the fictional dimension of historical understanding. The boundaries between fiction and history become blurred because our memory of facts depends on the significance we attribute to them, so that, in a traditional oral culture at least, facts tend to gravitate around the associative complexes which historical myths represent. Just as Newman had argued that the religious truth of a doctrine was shown by its vitality, or ability to assimilate to itself the culture that surrounded it,[154] so too J.A. Froude suggests that the 'truth' of hagiography must be regarded as consisting in the 'religious impression' it was designed to create, rather than in its literal adherence to facts, implying that the same could be said of any form of historical writing. This is of course intellectual territory which is not far removed from Oscar Wilde's claim that 'the primary aim of the critics is to see the object as in itself it really is not',[155] where the cogency of the critic's or historian's vision is made to outweigh the issue of fidelity to sources.

The blurring of the distinction between the world presented in the text and the world inhabited by the reader outside the text which Thompson notes as characteristic of nineteenth-century critical re-

153 Excerpted in Owen Chadwick, *The Mind of The Oxford Movement* (London: Adam and Charles Black, 1960), 173–8.
154 Newman, *Development of Christian Doctrine*, 131.
155 Oscar Wilde, 'The Critic as Artist', in *Complete Works*, intro by Vyvyan Holland (London and Glasgow: Collins, 1966), 1030.

sponses to Yonge is reflected in Froude's problematization of the distinction between fiction and history, in a gesture which can ultimately be traced back to Keble's elision of the boundaries between Biblical typology and the natural world in *On the Mysticism which has been Attributed to some Early Fathers of the Church.*[156] But if fiction for Yonge can be in certain ways more 'real' than the reader's everyday world, conversely she identifies moral maturity with an attitude which regards the everyday world as in some ways 'fictional', in the sense that it recognizes the extent to which that world is a projection of desires which are inherently unrealizable. This sense of the 'fictionality', or typological aspect, of the world we inhabit appears clearly in Yonge's concept of the *bild* and its relationship to idolatry, which informs her treatment of relationships in several novels (notably *Hopes and Fears*, where it is referred to by name)[157] but is most clearly articulated in an 1853 letter to Marianne Dyson, the friend who supplied the plot idea which formed the germ of *The Heir of Redclyffe.*[158]

Yonge uses the German word *bild* to refer to the object of that modelling of the self on the mind's idea of an other which Carlyle referred to as 'hero-worship', but as is indicated by the introductory comment that the 'Bild-worship question is [...] a puzzle to me',[159] her attitude to this form of psychological identification is complex and nuanced:

> Of course, example and all we are told about it shows that, to a certain extent, Bilds are right, but somehow, whether it may be coldness or self-sufficiency I don't know; I don't think I go as far in it as you do in theory. I know women have a tendency that way, and it frightens me, because the most sensible and strong-minded are liable to be led astray; but I do not think it is such an order of nature as to make it a thing to be preached against and struggled against. I always remember one of Dr Pusey's letters that speaks of the desire for guidance, a good thing in itself, turning to be a temptation. I am very much

156 Keble, *On the Mysticism*, 171–4.
157 Yonge, *Hopes and Fears, or Scenes from the Life of a Spinster* (London: Macmillan, 1889), 524 (Ch.30).
158 Christabel Coleridge, *Charlotte Mary Yonge: Her Life and Letters* (London: Macmillan, 1903), 162.
159 Ibid., 189–95.

afraid of live Bilds ; you say, what makes you safe, have a standard external to your Bild, and do not make the Bild the standard, but I think considering the way of womenkind, that should be the prominent maxim, not only the qualifying one. You being strong and sensible yourself, the Bild worship has done you no harm, but for women with less soundness, to carry it as far as you do would be dangerous; I believe that is the mind of your impertinent Slave. The holy saving example in living people is what I fully recognise as you spoke of it, and I think you will see it in what Dorothea is to Lucy, or what Guy was to Charles, but there I think it ought to stop, and pope-making be treated in different degrees as silly, melancholy, or wrong, an infirmity.[160]

Yonge's reservations about the psychology of the *bild* here are obviously related to her sense that women are especially prone to 'the idolatry of affection',[161] which we discussed earlier in this chapter. The reference to making 'popes' of people, an idea which frequently appears in Yonge's novels,[162] places the discussion within the context of the conversions of prominent Tractarians such as Newman to Roman Catholicism, in the early 1850s still a very sensitive topic in the circles in which Yonge moved, a context which also seems relevant to Yonge's reference to Pusey's remark that the 'desire for guidance' could itself turn out to be a temptation – essentially the same argument which we have seen Keble made against Newman.[163] These remarks follow on from a discussion of an early version of *Hopes and Fears* which makes it clear that the essential problem Yonge sees in excessive 'Bild-worship' is that it is bound to end in disappointment since, as she puts it in her discussion of idolatry, 'our guides are but men'.[164] For a morally healthy form of 'Bild-worship' to be possible, what is required, Yonge seems to be suggesting, is a recognition of the fictionality or projective character of the *Bild*. This view also seems to inform Yonge's somewhat critical treatment in

160   Ibid.
161   Yonge, 'Conversations on the Catechism: Conversation XXXI. The Second Commandment', *MP* 9 (1855): 181.
162   E.g. Yonge, *The Three Brides* (London: Macmillan, 1900), 281 (Ch.32), Yonge, *Heartease*, p.370 (Part 3 Ch.12), Yonge, *Hopes and Fears*, 15 (Part 1 Ch.1).
163   Keble, *Sermons*, lxvi–lxviii.
164   Yonge, 'Conversations on the Catechism: Conversation XXXI. The Second Commandment', *MP* 9 (1855): 181.

Hopes and Fears of ritualist tendencies in Tractarianism; whilst ritualism, Yonge suggests, has a valuable moral influence on the character of the rather vague and unintellectual spinster Honora Charlecote, it leads her protegé the young Owen Sandbrook into a crisis of faith because Honora has not 'drawn the line more strongly between doctrine and opinion, fact and allegory, the true and the edifying'.[165] The difference between Honora and the young Owen seems to be that Honora has received ritualist practices as a *Bild*, that is as fictions standing in a typological relationship to essentially immaterial moral intuitions, whereas for Owen they have been ends in themselves, and hence idolatrous.

Yonge's reference to Guy acting as Charles Edmonstone's *Bild*[166] shows that she envisaged the relationships in *The Heir of Redclyffe* in the terms set out in this letter, and her reference to the need to have 'a standard external to your Bild' echoes, of course, the conversation in the novel where the nature of Amy and Guy's relationship is contrasted to the idolatrous and limiting projection of self that is the basis of the relationship between Philip and Laura.[167] In the terms of contemporary psychoanalysis, it could be said that in suggesting the need to recognize limitations to the extent to which any *Bild* can actually represent one's ego-ideal, Yonge is advocating an awareness of the essentially transferential nature of all relationships. From this viewpoint, Philip's disastrous over-investment in his romantic relationship with Laura could be seen to repeat his earlier mistake in idolizing the older sister who, we are told, 'brought him up in great part after his mother died':[168] Philip's bitter disappointment with her marriage seems a rather excessive reaction, in a way which recalls Freudian accounts of *Hamlet*.[169]

Yonge certainly published fiction in the *Monthly Packet* which employs an appeal to the typological relationships established by the

165   Yonge, *Hopes and Fears*, 557.
166   Cf. Coleridge, *Yonge*, 175.
167   Yonge, *Heir*, 553–4 (Ch.42).
168   Ibid., 56 (Ch.4).
169   Cf. T.S. Eliot, 'Hamlet', in Frank Kermode (ed.), *Selected Prose* (London: Faber and Faber, 1975), 48–9.

imagination to explore issues of transference,[170] and in her late reworking of the story of Cupid and Psyche, *Love and Life*, Yonge seems to be employing the concept of transference in order to resolve the plot. In Yonge's version of the story, the Psyche figure Aurelia Delavie thinks she has entered into a clandestine marriage with Mr Amyas Belamour, an elderly hypochondriac whom she has never actually seen because he is unable to leave his darkened room. Unbeknownst to her, however, she has actually married his young nephew, Sir Amyas Belamour, and towards the end of the novel her spinster older sister Betty complicates the fairy-tale plot by suggesting that Aurelia might really love the uncle who 'has been kind to her for a whole twelvemonth' rather than the 'charming boy' to whom she has barely spoken.[171] The uncle, however, proposes to Betty herself, pointing out that he had never actually seen Aurelia until the previous day, but that 'the voice, the goodness, the amiability, in fact all that I did truly esteem and prize in her I had already found matured and mellowed together'[172] in Betty herself, who has been responsible for Aurelia's upbringing. The substitutable nature of the relationships in the book suggests an awareness on Yonge's part of love as a form of transference, as well as reflecting what seems to have been the common Victorian practice of young men transferring their attentions to the sister if the initial object of their affections proved unavailable, a situation which is hinted at in the suggestion of romance between Guy and Laura which precedes Guy's attachment to Amy.

170   Margaret Gatty, 'Rabbit Tails', *Monthly Packet* 16 (Series 1 1858): 400–1.

171   Yonge, *Love and Life, An Old Story in Eighteenth Century Costume* (London: Macmillan, 1900), 395 (Ch.35).

172   Ibid., 415 (Ch.36).

Language and the Unconscious: Yonge's Critique of Utilitarianism

If we accept that Philip's behaviour in *The Heir of Redclyffe* is dominated by an unconscious infantile transference in which Laura plays the role of mother-substitute and Guy that of the father whom Philip longs to displace, then the critique of Utilitarianism which Barbara Dennis has noted in the novel can be seen to be directed above all at Utilitarianism's failure to acknowledge the unconscious dimension of human behaviour. In its portrayal of Philip, Yonge's novel anticipates the claims of Adorno and Horkheimer in *The Dialectic of Enlightenment* about the implicit totalitarianism of the Enlightenment project,[173] since, as the narrator's comment that 'Philip had been used to feel men's wills and characters bend and give way before his superior force of mind'[174] makes clear, Philip's rationalistic phantasy of infantile omnipotence requires nothing less than total domination. This aspect of the novel reflects a wider nineteenth-century response to the philosophical basis of Utilitarianism, as set out in J.S. Mill's *A System of Logic*, by thinkers sympathetic to an intuitionist standpoint. These reviewers of Mill find his philosophy lacking in its failure to acknowledge any unconscious or intuitive dimension to mental life, in a way which suggests that the typological presentation of unconscious forms of motivation which we have been examining in Yonge's realist fiction taps into the deep currents of nineteenth-century thought which are flowing in the direction of Modernist exploration of the unconscious.

The fact that a number of the major reviews of Mill's *Logic* are by associates of Newman suggests that the association of Philip with Utilitarianism in *The Heir of Redclyffe* can reasonably be viewed as a critique specifically of Mill, especially as Yonge is at pains to stress the humiliation of the repentant Philip's logical nature before the

---

173 Theoder Adorno and Max Horkheimer, *Dialectic of Enlightenment*, trans. John Cumming (London: Verso, 1979), *passim*.

174 Yonge, *Heir*, 255 (Ch.19).

good-hearted but puzzle-headed Mr Edmonstone.[175] The *Dublin Review*[176] in particular emphasizes the tendency of the Protestantism of which it sees Mill's *Logic* as symptomatic to intoxicate the mind, placing it in 'an unreal transcendental world of which each one might fancy himself the presiding deity',[177] a description of the frame of mind of the German Idealists which might also be applied to Philip's own conceited little mental world.[178] W.G. Ward's lengthy review of Mill's *Logic* in the *British Critic*, a periodical which we know Yonge read,[179] argues against Mill's depreciation of formal, syllogistic logic and emphasis on induction from experience as characterizing all productive forms of reasoning by stressing 'the prodigious complexity of human consciousness; the incalculable number of synthetical judgements, which we are forming *inadvertently* every hour of the day',[180] an argument which appeals against Mill's rationalistic outlook to the role of the unconscious in mental processes.

For Ward, as for Newman, religious and moral truth is essentially inarticulable in rational terms, so that it is only representable at all by that kind of typological fiction or myth which Newman describes as an 'economy':[181]

> Viewing then the Church collective starting after the apostles' death on her aggressive course, we find her, as might have been expected, fully possessed of, and energizing in, those doctrines, which are the cardinal points of faith; eg the Trinity, the Incarnation, the Eucharistic Presence [...] Her *idea* of them, the *impression* they form on her mind, is infinitely indeed below the original truths themselves, yet is it 'the nearest approach to them which our present state allows;' as being received by the *moral* faculty: that faculty, which is more

---

175 Ibid., 479–80, 535 (Chs 36, 40).
176 William Jennings, 'Tendencies of Modern Logic', *Dublin Review* 36 (1854): 419–51. Given that Jennings was based at Maynooth College, and that Newman was rector of the newly established Catholic University of Ireland at this point, it is reasonable to assume that Jennings was influenced by Newman when he wrote this review.
177 Jennings, 'Modern Logic', 450.
178 Yonge, *Heir*, 521 (Ch.39).
179 Romanes, *Yonge: An Appreciation*, 138–44.
180 W.G. Ward, Review of *A System of Logic* by J.S. Mill, *British Critic* 34 (1843): 358.
181 Newman, *University Sermons*, 342–3.

truly heavenly in its origin, and in its nature more akin to heaven, than any other part of man's constitution. On these subjects, then, the task which remains for her is, to bring before her own notice one particular after another of her complex and mysterious consciousness, to regard it steadily and distinctly, to project it, as it were from the moral on the intellectual faculty, to express in accurate language the result of such projection, and to follow out the result so obtained into those intellectual consequences which necessarily flow from it.[182]

In suggesting that our intellectual apprehension of 'ineffable and transcendent'[183] moral truths can amount to no more than a 'projection', Ward incidentally provides a rationale for regarding fiction as a source of moral knowledge, rather than mere entertainment. Within Mill's empiricist epistemology, where all valid forms of knowledge are supposed ultimately to be reducible to inductions from sense-experience, fiction, which by definition is not a direct representation of experience, cannot perform any intellectual function. But within the epistemological framework suggested by Ward (which is recognizably derived from Common Sense philosophy), abstract philosophizing on moral questions is just as much a fiction as a novel like *The Heir of Redclyffe*, which seeks to embody moral stances in the characters it presents. This intuitionist epistemology is clearly to the advantage of a woman writer such as Yonge, because it implies that it is less important for the novelist to represent a wide variety of experience than to present their material in such as way that it prompts an awareness in the reader of the moral intuitions that inform their response to the novel. The very process of fiction-making and reading becomes a source of moral knowledge in its own right.

Ward's argument for the value of formal logic can thus also be read as an argument for the value of fiction, given that, in Ward's terms, the very attempt to devise a verbal form to convey the 'ten thousand lessons of practical wisdom' which are 'the results [...] of personal experience'[184] can and should be regarded as a legitimate contribution to knowledge, since the value derived from such representations derives in any case from the '*internal* evidence' which

182   Ward, 'Review of Mill's *Logic*', 403.
183   Ibid., 359.
184   Ibid., 378 (incorrectly paginated as 398).

206

the audience's minds 'furnish of themselves',[185] a point echoed in other reviews of Mill's *Logic*.[186] From the intuitionist standpoint represented by Ward and other reviewers, what is valuable about the practice of formal logic lies less in its effort after abstraction than in its grappling with the question of how to represent unconscious intuitions in the verbal medium, a characteristic which it shares with fiction. The review of Mill's *Logic* in the Catholic periodical *The Month*, for example, criticizes Mill for failing to account for the productive role which language plays in human thought: since, as the reviewer notes, all arguments would appear tautological 'to an intelligence that saw the full import of its own perceptions',[187] verbal reasoning must be regarded as 'a process adapted to the nature of a being, that does not always know the truth when it has it'.[188] Language in this view is a progressive revelation of the unconscious, a conception of the transcending of human intentionality by language with which Yonge's agreement is shown by Ethel's argument in *The Daisy Chain* against the liberalizing tendencies of the Stoneborough Ladies Committee, who are hostile to rote-learning of the catechism and other religious texts:

> 'What do you think, Ritchie?' asked Ethel. 'Is it not too bad that they should have it all their own way, and spoil the whole female population? Why, the last thing they did was to leave off reading the Prayer-book prayers morning and evening! And it is much expected that next they will attack all learning by heart.'
> 'It is too bad', said Richard, 'but Flora can hardly hinder them.'
> 'It will be one voice', said Ethel; 'but oh! if I could only say half what I have in my mind, they must see the error. Why, these, these – what they call formal – these the ties – links on to the Church – on to what is good – if they don't learn them soundly – rammed down hard – you know what I mean – so that they can't remember the first – remember when they did not know them – they will never get to learn – know – understand when they can understand!'

185   Ibid., 393.
186   Cf. Anon., Review of *A System of Logic* by J.S. Mill, *Prospective Review* 6 (1850): 93; Anon., Review of *A System of Logic* by J.S. Mill, *British Quarterly Review* 4 (1846): 7.
187   Anon., 'The Revolution – in Logic', *The Month* 15: 401.
188   Ibid., 400.

'My dear Ethel, don't frown so horribly, or it will spoil your eloquence', said Margaret.

'I don't understand either', said Richard gravely. 'Not understand when they can understand? What do you mean?'

'Why, Ritchie, don't you see? If they don't learn them – hard, firm, by rote when they can't – they won't understand when they can.'

'If they don't learn when they can't, they won't understand when they can?' puzzled Richard, making Margaret laugh; but Ethel was too much in earnest for amusement.

'If they don't learn them by rote when they have strong memories. Yes, that's it!' she continued; 'they will not know them well enough to understand them when they are old enough!'

'Who won't learn and understand what?' said Richard.

'Oh, Ritchie, Ritchie! Why the children – the Psalms – the Gospels – the things. They ought to know them, love them, grow up to them, before they know the meaning, or they won't care. Memory, association, affection, all those come when one is younger than comprehension!'

'Younger than one's own comprehension?'

'Richard, you are grown more tiresome than ever. Are you laughing at me?'

'Indeed, I beg your pardon – I did not mean it', said Richard. 'I am very sorry to be so stupid.'

'My dear Ritchie, it was only my blundering – never mind.'

'But what did you mean? I want to know, indeed, Ethel.'

'I mean that memory and association come before comprehension, so that one ought to know all good things – fa – with familiarity before one can understand, because understanding does not make one love. Oh! one does that before, and, when the first little gleam, little bit of a sparklet of the meaning does come, then it is so valuable and so delightful.'

'I never heard of a little bit of a sparklet before', said Richard, 'but I think I do see what Ethel means; and it is like what I heard and liked in a university sermon some Sundays ago, saying that these lessons and holy words were to be impressed on us here from infancy on earth, that we might be always unravelling their meaning, and learn it fully at last – where we hope to be.'

'The very same thought!' exclaimed Margaret, delighted; 'but', after a pause, 'I am afraid the Ladies' Committee might not enter into it in plain English, far less in Ethel's language.'[189]

The comedy of Ethel's incoherent expression here mimes the process which she is describing, whereby language progressively articulates unconscious intuitions; the 'university sermon' to which

189   Yonge, *Daisy Chain*, 254 (Part 1 Ch.24).

Richard refers in order to sum up her argument is presumably one of Newman's. Just as in Ward's argument about 'the incalculable number of synthetical judgements, which we are forming *inadvertently* every hour of the day',[190] so too Yonge insists on the priority of unconscious moral intuitions to rational comprehension, because 'understanding does not make one love'. This position is reflected in the numerous deathbed scenes in Yonge's novels where the suffering of the dying is lessened by the repetition of texts which they know by heart.[191]

The connection between language and unconscious moral intuition which I have been suggesting forms the basis for mid-nineteenth-century critiques of Mill's *Logic*, and underlies the theory of fiction as a means to moral knowledge which is embodied in Yonge's novelistic technique, can also be found in the work of the influential mid-Victorian aesthetic theorist E.S. Dallas, in a way that illustrates the continuity I have been claiming between Yonge's narrative mode of typological realism and later Symbolist and Modernist exploration of the unconscious. Dallas stresses the connection between the unconscious dimension of the mind and the wholeness of apprehension characteristic of the aesthetic,[192] referring to Common Sense philosophers such as Thomas Brown and Dugald Stewart in support of his argument.[193] Dallas's argument can be compared to Ward's claim that 'those mysterious feelings which are called forth by the sense of beauty' are evidence for the way in which the 'innate moral sense [...] enters as an important element in a vast number of judgements, even in the minds of those who most resolutely discredit its existence'.[194]

Ward interprets the relationship between aesthetics and the moral sense within a typological frame of reference, characterizing aesthetic emotions as 'media, by which heavenly and supernatural truths are, in

190 Ward, Review of Mill's *Logic*, 358.
191 E.g. Yonge, *Heir*, 467 (Ch.35).
192 E.S. Dallas, *The Gay Science*, 2 vols (London: Chapman and Hall, 1866), 1: 305.
193 Ibid., 1: 185, 187.
194 Ward, Review of Mill's *Logic*, 398.

various measure, shadowed forth to the believer's mind',[195] and religious references also play a significant role in Dallas's argument. Echoing Keble's account of poetry, Dallas sees in 'the theory of mysticism' evidence that:

> The theory of a hidden mental life which is only now beginning to be understood, has, although misunderstood, been always fully recognized in philosophy as one of the great facts of our moral nature, and as such has been the seed of many a strange, many a potent system of thought.[196]

Ultimately, however, Dallas's viewpoint is more secular, since he interprets the religious claim that we must 'accept the Christian doctrine before we see it to be true, and as the first step to a recognition of its truth'[197] merely as one manifestation of the more general phenomenon of unconscious mental function, rather than as something which shows the intrinsically religious nature of the unconscious as assumed by Tractarians such as Newman and Yonge. Dallas's aesthetics implicitly anticipate the controversial claim that art has no moral function made by leading members of the Aesthetic Movement such as Wilde and Whistler later in the nineteenth century, distinguishing between the non-rational intuitions represented by art and the promptings of the moral sense in a way which is not done by earlier writers such as Ward.

The relationship between language and the unconscious in nineteenth-century thought suggests the further possibility that Yonge may have conceived of her novels' effect on readers as akin to mesmeric influence. Nineteenth-century medical thought regarded novels as directly affecting readers' nerves, in a way which threatened to induce a condition of nervous debility through overstimulation,[198] and this conception of the intimate connection between language and the nerves also underlies Keble's contrasting claim that poetry has a

---

195 Dallas, *Gay Science*, 398.
196 Ibid., 1: 247.
197 Ibid.
198 Thomas Beddoes, *Hygeia, or Essays Moral and Medical on the Causes Affecting the Personal State of Our Middling and Affluent Classes*, 3 vols (Bristol: Phillips, 1802-3), 3: 164.

210

'soothing' effect.[199] In view of the emphasis on 'the incalculable number of synthetical judgements, which we are forming *inadvertently* every hour of the day'[200] which we have found in Ward, however, it would have been possible for an author such as Yonge to view the overwhelming flood of sensory detail characteristic of the novel, usually regarded as harmful by nineteenth-century thinkers, as connecting directly with that unconscious faculty of moral intuition which was constantly making responses to the demands of everyday life. In the hands of an author who sought to integrate realist detail through the associative coherence of typology, as I have argued Yonge does, the novel could become a means of educating the reader's moral intuition by unconsciously conveying a consistency of moral response, without ever being explicitly didactic. The relationship between writer and reader could thus be compared to that between the mesmerist and his subjects, who manifested previously unsuspected intuitive powers such as clairvoyance whilst under his influence.[201]

Nicola Thompson's conclusion that in nineteenth-century reviews '*The Heir of Redclyffe* is feminized, functioning in the public eye as a metonymical representation of the ideal woman, and like her, achieving transcendence through a spiritual path that short-circuits structures of temporal power, value, judgement, or hierarchy',[202] supports this interpretation of Yonge's novels as mesmeric texts. In the following chapters, I will look more closely at the relationship between Yonge's portrayal of women, nineteenth-century medical ideas about the relationship between nerves and mesmerism, and the Tractarian emphasis on the pursuit of holiness through discipline of the self in order to show that the preoccupation with the effects of the unconscious which I have been arguing characterizes Yonge's writing at a formal level is also present at a thematic level in her work.

---

199 Keble, *Keble's Lectures on Poetry, 1832–1841*, 2 vols, trans. Edward Kershaw Francis (Oxford: Clarendon Press, 1912), 1: 25.
200 Ward, Review of Mill's *Logic*, 358.
201 Alison Winter, *Mesmerized: Powers of Mind in Victorian Britain* (Chicago: University of Chicago, 1998), 77–8.
202 Thompson, *Reviewing Sex*, 100.

Section Three
Tractarianism, Feminism and the Nervous Female Body in Yonge's Domestic Fiction

Critics have often described Yonge as an 'antifeminist', but this characterization fails to do justice to the duality of Yonge's Tractarian position, in which an acceptance of women's natural physical inferiority to men is balanced by a claim that this very physical weakness makes women potentially more receptive to the immaterial intuitions of divine grace. A similar duality is typical of Victorian domestic ideology, in which the receptivity to the feelings of others which makes it impossible for women to survive the competitive pressures of the public sphere is precisely what makes the private female realm of home represent a moral ideal superior to the public sphere. Tractarian doctrinal emphasis on the Incarnation, however, implies that the Church bridges the realms of natural and supernatural in a way that makes the integration of the split female subject representative of Christian moral struggle in general. The Tractarian perspective radicalizes both domestic ideology and the common Victorian belief in women's immaterial moral 'influence' by suggesting that moral progress is only possible on the basis of a feminization of society in which immaterial moral values become incarnate in social institutions in the way that is characteristic of the home.

In this context, Yonge's emphasis on the need for women to develop their capacity for self-control, which reflects the Tractarians' reconceptualization of religious practice in the terms of associationist psychology, represents a discourse of female empowerment. The ability to manage the home, for which Ethel May in *The Daisy Chain* gives up her study of Latin and Greek in an episode often characterized by present-day feminist critics as 'repressive', in Yonge's fictional world spills over into the transformation of the society around the home, since female self-discipline in this respect constitutes an organizing associative centre around which cohesive social institutions gradually coalesce.

In line with nineteenth-century medical thinking, Yonge regarded self-control as presenting particular problems for women due to their irritable nerves, but her fiction holds out the promise that such self-discipline will be rewarded by the quasi-supernatural power of female 'influence', a concept which I suggest has strong links with the Victorian discourse of mesmerism which makes its appearance in her novels. Yonge's heroines, I argue, show a consistent pattern of development from a state of nervous irritability, which they learn to recognize and master, to a condition of moral empowerment described in terms which have supernatural or mesmeric overtones.

Chapter Six
Tractarian Feminism in Yonge

Was Yonge an Antifeminist? Religious Feminism in *Womankind*

Yonge's critics have often expressed some unease about her views on the proper role of women. In her 1943 biography, Georgina Battiscombe found Yonge's *Womankind*, the advice manual for young ladies she published in the early 1870s, simply laughable,[1] and later feminist critics have resorted to reading against the grain of her fiction in order to identify coded or repressed feminist impulses. Catherine Sandbach-Dahlström, for example, suggests that the recurrence of crippled characters in Yonge's work unconsciously expresses an internalized anger at the restricted life open to middle-class women,[2] a mode of interpreting her novels against which Alethea Hayter protests as one which 'disintegrates, rather than deconstructs, her work' in a search for 'a more fashionable sub-text'.[3]

Hayter, however, also feels uncomfortable with Yonge's 'degree of male chauvinism' and 'the demands for womanly submission made throughout her works'.[4] Although protesting against the 'determination to find fault with every aspect of Miss Yonge's work' in feminist critics such as Juliet Dusinberre and Elaine Showalter, which she shows is often based on rather a limited acquaintance with Yonge's life and work,[5] Hayter attributes Yonge's apparently conflict-free

---

1 Georgina Battiscombe, *Charlotte Mary Yonge: The Story of an Uneventful Life* (London: Constable, 1944), 148–50.
2 Catherine Sandbach-Dahlström, *Be Good Sweet Maid: Charlotte Yonge's Domestic Fictior A Study in Dogmatic Purpose and Fictional Form* (Stockholm: Almqvist & Wicksel, 1984), 171–6.
3 Alethea Hayter, *Charlotte Yonge* (Plymouth: Northcote House, 1996), 14.
4 Ibid., 56–61.
5 Ibid., 56.

acceptance of male dominance to a 'special temperament' which found emotional satisfaction in 'non-sexual companionship with able and dominating elder men'.[6] Hayter suggests that this 'special temperament' constitutes a limitation in Yonge's moral outlook, in that she 'extrapolated from her own experience' in 'thinking that such parental rule was mandatory for all women in all circumstances', although she does note that Yonge has remarkably little time for 'soft submissive helpless women'.[7]

Hayter's emphasis on Yonge's 'special temperament' makes her seem like a psychological anomaly, and does little to explain the popularity and lasting appeal of Yonge's fiction to young Victorian women. The symptomatic reading of Yonge which Sandbach-Dahlström proposes, however, is not really any more satisfactory. The problem with analysing Yonge's fiction in terms of symptoms of displaced emotion is that Yonge is too psychologically aware for the suggestion that particular themes unconsciously convey her own repressed anger to be particularly convincing. Psychological processes of displacement and transference are frequently portrayed in her novels,[8] and given Yonge's own regular practice of psychological self-scrutiny,[9] it is hard to imagine that the psychological significance of her own recurrent fictional themes would simply have escaped her. This is not to rule out the possibility that Yonge projected aspects of her own personality into her characters, nor that, given Victorian medicine's pervasive emphasis on psychosomatic causes of illness,[10] the crippled condition of some of her characters may reflect feelings

6   Ibid., 62.

7   Ibid., 62–5.

8   E.g. Charlotte M. Yonge, *The Two Guardians, or Home in This World* (London: Masters, 1885), 74 (Ch.5); Yonge, *Hopes and Fears, or Scenes from the Life of a Spinster* (London: Macmillan, 1889), 491–2 (Part 2 Ch.27).

9   Christabel Coleridge, *Charlotte Mary Yonge: Her Life and Letters* (London: Macmillan, 1903), 232–4.

10   Janet Oppenheim, *'Shattered Nerves': Doctors; Patients and Depression in Victorian England* (New York: Oxford University Press, 1991), 44–9; Yonge's familiarity with this aspect of Victorian medicine is shown by the reference to hypochondria in *Love and Life, An Old Story in Eighteenth Century Costume* (London: Macmillan, 1900), 147 (Ch.14).

of frustration.[11] Yonge would have regarded it, however, as her own duty, quite as much as that of her characters, to become aware of the influence of such feelings, and to struggle against them as the temptations belonging to her own particular condition,[12] just as Charles Edmonstone in *The Heir of Redclyffe* struggles against the temperamental irritability associated with his diseased hip.

Critical characterizations of Yonge as an antifeminist writer are based not so much on her novels as on *Womankind*, which opens with what seems an uncompromising statement that 'I have no hesitation in declaring my full belief in the inferiority of women, nor that she brought it on herself'.[13] It would be a mistake, however, to assume that Yonge's acceptance of women's natural inferiority (shared even by writers who have been accepted into the feminist canon)[14] is all there is to her thinking. Yonge's allusion to the consequences of the Fall is followed by an account of the elevation of woman from the 'squaw' of 'savage life' to 'her rightful position of help-meet' under Christianity, where 'the Blessing conferred upon the holy Mother of our Lord became the antidote to the punishment of Eve's transgression',[15] an account which can be compared to the historical narrative offered by other nineteenth-century women writers in support of a feminist stance.[16] Yonge then proceeds to pose 'the woman's question of the day':

> Is she meant to be nothing but the help-meet? If by this is meant the wife, or even the sister or daughter, attached to the aid of some particular man, I do not think she is. It is her most natural, most obvious, most easy destiny; but one of

11 Yonge confessed in a letter to Christabel Coleridge that she didn't feel she lived up to the 'goodness' of her characters (Coleridge, *Yonge*, 125–8).

12 For Tractarians, it was a religious duty to undertake severe self-scrutiny in order to identify the unconscious tendencies leading you into sin, see Pusey's sermon 'The Besetting Sin' in *Parochial Sermons*, 3 vols (London: Walter Smith, 1883), 2: 132–42.

13 Yonge, 'Womankind', *Monthly Packet* 17 (Series 2 1874): 24.

14 E.g. Mary Wollstonecraft, *Vindication of the Rights of Woman*, Miriam Brody (ed.) (Harmondsworth: Penguin, 1982), 109, 123–4.

15 Yonge, 'Womankind', *MP* 17 (1874): 25–6.

16 Cf. Margaret Fuller, *Woman in the Nineteenth Century* (Oxford: Oxford University Press, 1994), 29–34.

the greatest incidental benefits that Christianity brought the whole sex was that of rendering marriage no longer the only lot of all, and thus making both the wife and the maiden stand on higher ground [...] Wifehood was dignified by becoming a faint type or shadow of the Union of the Church with her Lord. Motherhood was ennobled by the Birth that saves the world; and Maidenhood acquired a glory it had never had before, and which taught the unmarried to regard themselves not as beings who had failed in the purpose of their existence, but as pure creatures, free to devote themselves to the service of their Lord; for if His Birth had consecrated maternity, it had also consecrated virginity.[17]

From Yonge's Tractarian perspective, the coming of Christ has cancelled out the natural inferiority of women at the same moment that it has cancelled out original sin. The order of grace has superseded the order of nature in a way that is expressed by the new typological significance taken on by the position of women, whether married or unmarried. It is Laura's neglect of this 'higher ground' in *The Heir of Redclyffe*, as we have seen in the previous chapter, that makes her a man's 'slave and automaton'.[18]

This interpretation of *Womankind* suggests that Yonge is best characterized as a religious feminist comparable to Christina Rossetti, rather than as an antifeminist. The articles which Yonge chose to publish in the *Monthly Packet* (of which it is not unlikely that the young Christina Rossetti may have been a reader)[19] strongly support a case for Yonge's feminism. In the very first number, for example, Yonge republishes a letter to the eighteenth-century bluestocking Elizabeth Carter, emphasizing Carter's scholarship whilst characteristically reminding her readers that 'she fulfilled all her homely housewifely duties without despising them';[20] that Carter was not just a passing interest of Yonge's is shown by her appearance at the conclusion of Yonge's late allegorical romance *Love and Life*, as the

17   Yonge, 'Womankind', *MP* 17 (1874): 26–7.
18   Yonge, *The Heir of Redclyffe*, Barbara Dennis (ed.) (Oxford: Oxford University Press, 1997), 553, 447 (Chs 42, 34)
19   I would like to thank my PhD student, Serena Trowbridge for pointing out this possibility.
20   Anon., 'An Old Letter', *Monthly Packet* 1 (Series 1 1851): 127. This article is probably by Yonge herself.

recipient of a letter from Elizabeth Montagu.[21] In other early numbers, 'The Cardioscope', a whimsical short story modelled on Addison's *Spectator* allegories, contains a mother who states bluntly that marriage is 'unworthy to be the ultimate object of an immortal being',[22] and 'Minor Cares', a fictionalized series on moral dilemmas in domestic life, has its exemplary role model describe how she has managed to escape the empty-headed existence implicit in being 'nothing but a fashionable young lady'.[23] Slightly later numbers start to contain positive references to 'sisterhoods',[24] all-female communities of women in Protestant countries devoted to charitable works – a highly controversial topic in Britain during the 1850s, in part because of the gender politics involved.[25]

Yonge rehearses at greater length many of the arguments to which she alludes in the first chapter of *Womankind* in one of her 1857 articles on the catechism. In a discussion of 'the law of purity' (i.e. the prohibition of adultery) in the Seventh Commandment she contrasts the condition of women under Christianity, where 'her submission becomes merely the safe and happy obedience of love', with that of women in 'civilized nations with a false religion', where wives are treated as 'distrusted and jealously guarded playthings', adding that with 'the later corrupt philosophy' of the Roman Empire 'came irregular marriages, perpetual divorces, and womanhood degraded, the sure sign of the decay of a nation'.[26] Given the pervasively typological frame of reference of the *Monthly Packet*, these references to the detrimental effects of 'false religion' and 'corrupt philosophy' on the position of women would have been read as allusions to the Britain of Yonge's own day – not a great interpretative leap for

---

21 Yonge, *Love and Life*, 426 (Ch.37)
22 Anon., 'The Cardioscope', *Monthly Packet* 2 (Series 1 1851): 24.
23 Anon., 'Minor Cares', *Monthly Packet* 7 (Series 1 1854): 123.
24 Anon., 'Likes and Dislikes', *Monthly Packet* 11 (Series 1 1856): 436; 'Likes and Dislikes', *Monthly Packet* 12: 360.
25 Robert P. Fletcher, '"Convent Thoughts": Augusta Webster and the Body Politics of the Victorian Cloister', *Victorian Literature and Culture* 31, no.1 (2003): 297–8.
26 Yonge, 'Conversations on the Catechism', *Monthly Packet* 14 (Series 1 1857): 229.

Victorian readers to make, as is shown by the example of Bulwer-Lytton's historical novel *The Last Days of Pompeii*, which was widely understood as a commentary on contemporary society.[27] The danger of such 'corrupt philosophy' to women is central to Yonge's early novel *The Two Guardians*, which turns on the impossibility of any truly equal relationship with a man who has taken up 'Germanism', and regards Christianity as 'all very well now for women and weak-minded people'.[28]

Yonge's discussion of adultery and its causes is far removed from critical stereotypes of Victorian 'hypocrisy', and anticipates in some respects the feminist 'social purity' campaigns of the 1870s:[29]

> Truly this sin, which makes woman a ruinous tempter, the degrader instead of the help-meet, the author and the victim of the worst miseries of this world – this sin has its chief root in feminine vanities and roving curiosity, 'the lust of the flesh and the lust of the eye', shown in the first sad example in holy Scripture. That brother and sister, Joseph and Dinah, stand out in strong contrast: the one holding no parley with temptation, but avoiding it, and simply calling it 'great wickedness', and a 'sin against God;' the other going forth from her father's tent to see the daughters of the land, and falling through her restless love of amusement – one keeping out of temptation, the other running into it; perhaps from the self-willed desire of frolic which is the bane of so many young girls, who will not obey because they do not see why. The not knowing *why* is the trial and the safeguard. Often, where there is much temptation and little protection, wilful pleasure leads to the worst consequences; and even among those whom their station shelters, eager love of diversion or admiration, and contempt of the advice of elders, is the very temper of Dinah. Nay, without stirring from home, prying or whispering gossip upon things 'not to be named' shows the same spirit. I do not mean knowledge of facts, but thinking of them [...]
>
> A woman whose high spirits or love of admiration lead her beyond what her parents, her husband, or her own sense of right show her to be prudent or decorous, may not in our time, or in our rank, come to actual disgrace, but is

27   J.I. Fradin, 'The Novels of Edward Bulwer-Lytton', University Microfilms, Ann Arbor, Michigan, facs. edn, 1973 Doctoral Dissertation Series, publication no.19,238 (Columbia University, 1956), 252–7.
28   Yonge, *Two Guardians*, 147 (Ch.9), 306–7 (Ch.16).
29   Elizabeth K. Helsinger, Robin Lauterbach Sheets and William Veeder, *The Woman Question: Society and Literature in Britain and America, 1837–1883*, 3 vols (New York: Garland, 1983), 2: 202

that owing to herself? Not, of course, that I mean that all gaiety deserves such condemnation, but what I would say is, that if we have ever found ourselves led by the intoxication of pleasure, or or receiving attention, into the borders of aught unmaidenly, then we have no right to 'cast the first stone', and should the more earnestly pray that our *hearts* may keep this law. When levity has been the destruction of many, should we be 'high-minded' because our homes are guarded?[30]

The story from Genesis to which Yonge alludes here ends with Dinah's brothers Simeon and Levi taking revenge despite the offer of marriage by Shechem, an offer which conventional Victorian morality would have regarded as compensating for his act of seduction.[31] The moral vocabulary in which Yonge couches her typological reading of this Biblical episode takes us recognizably (if somewhat anachronistically) into the world of her fiction, where a 'restless love of amusement' exposes Lucilla in *Hopes and Fears*, for example, to the unwanted and vaguely threatening attentions of the millionaire Mr Calthorpe,[32] and cautions against the 'intoxication of [...] receiving attention' are a regular occurrence.[33] Although Yonge does not treat adultery as an explicit theme in her novels, these parallels show her interest in exploring states of mind which she regards as morally equivalent to adultery, exposing the naïvety of the critical claim that issues of sexuality are absent from her writing.[34]

Yonge breaks with conventional Victorian moral rhetoric by refusing to demonize the fallen woman, arguing that her moral condition is identical to that of the nominally virtuous woman of fashion and suggesting that the ultimate outcome of 'what one is apt to think excusable and natural, the love of gaiety and pleasure' is irrelevant by religious standards, since it is dependent 'chiefly on the state of society, on the fear of man, not the fear of God'.[35] The moral equivalency Yonge finds between the condition of adultery and the surrender of self to fashionable life conveys a similar message to the

---

30 Yonge, 'Conversations on the Catechism', *MP* 14 (1857): 230–2.
31 Genesis, 34:1–31
32 Yonge, *Hopes and Fears*, 210 (Part 2 Ch.7)
33 Cf. Yonge, *Heir*, 177–8 (Ch.12)
34 Battiscombe, *Yonge*, 88.
35 Yonge, 'Conversations on the Catechism', 231.

comparison drawn in D.G. Rossetti's poem 'Jenny', where the speaker cannot distinguish in moral terms between the young prostitute and his cousin Nell, who is 'so mere a woman in her ways'.[36]

As in the case of later feminist 'social purity' campaigners, attitudes in Yonge that might at first sight appear repressive or puritanical can be seen to represent a form of protest against a male-dominated society's 'traffic in women';[37] the social norms of fashionable life are to be resisted because they implicitly favour male power, reducing even outwardly respectable women to the moral condition of prostitutes. In this context, respect for the advice of parents is the best safeguard for female independence, as we have already seen in relation to Yonge's portrayal of the way Laura in *The Heir of Redclyffe* is seduced by Philip into a condition of moral slavery.[38]

The Centrality of the Domestic in Tractarian Moral Thought

Despite her initial critical characterization of Yonge as an 'anti-feminist' writer,[39] June Sturrock draws attention to Yonge's indifference in her fiction to the conventional Victorian view that the lives of men and women should occupy 'separate spheres'. Sturrock argues that Yonge's novels evince 'a genuine distaste for the public realm as such, as dangerous both physically and spiritually', manifested, for example, in the way university education at Oxford is responsible for

36   D.G. Rossetti, 'Jenny', in *Poetical Works*, W.M. Rossetti (ed.) (London: Ellis and Elvey, 1895), l 186.

37   Cf. Gayle Rubin, 'The Traffic in Women: Notes on the "Political Economy" of Sex', in *Toward an Anthropology of Women*, R. Reiter (ed.) (New York: Monthly Review Press, 1975).

38   Yonge, *Heir*, 153–4 (Ch.10).

39   June Sturrock, *'Heaven and Home': Charlotte M Yonge's Domestic Fiction and the Victorian Debate Over Women*, English Literary Studies (Victoria, BC: University of Victoria, 1995), 13.

the religious doubts of Norman May in *The Daisy Chain*.[40] Male figures in Yonge's fiction, Sturrock suggests, are understood primarily in relationship to 'domestic values', and so are to this extent 'feminized',[41] with Dr May's 'nurturing qualities' as a doctor, fostered by his rejection of London practice, being portrayed as having played an important role in his professional success.[42] In support of Sturrock's view, one might also adduce the episode in *Hopes and Fears* where the aspiring slum priest Robert Fulmort is advised by Honora Charlecote not to reject the little feminine touches by which his sister Phoebe has endeavoured to make his rooms more comfortable, because without these concessions to domesticity 'you will never do your work efficiently'.[43] Later on in the novel, Robert's acceptance of domesticity is shown to have benefited him morally, in that he has become less 'stern' in judging others.[44]

Sturrock argues that the emphasis on domesticity in Yonge's novels is linked to their moral preoccupations. The moral importance of the trivial is emphasized in the fragment of verse which is repeatedly echoed in *The Heir of Redclyffe* ('Little things/On little wings/Bear little souls to heaven'),[45] and Sturrock notes that this is reflected in 'Guy's delicately-tuned conscience and exaggerated penance', for which the model was Hurrell Froude, described by Sturrock as 'guilt-ridden over scruples of conscience and minutiae of thought and behaviour'.[46] Sturrock draws attention to the way in which Yonge's writing benefits from the moral weight attached to surmounting everyday trials by Froude and Keble, since 'the spiritual significance of the practical, and of the apparently trivial and the minute, validates domestic fiction; it also validates the traditionally feminine, because of the traditional cultural association between the feminine and the particular'.[47] Although Sturrock recognizes some

40 Sturrock, *Heaven and Home*, 98.
41 Ibid., 98–104.
42 Ibid., 46.
43 Yonge, *Hopes and Fears*, 239 (Part 2 Ch.10).
44 Ibid., 476 (Part 2 Ch.26).
45 Yonge, *Heir*, 41, 103–4, 497 (Chs 4, 7, 37).
46 Sturrock, *Heaven and Home*, 98–104.
47 Ibid., 109.

important implications of Tractarianism for Yonge as a woman writer, she tends to underplay the wider cultural resonance of this focus on the moral demands of domestic life by describing Froude and Keble in terms which imply that they were merely fussy, or morbidly introspective – a gesture which, self-defeatingly for an argument claiming significance for Yonge's novels, minimizes these writers' importance for our understanding of Victorian culture by feminizing them. But rather than just being an aspect of Froude's or Keble's personal scrupulosity, an emphasis on the need to attend to the moral quality of one's response to quotidian vexations is thoroughly characteristic of the thought of all the Tractarians, and is reflected in their preaching.

Pusey, for example, in the sermons originally published as part of a companion series to the *Tracts for the Times*, suggests that the very phrase 'the "crosses" of daily life' is 'a witness against us, how meekly we ought to bear them, in the blessed steps of our Holy Lord', arguing that such checks are particularly morally beneficial in 'our earliest years, since then we are most subject to the wills of others; and to those, who are yet young, every contradiction of their will, whether from elders or from the rudenesses of those of their own age, every little ailment, every petty disappointment, will, if they take it cheerfully, become a blessing'.[48] The fact that Pusey specifies the period of youth as one in which frustration from parents or school-fellows is likely to prove a hidden boon indicates the basis of Tractarian moral theology in associationist thinking: external restraint providentially teaches self-restraint, and so develops that control of the will which the Victorians had particularly in mind when they referred to 'character', a view which helps to explain the consistent emphasis on submission to parents in Yonge's fiction. Yonge herself seems to be thinking in these terms when in a letter she expresses regret that since the death of her mother (her last surviving parent) she no longer has anyone at home to get regularly irritated by – in Tractarian terms, the absence of need for self-control is not a good thing.[49] Just how disastrous unchecked self-will can be is the subject

48 Pusey, *Parochial Sermons*, 3: 61–2.
49 Battiscombe, *Yonge*, 125–8.

of Yonge's early novel, *Henrietta's Wish* where the heroine, by getting her own way, unintentionally causes the death of her mother.[50]

Pusey's claim that having your will thwarted is a blessing in disguise is not just conventional piety, but is grounded at once in his theology of sin and in early nineteenth-century psychological theory. Pusey stresses that no sin takes place in isolation from the development of character as whole, in a way that he suggests can have significant repercussions for one's state of mental health:

> Consider also, how seldom sins are single! [...] Sins [...] are interwoven together in a sad chain, so that one sin opens the door for others, draws them in after it, spots and pollutes every thing else, even what, but for this, might have been acceptable service, even when it does not draw the whole man to perdition. There have been, who have given way to one wrong habit, only half knowing that it was wrong, not realizing that it was sin, except that they resolved against it; and these have, towards the close of life, had their eyes opened, seen their sin. But then they saw also how it had spoiled the whole of their conduct, how it spread like a cancer, eating out and corrupting what was good; how what they fell short in could be traced to this one sin; how the evil they at any time did was its bitter fruit [...] Whoever has been awakened to see in himself any one such sin, and has traced it through his life, has been amazed to see how on every side it branched off into other sin, how it spoiled his whole self [...] Thus does conscience itself, thus does our own implanted sense of right bear witness to the text; and not less our daily judgement in the things of this life. We count him a madman, who though in his senses on all points but one, is on that one point insane.[51]

Pusey is alluding here to the well-known psychological theory of 'moral insanity' put forward by J.C. Prichard in the 1830s, according to which the mind could suffer from a localized complex of ideas which constituted an obsession, or 'monomania', with the result that a person could manifest perfectly correct conduct in all other respects, and yet in one particular situation have an irresistible impulse to perverse or evil behaviour – a Victorian equivalent to syndromes such

---

50 Ethel Romanes, *Charlotte Mary Yonge: An Appreciation* (London: Mowbray, 1908), 42–4.

51 Pusey, *Parochial Sermons*, 3: 84–6.

as kleptomania or obsessive compulsive disorder.[52] For Pusey, however, in keeping with an associationist standpoint, it is impossible for quirks of this kind to remain merely localized; unless actively combated by the will, their obsessive nature must gradually derange one's whole moral being, a kind of moral downfall graphically portrayed in Dean Farrar's notorious school story *Eric, or Little by Little*. A similar anxiety permeates Yonge's fiction, underlying, for example, Marian's fear in *The Two Guardians* that her brother Gerald will become morally corrupted by hanging round their guardian Mr Lyddell's stables.[53] In *Love and Life*, Yonge even suggests that Lady Belamour's villainous behaviour reflects a condition of complete moral insanity.[54]

'Moral insanity' was a notoriously slippery concept, and many nineteenth-century doctors might have been prepared to concede that everyone exhibited it in some form or other.[55] Pusey exploits this potential ubiquity of moral insanity in his psychologization of the religious category of sin, laying particular stress on the concept of a 'besetting sin', different for each person, which constitutes the germ from which all their other sins grow, and continued struggle with which can therefore transform their character:

> What then, is the one sin which doth so easily beset us? It is that we are mostly born with one special temptation; we have not, all, the same trials; but we have, each, one special weakness or passion or evil inclination, which besets us again and again, is ever twining itself around us, and from which until we disentangle ourselves we make but little progress. It is the occasion of our stumbling, our falling, our slowness in heavenly things. It comes upon us, sometimes in the very same shape, sometimes in another. It takes us sometimes by surprise, sometimes by storm; sometimes in acts so slight that we heed them not, sometimes, in temptations so vehement, that they carry us off our feet. It comes to us [...] mostly in a few ways, but these so in and out, as it were, sometimes in

---

52   James Cowles Prichard, *A Treatise on Insanity and Other Disorders Affecting the Mind* (London: Sherwood, Gilbert, and Piper, 1835) in Sally Shuttleworth and Jenny Bourne Taylor (eds), *Embodied Selves: An Anthology of Psychological Texts 1830–1890* (Oxford: Clarendon Press, 1998), 252–4.

53   Yonge, *Two Guardians*, 98–9 (Ch.6).

54   Ibid., *Love and Life*, 404 (Ch.36).

55   Oppenheim, *Shattered Nerves*, 49–53.

the one, sometimes in the other, that till men examine it slowly, and take it away piece by piece, it seems much stronger and more manifold than it is [...]

For thy besetting sin lies most deeply in thy whole nature. It springs from the most corrupt part of thyself. It hurts thee the most, because it is the sin thou hast most love for. Other faults lie on the surface; this goes to the very depth of thy soul. Other faults are not so done with thy whole heart. Thou art in most peril as to thy besetting sin, that it take up thy whole heart, master thy affections, occupy thy imagination, fill thy thoughts, engross thy time, enslave thyself.[56]

Despite the baroque style of his religious prose, the terms in which Pusey describes the besetting sin as a bias in one's thought which will grow into an overmastering obsession unless actively identified and resisted reflect Prichard's claim that monomania can give rise a moral insanity of which the sufferer can be entirely unaware. Even the moralistic frame of reference within which Pusey places this psychological phenomenon would have been familiar to those familiar with Victorian manuals on mental health, which often emphasize that patients are responsible for the state of their own minds, regarded as a product of how their will has been exerted.[57] A similar identification of a state of besetting sin with monomania can be found in the writings of 1830s anti-slavery campaigners, which attribute West Indian planters' inability to perceive the 'self-evident' truth that they would be economically better off if slavery were abolished in favour of a free-market system to a monomania of lust induced by their ability sexually to exploit their female slaves.[58]

The Tractarian emphasis on struggle with a besetting sin as the central focus of one's moral life informs the characterization in Yonge's novels, whose interest in exploring unconscious aspects of the mind reflects Pusey's argument that since Satan will 'use whatever our temper be, our security or our timidity, our energy or our listlessness',[59] it is the Christian's duty to bring all their motivations to consciousness.[60] At its most obvious, the way in which Yonge defines

---

56   Pusey, *Parochial Sermons*, 2: 132–3.
57   John R. Reed, *Victorian Will* (Athens: Ohio University Press, 1989), 134–8.
58   Charles Stuart, *The West India Question* (London, 1832), 12–13, 28–9, 31.
59   Pusey, *Parochial Sermons*, 3: 37–8.
60   Ibid., 2: 101.

character by relationship to temperamental weakness is shown by her occasional use of 'flat' characters,[61] such as gluttonous Augusta Fulmort[62] and the 'acid' Juliana Fulmort[63] in *Hopes and Fears*. Like Austen, though, Yonge has the ability briefly to unsettle the comic perspective in which such characters are usually regarded, such as when in describing the reaction to Juliana's death she comments that 'those who have so lived as to make themselves least missed, are perhaps at the first moment the more mourned by good hearts for that very cause'.[64]

More extended forms of characterization in Yonge's novels often dramatize the process by which a character comes to realize the nature of their central moral failing, or chronicle their struggle against a besetting sin. This is obviously the case with Yonge's description of Guy's struggle against the irritable Morville temperament in *The Heir of Redclyffe*, for example, but can also be seen, often in more complex and nuanced forms, in other novels. Yonge portrays Robert Fulmort, for instance, as prone to severity and sternness, and this is shown to be a fault against which he has to struggle in his life as a priest; towards the end of *Hopes and Fears* the narrator notes that 'his greatest effort was against being harsh and unsympathizing, even while his whole career was an endeavour to work through charities of deed and word into charities of thought and judgment'.[65] At the same time, however, Yonge suggests that Robert Fulmort's temperamental severity is exactly the quality which makes him capable of choosing, in preference to an engagement to the unsuitably flighty Lucilla, to undertake the demanding mission to the London slum of Whittingtonia which is to atone for the corrupting influence of the gin palaces on which his family's wealth depends. When Robert definitively renounces all thoughts of Lucilla in a conversation with his sister Phoebe, Yonge comments on the mixed nature of his motives:

61   See E.M. Forster, *Aspects of the Novel* (Harmondsworth: Penguin, 1962), in Michael J. Hoffman and Patrick D. Murphy (eds), *Essentials of the Theory of Fiction* (London: Leicester University Press, 1996).
62   Yonge, *Hopes and Fears*, 112–13 (Part 2 Ch.2).
63   Ibid., 423 (Part 2 Ch.22).
64   Ibid., 440 (Part 2 Ch.24).
65   Ibid., 522 (Part 2 Ch.29).

He spoke as a man whose steadfastness had been defied, and who was piqued on proving it to the utmost. Such feelings may savour of the wrath of man, they may need the purifying of chastening, and they often impel far beyond the bounds of sober judgment; but no doubt they likewise frequently render that easy which would otherwise have appeared impossible, and which, if done in haste, may be regretted, but not repented, at leisure.

Under some circumstances, the harshness of youth is a healthy symptom, proving force of character and conviction, though that is only when the foremost victim is self. Robert was far from perfect, and it might be doubted whether he were entering the right track in the right way, but at least his heart was sound, and there was a fair hope that his failings, in working their punishment, might work their cure.[66]

Yonge emphasizes the morally ambivalent nature of a forcefulness of which it is possible, as Pusey comments, that Satan might 'use even the energy which God infuses, to hurry us beyond the boundaries prescribed by God',[67] but which also might turn out to be an instrument of Providence if Robert is capable of attaining, through the experience of restraints to his own self-will, to an awareness of the nature of his own motivations – something he begins to do in the episode where he grudgingly accepts Phoebe's domestic touches in his rooms, to which we have already referred. Robert's ultimate success in subduing his besetting sin is hinted at by the redemptive language in which Yonge describes the orphan children he conducts on a railway excursion to the family estate as 'his most hopeful conquest from the realm of darkness',[68] but although his actions are admirable, a continuing unsympathetic rigidity in his character is implied by Lucilla's perception of him as a 'medieval saint in cast-iron'.[69] The complexity of Yonge's portrayal of a man who embodies a degree of religious and social commitment which on a theoretical level she would have wholeheartedly approved bears comparison with Charlotte

---

66   Ibid., 221 (Part 2 Ch.9).
67   Pusey, *Parochial Sermons*, 3: 37.
68   Yonge, *Hopes and Fears*, 481 (Part 2 Ch.25).
69   Ibid., 521 (Part 2 Ch.29).

Brontë's similarly ambivalent depiction of the missionary St John Rivers in *Jane Eyre*.[70]

Tractarian Feminism and Victorian Domestic Ideology

The stress laid by Tractarian preachers on the pervasive nature of one's besetting sin, and on the way in which it can manifest itself and ramify in the most trivial actions, shows that the encouragement of an implicitly feminizing concentration on domesticity noted by Sturrock is not incidental to Tractarianism as a movement, but represents an integral part of its cultural and theological significance. Tractarian ideology makes the home into a moral theatre where struggles of the utmost importance for one's future destiny are played out, a moralization of domesticity which coincides with other important Victorian cultural trends which tend to identify the private realm of home, rather than a degraded public sphere, as the locus of moral and social progress.

To illustrate this mutual reinforcement between Tractarianism and a wider Victorian domestic ideology in which the role of women is identified as crucial, we may use the example of Sarah Ellis's 1839 book, *The Women of England*, identified by critics as representative of the Victorian cult of home.[71] What is striking about Ellis's writing is the extremely negative portrayal of the newly commercialized public sphere within which men must operate:

> The great facilities of communication, not only throughout our own country, but with distant parts of the world, are rousing men to every description to tenfold exertion in the field of competition in which they are engaged; so that their whole being is becoming swallowed up in efforts and calculations related to their pecuniary success. If to grow tardy or indifferent in the race were only to lose the goal, many would be glad to pause; but such is the nature of

70   Charlotte Brontë, *Jane Eyre*, Margaret Smith (ed.) (Oxford: Oxford University Press, 1993), 369–71.
71   Helsinger, Sheets and Veeder, *Woman Question*, 1: xiv.

230

commerce and trade, as at present carried on in this country, that to slacken in exertion, is altogether to fail. I would fain hope and believe of my countrymen, that many of the rational and enlightened would now be willing to reap smaller gains, if by doing so they could enjoy more leisure. But a business only half attended to, soon ceases to be a business at all; and the man of enlightened understanding, who neglects his, for the sake of hours of leisure, must be content to spend them in the debtor's department of a jail. Thus, it is not with single individuals that the blame can be made to rest. The fault is in the system; and happy will it be for thousands of immortal souls, when this system shall correct itself. In the mean time, may it not be said to be the especial duty of women to look around them, and see in what way they can counteract this evil, by calling back the attention of man to those sunnier spots in his existence, by which the growth of his moral feelings have been encouraged, and his heart improved?[72]

Ellis's concern at the moral effects of capitalism was widely shared in the 1830s, with medical writers attributing a rise in cases of insanity to the relentless competitive pressures which she describes,[73] a pathological form of social modernity which forms the background to Tennyson's *Maud*. The remedy Ellis proposes for the dehumanizing effects of a capitalism in which 'we almost fail to recognize the man in the machine',[74] is to enhance the quality of moral response to the details of domestic life. Ellis recommends close attention by middle-class women to management of the home not on the utilitarian grounds that it will result in smoother functioning of domestic arrangements, but as a form of discipline and self-cultivation which will bring forth a 'moral power' in these women which can in practice be superior to that of men, whose 'moral feelings are [...] liable to be impaired by [...] pecuniary objects'.[75]

72   Sarah Ellis, *The Women of England: Their Social Duties and Domestic Habits* (London and New York, 1839), 52–7.
73   Cf. C.T. Thackrah, *The Effects of Arts, Trades, and Professions, and of Civic States and Habits of Living: With Suggestions for the Removal of Many of the Agents Which Produce Disease, and Shorten the Duration of Life*, 2nd edn (London: Longman, 1832) in Shuttleworth and Taylor, *Embodied Selves*, 293–4.
74   Ellis, *Women of England*, 52–7.
75   Ibid., 48–52.

For Ellis, the moral power developed in a woman by her continual concern for others is something that is communicated to her menfolk through 'home-associations', making her 'influence [...] so potent as to mingle with the whole existence of those whom she loves'.[76] Domesticity, in Ellis's conception, is a kind of lived poetry. Like the landscape of Wordsworth's 'Tintern Abbey', domesticity, recollected 'mid the din / Of town and cities', imparts:

> In hours of weariness, sensations sweet
> Felt in the blood and felt along the heart,
> And passing even into my purer mind
> With tranquil restoration: – feelings too
> Of unremembered pleasure; such, perhaps,
> As may have had no trivial influence
> On that best portion of a good man's life;
> His little, nameless, unremembered acts
> Of kindness and of love.[77]

Ellis's version of this Wordsworthian restorative effect is the fireside chat, where the domestic woman's conversational 'freshness and [...] charm' serves as a mild stimulant in 'moments when the wearied frame is most in need of exhilaration, when the wearied mind is thrown back upon its own resources for the restoration of its exhausted powers, and when home-associations and home-affections are the balm which the wounded spirit needs'.[78] In view of 1830s anxieties that capitalist competition led to insanity, it is clear that Ellis envisages the domestic woman as the preserver of her husband's mental health, in much the same way as J.S. Mill attributed his recovery from nervous breakdown to the 'culture of the feelings' imparted by Wordsworth's poetry.[79] For Ellis, the domestic woman is

76   Ibid., 32, 57.
77   William Wordsworth, 'Lines Written a Few Miles Above Tintern Abbey', in *The Oxford Authors: William Wordsworth*, Stephen Gill (Oxford: Oxford University Press, 1984), ll 26.
78   Ellis, *Women of England*, 32.
79   See the discussion of Mill's *Autobiography* in Antony H. Harrison, *Victorian Poets and the Politics of Culture: Discourse and Ideology* (Charlottesville and London: University Press of Virginia, 1998), 13–16.

even capable of preventing her husband of succumbing to the moral contagion of capitalism when he is not by her side:

> So potent may have become this secret influence, that he may have borne it about with him like a kind of second conscience, for mental reference, and spiritual counsel, in moments of trial; and when the snares of the world were around him, and temptations from within and without have bribed over the witness in his own bosom, he has thought of the humble monitress who sat alone, guarding the fireside comforts of his distant home; and the remembrance of her character, clothed in moral beauty, has scattered the clouds before his mental vision, and sent him back to that beloved home, a wiser and a better man.[80]

The domestic woman here represents a kind of associative centre in the man's life, akin to Wordsworth's 'spots of time' with their 'renovating virtue',[81] which is capable of enabling him to resist the moral sickness of contemporary society. Similar ideas about the moral effects of domesticity are present in Yonge's fiction. As has already been pointed out, Philip's self-deception in *The Heir of Redclyffe* is attributed by Yonge to a lack of exactly the kinds of 'home-associations' to which Ellis is referring,[82] a view of the morally stabilizing effects of the domestic woman which also underlies Edmund's remark to Marian in *The Two Guardians* that 'many a man has owed everything to a sister's influence'.[83] In the context of nineteenth-century medicine's tendency to link bodily disorder with mental perturbation, Ellis's claim that 'thought of the humble mon-itress' can prevent her husband's moral infection by capitalism resembles the assumption in Charles Kingsley's novel *Two Years Ago*, that non-enthusiastic religious faith nurtured by the practice of regular prayer can shield its possessors from the contagion of cholera.[84] In Yonge's *Three Brides* there is a similar emphasis on the immunizing

---

80   Ellis, *Women of England*, 52.
81   William Wordsworth, *The Prelude 1799, 1805, 1850*, Jonathan Wordsworth, M.H. Abrams and Stephen Gill (ed.) (New York and London: Norton, 1979), 12: ll 208–10 (1850 text).
82   Yonge, *Heir*, 56–7, 246–7 (Chs 4, 18).
83   Yonge, *Two Guardians*, 98 (Ch.6).
84   Charles Kingsley, *Two Years Ago* (London: Macmillan, 1886), 304–10 (Ch.17)

effects of domestic regularity in the episode where Rosamund insists that her clergyman husband Julius eat a good dinner in order to protect him from the typhus epidemic that has broken out; Julius later realizes that it is for want of this 'cherishing care' that his bachelor curate Herbert has taken the infection.[85]

The Yonge novel which most fully embodies the kind of domestic ideology represented by Ellis is *The Daisy Chain*, something which perhaps explains its enormous popularity in the Victorian period. Shortly after the death of his wife early on in the book, Dr May tells his eldest daughters about his dream of a 'mêlée, a sense of being crushed down, suffocated by the throng of armed knights and horses – pain and wounds – and I looked in vain through the opposing overwhelming host for my – my Maggie',[86] a dream which seems to correspond to Ellis's description of the competitive pressures besetting Victorian masculinity. During the novel, the awkward and bookish daughter Ethel (agreed by many critics to be a self-portrait on Yonge's part)[87] develops into 'Papa's best companion and friend'[88] through a process which is summed up by her invalid elder sister Margaret towards the end of the novel:

> 'I expected to be struck with Ethel', said Mrs Arnott; 'and –'
>
> 'Well', said Margaret, waiting.
>
> 'Yes, she does exceed my expectations. There is something curiously winning in that quaint, quick, decisive manner of hers. There is so much soul in the least thing she does, as if she could not be indifferent for a moment.'
>
> 'Exactly – exactly so', said Margaret, delighted. 'It is really doing everything with all her might. Little, simple, everyday matters did not come naturally to her as to other people, and the having had to make them duties has taught her to do them with that earnest manner, as if there were a right and a wrong to her in each little mechanical household office.'[89]

85   Yonge, *Three Brides*, 230–1, 236, 271 (Chs 26, 27, 31).

86   Yonge, *Daisy Chain*, 62 (Part 1 Ch.7).

87   Barbara Dennis, *Charlotte Yonge (1823–1901), Novelist of the Oxford Movement: A Literature of Victorian Culture and Society* (Lewiston, NY: Edwin Mellen, 1992), 18–21; Hayter, *Yonge*, 5.

88   Yonge, *Daisy Chain*, 318 (Part 1 Ch.29).

89   Ibid., 629 (Part 2 Ch.24).

By following the rules she has set out for herself (the first of which is the punning and self-abnegating one, 'MUSTS – to be first consulted. – Mays – last. Ethel May's last of all')[90] Ethel, in her willed absorption in domesticity, has attained the condition of moral power which Ellis describes. This is shown by Ethel's relationship with the morbidly sensitive governess, Miss Bracy,[91] who by the end of the novel has come to have a 'healthier mind' as a result of Ethel's advice, even though Ethel is not conscious of exerting 'influence'.[92]

Feminist critics have often characterized *The Daisy Chain* as a fundamentally repressive novel,[93] citing the episode where Ethel has reluctantly to decide to give up her study of Latin and Greek, because it leads her into 'careless habits' around the home.[94] It would be a mistake, however, to regard Yonge as opposed to female learning; even when Ethel has given up the attempt to keep up with her brother Norman's classical studies, she still intends, with Margaret's approval, to devote half-an-hour a day to Greek, and as we have seen, Yonge holds up the bluestocking Elizabeth Carter for approval in the *Monthly Packet*.[95] This episode, moreover, has been carefully prepared for by a conversation between Ethel and her father in which, after rebuking her for letting her little brother set alight to his clothes, he reveals his fear that she may develop the very 'ingrain, long-nurtured habits' of 'inbred heedlessness' to which he has succumbed himself, and which were the cause of the driving accident in which her mother died.[96] Given the emphasis in the novel on the temperamental similarity between Ethel and her father,[97] it seems to be Ethel's renunciation of activities to which she has a bent, in favour of duties which, as Margaret comments, do not 'come naturally', that makes her morally

---

90   Ibid., 409 (Part 2 Ch.7).
91   Ibid., 353 (Part 2 Ch.2).
92   Ibid., 619–20 (Part 2 Ch.23).
93   Alethea Hayter gives a summary of this liberal feminist interpretative tradition in *Yonge*, 56–61.
94   Yonge, *Daisy Chain*, 180–1 (Part 1 Ch.18).
95   Anon., 'Old Letter'.
96   Yonge, *Daisy Chain*, 136–7 (Part 1 Ch.14).
97   Ibid., 49 (Part 1 Ch.5).

exemplary for Yonge, without this incident having implications which are necessarily antifeminist in the way assumed by some critics.

It should also be noted that the choice with which Ethel is presented at this point is not simply between classical scholarship and domestic duties. Ethel has also taken on work as a teacher in the benighted village of Cocksmoor, and it is ultimately this commitment outside the home which makes it impossible for her to continue studying. This aspect of the novel, in which Ethel's 'steadiness'[98] ultimately leads to the building of a church in Cocksmoor, subsumes Victorian domestic ideology under the Tractarian social mission in a way which can be compared to *The Heir of Redclyffe*'s enlisting of Byronic romantic love in the service of the Christian ideal. As we have seen, Yonge suggests that Philip's and Laura's error consists in their failure to acknowledge any transcendent reference point outside their relationship,[99] and a conversation in *The Daisy Chain* makes a similar point about the relation between commitment to the socially deprived Cocksmoor and the Mays' family life:

'You said how Cocksmoor had been blessed to Margaret – I think it is the same with them all – not only Ethel and Richard, who have been immediately concerned; but that one object has been a centre and aim to elevate the whole family, and give force and unity to their efforts. Even the good doctor, much as I always looked up to him – much good as he did me in my young days – I must confess that he was sometimes very provoking.'

'If you had tried to be his keeper at Cambridge, you might say so!' rejoined Dr Spencer.

'He is so much less impetuous – more consistent – less desultory; I dare say you understand me', said Mr Wilmot. 'His good qualities do not entangle one another as they used to do.'[100]

In a gesture which significantly revises the rather privatized domestic ideology put forward by Ellis, Yonge makes the blessings of domesticity dependent on social aspirations outside the home. It is not so much commitment to domesticity that has improved Ethel's character, as her will to improve conditions at Cocksmoor, a point made

98   Ibid., 558 (Part 2 Ch.19).
99   Yonge, *Heir*, 553 (Ch.42).
100   Yonge, *Daisy Chain*, 587–8 (Part 2 Ch.21).

by Margaret, when she comments that 'Cocksmoor was the stimulus, and made Ethel what she is.'[101] Instead of the woman forming the associative centre of the home, as in Ellis's model of domesticity, for Yonge commitment to ideals beyond the home represents that centre, and this is shown to have developed the character of Dr May himself, making him 'less desultory'. By the end of the novel, Ethel herself has come to recognize the inadequacy of domesticity as a source of value, with Yonge commenting that 'her eyes had been opened to see that earthly homes may not endure, nor fill the heart'.[102] The associative centre has shifted from the home to the church, as becomes apparent when the effect of the newly built church on Cocksmoor is described:

> It was not a desolate sight as in old times, for the fair edifice, rising on the slope, gave an air of protection to the cottages, which seemed now to have a centre of unity, instead of lying forlorn and scattered. Nor were they as wretched in themselves, for the impulse of civilisation had caused windows to be mended and railings to be tidied, and Richard promoted, to the utmost, cottage gardening, so that, though there was an air of poverty, there was no longer an appearance of reckless destitution and hopeless neglect.[103]

Yonge's description emphasizes the change from the inadequate individualism of the domestic ideology, which left the cottages 'forlorn and scattered', to a model in which religion is the 'centre of unity', and therefore can promote a successful domesticity, as shown by the spread of 'cottage gardening'. A similar point is conveyed by the contrast between Ethel and her 'worldly' sister Flora.[104] For much of the novel, it is Flora who is the embodiment of domesticity, being 'the only practically useful person in the family',[105] but because her aim is only to shine in the domestic sphere (to be 'everywhere liked and sought after',[106] as her mother puts it in a letter), she ends up spectacularly failing in her domestic duties when her baby dies of

---

101   Ibid., 629 (Part 2 Ch.24).
102   Ibid., 666 (Part 2 Ch.27).
103   Ibid., 631 (Part 2 Ch.24).
104   Ibid., 392–3 (Part 2 Ch.6).
105   Ibid., 402 (Part 2 Ch.7).
106   Ibid., 50 (Part 1 Ch.5).

opium withdrawal after having been dosed with Godfrey's Cordial by an ignorant nurse.[107]

Domesticity as Moral Empowerment

For Sarah Ellis, in a statement that tellingly implies the doctrine of 'separate spheres', the function of the domestic woman is to cultivate in her husband 'that higher tone of feeling, without which he can enjoy nothing beyond a kind of animal existence – but with which, he may faithfully pursue the necessary avocations of the day, and keep as it were a separate soul for his family, his social duty, and his God.'[108] For Yonge, on the other hand, it is impossible to cordon off one's 'soul' in this way: Ethel's moral commitment to her work in Cocksmoor is precisely what enables her to become adequate to the domestic realm, because she does 'everything with all her might'. Yonge consistently emphasizes in her fiction the moral value of undivided attention, as that which will reveal our duty in the circumstances that surround us: the difference made by this kind of attention is shown in *The Daisy Chain*, when Meta is discussing Ethel with her brother Norman, and responds to his comment that 'Circumstances have formed Ethel' by remarking 'Circumstances! What an ambiguous word! Either Providence pointing to duty, or the world drawing us from it.'[109] The suggestion is that the habit of attention is what has enabled Ethel to perceive her providentially ordained role in life, since, as Ethel herself comments early on in the novel, 'One sees more with one's mind than one's eyes'.[110] In *Hopes and Fears*, Yonge makes a similar point in relation to the exemplary Phoebe, when the narrator comments that 'the key of Phoebe's character' was her remark, ignored by her dissolute brother Mervyn, that the chief thing

107   Ibid., 566–7 (Part 2 Ch.20).
108   Ellis, *Women of England*, 57.
109   Yonge, *Daisy Chain*, 600–1 (Part 2 Ch.22).
110   Ibid., 54 (Part 1 Ch.6).

taught by her governess Miss Fennimore was 'to attend to what we are doing'.[111]

Yonge's rejection of the assumption underlying the conventional Victorian domestic ideology of Mrs Ellis, that the moral consequences of actions in the public sphere of business can simply be discarded once at home, is shown by the general malaise afflicting the Fulmorts in *Hopes and Fears*, whose wealth, with its morally questionable origin in a distillery, fragments the family, resulting in Mervyn's lack of a moral centre and the consequent addiction to 'excitement' which threatens to wreck his health.[112] Yonge's Tractarianism effects a transvaluation of domestic ideology in which the home, in order truly to *be* a home, must transform the world surrounding it. Her novels' focus on domestic life is in this respect comparable to the transgressive domesticity of Elizabeth Gaskell's *North and South*, where the genuine, if rather shabby, domesticity of the Hales is contrasted with the sterile luxury of the Thornton household, and shown to represent values which are capable of transforming the 'cash nexus' of the public world represented by Thornton's factory.[113]

Far from being merely 'repressive', then, the emphasis on domesticity in novels such as *The Daisy Chain* can be seen as a form of social critique, in that the Victorian cult of home is adopted only to be universalized in a gesture which implies the centrality of the role of women. This understanding of the political significance of domesticity is of course not unique to Yonge; it is already implicit, for example, in Peter Gaskell's 1830s observations on the breakdown of family structures among the working class in Manchester under the pressures of capitalism.[114] Yonge, however, was an active participant in the process whereby a transvalued domestic ideology evolved in the mid-nineteenth century into practical initiatives which not only provided

111 Yonge, *Hopes and Fears*, 397–403 (Part 2 Ch.20).
112 Ibid., 104, 255, 386 (Part 2 Chs 1, 10, 19).
113 Elizabeth Gaskell, *North and South*, Dorothy Collin (ed.) (Harmondsworth: Penguin, 1970), 119–20, 525 (Chs 10, 51).
114 Peter Gaskell, *The Manufacturing Population of England, Its Moral, Social, and Physical Conditions, and the Changes Which Have Arisen from the Use of Steam Machinery*, London: Parker 1836 (facs. edn) (London: Cass, 1968), 62–9, 72–3.

employment for women, but also represented the beginning of the modern conception of 'social work'.

From 1859 onwards, the *Monthly Packet* regularly featured reports on institutions that are sometimes suggestively named 'Industrial Homes',[115] where working-class girls can be trained for domestic service in the context of all-female communities modelled on continental societies of deaconesses.[116] In *The Clever Woman of the Family*, there seems to be an allusion to such initiatives when the old blind clergyman, Mr Clare, takes Rachel, the repentant heroine, 'to lunch with an old friend, a lady who had devoted herself to the care of poor girls to be trained as servants', an undertaking which the narrator describes as 'one of the many great and good works set on foot by personal and direct labour'.[117]

A major purpose of such ventures seems to have been the preventing of abusive marriages, since, as one contributor noted, 'girls do not sufficiently respect themselves, are too ready, especially if they are not very attractive, to accept the first that offers'.[118] The theme of women's self-respect as a safeguard against male exploitation regularly appears in Yonge's fiction; in *The Two Guardians*, Caroline nearly succumbs to the unbelieving Mr Faulkner because 'her consent was assumed',[119] and in *Hopes and Fears* Yonge describes Phoebe's avoidance of the younger Owen Sandbrook's duplicitous attentions at the ball from which he clandestinely elopes with the governess, Miss Murrell, as 'the shoal past which her self-respect had just safely guided her'.[120]

This inversion of domestic ideology, in which the home, rather than being a retreat from the public sphere, comes to represent the standard by which the public sphere should be judged, obviously draws on the commonplace Protestant emphasis on the home as a kind of church, an emphasis which Tractarianism, with its promotion of

---

115   Anon., 'Church of England Industrial Home', *Monthly Packet* 14 (Series 1 1857): 657–9.

116   Anon., 'Sandwell', *Monthly Packet* 17 (Series 1 1859): 333.

117   Yonge, *Clever Woman*, 345 (Ch.28).

118   Anon., 'Life Among the Factories', *Monthly Packet* 18 (Series 1 1859): 549.

119   Yonge, *Two Guardians*, 247 (Ch.14).

120   Ibid., *Hopes and Fears*, 187 (Part 2 Ch.7).

morning and evening household prayer, sought to revive.[121] There are other, more distinctive features of Tractarianism, however, which make the tactic of domesticizing the public sphere a peculiarly powerful one for Yonge in comparison to other women writers. For the Tractarians, the whole purpose of religious observance is to achieve sanctity, in a way which makes the home a prime site of moral struggle and so tends to equalize the position of men and women.

As part of its doctrine of 'reserve', Tractarianism laid particular stress on the role of behaviour, as opposed to preaching, in the communication of religious truth. In Froude's *Remains*, for example, which was edited by Keble and Newman, the following conversation is reported:

> N.'s maxim that [*in ordinances, public acts, &c.*] we should consult for the few good, and not the many bad, cuts very deep. [*Objection was made to its application to church building, as if to sacrifice some beauty to the accommodation of numbers where there was a large population.*] I would build as perfect a church as I could for my money, whatever that money was..... Well, R. do you think that any but a very small portion of those who would go to your large church would get any good from it. [*His friend protested.*] Can you think that any would get good (as a general rule) who do not attend the Sacrament. [ANS. *Yes, very many.*] Really! I though obedience was the very condition of receiving benefit from prayer. [ANS. *They are not deliberately disobedient, and, besides, the seeing and hearing the prayers does them good.*] Ah! the regular Protestant way..... You want a church to preach the prayers in..... Depend upon that is not the way to get at the bad, but exertion in private, and showing you care for them. For them a pudding is worth twenty prayers. What a profane sentence some people would think that! And so it is in one sense. No, R; make two or three saints, that is the way to set to work.[122]

Given that 'Protestant' was a pejorative term in Froude's vocabulary, it is clear that the role of preaching here is being very much downgraded in favour of personal contact. Froude's conception of religious effectiveness can be compared to present-day 'viral mar-

---

121   E.g. Yonge, *Two Guardians*, 39–40 (Ch.4). This aspect of Tractarianism, of course, owed much to Evangelical influence, see Elizabeth Jay, *The Religion of The Heart: Anglican Evangelicalism and The Nineteenth Century Novel* (Oxford: The Clarendon Press, 1979), 140–4.

122   Froude, *Remains*, 1: 435–6.

keting'; authentic religion will propagate itself through 'two or three saints' in a way that will attract a far deeper level of commitment than merely being preached at. In practical terms, as a series of articles in the *Monthly Packet* makes clear,[123] this strategy meant attaching a high level of importance to district visiting, even in urban areas where an overwhelming ratio of parishioners to clergy had built up.[124] Since district-visiting was almost exclusively the province of women, the Tractarian emphasis on personal contact as the means by which religious truth is to be communicated very much privileged women's role in the church. This is the implication, for example, of the episode in *The Daisy Chain* where Ethel learns by letter of the pious deathbed of one of the poor Irish children she has taught at Cocksmoor, Una McCarthy.[125]

For the Tractarians, as Froude makes clear in his sermons, the authentic religion of the saint consists in constant practical action, rather than in mere talk or feeling.[126] One particular form of action that is available to everyone, as Froude points out, is that resistance to our own inclinations which constitutes self-command, and Froude suggests that it might be a good thing deliberately to go against one's own preferences even in matters where the outcome has no particular moral significance, in order to strengthen one's habit of self-command for when it is truly needed, since 'every victory gained over our inclinations will make the next struggle easier'.[127] This denial of pleasure, simply because it *is* pleasure, which can easily appear masochistic or perverse to the modern reader, is a central theme of Yonge's fiction; as the exemplary heroine Marian sums it up in *The Two Guardians*, 'self-denial is always best, and in a doubtful case, the most disagreeable is always the safest.'[128] Yonge, however, often invokes the principle in order to warn against false kinds of self-denial, such as when, in *The Heir of Redclyffe*, Guy, having caused

123   Cf. Anon., 'Will No One Do Likewise? A Tale of East London Life', *Monthly Packet* 17 (Series 1 1859): 289–302; 401–23; 505–24; 18: 181–92; 290–304.
124   Anon., 'Will No One Do Likewise?' *MP* 17 (1859): 419.
125   Yonge, *Daisy Chain*, 374–6 (Part 2 Ch.4).
126   Froude, *Remains*, 2: 26–8, 76–8, 95–9.
127   Ibid., 2: 20–1.
128   Yonge, *Two Guardians*, 80 (Ch.5)

offence by not attending a ball because he thought he would enjoy it too much, concludes there would be more true self-denial in enduring his neighbours' attentions in the knowledge that they were elicited by his social rank, rather than his personal qualities.[129]

The Tractarian emphases on self-denial for its own sake and on practical action as means to moral progress are not only compatible with Victorian domestic ideology, as represented by Sarah Ellis, but in this context could even be seen to imply the general moral superiority of women to men. For Ellis, the domestic woman attains 'moral power' through her constant thought for others, in a process of moral self-cultivation which is comparable to the Tractarian account of the development of sanctity through a habit of self-denial. Ellis likewise insists on the necessarily practical manifestations of the domestic woman's concern for others, in much the same way as Tractarians such as Froude argue that the only criterion for the authenticity of personal religion is its issue in action.[130] Within a Tractarian frame of reference, women's role within the domestic world affords an opportunity for the development of sanctity which is much less obviously available in the public sphere, so that men's comparative freedom from domestic restrictions becomes in religious terms a disadvantage.

Tractarian Feminism in Yonge's 'The Six Cushions'

The connection between Tractarian religion and female self-assertion for which I have been arguing in this chapter may be illustrated by Yonge's tale 'The Six Cushions', first published in the *Monthly Packet* during 1866. The local clergyman, Dr Henderson, commissions embroidered covers for altar-rail cushions from a group of six young ladies, explaining that the task must be 'a work of self-denial, or it would lose its very essence'.[131] The six heroines' struggle to

129 Yonge, *Heir*, 141 (Ch.10)
130 Froude, *Remains*, 2: 76.
131 Yonge, 'The Six Cushions', *Monthly Packet* 1 (Series 2 1866): 208.

finish the embroidery becomes a test of their characters: in a typically Yongean twist, the self-righteous Mary Rose, who is sure of her moral superiority to the 'concerts and parties and croquet and pic-nics'[132] attended by the other girls, turns out to be the only one who doesn't manage to complete the work. As Dr Henderson points out, she has been reading too many Evangelical tracts:

> See, here, Mary. If this was a story such as you have often read, the widow's daughter in the little house, who never goes to parties, would be superior to all the grand young ladies. The tortoise would beat the hare. It is very gratifying; and tortoises sometimes do. But then they are tortoises that go on: of the two, I had rather have a hare asleep than a tortoise asleep – or a tortoise too sure of the race to bestir himself – eh?[133]

Mary Rose is, on a small scale, a version of Philip in *The Heir of Redclyffe*, a character whose family has fallen on hard times and, by way of reaction and class envy, becomes so sure of their own virtue that they are incapable of seeing that of anybody else. Yonge's reference to a recognizably Evangelical genre of fiction here critiques popular Protestantism's tendency to make the moral standard consist in inward feeling, rather than in actions, a theme which can be found in other Tractarians: Pusey, for example, objects to theological emphases on justification by faith alone, because it makes the mind's own feelings the exclusive object of attention and so leads to religious morbidity and despair.[134] But Yonge is also drawing attention to dangers that were widely regarded to be inherent in the novel form itself, in that by exciting feelings for their own sake it tended to substitute self-consciousness for action.[135] Within a Tractarian frame of reference, the problem represented by the novel was that it seemed to be inherently inimical to the doctrine of reserve: Froude comments early on in his Journal, for example, in a remark that suggestively echoes Keble's theory of poetry, that 'Not allowing oneself to talk of an opinion, is one of the surest helps to acting upon it, as it will find

132 Yonge, 'Six Cushions' *MP* 2 (1866): 547
133 Ibid., 548
134 Pusey, *Parochial Sermons*, 2: 183–95.
135 B.L.K., 'Imagination', 472–3; see also H.L. Mansel, 'Sensation Novels', 483–502.

some vent. Communicating it is like opening the valve of a steam boiler.'[136] The problem with the demonstrative Evangelicalism of Mary Rose and her mother is that it is precisely the opposite of the 'hidden life'[137] which for the Tractarians constituted saintliness, something shown in 'The Six Cushions' by their failure to provide any real help when Clara, one of the other heroines, is laid up: as her father tells Dr Henderson:

> Those two set themselves down in the drawing-room, and never attempted a useful thing; crept up to Clara's room now and then, and worried her to tears or fever; but almost always, from morning to night, there they were, doing nothing, wherever they could be most in the way.[138]

At one level, 'The Six Cushions' is a justification of the Tractarian emphasis on decoration in churches: the Scottish Lady Euphemia, who Yonge makes clear 'had no personal likings for the school of doctrine to which Dr. Henderson belonged',[139] nevertheless confides in him that the embroidery has prevented her girls being taken in by a 'plausible' lad who 'was for daffing – as we say in Scotland – with any girl that would attend to him'.[140] The significance of the embroidery, however, is not just that it has been a safeguard against flirtation, but more widely that it has served as a focus which has prevented the lives of the heroines from being dominated by male selfishness. Early on in the story, there is a council of war where various young male relatives of the heroines, who are home on holiday, agree, in the language of the popular Protestantism which was often invoked against Tractarian innovations,[141] that the embroidery constitutes 'spiritual despotism' on Dr Henderson's part, which 'it is the duty and pride of every free-born Briton to resist', since, as one comments, 'if the women-folk won't condescend to make themselves pleasant in the holidays, what do they get board and lodging for, I'd

---

136 Froude, *Remains*, 1: 33.
137 Yonge, *The Castle Builders; or, The Deferred Confirmation* (London: Mozley, 1854), 214–15.
138 Yonge, 'Six Cushions', *MP* 2 (1866): 543.
139 Yonge, 'Six Cushions', *MP* 2 (1866): 232
140 Yonge, 'Six Cushions', *MP* 2 (1866): 544
141 Cf. John Shelton Reed, *Glorious Battle*, 235–6.

like to know?'[142] They vow to make the heroines abandon the embroidery, not by bullying them out of it, since 'civilization has surer methods',[143] but simply by distracting them. Although Yonge writes the scene as comedy, it later takes on darker overtones, since Clara's little brother Freddy, who is present, eventually ends up throwing lime into her face and nearly blinding her permanently, as part of the campaign to prevent her doing the embroidery to which he has been egged on by this conversation.

The 'work of self-denial' represented by the embroidery thus constitutes in 'The Six Cushions' a means of female emancipation not only from the selfish demands of men, but also, more fundamentally, from the self. Whilst the other heroines successfully resist their menfolk's attempts to waylay them, Mary Rose fails to complete the embroidery, as Dr Henderson points out, because sustaining the emotional investment in a particular representation of self takes all her energy. This is a psychological danger to which Pusey draws attention in a letter:

> It might be better to concentrate yourself on some few points, to get rid of this all-destroying self-reflection. You never can make any solid progress until you have uprooted this. It may be unfit that you should, else you might make even good minister to evil, and become worse through what would in itself have been good. It is the worst form of idolatry, setting up yourself as the idol in God's stead, and using any good thoughts from Him to deck out your idol; referring God to self instead of yourself to God.[144]

As Yonge herself comments, selfishness is at bottom a form of idolatry[145] in which all emotional reality becomes absorbed into representation, what Yonge in her letters frequently refers to (using the German word for picture) as a 'bild'.[146] This may not at first sight seem a very feminist message, but in 'The Six Cushions', Yonge

---

142   Yonge, 'The Six Cushions', *Monthly Packet* 2 (Series 2 1866): 414.

143   Ibid.

144   E.B. Pusey, *Spiritual Letters*, ed. Rev. J.O. Johnstone and Rev. W.C.E. Newbolt (London: Longmans, Green & Co, 1898), 24.

145   Yonge, 'Conversations on the Catechism: Conversation XXX. The First Commandment', *Monthly Packet* 9 (1st series 1855): 18.

146   Coleridge, *Yonge*, 189–95.

246

aligns the need to escape from self and its representations with the need to escape from male-centred definitions of women's domestic role, in a way that suggests the fundamental equivalence of the two. Women's identification with the work of the church, Yonge suggests, emancipates them not only from male domination as it is inscribed in the social structures of patriarchy, but also, more radically, from their own internalization of gender roles.

When Dr Henderson is trying to open Mary Rose's eyes to her own self-deception, he notices that her self-excusing replies are uttered 'exactly in her mother's tone',[147] so that his attempt to awake in her some insight into her own 'besetting sin'[148] also represents a project to emancipate her from her mother's perspective. Yonge portrays the faults of Mary Rose and her mother as the typically female ones of gossip and a love of excitement which figure elsewhere in writings by her associates,[149] so that in suggesting that Mary needs to free herself from a self-centred mindset in which her characteristic faults are dressed up as virtues, Dr Henderson is also engaging in what feminists in the 1970s used to call 'consciousness-raising', in that he is encouraging to Mary realize that she can't appeal to a 'feminine mystique'[150] in order to excuse herself from meeting obligations. One of the principal reasons Mary gives for her failure to complete the embroidery is that 'I thought hardly anyone else would finish so soon, and then it would not signify',[151] something which suggests that she doesn't have a very high opinion in general of her fellow women's capacity to persevere.

Although Yonge insists on the natural inferiority of women, this does not mean she is an 'antifeminist', since from her Tractarian perspective the whole purpose of the moral striving inherent in the Christian life is to go against Nature; Yonge, like the later Coleridge,

---

147   Yonge, 'Six Cushions', *MP* 2 (1866): 546.
148   Pusey, *Parochial Sermons*, 2: 132–42.
149   Author of 'Gentle Influences', 'Gossip', *MP* 17 (1859): 77–8; Anon., 'Shadow and Substance', *Monthly Packet* 22 (Series 1 1861): 596–9.
150   Cf. Betty Friedan, *The Feminine Mystique* (Harmondsworth: Penguin, 1992).
151   Yonge, 'Six Cushions', *MP* 2 (1866): 547.

thinks of Nature as 'the devil in a strait waistcoat'.[152] For Yonge, as for many other Victorians, women are at once naturally inferior to men and, potentially, morally superior to them because of their very weakness; in the context of the domesticizing of the public sphere which I have suggested is taking place in the mid nineteenth century, this is a politically powerful position. The complexities of this Victorian gender ideology are played out in Yonge's novels particularly in relationship to the ideologically important concept of the healthy body,[153] and it is to the relationship between Yonge's female characters and nineteenth-century medical ideas that I should like to turn in the following chapter.

152   Cf. Raimonda Modiano, *Coleridge and the Concept of Nature* (London and Basingstoke: Macmillan, 1985), 99 fn.
153   Cf. Bruce Haley, *The Healthy Body and Victorian Culture* (Cambridge, MA: Harvard University Press, 1978), 19.

Chapter Seven
Mesmerism, Tractarianism and Woman's Mission

Women and Nervous Irritability in Yonge's Novels

Victorian assumptions about the natural inferiority of women of the kind which, as we saw in the previous chapter, Yonge endorsed in a qualified way in her advice manual *Womankind*, did not stem wholly, or even mainly, from religious doctrine. As feminist critics such as Diana Basham have explored, nineteenth-century medical understandings of the female body, and in particular of menstruation, played a key role in the period's thinking about the social role of women.[1] Medical ideas play a significant part in Yonge's plots and characterization, as they do in the work of other Victorian novelists.[2] The reference of a correspondent to the 'physiological robustness' in the portrayal of her characters shows that this was recognized by Yonge's contemporaries.[3]

Medical concepts are particularly important in Yonge's characterization of women, which, as I hope to show in this chapter, tend to fall into the two opposing types of the 'mesmeric' woman on the one hand, and the 'irritable' woman on the other. While this kind of typology of female character can be found in other Victorian nov-

---

1   Diana Basham, *The Trial of Woman: Feminism and the Occult Sciences in Victorian Literature and Society* (Basingstoke: Macmillan, 1992).

2   Cf. Sally Shuttleworth, *Charlotte Brontë and Victorian Psychology* (Cambridge: Cambridge University Press, 1996); Jenny Bourne Taylor, *In the Secret Theatre of Home: Wilkie Collins, Sensation Narrative and Nineteenth Century Psychology* (Routledge: London and New York, 1988). To my knowledge, no previous critic has commented on the role of medical discourse in Yonge's novels.

3   The German correspondent uses the expression 'physiologische rustige Durchfuhrung' to describe Yonge's characterization, see Christabel Coleridge, *Charlotte Mary Yonge: Her Life and Letters* (London: Macmillan, 1903), 348–52.

elists, Yonge is distinctive in making the struggle with bodily temperament central to the development of her characters, and this reflects the religious feminism implicit in her Tractarian beliefs. Although in Yonge's novels such moral struggles are not confined to women, the male characters who go through them are almost always either adolescent or invalid, and so, as Sturrock has suggested,[4] can be regarded as feminized. This applies even to the apparent exception of Dr May in *The Daisy Chain*, whose adolescent qualities are indicated by Yonge's description of him as possessing a 'boyish character that seemed as if it could never grow older'.[5]

J.G. Millingen's 1848 book *The Passions: or Mind and Matter* has been identified by Sally Shuttleworth as representative of Victorian medical ideas about women.[6] The rhetorical nature of Millingen's language shows the book is addressed to a popular audience:

> If corporeal agency is [...] powerful in man, its tyrannic influence will more frequently cause the misery of the gentler sex. Woman, with her exalted spiritualism, is more forcibly under the control of matter; her sensations are more vivid and acute, her sympathies more irresistible. She is less under the influence of the brain than the uterine system, the plexi of abdominal nerves, and irritation of the spinal cord; in her, a hysteric predisposition is incessantly predominating from the dawn of puberty. Therefore is she subject to all the aberrations of love and religion; ecstatic under the impression of both, the latter becomes a resource when the excitement of the former is exhausted by disappointment, infidelity, and age – when, no longer attractive, she is left by the ebb of fond emotions on the bleak shore of despondency; where, like a lost wanderer in the desert, without an oasis upon earth on which to fix her straining eyes, she turns them to heaven, as her last consolation and retreat.[7]

In making the point that women are less rational than men, in that their minds respond more to bodily nerves than to the brain,

---

4   June Sturrock, *'Heaven and Home': Charlotte M. Yonge's Domestic Fiction and the Victorian Debate Over Women*, English Literary Studies (Victoria, BC: University of Victoria, 1995), 98–104.

5   Charlotte M. Yonge, *The Daisy Chain, or Aspirations* (London: Macmillan, 1886), 8 (Part 1 Ch.1).

6   Shuttleworth, *Charlotte Brontë and Victorian Psychology*, 71–6.

7   J.G. Millingen, *The Passions: Or Mind and Matter* (London: Hurst, 1848), 157–9.

Millingen is not simply being a misogynist, as Shuttleworth implies.[8] One of the things that distinguishes Victorian culture from our present-day attitudes is the greater value it sets on personal qualities other than pure reasoning capacity; this has often been caricatured in twentieth-century criticism as Victorian 'anti-intellectualism',[9] but represents a recognition of a set of abilities that contemporary Anglo-American society is currently rediscovering under the label of 'emotional intelligence'.[10] The Victorian suspicion of mere intellect, unaided by other personal qualities, is reflected in Newman's argument that 'moral Truth will be least skilfully defended by those [...] who are the genuine depositories of it',[11] and this sense that fluency in reasoning is in inverse proportion to genuine and practical conviction, which underlies Froude's suspicion of talk about religious matters,[12] can also be found in Yonge's novels. Norman in *The Daisy Chain*, for example finds that the very cleverness of his arguments in defence of religion tends to undermine his actual faith,[13] and, conversely, the rationalistic governess Miss Fennimore in *Hopes and Fears* remarks admiringly to Robert Fulmort (whose example later leads to her conversion) 'You cannot argue – you can only act'.[14]

When Millingen, then, suggests that the 'exalted spiritualism' of women is in conflict with 'the control of matter', we should take both poles of this opposition between the spiritual and the material seriously. It is easy to assume that Millingen is referring to the kind of religious self-delusion Flaubert described in *Madame Bovary*, a novel whose intellectual affinity to the medical ideas behind Yonge's

8   Shuttleworth, *Charlotte Brontë and Victorian Psychology*, 76.
9   Joseph Ellis Baker, *The Novel and the Oxford Movement* (New York: Russell and Russell, 1965), 114–19.
10   Cf. Daniel Goleman, *Emotional Intelligence: Why It Can Matter More Than IQ* (New York: Bantam Books, 1995).
11   John Henry Newman, *Newman's University Sermons: Fifteen Sermons Preached Before the University of Oxford 1826–1843*, intro by D.M. MacKinnon and J.D. Holmes (London: SPCK, 1970), 84.
12   Richard Hurrell Froude, *Remains of the Late Reverend Richard Hurrell Froude MA, Fellow of Oriel College, Oxford*, 2 vols (London: Rivington, 1838), 1: 33.
13   Yonge, *Daisy Chain*, 515–18 (Part 2 Ch.16).
14   Yonge, *Hopes and Fears, or Scenes from the Life of a Spinster* (London: Macmillan, 1889), 365 (Part 2 Ch.17).

writing was recognized by at least one nineteenth-century reader.[15] The 1840s American feminist Margaret Fuller, however, who cannot be suspected of this kind of reductionism, refers to women in a very similar way,[16] and claims for the superior spirituality of women are a truism of nineteenth-century critical writing about the poetess tradition.[17]

Millingen's claims about the mental weakness of women are based on the widely held nineteenth-century assumption that concentrated thought demanded a greater supply of blood to the brain, which competed with the requirements of other bodily organs. Even in the case of men, severe study was thought to be the cause of health problems, such as indigestion,[18] and could lead to a dangerous state of mental overstimulation, in which certain parts of the brain became 'morbid' and so required ever-increasing supplies of blood in order to keep up their level of stimulation, eventually terminating either in insanity or in complete physical breakdown.[19] Dr May's concern in *The Daisy Chain* over the 'funny state'[20] the brilliant Norman gets into, and which allows him intellectually to outperform all his contemporaries, reflects these medical ideas, which originate in the Brunonianism of the late eighteenth century.[21] Dr May suspects that Norman may be heading for the potentially fatal 'brain fever'[22] which

---

15   See the letter from Henry Sidgwick to Roden Noel, quoted in Ethel Romanes, *Charlotte Mary Yonge: An Appreciation* (London: Mowbray, 1908), 93–4.

16   Margaret Fuller, *Woman in the Nineteenth Century* (Oxford: Oxford University Press, 1994), 66.

17   Charles LaPorte, 'George Eliot, the Poetess as Prophet', *Victorian Literature and Culture* 31, no.1 (2003): 160–1.

18   Alexander Crichton, *An Inquiry Into the Nature and Origin of Mental Derangement*, 2 vols (London: Cadell and Davies, 1798), 2: 29–33.

19   Ibid., 35–9.

20   Yonge, *Daisy Chain*, 109 (Part 1 Ch.11).

21   Janet Oppenheim, *'Shattered Nerves': Doctors; Patients and Depression in Victorian England* (New York: Oxford University Press, 1991), 94–9.

22   Yonge, *Daisy Chain*, 110 (Part 1 Ch.11).

figures in numerous Victorian novels,[23] as well as in many Victorian memoirs.[24]

The Victorians regarded women as even more liable to face these kinds of health problems if their brains were overtaxed, because in their case the brain competed not only with the digestive system but with the reproductive organs,[25] menstruation being regarded as requiring substantial supplies of blood.[26] Victorian medicine's obsession with the need for regular menstruation[27] stemmed from this assumption that blood flow could be impeded by unhealthily active mental processes, and was lent support by the notoriously high incidence of nervous disease among middle-class Victorian women.[28] The onset of menstruation was regarded as a particularly crucial period in a woman's life, when the state of her future health would be determined,[29] and this may explain the Victorian practice of withdrawing girls from the schoolroom (where they would be educated alongside their brothers) at about the age of fifteen, and Yonge's own focus on the period of 'young ladyhood' (which she defined as the ages between fifteen and twenty-five)[30] both in her novels and in her definition of her audience.[31]

Yonge's acceptance of these medical ideas is shown by her description in *Hopes and Fears* of Miss Fennimore's effect on her young charges:

23   E.g. Edward Bulwer-Lytton, *A Strange Story* (London: Routledge, 1897), 58 (Ch.10).

24   Oppenheim, *Shattered Nerves*, 3–8.

25   Elizabeth K. Helsinger, Robin Lauterbach Sheets and William Veeder, *The Woman Question: Society and Literature in Britain and America, 1837–1883*, 3 vols (New York: Garland, 1983), 2: 81.

26   Justus Liebig, *Animal Chemistry, or Organic Chemistry in Its Applications to Physiology and Pathology*, trans. William Gregory (London: Taylor and Walton, 1842), 38–40.

27   Shuttleworth, *Charlotte Brontë and Victorian Psychology*, 85–90.

28   Oppenheim, *Shattered Nerves*, 187–93.

29   Ibid.

30   E.g. Charlotte M. Yonge, *The Clever Woman of the Family* (London: Macmillan, 1892), 1 (Ch.1).

31   Yonge, 'Introductory Letter,' *Monthly Packet* 1 (Series 1 1851): i (second sequence of roman numerals).

As a teacher she was excellent; but her own strong conformation prevented her from understanding that young girls were incapable of such tension of intellect as an enthusiastic scholar of forty-two, and that what was sport to her was toil to a mind unaccustomed to constant attention. Change of labour is not rest, unless it be through gratification of the will. Her very best pupil she had killed. Finding a very sharp sword, in a very frail scabbard, she had whetted the one and worn down the other, by every stimulus in her power, till a jury of physicians might have found her guilty of manslaughter; but perfectly unconscious of her own agency in causing the atrophy, her dear Anna Webster lived foremost in her affections, the model for every subsequent pupil. She seldom remained more than two years in a family. Sometimes the young brains were over-excited ; more often they fell into a dreary state of drilled diligence but she was too much absorbed in the studies to look close into the human beings, and marvelled when the fathers and mothers were blind enough to part with her on the plea of health and need of change.[32]

Miss Fennimore, who is consistently presented in the novel as excessively intellectual (with all the moral limitations which that implies in Yonge's fictional world), has 'killed' her former pupil by the remorseless over-stimulation of her brain, and Yonge implies that her present pupil Phoebe Fulmort, to whom 'each study was a duty, and not a subject of zeal',[33] only escapes her blighting influence by being resolutely uninterested in intellectual questions for their own sake. A similar medical rationale seems to underlie Yonge's portrayal of the harmful effects of the secret engagement between Philip and Laura in *The Heir of Redclyffe*, which we examined in a previous chapter. The very secrecy of the engagement seems permanently to impair the condition of Laura's nerves by encouraging her to dwell obsessively on her relationship with Philip, so that even when at the close of the novel she is getting married, she is still described as suffering from 'the oppression of dejection and anxiety'.[34] Philip's encouragement to Laura to strengthen her mind,[35] of course, only makes matters worse, since the mental overstimulation caused by concealment of her emotions is at the root of her problems.

32   Yonge, *Hopes and Fears*, 107 (Part 2 Ch.2).
33   Ibid., 108 (Part 2 Ch.2).
34   Ibid., *The Heir of Redclyffe*, Barbara Dennis (ed.) (Oxford: Oxford University Press, 1997), 591 (Ch.44).
35   Ibid., 153 (Ch.10).

Mental over-exertion, caused by perplexities over the household accounts, is a major cause of Violet's collapse early on in *Heartsease*, where Yonge seems to imply that the heroine's brain has been vying with the demands placed on her circulatory system by pregnancy.[36] The female health problems caused by 'irritation of the spinal cord' to which Millingen refers also appear frequently in Yonge's novels. In *The Daisy Chain*, for instance, the invalid Margaret, who suffers spinal injury in the same accident that kills her mother, has her spine problems worsened through the nervous agitation caused her by a practical joke played by her brother Harry,[37] and Sophy Kendal in *The Young Stepmother* also unites a nervous 'morbid state'[38] with a spine condition diagnosed by the similarly afflicted clergyman's wife, Mrs Dusautoy.[39] The diagnosis of spine problems was so common in the Victorian period that one of the characters in *Magnum Bonum* can refer knowingly to having a 'spine';[40] Victorian anxieties about the potential for the shock and excitement of high-speed railway travel to give rise to this condition show that it was understood as caused by nervous overstimulation.[41]

This catalogue of female ailments in Yonge's novels may give the misleading impression that she was a stereotypical Victorian lady novelist with a stock-in-trade of languishing heroines who, as Georgina Battiscombe rather aggressively puts it, 'deserved to be slapped'.[42] In fact, Yonge herself was remarkably healthy, despite her gruelling writing schedule,[43] and often suggests that her female characters are at least partly responsible for their own ill-health: she

---

36   Ibid., *Heartsease, or the Brother's Wife* (London: Macmillan, 1891), 83 (Part 2 Ch.2).

37   Ibid., *Daisy Chain*, 263–7 (Part 1 Ch.25).

38   Ibid., Yonge, *The Young Stepmother, or A Chronicle of Mistakes* (London: Macmillan, 1889), 97–8 (Ch.8).

39   Ibid., 99–100 (Ch.8).

40   Ibid., *Magnum Bonum, or Mother Carey's Brood*, 3 vols (London: Macmillan, 1879) (Ch.35).

41   See Nicholas Daly, 'Railway Novels: Sensation Fiction and the Modernization of the Senses,' *English Literary History* 66, no.2 (1999): 461–87.

42   Georgina Battiscombe, *Charlotte Mary Yonge: The Story of an Uneventful Life* (London: Constable, 1944), 63–7.

43   Coleridge, *Yonge*, 234, 288–91.

suggests, for example Margaret's morbid nervousness is the product of 'fears which, perhaps, had not been sufficiently combated in her days of health, and now were beyond control'.[44] Violet's breakdown in *Heartsease* is also presented as something that could have been avoided, if she had been better instructed at home; as Yonge comments, 'She did not know the use of change of scene, and the bracing effect of resolution, – she had no experience of self-management, and had not learnt that it was a duty not to let herself pine.'[45] The need for this kind of 'self-management' is a recurrent theme in the *Monthly Packet*.[46] In *The Young Stepmother*, there is a more extended scene to this effect, where the heroine Albinia, who has just given birth, is told off by her clergyman brother Maurice for fretting in a way which is damaging her health:

'Albinia, this is not right. It is not thankful or trustful. No, do not cry, but listen to me. Your child is as likely to do well as any child in the world, but nothing is so likely to do him harm as your want of composure.'

'I tell myself so,' said Albinia, 'but there is no helping it.'

'Yes, there is. Make it your duty to keep yourself still, and not be troubled about what may or may not happen, but be glad of the present pleasure.'

'Don't you think I am?' said Albinia, half smiling; 'so glad, that I grow frightened at myself, and –' As if fain to leave the subject, she added, 'And it is what you don't understand, Maurice, but he can't be the first to Edmund as he is to me – never – and when I get almost jealous for him, I think of Gilbert and the girls – and oh! there is so much to do for them – they want a mother so much – and Winifred won't let me see them, or tell me about them!'

She had grown piteous and incoherent, and a glance from Winifred told him, 'this is always the way.'

'My dear,' he said, 'you will never be fit to attend to them if you do not use this present time rightly. You may hurt your health, and still more certainly, you will go to work fretfully and impetuously. If you have a busy life, the more reason to learn to be tranquil. Calm is forced on you now, and if you give way to useless nervous brooding over the work you are obliged to lay aside for a time, you have no right to hope that you will either have judgment or temper for your tasks.'

44   Yonge, *Daisy Chain*, 269 (Part 1 Ch.25).

45   Ibid., *Heartsease*, 72 (Part 2 Ch.1).

46   E.g. Anon., 'Sunlight in the Clouds,' *Monthly Packet* 1 (Series 1 1851): 149–51, Anon., 'The Country Visit,' *Monthly Packet* 14 (Series 1 1857): 171.

'But how am I to keep from thinking, Maurice? The weaker I am, the more I think.'

'Are you dutiful as to what Winifred there thinks wisest? Ah! Albinia, you want to learn, as poor Queen Anne of Austria did, that docility in illness may be self-resignation into higher Hands. Perhaps you despise it, but it is no mean exercise of strength and resolution to be still.'[47]

Yonge's point here is that it is Albinia's duty, through the exercise of her will, to control her naturally irritable temperament, since in her enfeebled state of health it threatens to bring on what Brunonian medicine would have called a condition of asthenia[48] (a label which later in the century evolved into 'neurasthenia')[49] in which the overstimulated brain takes up an ever-increasing amount of the blood supply, thus bringing on the puerperal fever from which so many Victorian women died after childbirth[50] – a danger which is indicated by Albinia's comment that 'the weaker I am, the more I think'. Ultimately, Yonge shows, Albinia is morally responsible for the state of her own health, and in the context of *The Young Stepmother* this episode represents merely one aspect of Albinia's continuing struggle with the 'besetting sin'[51] into which her irritable temperament leads her, responsible for many of her *faux pas* during the novel.[52]

47   Yonge, *Young Stepmother*, 71–2 (Ch.7).
48   John Brown, *The Works of Dr John Brown*, 3 vols, intro by William Cullen Brown (London: Johnson and Symonds, 1804), 1: 110–16.
49   Oppenheim, *Shattered Nerves*, 94–9.
50   Ibid., 187–93.
51   E.B. Pusey, *Parochial Sermons*, 3 vols (London: Walter Smith, 1883), 2: 132–42.
52   Yonge, *Young Stepmother*, 83–4 (Ch.8).

The Mesmeric Woman in Victorian Culture

An aspect of Victorian attitudes towards women that has received far less critical attention than the claims about women's mental weakness and susceptibility to nervous attacks which we have been examining is the emphasis on greater female awareness of immaterial forces which is implied by Millingen's allusion to women's 'exalted spiritualism', and which is also hinted at by Sarah Ellis's references to women's 'moral power', which we examined in the previous chapter. There is a tendency among many twentieth-century critics to regard such claims, and the pervasive references to women's 'influence' in Victorian culture,[53] as mere sentimentality on the part of the Victorians, but this is to ignore the very significant Victorian interest in the phenomena of mesmerism, which were often identified with the poorly understood immaterial forces of magnetism and electricity.[54] As Alison Winter has shown, during the 1840s, mesmerized female subjects were thought capable of perceiving the immaterial 'vital force' and so of intuitively diagnosing a patient's condition,[55] and a dominant female role continued to be characteristic of the subsequent closely related nineteenth-century Spiritualist movement.[56]

The relevance of ideas about mesmerism to Yonge's Tractarian milieu is illustrated by the fact that one of the leading figures promoting mesmerism in the 1830s and 1840s was Richard Whately, the mentor of most of the leading Tractarians at Oriel College, who, as Helen Small comments, 'yoked an understanding of mesmeric phenomena with theology to produce an influential account of the

---

53   Alison Chapman, 'Phantasies of Matriarchy in Victorian Children's Literature', in *Victorian Women Writers and the Woman Question*, Nicola Thompson (ed.) (Cambridge: Cambridge University Press, 1999), 60–6.

54   Basham, *Trial of Woman*, 207.

55   Alison Winter, *Mesmerized: Powers of Mind in Victorian Britain* (Chicago: University of Chicago, 1998), 85.

56   Marlene Tromp, 'Spirited Sexuality: Sex, Marriage and Victorian Spiritualism', *Victorian Literature and Culture* 31, no.3 (2003): 68–70.

workings of the divine spirit'.[57] The connection between mesmerism and nineteenth-century medical ideas about the dominant role of the nerves, rather than the brain, in the female body is illustrated by Margaret Fuller's insistence on the 'electric' nature of women.[58] Although Fuller doesn't elaborate on this description, she seems to conceive of the female nervous system as something rather like a radio transmitter whose vibrations can be picked up by other people's nerves; in the case of women who suffer from nervous agitation, this tends to antagonize the people around them, since these women literally 'get on their nerves'.[59] Yonge seems to hint at this kind of corporeal transmission of nervous irritability in *The Young Stepmother*, where an encounter with the nervous Miss Meadows always leaves Albinia 'tingling with irritation'.[60]

Since the 'passes' by which early nineteenth-century mesmerism was understood to operate relied on a close physical proximity analogous to the slightness of the gap which permits an electric spark, mesmerism seems to have been conceived of as just such a transmission of nervous force (or magnetic or electric 'fluid') from the mesmerizer to the subject's nerves.[61] In this context, women's notoriously greater susceptibility to mesmerism than men[62] would reflect the greater dominance of the nerves in the female body, on which Millingen comments. As is indicated by Fuller's reference to the effect of nervously irritable women in 'jamming' other people's nerves, however, women appear not to have been conceived merely as passive recipients of mesmeric energy, but as actively exerting it, a view which also seems to underlie Victorian references to women's 'influence', a term strongly associated with mesmerism. The close relationship between these ideas about mesmerism and Victorian

57 Helen Small, *Love's Madness: Medicine, the Novel and Female Insanity 1800–1865* (Oxford: Clarendon Press, 1996), 167–73.
58 Fuller, *Woman*, 66.
59 Ibid., 67.
60 Yonge, *Young Stepmother*, 28.
61 Winter, *Mesmerized*, 2–3.
62 Fred Kaplan, *Dickens and Mesmerism: The Hidden Springs of Fiction* (Princeton: Princeton University Press, 1975), 34.

attitudes to sexuality[63] is apparent in Louisa Alcott's *Little Women*; when the nervously irritable Jo hugs Laurie in relief at hearing he has already telegraphed her mother about Beth's illness, she is described as 'electrifying' him.[64]

The Victorian association between women and mesmerism reinforces the religious feminism which we examined in the previous chapter, in that both appeal to personal contact as a means of conveying intuitions which can't be adequately stated in rational terms. This connection between mesmerism and religious belief underlies, for instance, George Eliot's lengthy description of Dinah Morris's Methodist preaching in *Adam Bede*. The mesmeric nature of Dinah's gaze is hinted at by Eliot's comment that her eyes 'had the liquid look which tells that the mind is full of what it has to give out, rather than impressed by external objects',[65] and Bess Cranage, who is suddenly moved to renounce the earrings which represent her vanity, is described as showing 'an unwonted quietude and fixity of attention', something which enables Dinah to communicate to her 'that belief in visible manifestations of Jesus which is common among the Methodists'.[66] The reference to 'visible manifestations' suggests that Eliot may well have had the model of the spiritualist séance in mind when describing this scene, a very topical phenomenon when she was writing the novel.[67]

Eliot describes Dinah as exerting this mesmeric influence through her 'mellow treble tones, which had a variety of modulation like that of a fine instrument touched with the unconscious skill of musical instinct',[68] an artistic analogy which suggests the relationship between nineteenth-century ideas about mesmerism and Romantic poetics, since Coleridge and Wordsworth, for example, were well-

---

63   See Gavin Budge, 'Mesmerism and Medicine in Bulwer-Lytton's Novels of the Occult', in *Victorian Literary Mesmerism*, Martin Willis and Catherine Wynne (eds) (Amsterdam and New York: Rodopi, 2006), 42–3.

64   Louisa May Alcott, *Little Women*, Elaine Showalter (ed.) (Harmondsworth: Penguin, 1989), 187.

65   George Eliot, *Adam Bede*, Carol A. Martin (ed.) (Oxford: Clarendon, 2001), 23.

66   Ibid., 28.

67   Winter, *Mesmerized*, 277–87, 293.

68   Eliot, *Adam Bede*, 26.

260

known for holding audiences spell-bound by the recitation of their works in a quasi-musical chant.[69] In this context, the Wordsworthian tropes used by Sarah Ellis to describe women's ability to convey renewed perceptions to their menfolk,[70] on which we commented in the previous chapter, acquire fresh significance. The connection between femininity, a mesmeric power of inexplicable suggestion, and a Wordsworthian poetic is more explicitly made in an 1830s review of Mrs Hemans by Francis Jeffrey, which comments on the 'peculiar charm' of Hemans's imagery:

> The very essence of poetry [...] consists in the fine perception and vivid expression of that subtle and mysterious analogy which exists between the physical and the moral world – which makes outward things and qualities the natural types and emblems of inward gifts and emotions, and leads us to ascribe life and sentiment to every thing that interests us in the aspects of external nature [...] it strikes vividly out, and flashes at once on our minds, the conception of an inward feeling or emotion, which it might otherwise have been difficulty to convey, by the presentment of some bodily form or quality, which is instantly felt to be its true representative, and enables us to fix and comprehend it with a force and clearness not otherwise attainable [...] This magical operation the poet [...] performs, for the most part, in one of two ways – either by the direct agency of similes and metaphors, more or less condensed or developed, or by the mere graceful presentment of such visible objects on the scene of his passionate dialogues or adventures, as partake of the character of the emotion he wishes to excite, and thus form an appropriate accompaniment or preparation for its direct indulgence or display.
>
> The former of those methods has perhaps been most frequently employed, and certainly has attracted most attention. But the latter, though less obtrusive, and perhaps less frequently resorted to of set purpose, is, we are inclined to think, the most natural and efficacious of the two; and is often adopted, we believe, unconsciously by poets of the highest order; – the predominant emotion of their minds overflowing spontaneously on all the objects which present themselves to their fancy, and calling out from them, and colouring with its own hues, those that are naturally emblematic of its character, and in accordance with its general expression [...]

69   Cf. S.T. Coleridge, *Biographia Literaria*, 2 vols, James Engell and W. Jackson Bate (ed.) (Princeton University Press, 1983), 2: 239.

70   Sarah Ellis, *The Women of England: Their Social Duties and Domestic Habits* (London and New York, 1839), 28–32.

> We think the fair writer before us is eminently a mistress of this poetical secret [...] Almost all her poems are rich with fine descriptions, and studded over with images of visible beauty. But these are never idle ornaments: All her pomps have a meaning; and her flowers and her gems are arranged, as they are said to be among Eastern lovers, so as to speak the language of truth and of passion. This is peculiarly remarkable in some little pieces, which seem at first sight to be purely descriptive – but are soon found to tell upon the heart, with a deep moral and pathetic impression.[71]

The terms in which Jeffrey describes poetry, as conveying 'inward feeling or emotion' by virtue of a 'mysterious analogy' between 'the physical and moral world' are remarkably similar to Keble's aesthetic of 'reserve'. In both, poetry expresses emotions which can't be openly articulated by virtue of a displacement onto 'emblematic' objects. Jeffrey's reference to the language of flowers also indicates the closeness of this poetic to the typological habits of reading encouraged by Yonge's *Monthly Packet*, which in its early numbers featured a number of articles on the significance of flowers.[72]

Jeffrey's emphasis on the spontaneous and unconscious way in which the poet's mind colours the objects which are described, however, tends to feminize the process of producing poetry, so that it becomes similar to women's unconscious exertion of 'moral power' as described by Ellis. For Jeffrey, poetry becomes a mesmerizing process of unconscious self-revelation, similar to what George Eliot has in mind when she describes Dinah's sermon as possessing 'the sort of fascination in all sincere, unpremeditated eloquence, which opens to one the inward drama of the speaker's emotions',[73] constituting a kind of discourse which can be compared to the Italian tradition of improvization celebrated by the poetess Laetitia Landon (LEL) in 'The Improvisatrice'. This conception of poetry as an intuitive externalization of the poet's *ethos*, when coupled with Vic-

---

71   Francis Jeffrey, 'Review of "Records of Woman" and "The Forest Sanctuary"', *Edinburgh Review* 50 (October 1829) in Caroline Franklin (ed.), *The Wellesley Series: British Romantic Poets* (London and Bristol: Routledge/Thoemmes, 1998), 3: 1362–4.

72   E.g. Anon., 'The Voices of Spring Flowers,' *Monthly Packet* 2 (Series 1 1851): 314–20.

73   Eliot, *Adam Bede*, 31.

torian claims for women's greater 'moral power', lead naturally to the quasi-religious prophetic stance which critics have noted is characteristic of the Victorian poetess tradition.[74]

At least one Evangelical critic objected to the Tractarian revival of Catholic religious ritual on the grounds that it was a kind of mesmerism, describing 'the monotony, the mesmeric continuousness, the sensible mechanism of the Popish chant'[75] which in his view was closely allied with sceptical materialism.[76] A similar characterization of Catholicism as inherently mesmeric can be found in Oscar Wilde's letters, which repeatedly emphasize the 'fascination' of Catholicism.[77] The association of Catholic religious practice with a mesmeric power of which women are the representative seems to underlie Anna Jameson's view, in *Legends of the Madonna*, of the worship of the Madonna as prophetic of female empowerment:

> Every where it seems to have found in the human heart some deep sympathy – deeper far than mere theological doctrine could reach – ready to accept it; and in every land the ground prepared for it in some already dominant idea of a mother-Goddess, chaste, beautiful and benign [...] Others will have it that these scattered, dim, mistaken – often gross and perverted – ideas which were afterwards gathered into the pure, dignified, tender image of the Madonna, were but as the voice of a mighty prophecy, sounded through all the generations of men, even from the beginning of time, of the coming moral regeneration, and complete and harmonious development of the whole human race, by the establishment, on a higher basis, of what has been called the 'feminine element' in society. And let me at least speak for myself. In the perpetual iteration of that beautiful image of the woman highly blessed – *there*, where others saw only pictures or statues, I have seen this great hope standing like a spirit beside the visible form: in the fervent worship once universally given to that gracious presence, I have beheld an acknowledgement of a higher as well as gentler power than that of the strong hand and the might that makes the right, – and in

---

74   LaPorte, 'Poetess as Prophet', 164–5.
75   Edward Young, *The Harp of God: Twelve Letters on Liturgical Music: Its Import, History, Present State, and Reformation* (London: Nisbet, 1861), 149.
76   Young, *Harp of God*, 192.
77   Ellis Hanson, *Decadence and Catholicism* (Cambridge, MA: Harvard University Press, 1997), 263–70.

263

every earnest votary one who, as he knelt, was in this sense pious beyond the reach of his own thought, and 'devout beyond the meaning of his will'.[78]

Yonge's familiarity with Jameson's work is shown by the episode in *The Two Guardians* where Marian refuses to go to a fancy-dress ball in order that she may have enough money to buy the first two volumes of Jameson's *Sacred and Legendary Art*, the series in which *Legends of the Madonna* was the third instalment.[79] Jameson's suggestion that the very repetition of the image of the Madonna in Western art tends to dematerialize it, making it stand for an immaterial moral power, and her description of this tradition as 'the voice of a mighty prophecy', aligns Madonna-worship with the prophetic discourse of the poetess tradition. The association with mesmerism implicit in this description is reinforced later, when Jameson replies to those who would characterize 'the Madonna subject [...] a mon-otonous theme' by emphasizing, in Ruskinian fashion, that 'a picture [...] is worth nothing except in so far as it has emanated from mind, and is addressed to mind'.[80]

For Jameson, the process of understanding art itself constitutes a kind of mesmerism, in which meanings that cannot be conveyed directly through language are transmitted from the mind of the artist into the minds of the spectators. The representation of the Madonna becomes an exemplification of this mesmeric power, in that its very monotony testifies to the way in which a significance beyond the sensory flows through art. Jameson's argument anticipates later nineteenth-century aestheticism, since 'the higher as well as gentler power' of which she sees the figure of the Madonna as prophetic is as much the power of art as it is the power of women, both being characterized in the language of mesmerism.

78   Anna Jameson, *Legends of the Madonna, as Represented in the Fine Arts* (London: Longman, Brown, Green and Longmans, 1852), xix–xx, in Gavin Budge (ed.), *Aesthetics and Religion in Nineteenth-Century Britain*, 6 vols (Bristol: Thoemmes, 2003), Vol.5.

79   Yonge, *The Two Guardians, or Home in This World* (London: Masters, 1885), 216 (Ch.5).

80   Jameson, *Madonna*, lxvi in Budge, *Aesthetics and Religion*, Vol.5.

Mesmerism in Yonge's Fiction

One of the most famous examples of mesmerism in the Victorian novel is the moment towards the end of *Jane Eyre* where Jane mysteriously 'hears' Rochester's voice calling to her, which later, when she arrives at the remote house to which Rochester has withdrawn after the fire in which his mad wife Bertha has died, she finds corresponded to a moment where Rochester has prayed in anguish to be reunited with her.[81] Yonge's interest in mesmerism is shown by the presence of a very similar moment in *The Heir of Redclyffe*, which has so far escaped the attention of her commentators. When Guy is spending Christmas Eve alone on the Redclyffe estate, having been banished the Edmonstone house as a result of Philip's unjust accusation of gambling, he sings to himself a carol he has sung with Amy, a moment which the narrator indicates is a spiritual watershed by commenting that 'the anguish of feeling, the sense of being in the power of evil, had insensibly left him'.[82] When Amy's Christmas Eve is described slightly later, it becomes apparent that she is in a mesmeric state:

> She took up a book of sacred poetry, and began to learn a piece which she already nearly knew; but the light was bad, and it was dreamy work; and probably she was half asleep, for her thoughts wandered off to Sintram and the castle on the Mondenfelsen, which seemed to her like what she had pictured the Redclyffe crags, and the castle itself was connected in her imagination with the deep, echoing porch, while Guy's own voice seemed to be chanting –

> Who lives forlorn,
> On God's own word doth rest;
> His path is bright
> With heavenly light,
> His lot among the blest.[83]

---

81   Charlotte Brontë, *Jane Eyre*, Margaret Smith (ed.) (Oxford: Oxford University Press, 1993), 471–2.

82   Yonge, *Heir*, 295 (Ch.22).

83   Ibid., 317 (Ch.24).

Typically, Yonge doesn't belabour the point in the way that Brontë does, but that there has been some mysterious mesmeric communication between Guy and Amy in her altered state of consciousness is clear from the correspondence of the words from the carol, which are also quoted in the initial passage when Guy is described singing it. Given the linkage between mesmerism and sexuality in the Victorian mind,[84] it is clear that one of the functions of this episode is to establish the depth of the relationship between Guy and Amy.

Towards the end of *The Three Brides*, a similar, if more melodramatic, episode occurs where the connection with mesmerism is made more explicit. On his deathbed, Raymond warns his somewhat puritanical sister-in-law Anne not to 'hang back from Miles's friends and pleasures' because 'if you leave him to himself, then will every effort be made to turn him from you', adding darkly that 'mesmerism has its power over whoever has been under the spell'.[85] This alienation from his spouse is of course exactly what has been undergone by Raymond, whose old flame Lady Tyrrell has been encouraging his young wife Cecil to assert her independence against Raymond's invalid mother, who lives with them. Immediately after Raymond's warning, he has a vision of Lady Tyrrell, exclaiming 'Yes, Camilla, you have had your revenge. Let it be enough. No – no; I forgive you; but I forbid you to touch her.'[86] Slightly later, after Raymond's death, Lady Tyrrell's sister Eleonora, is shocked to hear from his clergyman brother Julius the time of this fatal hallucination:

'Twelve!' Eleonora laid her hand on his arm, and spoke in a quick agitated manner. 'Camilla was much better till last night, when at twelve I heard such a scream that I ran into her room. She was sitting up with her eyes fixed open, like a clairvoyante, and her voice seemed pleading – pleading with *him*, as if for pardon, and she held out her hands and called him. Then, suddenly, she gave a terrible shriek, and fell back in a kind of fit. Mr. M'Vie can do nothing, and

---

84   Budge, 'Mesmerism and Medicine in Bulwer-Lytton's Novels of the Occult', 42–3.
85   Yonge, *The Three Brides* (London: Macmillan, 1900), 253–4 (Ch.39).
86   Ibid., 254 (Ch.29).

though she is conscious now, she does nothing but ask for you and say that he does not want you now.'[87]

The implication of these scenes is Raymond and Lady Tyrrell are still mesmerically attuned as a result of their earlier engagement (although presumably Raymond has been resisting Lady Tyrrell's influence through an act of will), a point underscored by the narrator's comment that Eleonora and Julius 'both felt how those two spirits must have been entwined, since these long years had never broken that subtle link of sympathy which had once bound them'.[88]

The almost demonic way in which Lady Tyrrell is subsequently described as having a 'weird tragic head with snake-wreathed brows' and eyes that 'burned with a strange fire that almost choked back Julius's salutation of peace'[89] brings this character close to the figure of the *femme fatale*,[90] and suggests, in view of the nineteenth-century discourse of female influence, that other powerful and morally dubious women in Yonge's fiction could be seen as belonging to a general type of 'the mesmeric woman'. The omnicompetent Flora in *The Daisy Chain*, for example, is described as 'conscious of power'[91] in her dealings with the Stoneborough Ladies' Committee, and Dr May is strangely unaware of the 'worldly motives'[92] in her behaviour which are quite apparent to Ethel.

The 'impenetrability of Flora's nature'[93] is similar to that which Alick Keith in *The Clever Woman of the Family* detects in his sister Bessie. Alick sets out the moral dangers of this kind of temperament in a conversation with the heroine Rachel:

87   Ibid., 257 (Ch.29).
88   Ibid.
89   Ibid.
90   See Nina Auerbach, *Woman and the Demon: The Life of a Victorian Myth* (Cambridge, MA: Harvard University Press, 1982).
91   Yonge, *Daisy Chain*, 369 (Part 2 Ch.4).
92   Ibid., 392–3 (Part 2 Ch.6).
93   Ibid., 393 (Part 2 Ch.6).

Rachel continued, 'I do envy that power of saying the right thing to everybody!'

'Don't – it is the greatest snare,' was his answer, much amazing her, for she had her mind full of the two direct personal blunders she had made towards him.

'It prevents many difficulties and embarrassments.'

'Very desirable things.'

'Yes; for those that like to laugh, but not for those that are laughed at,' said Rachel.

'More so; the worst of all misfortunes is to wriggle too smoothly through life.'[94]

Alick's view of his sister is borne out after her death when his cousin Colonel Keith remarks to Rachel, as they are going through the 'accumulation of expensive trinkets'[95] for which 'poor Bessie had sold herself',[96] that 'one would rather have one's faults come to light in one's life than afterwards',[97] a comment which, as is implied by the narrator's description of it as connected with a 'terrible truth',[98] strongly suggests that we are to regard Bessie as damned – a fate also implicit in the unquiet deathbed of Lady Tyrrell in *The Three Brides*. During her lifetime, however, Alick is alone in regarding his sister in this light, something which the narrator's comment that 'there was a charm about her which no one but her brother ever resisted, and even he held out by an exertion that made him often appear ungracious',[99] and a later reference to her 'witcheries',[100] suggest is due to Bessie's mesmeric influence. Alick attributes his immunity from Bessie's fascinations to his nervous irritability as an invalid, which 'sharpened my perceptions',[101] and the connection this suggests between mesmeric influence and the state of one's nerves also seems to underlie his comment that Bessie 'is one of those selfish people who are infinitely better liked than those five hundred times their worth,

94   Yonge, *Clever Woman*, 182 (Ch.14).
95   Ibid., 339 (Ch.28).
96   Ibid., 342 (Ch.28).
97   Ibid.
98   Ibid.
99   Ibid., 304 (Ch.25).
100   Ibid., 341 (Ch.28).
101   Ibid., 189 (Ch.15).

because they take care to be always pleased'.[102] Bessie exerts her mesmeric influence precisely because she is so self-satisfied, since this ensures that her nervous system only transmits vibrations that other people find soothing, in the way that poetry itself is soothing within Keble's aesthetics.[103]

A contrast between the two main female characters of *The Clever Woman of the Family* is indicated by the ambiguity of the title, which initially seems to refer to the 'strong-minded'[104] heroine Rachel, but by the novel's end has taken on a reference to Bessie Keith, who is too clever by half.[105] Bessie, as we have seen, represents an identifiable type of 'mesmeric woman' appearing in a number of Yonge's novels, the woman who uses her potent influence to achieve selfish ends; as Lionel remarks in *The Two Guardians* in relation to his sister's and the governess's decision to read Marian's letter behind her back, 'if you were boys you would never hold up your heads again; but girls can do anything, and that is the reason they have no shame'.[106] As the example of Rachel shows, however, an opposite female type also features very frequently in Yonge's fiction, a woman whose tendency to over-enthusiasm or headlong unconsidered action reflects what nineteenth-century medicine called an 'irritable temperament'.[107] Yonge's own account of her childhood indicates that she regarded herself as belonging to this latter category,[108] and a central theme of her fiction is the potential for women who struggle with their irritability to become the kind of morally powerful forces for good envisaged by the Victorian domestic ideal. As we shall see, it is this emphasis on a morally enabling struggle with one's own temperament which unites Yonge's Tractarianism with what I have argued in the previous chapter deserves to be regarded as her feminism.

---

102 Ibid., 188 (Ch.15).
103 John Keble, *Keble's Lectures on Poetry, 1832–1841*, 2 vols, trans. Edward Kershaw Francis (Oxford: Clarendon Press, 1912), 1: 25 in Budge, *Aesthetics and Religion*, Vol.1.
104 Yonge, *Clever Woman*, 172 (Ch.13).
105 Ibid., 367 (Ch.30).
106 Ibid., *Two Guardians*, 72 (Ch.5).
107 Cf. Oppenheim, *Shattered Nerves*, 206–11.
108 Coleridge, *Yonge*, 56–62, 82–3.

Irritable and Mesmeric Women in Yonge

Although for analytical purposes I have distinguished between the types of the 'mesmeric woman' and the 'irritable woman' in Yonge's fiction, I do not mean to suggest that these types are totally separate. In *The Clever Woman of the Family*, for instance, Rachel, many aspects of whose character exemplify the type of the 'irritable woman' nevertheless experiences a moment of mesmeric intuition: listening to a conversation between Alick and Bessie Keith about people who are 'obnoxiously sage' she has 'a sort of odd dreamy perception that Bessie Keith had unconsciously described her (Rachel's) own aspect, and that Alick was defending her'.[109] That Rachel's insight results from a developing mesmeric attunement between her and Alick is suggested by Yonge's use of the keywords 'odd' and 'dreamy', and the episode is obviously intended to suggest some sexual attraction between Rachel and Alick, so that his later proposal of marriage after Rachel's plans for a charitable institution for poor children have gone disastrously awry does not seem to the reader merely 'chivalry', as his fellow officer suspects it is.[110]

Yonge suggests that Rachel's rather nebulous religious doubts are largely overcome by Alick's quasi-mesmeric 'influence' once she has become his wife, though Rachel protests at the assumption that her doubts are so 'vague and shallow' as simply to evaporate.[111] This link between personal influence and the development of faith occurs in other novels by Yonge, and also forms part of the message of Newman's *University Sermons*. Here, however, I would like to draw attention to the similarity of Yonge's mesmeric model of gender roles to that of another popular mid nineteenth-century novel, Edward Bulwer-Lytton's *A Strange Story*, in which the relationship between mesmerism and female nervous irritability is fundamental to the plot.

---

109 Yonge, *Clever Woman*, 115 (Ch.8).
110 Ibid., 272 (Ch.23).
111 Ibid., 322 (Ch.26).

Whilst *The Clever Woman of the Family* consistently emphasizes Rachel's 'superabundant' strength,[112] from the point of view of the Brunonian tradition of nineteenth-century medicine such a condition was potentially as dangerous as the weakened physical state we have seen Yonge describe in the cases of *The Young Stepmother*'s Albinia, and Violet in *Heartsease*, since it contained the potential for the development of 'sthenia', a condition whose symptoms were hard to distinguish from those of 'asthenia'.[113] When Rachel is suffering from 'nervous fever' after the court case which the failure of her attempt to set up a children's home has brought about, Alick recognizes her state as one of the excessive energy of 'sthenia' when he disagrees with her doctor's orders for 'quiet' to combat 'the strain on her nerves', commenting 'I know that sort of quiet, the best receipt for distraction!'[114]

A parallel can be found in Bulwer-Lytton's 1862 occult novel *A Strange Story*, where the heroine Lilian throughout most of the novel is suffers from a condition of sthenia, where excessively developed nerves[115] compete with the other organs for supplies of blood, a condition exacerbated by the increased requirements of the reproductive organs with the onset of menstruation, and whose major symptom is her tendency to prolonged day-dreaming.[116] As the novel's mesmeric villain Margrave makes clear, it is precisely this condition of nervous irritability which makes Lilian the perfect mesmeric subject, which is why he pursues her.[117] Lilian's condition can only finally be cured, the novel suggests, through a marriage in which both partners to some degree take on each other's gender characteristics, with her doctor lover shedding some of his excessive rationalism, whilst Lilian becomes less exclusively intuitive and imaginative.[118]

---

112   Ibid., 121 (Ch.8), ibid., 266 (Ch.22).
113   Brown, *Works*, 1: 110–16.
114   Yonge, *Clever Woman*, 273 (Ch.23).
115   Bulwer-Lytton, *Strange Story*, 58 (Ch.9).
116   Budge, 'Mesmerism and Medicine in Bulwer-Lytton's Novels of the Occult', 54–55.
117   Bulwer-Lytton, *Strange Story*, 146–8 (Ch.26).
118   Budge, 'Mesmerism and Medicine in Bulwer-Lytton's Novels of the Occult', 54–6.

The trope of mesmeric correspondence in *A Strange Story* implies the exchange of gender characteristics in a way that is meant to show the complementarity of the sexes. A similar point could be made about *The Clever Woman of the Family*, though with the complication that instead of the gender stereotypes of the dreamy imaginative woman and the rationalistic man on which Bulwer-Lytton's narrative relies, Yonge appeals to notions of gender inversion. Rachel's 'vigorous health and strength'[119] make her a rather tomboyish figure (something also implied by the comment that 'her turn had always been for boys'),[120] whereas the novel's emphasis on Alick's 'languid' manner[121] tends to feminize him, as does of course his invalid status.

Rachel's masculine characteristics are precisely what Alick prizes in her, as is shown by the conversation with Colonel Keith, his fellow-officer, when he praises her 'nobleness', and significantly comments that 'I liked her that first evening, when she was manfully chasing us off for frivolous danglers round her cousin.'[122] Alick rejects the suggestion, corresponding to conventional Victorian gender ideology, that he might 'lead her and work upon her', replying 'rather resentfully' that it is 'sympathy that she wants'.[123] The implication is that Rachel's marriage with Alick makes her into the morally powerful person she has become by the novel's close[124] not through any explicit guidance on her husband's part, but by the action of his 'sympathy' in aligning and channelling the qualities she already possesses, much in the way that a piece of metal becomes magnetized through the alignment of its magnetic poles by another magnet. Through this process, the novel implies, Rachel can change from being an ineffective and off-putting 'irritable woman' to being a 'mesmeric woman' who exerts a morally uplifting influence, a potential implied near the novel's beginning when Rachel is described

---

119   Yonge, *Clever Woman*, 121 (Ch.8).
120   Ibid., 46 (Ch.3).
121   Ibid., 80 (Ch.6).
122   Ibid., 273 (Ch.23).
123   Ibid.
124   Ibid., 364–5 (Ch.30).

as exerting 'a sort of fascination in her overpowering earnestness'.[125] Dr May in *The Daisy Chain* is shown to have undergone a similar process of personal moral realignment under his daughter Ethel's influence when an onlooker remarks that 'his good qualities do not entangle one another as they used to do'.[126]

Yonge's analysis of the process of moving from irritability to mesmerism reflects her distinctive emphasis on character development, but the female types of the 'irritable woman' and the 'mesmeric woman' can be found in other mid-Victorian novelists. We have already seen that the 'mesmeric woman' is central to Bulwer-Lytton's *A Strange Story*, and the same novelist's *Lucretia*, which controversially described the machinations of a female poisoner, can be seen as a portrait of a woman of irritable temperament – the fact that she goes mad at the end of the novel is consistent with this diagnosis.[127] As Sally Shuttleworth has pointed out, many of Charlotte Brontë's characters can be understood as studies in female irritability, from the young Jane Eyre's ungovernable temper to Lucy Snowe's phantasmagoric experiences in *Villette*, and Caroline Helstone's nervous decline through unrequited love in *Shirley*.[128] Brontë also depicts mesmeric female figures, notably Shirley Keeldar, whose combination of masculine characteristics with mystical communing with a feminized Nature testifies to a nervous force which communicates itself to other characters.[129] Brontë presents a female character who has exchanged an irritable for a mesmeric temperament in *Villette*'s Paulina de Bassompierre, but the growth in 'harmony and consistency' which has led to her transformation from an irritable child to a woman whose 'refined and tender charm' consists in 'a subdued glow from the soul outward'[130] is not explored in the novel.

125 Ibid., 12 (Ch.1).
126 Ibid., *Daisy Chain*, 588 (Part 2 Ch.21).
127 Edward Bulwer-Lytton, *Lucretia, or The Children of Night* (London: Routledge, n.d.), 355–9, 414–18 (Part 2 Chs 18, 27).
128 Shuttleworth, *Charlotte Brontë and Victorian Psychology, passim.*
129 Brontë, *Shirley*, Andrew Hook and Judith Hook (eds) (Harmondsworth: Penguin, 1974), 213, 218, 222, 250, 315–16 (Chs 11, 12, 13, 18).
130 Brontë, *Villette*, pp.316–17 (Ch.24).

Jane Eyre herself is also arguably a character who has moved from a condition of irritability to a condition of mesmeric force. Brontë presents her development through an episode in which Jane returns to the deathbed of her cruel aunt Mrs Reed, one of whose daughters has grown into a rigid Tractarian, and the other into a *belle* whose only interest is in 'fashionable life'[131] – both are shown to be equally selfish. The two sisters can be seen to represent what in the Brunonian terms of nineteenth-century medicine are the 'sthenic' and 'asthenic' kinds of irritable temperament,[132] Eliza seeking an outlet for her excessive nervous energy through 'rigid regularity',[133] Georgiana craving after 'excitement'[134] to stimulate her languid nerves. Jane, by contrast, is shown as capable of occupying herself, unlike Georgiana, but also of responding to the needs of others, unlike Eliza: the two sisters represent alternative nervous syndromes which Jane might have developed had she stayed in the Reed household, and so show, by implication, what she owes to the capacity for self-control instilled at Lowood School. A comparable contrast between sthenic and asthenic forms of irritable temperament can be found in Yonge's *Hopes and Fears*, where the dashing harum-scarum (and therefore sthenic) Ratia ends the novel by embracing the disciplined life of a Plymouth Sister,[135] whilst her companion Lucilla's craving for 'excitement' has been shown to be the result of weak nerves that require stimulation (i.e. a condition of asthenia).[136]

---

131 Brontë, *Jane Eyre*, 245 (Vol.2 Ch.6).
132 Brown, *Works*, 1: 110–16.
133 Brontë, *Jane Eyre*, 247 (Vol.2 Ch.6).
134 Ibid.
135 Yonge, *Hopes and Fears*, 464 (Part 2 Ch.25).
136. Ibid., 277 (Part 2 Ch.11).

Tractarianism and the Integration of the Female Self

Brontë's message that women's virtue depends on their will's ability to exercise control over a natural nervous irritability reflects widely-held nineteenth-century medical beliefs. J.G. Millingen, for example, cites 'one of our most able and philosophic physiologists' in support of a claim that women are subject to an excessive intensity of feeling:

> With less of the volitional power that man possesses, she has the emotional and instinctive in a much stronger degree. The emotions therefore predominate, and more frequently become the leading springs of action than they are in man [...] They [...] act as powerful motives on the will; and, when strongly called forth, produce a degree of vigour and determination which is very surprising to those who have usually seen the individual under a different aspect. But this vigour, being due to the strong excitement of the feelings, and not to any inherent strength of intellect, is only sustained during the persistence of the motive, and fails as soon us it subsides. The feelings of woman being frequently called forth by the occurrences she witnesses around her, are naturally more disinterested than those of man; his energy is more concentrated upon one object, and to this his intellect is directed with an earnestness that too frequently either blunts the feelings, or carries them along in the same channel, thus rendering them selfish.[137]

For Millingen's source, the decentred subjectivity characteristic of women, located not primarily in the brain but in the diffuse nervous system, makes them at once less selfish and less effective than men: their efforts are essentially spasmodic, because they are dependent on a transient 'excitement of the feelings', but this emotional lability also makes them more responsive to others' needs. Given the similarity which nineteenth-century thinkers perceived between the female and poetic temperaments,[138] one might sum up this view of women using Matthew Arnold's description of Shelley as a 'beautiful and inef-

---

137 Millingen, *Passions*, 159–61.
138 Dugald Stewart, *Collected Works*, orig pub 1854, 11 vols, William Hamilton (ed.), intro by Knud Haakonssen (Bristol: Thoemmes, 1994), 4: 222–33, 238–43.

fectual angel, beating in the void his luminous wings in vain'.[139] As reviews of the so-called 'spasmodic poets' in the early 1850s indicate, poets were also liable to be accused of being incapable of sustained attention in the same way this passage suggests women are mentally hobbled by their physiology.[140]

Yonge's early novel *The Castle-Builders* reflects this view of women's natural capacities in its depiction of the two flighty heroines, who run through a series of short-lived enthusiasms without ever having the sticking power to achieve anything. Crucially, however, Yonge suggests that the underlying cause of their desultory ways is a failure to seek confirmation.[141] In this, Yonge reflects a Tractarian emphasis on the grace originally imparted by baptism, and subsequently by the regular communion which her heroines have not valued.[142] Yonge, however, interprets this grace in a surprisingly practical way, as a mental influence which can enable women to counteract the effects of their own biology. For Yonge, religion and feminism ultimately come down to the same thing, since they are both about resisting nature.

In the previous chapter, we noted that within Victorian domestic ideology a key function of women was to represent an associative centre for their menfolk which would exert a 'renovating virtue' akin to the Wordsworthian 'spots of time',[143] a conception which underlies Victorian invocations of the home as an antidote to the effects of industrial capitalism. We also found that Tractarianism's focus on personal moral struggle promoted the extension of domestic ideology beyond the home, so that the function of providing an associative

---

139   Matthew Arnold, 'Byron', *Essays in Criticism*, Second Series, Macmillan: London 1930, pp.116–44, pp.143–4.

140   Mark A. Weinstein, *William Edmondstoune Aytoun and the Spasmodic Controversy* (New Haven and London: Yale University Press, 1968), 153–7.

141   Yonge, *The Castle Builders; or, The Deferred Confirmation* (London: Mozley, 1854), 331 (Ch.21).

142   John Henry Newman, *Parochial Sermons* (London and Oxford: Rivington and Parker, 1835), 2: 70–5, 86.

143   William Wordsworth, *The Prelude 1799, 1805, 1850*, Jonathan Wordsworth, M.H. Abrams and Stephen Gill (ed.) (New York and London: Norton, 1979), 12: ll 208–10 (1850 text).

centre became identified with religion itself in a way that enhanced the role of women, a message we saw was implicit in the description of the church at Cocksmoor at the end of *The Daisy Chain*. I am now going to suggest that, paradoxically, it is the very lack of a naturally centred subjectivity in women, according to nineteenth-century thinking, that makes their role in elaborating the associative centres of home and church so central to Victorian culture.

The decentred nature of female subjectivity, as writers such as Millingen describe it, diffused as it is throughout the nervous system, means that women can only develop the consistency of action in which the nineteenth century thought virtue consisted[144] by developing an internal associative centre to which all their feelings are referred, a process which Yonge depicts in the development of the character of Ethel in *The Daisy Chain*. Virtuous women can make the locations of home and church into associative centres which will exert influence over the public realm of men because they have already had to develop these associative centres within themselves. Women's moral power is thus a projection of the inward associations that bind together their moral being in a way which is comparable to the 'culture of the feelings' which J.S. Mill found in the Wordsworthian poetic.[145] Conversely, moral failure for women, at least within the fairly circumscribed social world of Yonge's novels, consists in the failure to develop an associatively unified self, a condition imaged in the incoherent and aimless 'accumulation of expensive trinkets' which Ethel finds in Bessie Keith's belongings after her death.[146]

Achieving the moral power which I have suggested is associated in Yonge's fiction with the influence of the mesmeric woman is ultimately a matter of integrating the self through association, a process which also makes that self available to be transmitted to others through the very associations which give it unity. The recurrent

144 Cf. S.T. Coleridge, *The Friend*, 2 vols, Barbare E. Rooke (ed.) (Princeton: Princeton University Press, 1969), 1: 315.
145 Antony H. Harrison, *Victorian Poets and the Politics of Culture: Discourse and Ideology* (Charlottesville and London: University Press of Virginia, 1998), 13–16.
146 Yonge, *Clever Woman*, 339 (Ch.28).

theme in Yonge's fiction in which a nervously irritable and impetuous heroine, such as Rachel in *The Clever Woman of the Family* or Ethel in *The Daisy Chain*, manages to develop into an effective or even a mesmeric woman, embodies this process of self-realization. In keeping with the Tractarians' sacramental interpretation of natural theology, the transformation of female nervous irritability into moral power in Yonge's novels is portrayed in naturalistic psychological terms which nevertheless can also be seen to suggest a supernatural dimension. It is in this encoding of the supernatural within the natural that Yonge's fiction corresponds to the Tractarian doctrine of reserve.

The narrator's comment in *Hopes and Fears* that the key to the exemplary Phoebe Fulmort's character was her ability to attend to what she was doing[147] indicates that Yonge regarded a key aspect of the realization of the female self as consisting in the development of the mental power of attention. In regarding deficiency of attention (or what in present-day language we would refer to as a short attention span) as particularly characteristic of women, Yonge was simply reflecting a widely-held nineteenth-century view, which is set out by Dugald Stewart:

> The scientific or the professional pursuits of young men, establish very early in their understandings the influence of the stricter and more philosophical principles of association; while the minds of young women, like those of well educated men of independent fortune, are left much more open to the effects of casual impressions, and of such associations as regulate the train of thought in a mind which has no particular object in view.
>
> To these early habits I think it is owing, that, in general, women are inferior to well educated men in a power of steady and concentrated attention; or in what Newton called a capacity for patient thought [...] As their early habits invite their attention constantly to sensible objects, their minds become singularly alive to things external, and of consequence more liable to those habits of inattention to the phenomena of the internal world, which, while, they damp their curiosity with respect to these phenomena, prevent the cultivation of that power of reflection, without which it is impossible to study them with success.[148]

147 Ibid., *Hopes and Fears*, 400 (Part 2 Ch.20).
148 Stewart, *Works*, 4: 238–43.

Yonge's novels echo Stewart's comparison of women to 'well educated men of independent fortune' through figures such as Guy Morville in *The Heir of Redclyffe* and Louis Fitzjocelyn in *Dynevor Terrace*, who initially suffer from markedly short attention spans which they have to learn to overcome, in Guy's case through more thorough study of classical languages.[149] Significantly, Louis's 'naturally fickle and indolent disposition'[150] is regarded by his father as 'unmanly'.[151] Stewart emphasizes the role of 'principles of association' in developing the power of attention, in a way that shows he does not regard women's intellectual abilities as necessarily inferior to men's, but he does note that women suffer from inherent bodily disadvantages as a result of their 'greater nervous irritability',[152] something which makes his position quite similar to the one Yonge expresses in *Womankind*.

The same emphasis on association as a means of developing the power of attention which is essential to an educated mind underlies the educational programme set out by John Abercrombie in his extremely popular *Inquiries concerning the Intellectual Powers and the Investigation of Truth*, a book with which Yonge was probably familiar, given her activities as an educator, and whose orientation towards the natural theology tradition makes it highly compatible with the Tractarian religious position. Abercrombie emphasizes the need to combat 'that listless inactive state of mind, which is occupied with trifles, or with its own waking dreams; or which seeks only amusement in desultory pursuits which pass away and are forgotten', arguing that 'nothing [...] appears to contribute more to progress in any intellectual pursuit, than the practice of keeping one subject habitually before the mind'.[153] It is, of course, exactly this undesirably 'listless inactive state of mind' which characterizes the heroines of *The Castle-Builders*, and the need to combat it not only for intel-

---

149 Yonge, *Heir*, 57–8 (Ch.5).
150 Ibid., Yonge, *Dynevor Terrace, or The Clue of Life* (London: Macmillan, 1888), 50 (Ch.5).
151 Ibid., 47 (Ch.5).
152 Stewart, *Works*, 4: 238–43.
153 John Abercrombie, *Inquiries Concerning the Intellectual Powers and the Investigation of Truth*, 13th edn (London: Murray, 1849), 98.

lectual, but also for religious reasons forms a major theme of Yonge's writings.

In the early issues of the *Monthly Packet*, where *The Castle-Builders* was serialized, this emphasis on the need to attain intellectual discipline shades over into criticism of the desultory nature of the life to which young Victorian middle-class women were expected to conform. One of the dialogues from the 'Minor Cares' series, for example, in the context of advice on what would now be called time-management, has a description of a typical middle-class family's day whose implications are fairly uncomplimentary:

> *F.* Breakfast is never over till half-past ten, and then come the letters, and reading them, and hearing each other's, takes ever so much time, and if it is fine, one wanders in the garden, or picks leaves off the geraniums in the green-house, or something, so that I never get settled down till nearly twelve, and it is a chance if I do then, for perhaps there is a poor person to be spoken to, or I have to go to school, or the children have to be taught, if mamma is busy – or perhaps I hve to help mamma, or read to grandmamma. There is no end to the things.
>
> *S.* But if you do settle down, what then? You surely do something.
>
> *F.* Oh! there are no end of letters to write, and I am so slow at writing letters. I hate it so. Or else Mary wants me to practice, or there is something in the way. My brothers come in, and any youth they may have staying with them, or some of the set from the manor, who have no mercy on one's morning, and so luncheon comes, and there's an end of everything.[154]

Whilst this dialogue (quite probably by Yonge herself, given her penchant for the form) portrays Fanny as somewhat lacking in will-power, it isn't clear that any of the other members of the family are really getting anything done either, and her more organized inter-locutor Sophy cites an older unmarried female friend, significantly positioned outside family life, as someone who could 'tell you how to put your day on its hinges better'.[155] The description of this forty-year-old as 'just like a girl getting eager about things'[156] suggests that she

154 Anon., 'Minor Cares,' *Monthly Packet* 7 (Series 1 1854): 121.
155 Ibid., 124.
156 Ibid., 123.

represents the type of the nervously irritable woman we have been examining in Yonge's novels, as well as serving to distance this figure from the stereotype of the frustrated spinster.

The splendidly titled *Monthly Packet* series, 'Gossip; or, the Domestic Demon' makes the implied criticism of the position accorded women in middle-class life more explicit, portraying a family whose female members have nothing better to do to occupy their energies than to indulge their 'inordinate love of news',[157] a propensity whose evil effects the conclusion sardonically remarks are:

> Slight to a certain degree [...] only a marriage that might have made the happiness of two lives defeated; a poor schoolmistress plunged into difficulties; a maid-servant's heart nearly broken; and valuable and peculiarly-gifted clergyman lost to a parish.[158]

The narrator's concluding advice to 'eschew all dealings with so dangerous a familiar as the Domestic Demon we have been speaking of',[159] suggests that the description of gossip as a 'demon' inhabiting middle-class life is not to be taken entirely metaphorically.

Women and Attention in Tractarian Spirituality

The emphasis of Yonge and the *Monthly Packet* on the need for women to acquire a capacity for disciplined attention does not simply reflect an educational programme, but also corresponds to Tractarian religious teaching. Pusey, for example, argues that the acquiring of mental discipline is a precondition of effective prayer:

> If [...] you would guard against wandering in prayer, you must practise yourself in keeping a check upon your thoughts at other times [...] If we let our senses wander after every thing which presents itself to them, we are forming in

---

157 Author of 'Gentle Influences', 'Gossip, or, The Domestic Demon', *Monthly Packet* 17 (Series 1 1859): 77.
158 Author of 'Gentle Influences', 'Gossip' *MP* 18 (1859): 86–7.
159 Ibid., 87.

ourselves a habit of distraction, which will oppress us in our prayers too [...] The compass of our mind is narrow at best and cannot hold many things; one thing thrusts out another; and if we admit these manifold things into our mind, we shall have small room for its true and rightful Owner and Inmate, God.[160]

Pusey warns against gossip, and even against 'excitement about things of religion',[161] not on the grounds that they are evil in themselves, but because 'if we will be busied and careful about many things, we cannot do the one thing needful, sit at Jesus' feet and hear His words'.[162] This emphasis on religious practice as an act of concentration is very much the message of the *Monthly Packet* series 'An Object in Life', which as well as reinforcing earlier advice about time-management[163] also includes a lengthy discussion which emphasizes that 'the way in which every minute of our time is spent, must have its effect upon ourselves either for good or ill',[164] so that even activities which don't achieve any 'visible results'[165] are still valuable for their effect in disciplining the mind.

Acquiring the ability to attend to what you are doing is then for Yonge an essential step on the pathway to spiritual authenticity, and one that is particularly necessary for the nervously irritable woman, because of her liability to distraction. From the Tractarian viewpoint, not only is disciplined attention a precondition of religion, but religion itself can be described as a form of disciplined attention.

In a sermon on the Eucharist, Keble describes the kind of influence which focussing mentally on a sacrament exerts on one's character, in terms which can be seen to be particularly relevant to the predicament of the nervously irritable woman:

In our moments of excitement and perplexity, more especially in our spiritual perplexities, – whither may we so well betake ourselves for soothing and support, as to the holy Eucharistical Services [...]?

---

160   Pusey, *Parochial Sermons*, 3: 273.
161   Ibid., 3:271.
162   Ibid., 3:272. This is an allusion to Luke 10:38–42, King James version.
163   Anon., 'An Object in Life', *Monthly Packet* 15 (Series 1 1858): 38–39.
164   Anon., 'An Object in Life' *MP* 15 (1858): 493.
165   Ibid., 490.

When our frail weak souls are, according to their natural infirmity, in a tumult of earnest feelings on any event, glad or sorrowful: – when moments to which we have long looked forward are come, and we know not how to meet them worthily, how to order our hearts and minds in the Presence of God and our Lord Jesus Christ and the Elect Angels, amidst the rush and strife of many contending emotions, hope and fear, penitence and thankfulness, deep reverence and overflowing love: – then may we discern and experience more clearly than usual the condescending mercy of our God and Saviour, in coming to us outwardly by His Sacraments, as well as inwardly by His Grace. We may discern His mercy in this among other respects, that He tells us what to think of, where to fix our minds for the time. He steadies and supports, strengthens and comforts us, by commanding us and enabling us to remember Him: not simply Him, but Him engaged in some one definite work or suffering for our sakes [...]

The Holy Church is not ignorant what a troublous world of thoughts and regrets, hopes, anxieties, and satisfactions, wishful and earnest longings and prayers, will naturally gather itself around such times as these: and to assuage and regulate and sanctify them all, she calls you from them by her authoritative voice. She bids you for a while forget yourself, and be wholly taken up with the Idea and Image of our Blessed Lord at those two most solemn times of His earthly humiliation, the Consecration of the Holy Communion, and the offering of Himself on the Cross. [166]

For Keble, the Eucharist is a remedy for nervous agitation and excitement, something to which, as we have seen Millingen suggest, the Victorians thought women particularly liable. Church services are often shown as having this effect in Yonge's writings: a good example is the consecration of the church at Cocksmoor towards the end of *The Daisy Chain*, where Ethel can 'lose the present grief of Margaret's fast approaching death, leaving with the sense of peace'.[167] Yonge's emphasis here on the 'soothing' effect of church services corresponds to the key role which the concept of the 'soothing' plays in Keble's aesthetics: it appears, for example, in Keble's characterization of the aim of *The Christian Year* as to reinforce 'that *soothing* tendency in the Prayer Book' which, it is implied, is productive of that 'sober standard of feeling' to which the Tractarians attached so much

---

166   John Keble, *Sermons Academical and Occasional* (Oxford and London: Parker and Rivington, 1848), 267–9.
167   Yonge, *Daisy Chain*, 641. (Part 2 Ch.25).

religious importance.[168] It is also arguably a central term in Keble's *Lectures on Poetry*, where poetry's 'healing force' is attributed to its ability to soothe the feelings both of poets and their readers.[169]

Keble emphasizes in particular that the soothing properties of the liturgy stem from the implicit obedience it embodies to Christ's command and the Church's 'authoritative voice'. This theme of the spiritual value of obedience forms a consistent thread in Yonge's novels, with the episode in *The Heir of Redclyffe* where Amy is saved from falling off a cliff by her habit of obedience being merely the most striking example.[170] Obedience for Yonge, however, is not just a matter of doing what other people say, but also of being able to follow spiritual intuitions, as a dialogue on the concept of 'Uniform Obedience' from an early number of the *Monthly Packet* illustrates:

> There is a Spirit continually working with our spirit – I am speaking upon an awful subject – to that Spirit we must yield. Can we imagine one who has implicitly obeyed every impulse of that Holy Spirit? Do we not feel how clearly such impulses would be understood, how it would, in fact, be only natural to obey, natural according to the nature of the new birth when it has subdued and absorbed the old Adam. We have lowered and lessened the privilege of our Baptism – mercy unspeakable that we still retain it, but it is lowered and lessened. In the same measure that we have resisted and disobeyed those holy impulses, our power of discerning them has grown dim and faint. Emma, this is very awful; I am almost afraid to speak of it; but is it not still more awful to live on day after day without seeking to realize that we are indeed temples of the Holy Ghost? that He works in us, that He strives with us, combating our evil dispositions, and leading us as far as we will be led, to good. Do we not feel that to obey here in all times, and places, and things, would be blessed indeed? But our perceptions have grown dim.[171]

168   Keble, *The Christian Year*, intro by J.C. Shairp (London and New York: Dent and Dutton, 1914), 1; cf. Newman, *Parochial Sermons*, 1: 133–41.
169   The original Latin title of Keble's *Lectures on Poetry* was *De Poeticae Vi Medica*, which translates as 'On the Healing Force of Poetry'; Keble, *Lectures on Poetry*, 1: 25 in Budge, *Aesthetics and Religion*, Vol.1.
170   Yonge, *Heir*, 392 (Ch.30).
171   R.W., 'A Discussion with Aunt Mena: Obedience', *Monthly Packet* 4 (Series 1 1852): 4–5.

Viewed as a condition of receptivity to spiritual impulses which is to be attained through an abnegation of one's own wilfulness, obedience is the means by which it becomes possible to discern God's will. The ability to do 'the duty that lies nearest',[172] which in Yonge's fiction an exemplary character such as Phoebe Fulmort in *Hopes and Fears* possesses, grows out of such obedience, which ensures an intuitive awareness of the course of action which will correspond to what is providentially ordained. Attaining this condition, in which the mind is intuitively attuned to the ways of Providence, constitutes the spiritual goal of the good characters in Yonge's novels, and corresponds to Tractarian definitions of sainthood.[173] But this goal of always doing your duty is presented in Yonge's novels as a very elusive one, since what constitutes 'duty' can only be defined in relation to the circumstances of the individual and cannot be reduced to general rules, as, for instance, Guy in *The Heir of Redclyffe* finds out when he offends the neighbourhood by not attending a ball.[174] Ultimately, the concepts of 'duty' and 'obedience' represent for Yonge the attainment of an absolute existential authenticity, although the conservative social and religious message of her fiction is that this personal authenticity is more likely to be attained within existing forms than by following potentially delusive individual feelings. This emphasis on the deceptiveness of feeling is, of course, a recurrent one in Tractarian writing.[175]

As the example of the frighteningly disciplined, but religiously at sea,[176] Miss Fennimore in *Hopes and Fears* might suggest, from Yonge's Tractarian viewpoint the capacity for disciplined attention is not by itself enough to transform the nervously irritable woman into a morally powerful or mesmeric figure. For Yonge, the concomitant of obedience to the doctrine of the Church is an ultimately supernatural grace which Miss Fennimore, as a Unitarian, cannot acquire before her conversion. A striking feature of the passage from the *Monthly*

---

172   Cf. Anon., 'Object in Life', *MP* 15 (1858): 38–9.
173   Newman, *University Sermons*, 91–7.
174   Yonge, *Heir*, 136–41 (Ch.10).
175   E.g. Froude, *Remains*, 2: 26–8.
176   Yonge, *Hopes and Fears*, 107, 416–17 (Part 2 Chs 2, 21).

Packet is the connection it suggests between the condition of uniform obedience and the traditional religious doctrine of the indwelling of the Holy Spirit which follows from baptismal regeneration, an emphasis on which came to be regarded in the nineteenth century as distinctively Tractarian.[177] Following the impulses of the Holy Spirit, it is suggested, constitutes an act of obedience, because those impulses come from outside the self; they are, in Matthew Arnold's phrase, the 'consciousness of *the not-ourselves which makes for righteousness*'.[178] In a similar way, Pusey insists on the externality of religious intuition to the self when he claims in a sermon that 'the thought to pray must come from Him; it cannot come from thyself or from the evil one'.[179]

177 Peter Benedict Nockles, *The Oxford Movement in Context: Anglican High Churchmanship, 1760–1857* (Cambridge: Cambridge University Press, 1994), 230.
178 Matthew Arnold, *Literature and Dogma*, in *Dissent and Dogma*, R.H. Soper (ed.) (Ann Arbor: University of Michigan Press, 1968), *Complete Prose Works*, 10 vols (Ann Arbor: University of Michigan Press, 1960–1974), Vol.6.
179 Pusey, *Parochial Sermons*, 3: 238.

Conclusion
Feminism and the Supernatural in Yonge

In *Woman and the Demon*, Nina Auerbach sums up her sense of the centrality of the figure of the *femme fatale* to nineteenth-century representations of woman by noting that 'the mobile and militant woman is the source of the placid self-renouncing paragon of official veneration; the demonic angel arises from within the angel in the house'.[1] My analysis of the relationship between medical ideas about female nervous irritability and the discourse of mesmerism in Yonge's fiction underscores Auerbach's claim that the figures of the *femme fatale* and the 'angel in the house' are two sides of the same coin, but suggests a revision of the political valency with which Auerbach endows them, at least for the period before the rise of the New Woman. Auerbach's equation of the 'angel' of the Victorian domestic ideal with 'the diluted woman of acceptable convention'[2] assumes the essentially repressive nature of Victorian domestic ideology, but it seems questionable whether the figure of the *femme fatale* was really politically empowering for most nineteenth-century women. As I hope my account of the role played by domestic ideology in Yonge's novels has suggested, the discourse of the 'angel in the house' could lead to female empowerment, provided that it remained open for appropriation by women themselves.

This variety of nineteenth-century feminism was conservative, in that it remained within the gender oppositions of Victorian culture, but at the same time it arguably possessed greater political efficacy than radical forms of feminism, in that it was harder to object to its subversive revoicing of the language of gender, which seemed simply to pursue the implications of gender opposition even more consistently than the dominant culture. Elizabeth Barrett Browning's

1   Auerbach, *Woman and the Demon*, 186.
2   Ibid.

287

poem, ' A Man's Requirements', can be seen as representative of this conservative feminist discursive tactic. The male speaker of the poem voices an ever more extreme set of idealizing demands of the mute object of his affection, whose patriarchal repressiveness is transformed by the final stanza:

> Thus, if thou wilt prove me, Dear,
> Woman's love no fable,
> *I* will love *thee* – half a year –
> As a man is able.[3]

Barrett Browning's deflation of the male speaker does not have the effect of simply invalidating the idealization of woman which occupies the bulk of the poem, but of framing it as a challenge to the male audience, something to which the man fails to live up.

A similar cultural politics of the ideal, in which the power of a dominant monologic discourse is reappropriated through a kind of mimicry, characterizes Tractarianism itself as a movement, which may be why Tractarian ideas, as I have suggested, consorted so easily with the conservative cultural feminism this study has identified in Yonge. Tractarians such as Newman managed in matters of religious practice to disobey what they knew to be the actual views of the Anglican hierarchy, whilst claiming simply to be pursuing the implications of Anglican doctrines more consistently than the rest of the church.[4] Tractarianism's ostensible reassertion of Anglican orthodoxy was simultaneously a radicalization of the church completely transforming its political significance, in the same way that I have argued that Yonge's espousal of domestic ideology in such novels as *The Daisy Chain* paradoxically radicalizes the domestic space as a model for society outside the home.

The feminist transformation of domestic ideology in writers such as Yonge depended crucially on the liminality of women's positioning in nineteenth-century culture, to appreciate which we need to accord full weight to both terms in the oppositions through which women's

3   Elizabeth Barrett Browning, 'A Man's Requirements', in *Poetical Works* (London: Smith, Elder, & Co, 1897), stanza 11.
4   Reed, *Glorious Battle*, 146.

place in that culture was articulated. It is easy, for example, for modern critics to fall into the habit of using a phrase such as 'the angel in the house' in a rather dismissive way, without pondering the profoundly disruptive implications it must have had for a poet and a public who believed in the possibility of religious transcendence which angels represent. Whilst modern critical invocations of the phrase emphasize exclusively the boundedness and limitation of the house as the place assigned to women, the ontological fracture marked by the phrase's conjunction of 'angel' with 'house' marks a potential for social transformation which is radical in the same way as the Carlylean invocation of the 'hero' as a figure who will rescue society from utilitarian 'machinery'.[5] A contemporary parallel for what I am arguing is the connection between feminism and the discursive rupture represented by the supernatural can be found in the parodic treatment of the 'angel in the house' motif in Angela Carter's novel, *Nights at the Circus*, where the ambiguous status of the circus *aerialiste* Fevver's wings consitutes an epistemological break with the masculinist discourse of realism, as represented by the newspaper reporter Walser's notebook, which Carter links to the new feminist era of the novel's turn of the century setting.[6]

As in the case of Carlylean hero-worship, the political effectiveness of the ideology of 'Woman's Mission', for which the 'angel in the house' stands, depends on women's ability to lay claim to a liminal position between materiality and immateriality (or transcendence). As Marlene Tromp's recent study of the role of women mediums in late nineteenth-century spiritualism shows, the ability to project a female power or 'influence' was intimately linked to a 'slippage in the boundaries of the self'[7] for which belief in a person's closer contact with the spiritual world was responsible. Both poles of the opposition between the material and the immaterial are necessary, however, in order for women to continue to lay claim to this power, since a reified conception of women as simply 'angels' (which sup-

---

5   Carlyle, 'Signs', 241.
6   Angela Carter, *Nights at the Circus* (London: Picador, 1985), 9–11.
7   Marlene Tromp, *Altered States: Sex, Nation, Drugs and Self-Transformation in Victorian Spiritualism* (Albany, NY: SUNY Press, 2006), 13, 133.

presses the binary opposition of 'the angel in the house') is just as disempowering as the claim which Victorians associated with 'Mahommedanism', that women were purely physical and 'had no souls'.[8] Tromp notes that when female mediums became unable to maintain a position of liminality, and were forced into occupying one side of the opposition between matter and spirit, they became liable to be exposed as 'imposters'.[9]

In the writings of Yonge and other mid nineteenth-century conservative feminists such as Margaret Fuller, an awareness of the threat to women's power posed by this kind of reification is reflected in warnings against the danger of 'idolatry' in sexual relationships,[10] an issue which this study has explored at length in relation to Yonge's portrayal of the character of Laura in *The Heir of Redclyffe*. Idolatry is disempowering for women such as Laura because its fixation on the particularity of its object blocks the passage between material and immaterial worlds inherent in non-idolatrous, typological relationships such as that between Guy and Amy. Again, a contemporary parallel can be found in Carter's *Nights at the Circus*, where the feminist power of the heroine Fevvers is repeatedly shown to be threatened by the reification inherent in various male interpretative systems, which endanger her liminal status through classification.[11]

As is suggested by the terms in which Tromp articulates her study of spiritualism, deconstruction represents the modern critical discourse which most clearly theorizes the unlocatable position of liminality the maintenance of whose possibility I have been suggesting is essential to Yonge's conservative feminism, and at points in this study I have suggested that a self-consciously ludic play of the signifier characterizes the typological mode of interpretation encouraged by Yonge's realist fiction. Achieving this utopian space of

8   John Polidori, *The Vampyre, and Other Tales of the Macabre*, Robert Morrison and Chris Baldick (ed.) (Oxford: Oxford University Press, 1997), 8.

9   Tromp, *Altered States*, 111.

10   Margaret Fuller Ossoli, *Woman in the Nineteenth Century, and Kindred Papers Relating to the Sphere, Condition and Duties of Woman*, facs. edn, orig pub 1855, Arthur B. Fuller (ed.), intro by Horace Greeley (Freeport, NY: Books for Libraries Press, 1972), 73.

11   Carter, *Nights*, 77–83, 190–2, 289–91.

liminality, however, in the way that a character such as Ethel does in *The Daisy Chain*, is not an end in itself in Yonge's fiction, something which distinguishes her Tractarianism from the discourse of late nineteenth-century Aestheticism to which it is often close.[12] For Yonge, as my analysis of her novels has suggested, the point of sustaining a position of liminality is because it provides a critical standpoint on Victorian society. Yonge's feminist strategy of liminality, then, is closer to Derrida's later emphasis, in such texts as *Specters of Marx*, on deconstruction as an enabler of political critique than to versions of deconstruction which celebrate an endless and anarchic sliding of the signifier over the signified. Recent critical developments emphasizing the 'prophetic' element in deconstruction, in such texts as John Caputo's *The Prayers and Tears of Jacques Derrida*,[13] suggest the possibility of a *rapprochement* between this contemporary form of ideology critique and the prophetic invocation of 'Woman' as the harbinger of a new kind of society to be found explicitly in such mid nineteenth-century 'separate spheres' feminists as Margaret Fuller and Anna Jameson, and which I have suggested is also present in a more indirect form in Yonge's emphasis on her heroines' ability to develop into 'mesmeric women'. It would be plausible to see the 'Radical Orthodoxy' formulated in the wake of deconstruction by theologians such as John Milbank as a contemporary rearticulation of the Tractarian position underlying Yonge's novels.[14]

This study has suggested that the recovery of an understanding of nineteenth-century conservative feminism as a position of social critique must be linked with a critical redefinition of realism in a way that opens it to the possibility of a dimension of typological or supernatural significance beyond the material world. The category of liminality allows us to see why these issues are connected. Just as the critical force of conservative feminism's discourse of Woman is dependent on female occupation of a position of liminality between

---

12   E.g. Yonge, *Pillars of the House*, 2: 155–61 (Ch.30)

13   John D. Caputo, *The Prayers and Tears of Jacques Derrida: Religion Without Religion* (Bloomington, IN: Indiana University Press, 1997).

14   John Milbank, *Theology and Social Theory* (Oxford: Blackwell 1990).

material and spiritual worlds, so too, as I have suggested, the critical force of the Victorian realist novel depends upon an aesthetic in which it is envisaged as mediating between a formless material world and the reality of a transcendent Ideal, an aesthetic which I have linked to the intuitionist (or Common Sense) philosophical school of Brown, Reid and Stewart which dominated British intellectual life up till the 1870s (a tradition which Victorianists have often misleadingly identified as 'Coleridgean' or 'Platonist').[15] The associationist terms in which I have suggested Yonge regarded her Tractarian aesthetic of character development constitute one example of the liminal position assumed by nineteenth-century novelistic realism. The 'slippage in the boundaries of the self'[16] which Tromp identifies in the practice of female mediums is also, as I have suggested, present in the reader's relationship to the development of Yonge's characters. When character is conceived in terms of the growth of associative complexes, then the hermeneutic process by which novelistic characters are understood becomes identifiable with the characters' own psychological processes, blurring the distinction between the mind of the character and the mind of the reader and, ultimately, between Yonge as an author and the texts she produces.

The dual emphasis on the combination of female nervous weakness with spiritual power which defines the liminal position of Yonge's conservative feminism also locates women on the aporetic threshold between bodily determinism and the freedom of an immaterial will. This aspect of conservative feminism makes it representative of the British intuitionist epistemological position in general, in a way which may help to account for the intellectually compelling nature of domestic ideology for many nineteenth-century thinkers. As formulated by the highly influential and popular philosopher Thomas Brown in the 1820s, this position reconciled a

---

15 E.g. David Newsome, *Two Classes of Men: Platonism and English Romantic Thought* (London: Murray, 1974). For a study which illustrates the importance of the Common Sense tradition in nineteenth-century British intellectual life, see Richard Olson, *Scottish Philosophy and British Physics, 1750–1880* (Princeton: Princeton University Press, 1975).

16 Tromp, *Altered States*, 113.

Humean approach to scientific causality in the material world, defined in anti-essentialist terms as the 'constant conjunction' of phenomena,[17] with an argument for the validity of the human sense of freedom in the immaterial realm of morality.[18] According to Brown's account, the nineteenth-century subject inhabited an epistemological/ontological crossroads between material determinism and immaterial moral freedom, a Victorian understanding of the self which has recently been explored in relationship to the nineteeenth-century discourse of scientific biography and autobiography by Elizabeth Green Musselman.[19] Green Musselman draws attention to the important role which the concept of self-control played in establishing the intellectual authority of the male scientist within this (auto)biographical discourse, in that it demonstrated the male scientific subject's freedom from the 'automatism'[20] of the nervous conditions of which many Victorian male intellectuals complained.

The dilemma of the Victorian subject, then, caught in the differend between the scientific discourse of determinism and the Carlylean existentialist assertion of moral freedom, finds itself exemplified in the predicament of Woman, who, as conservative feminism emphasized, suffered to a greater extent from the bodily tyranny of irritable nerves but benefited from clearer spiritual intuitions of an immaterial beyond. As this study has shown, a discourse of self-control similar to the one identified by Green Musselman informs the Tractarian synthesis of associationist psychology and religion, and underlies Yonge's depiction of heroines such as Rachel in *The Clever Woman of the Family*, who ultimately attain moral authority by learning to discipline their own tendencies to nervous irritability. From the viewpoint of Yonge's conservative feminism, however, the practice of self-control alone was not enough morally to empower women, because an exclusive emphasis on it endangered

17   Thomas Brown, *Inquiry Into the Relation of Cause and Effect*, 3rd edn (Edinburgh: Constable, 1818), 324.
18   Brown, *Cause and Effect*, 173–4; cf. Thomas Brown, *Lectures on the Philosophy of the Human Mind*, 4 vols (Edinburgh: Tait, 1824), 1: 144–5.
19   Elizabeth Green Musselman, *Nervous Conditions: Science and the Body Politic in Early Industrial Britain* (Albany, NY: SUNY Press, 2006).
20   Ibid., 6.

women's liminal position between the material and the immaterial. This is the implication, for example, of Yonge's portrayal of Laura in *The Heir of Redclyffe*, where the control of emotion counselled by Philip leads ultimately to a condition of permanent nervous disability,[21] and of her depiction of Janet Brownlow in *Magnum Bonum*, whose sustained capacity both for deceit about a lost will and for medical study suggests a high degree of self-discipline, but who is consistently described as unspiritual and lumpen.[22] In the absence of openness to the supernatural dimension of moral intuition, self-control for Yonge merely makes these female characters into lesser copies of men.[23]

Within the terms of reference adopted by Yonge and other nineteenth-century conservative feminists, the very possibility of feminism depends on the supernatural influence of religion, which is why, as I have commented, this kind of position is often characterized, from the purely naturalist position adopted by many present-day feminist critics, as patriarchal and repressive.[24] Since Yonge, like most other nineteenth-century thinkers, accepts women's natural and bodily inferiority to men, within the terms of a position which accepts no point of reference other than the natural, Yonge must appear to be 'antifeminist', although for consistency's sake such critics should also concede that by this criterion even iconic feminist figures such as Mary Wollstonecraft must be described as 'antifeminist'.[25] This problem with this kind of naturalist interpretative stance, as my study has suggested, is not only that it makes Yonge's fiction 'unreadable', but also that, if consistently applied, it would stand in the way of any appreciation of the achievement of a novelist such as Charlotte Brontë – as indeed it does in the work of Q.D. Leavis.[26]

21   Yonge, *Heir*, 591.
22   Ibid., *Magnum Bonum*, 182 (Ch.10; edition is through-numbered across volumes).
23   Cf. Yonge, *Young Stepmother*, 42 (Ch.4)
24   Schaffer, 'Mysterious Magnum Bonum', 247.
25   Cf. Barbara Taylor's emphasis on 'the central part played by religion in Wollstonecraft's thought' (*Mary Wollstonecraft and the Feminist Imagination* [Cambridge: Cambridge University Press, 2003], 4).
26   Leavis, *Fiction and the Reading Public*, 237.

The context of nineteenth-century natural theology in which the mind's capacity for moral intuition could be equated with a supernatural grace freeing the mind from the system of physical determinism is set out by John Abercrombie, who acknowledges the influence of Brown on his educational and psychological theory:[27]

The highest state of man consists in his purity as a moral being; and in the habitual culture and full operation of those principles by which he looks forth to other scenes and other times. Among these are desires and longings, which nought in earthly science can satisfy; which soar beyond the sphere of sensible things, and find no object worthy of their capacities, until, in humble adoration, they rest in the contemplation of God [...] There is now felt, in a peculiar manner, the influence of that healthy condition of the moral feelings, which leads a man not to be afraid of the truth. For, on this subject, we are never to lose sight of the remarkable principle of our nature [...] by which a man comes to reason himself into the belief of what he wishes to be true, – and shuts his mind against, or even arrives at an actual disbelief of, truths which he fears to encounter [...]

This condition of mind presents a subject of intense interest, to every one who would study his own mental condition, either as an intellectual or a moral being. In each individual instance, it may be traced to a particular course of thought and of conduct, by which the mind went gradually more and more astray from truth and from virtue [...] The first volition, by which the mind consciously wanders from truth, or the moral feelings go astray from virtue, may impart a morbid influence which shall perpetuate itself and gain strength in future volitions, until the result shall be to poison the whole intellectual and moral system [...]

Every candid observer of human nature must feel this statement to be consistent with truth; and by a simple and legitimate step of reasoning, a principle of the greatest interest seems to arise out of it. When this loss of harmony among the mental faculties has attained a certain degree, we do not perceive any power in the mind itself, capable of correcting the disorder which has been introduced into the moral system. Either, therefore, the evil is irremediable and hopeless, or we must look for an influence from without the mind, which may afford an adequate remedy. We are thus led to discover the adaptation and the probability of the provisions of the Christian revelation, where an influence is indeed disclosed to us, capable of restoring the harmony which has been destroyed, and of raising man anew to the sound and healthy condition of a moral being.[28]

27   Abercrombie, *Intellectual Powers*, 34.
28   Ibid., 340–2.

The combination of an associationist with an intuitionist model of the mind, which is characteristic of Brown's philosophical psychology, allows Abercrombie to map psychology onto theology. Abercrombie acknowledges the fundamental determinism of associationist accounts of the mind, in which one failing can end up by vitiating the whole 'moral system', a process most famously portrayed in Farrar's 1850s school story *Eric; or Little by Little* but also underlying moral tales by Maria Edgeworth such as 'Lazy Lawrence' and theorized in Paley's *Moral Philosophy*.[29] He is able, however to invoke a supernatural 'influence from outside the mind' to allow for the possibility of escaping this determinism. Sin becomes a state of irremediable subjection to a nightmarish materiality of the mind, whereas grace is a miraculous act of restoration to a 'healthy condition of the moral feelings'.

This appeal to an external supernatural influence of grace has important implications for the role of women within Tractarian thought, which allow Yonge to formulate her conservative feminism. The very decentredness of self which for the Victorians was the consequence of women's greater susceptibility to influences originating in the nervous system can, in this supernaturalist view, imply that women, instead of being necessarily subjected to the materiality of the body, are more capable than men of transcending this materiality through their greater sensitivity to moral intuition. This supernatural influence of grace has the potential to form the basis of a woman's whole character, given that this character represents an associative and rhizomatic complex of nervous impulses, rather than the more goal-directed and selfish subjectivity typical of men. The very lack of coherence which medical psychologists identify in the female character, subject as it is to the random impingements of external circumstances, makes it more likely than in the case of men that the divine consistency of grace will come to form the inner principle guiding female psychological development.[30]

29 Paley, *Works*, 147–8.

30 From an associationist viewpoint, the strength of such intuitions matters much less than their consistency. This Tractarian position could be seen as a religious reinterpretation of Hume's argument in the *Enquiry Concerning the Principles*

The psychologized supernaturalism characteristic of the Tractarians forms in this way the basis for a religious feminism. Isaac Williams, for instance, suggests that Christ 'has diffused throughout all the sex His strength [...] affording the measures of His grace, according to the measures of their infirmities and needs'.[31] Women's moral frailty becomes, paradoxically, the enabling condition of their moral power under the Christian dispensation, since the guiding influence of the Holy Spirit is capable of supplying their want of natural consistency.

Abercrombie's background as a doctor, and use of the language of health and disease, point to a troping of the spiritual and the bodily which is fundamental to Yonge's portrayal of her characters' moral progress. This is particularly, though not exclusively, true of her female characters, and I would like to conclude by suggesting that Yonge's attitude to gender difference can itself be regarded as a form of natural theology in which the material and the immaterial are at once sacramentally identified and essentially discontinuous in a way that reflects the Tractarian understanding of typology.

In a well-known passage from *The Clever Woman of the Family*, Yonge expresses her conception of the sexes' reciprocal moral influence, *a propos* of the effect on Rachel of helping the saintly blind clergyman Mr Clare with research for his sermon:

> Unwilling as she would have been to own it, a woman's tone of thought is commonly moulded by the masculine intellect, which, under one form or another, becomes the master of her soul. Those opinions, once made her own, may be acted and improved upon, often carried to lengths never thought of by their inspirer, or held with noble constancy and perseverance even when he himself may have fallen from them, but from some living medium they are

of Morals, that all that is necessary for benevolence to be regarded as forming the basis of moral judgements is 'some particle of the dove kneaded into our frame, along with the elements of the wolf and serpent' (David Hume, *Enquiries Concerning Human Understanding and Concerning the Principles of Morals*, P.H. Nidditch (ed.) [Oxford: Clarendon Press, 1975], 271). The references to Hume in Newman's *University Sermons* show that Hume is a point of reference for Tractarian thought.

31   Isaac Williams, *The Gospel Narrative of Our Lord's Passion Harmonized: With Reflections* (London: Rivington, 1842), 108.

almost always adopted, and thus, happily for herself, a woman's efforts at scepticism are but blind faith in her chosen leader, or, at the utmost, in the spirit of the age. And Rachel having been more than usually removed from the immediate influence of a superior man, had been affected by the more feeble and distant power, a leading that appeared to her the light of her independent mind; but it was not in the nature of things that, from her husband and his uncle, her character should not receive that tincture for which it had so long waited, strong and thorough in proportion to her nature, not rapid in receiving impressions, but steadfast and uncompromising in retaining and working on them when once accepted.[32]

In the context of Keble's injunction 'Don't be original',[33] where originality is implicitly equated with a sinful wilfulness, Yonge's insistence on the essentially reproductive nature of women's minds does not necessarily imply that they are secondary in moral status. The emphasis on Rachel's ability to retain 'impressions' which may be 'carried to lengths never thought of by their inspirer' suggests that the associative centre of her character, once formed, will be powerful enough to draw the world around Rachel into its orbit, something implied by Ermine's description of Rachel towards the novel's conclusion as 'a thorough wife and mother, all the more so for her being awake to larger interests, and doing common things better for being the Clever Woman of the family'.[34] Rachel's reformation of herself will ultimately translate into a reformation of the world around her, but her recognition that this is a process that can only come about through the unconscious influence of association, rather than through the self-assertion of the conscious will is indicated by Ermine's comment that 'it is beautiful to see her holding herself back, and most forbearing where she feels most positive'.[35]

The transformation of Rachel from a nervously irritable to a mesmeric woman is portrayed by Yonge as a product of the way in which a 'masculine intellect' has become 'the master of her soul'. This is a process which has parallels in other Yonge novels, for

32   Yonge, *Clever Woman*, 337–8 (Ch.28).
33   G.B. Tennyson, *Victorian Devotional Poetry: The Tractarian Mode* (Cambridge, MA: Harvard University Press, 1981), 80.
34   Yonge, *Clever Woman*, 365 (Ch.30)
35   Ibid.

example in the relationship between Miss Fennimore and Robert Fulmort in *Hopes and Fears*, and between Amy and Guy in the *Heir of Redclyffe*; in a negative way, this could also be said of the relationship between Laura and Philip. In Yonge's own life this is paralleled in her relationship with John Keble.[36] Yonge emphasizes that such a relationship is not merely a matter of conviction of the intellect by noting that even correct religious opinions require to be transmitted through the 'living medium' of another's personality.

Yonge's insistence on the ultimately male source of this formation of character at one level reflects the medical origin of nineteenth-century ideas about mesmerism, in which the more highly organized, brain-dominated male personality tends to be regarded as a transmitter of nervous force in localized, one-to-one situations, whereas the influence of the mesmeric woman tends to be seen as more public, and hence more a matter of the diffuse associations of crowd psychology,[37] a model of gender roles which can be seen in the contrast between the mesmeric personalities of M. Paul and the actress Vashti in Brontë's *Villette*, and which is fundamental to the plot of du Maurier's *Trilby*. Yonge's own adopted role as a publicist for the Oxford Movement[38] corresponds to this model, in which male influence becomes generally diffused through that transposition of the personal onto the public realm which I have suggested is characteristic of Victorian domestic ideology. Canon Moberly's funeral sermon for Yonge, preached on the text 'the desolate hath many more children than she which hath an husband',[39] suggests that others recognized in Yonge's life this kind of gendered intellectual role, in which women become central to the new mass culture that was emerging at the end of the nineteenth century.

But regarded in the context of the supernatural dimension which forms the other pole of Tractarian natural theology, Yonge's emphasis

36 Coleridge, *Yonge*, 126–31; Romanes, *Yonge: An Appreciation*, 7–13, 32.
37 For Victorian interest in crowd psychology, see Mackay, *Extraordinary Popular Delusions and the Madness of Crowds*, xiii, xv.
38 Dennis, *Yonge*, 122–7.
39 Galatians, 4:27. The sermon is discussed in Julia Courtney, 'Charlotte Mary Yonge: A Novelist and Her Readers', unpublished PhD thesis (London University, 1989), 18–23.

on the male origin of character formation reflects not so much a pragmatic acceptance of male dominance as a need to insist on a quasi-Modernist impersonality of the spiritual, the externality to the self of the grace represented by moral intuition. From this perspective, masculinity becomes the transcendent Other of the morbid and feminized nineteenth-century subject. A dialogue from the *Monthly Packet* series 'An Object in Life' sets out the Tractarian drive towards an elusive objectivity which underlies Yonge's fiction:

'You must let me set you right again, my dear,' Mr. Easton said; 'it is not only in spite of what we call our disadvantages that we may do well, but even *by means of them*. What we fancy hindrances may be, if rightly used, real helps, just what we really need to conform us to God's Will, to make us what He would have us to be.'

'Yes, I suppose it must be so,' Anstance said; 'the difficulty is how to feel that it is so.'

'Never mind that, only *act* upon your belief, and better feelings will come at last; and strive against doubting and discontented thoughts and feelings, as against sin, for such, indeed, they are. Try to do your duty in that state of life to which it has pleased God to call you, and don't torment yourself wtih considering how you *feel* about it.'

'That is more easily said than done; and, indeed, Uncle, I don't think you know how I do feel sometimes. It is better here, but when I am where I have no one to understand me and sympathize with me, that is the worst trial.'

'Can you bear a little more plain speaking?' her uncle asked.

'Oh, as much as you please, I shall only be thankful to you,' was her answer, and he went on.

'Well, I think you are rather too full of yourself, or at least of your own feelings; it is the way with young ladies now-a-days.'

It was not pleasant to be accused of selfishness, but it was still less pleasant to Anstace to be thus classed among 'young ladies, now-a-days,' in this indiscriminate way, and her tone betrayed a little mortification as she answered,

'I did not know I was selfish, Uncle.'

'I believe you did not; and I don't mean to accuse you of selfishness in the worst sense of the word. It is rather self-contemplation or self-consciousness, a habit of dwelling to a morbid extent on thoughts of self, one's own feelings, and so forth, which I am inclined to fancy a sort of mental epidemic among the young ladies of the present day.'[40]

---

40   Anon., 'Object in Life', 499–500.

Although Yonge's own disabling self-consciousness seems to be reflected in this passage,[41] the nineteenth-century reader would have recognized in this morbid subjectivity not just a 'mental epidemic among the young ladies' but a central theme of poems such as Tennyson's *Maud*. It is for this reason, I would suggest, that Yonge's Tractarian novels about young ladies found such a large public in the mid-nineteenth century. Women in Yonge's novels represent the site of a metaphysical and religious anxiety about the possibility of relationship between the material world and the immaterial realm of spirit,[42] in which the unavailability of a sphere beyond the material is figured as an immersion in the self – women, of course, function in this way in Yonge's fiction as a result of the greater medicalization of the female body in the nineteenth century, although, as we have noted, invalids such as Charles Edmonstone in *The Heir of Redclyffe* can fulfil a similar role. The moral threat in Yonge's novels is ultimately that of materiality itself: Rachel, in *The Clever Woman of the Family*, for example, comes to realize at a crucial moment 'her unconscious detachment from all that was not visible and material',[43] in a way which echoes Keble's warnings about the dangers of an 'unconscious rationalism' whose effect is 'to withdraw attention, and finally faith, from the unseen truths themselves, towards the process in our own minds, which is matter of feeling and experience'.[44] Yonge's *bildungsromanen* of female development, in describing the attainment of authentic relationship with others, typologically enact a transcendence of this materiality, and so reaffirm the psychologized natural theology of Tractarianism.

41   Romanes, *Yonge: An Appreciation*, 150.
42   Henry Longueville Mansel, *The Limits of Religious Thought Examined in Eight Lectures* (London: Murray, 1859), 55–8.
43   Yonge, *Clever Woman* (Ch.23), 286.
44   Keble, *Sermons*, 379.

Bibliography

Abercrombie, John. *Inquiries Concerning the Intellectual Powers and the Investigation of Truth*. 13th edn (London: Murray, 1849).

Abrams, M.H. *The Mirror and the Lamp: Romantic Theory and the Critical Tradition* (Oxford: Oxford University Press, 1971).

Adorno, Theoder and Max Horkheimer. *Dialectic of Enlightenment*. Translated by John Cumming (London: Verso, 1979).

Alcott, Louisa May. *Little Women*. Edited by Elaine Showalter (Harmondsworth: Penguin, 1989).

Anon. *Plain Sermons, by Contributors to the 'Tracts for the Times'* (London: Rivington, 1845).

——. Review of *A System of Logic* by J.S. Mill. *British Quarterly Review* 4 (1846): 1–38.

——. 'The Cardioscope'. *Monthly Packet* 2 (Series 1 1851): 16–28.

——. 'An Old Letter'. *Monthly Packet* 1 (Series 1 1851): 126–7.

——. 'Sunlight in the Clouds'. *Monthly Packet* 1 (Series 1 1851): 149–65.

——. 'The Voices of Spring Flowers'. *Monthly Packet* 2 (Series 1 1851): 314–20.

——. Review of *Heartsease; or, The Brother's Wife*. *Fraser's Magazine* 50 (1854): 489–503.

——. 'Minor Cares'. *Monthly Packet* 7 (Series 1 1854): 120–5.

——. 'Mythological Legends: The Legend of Glaucus and Polyidus'. *Monthly Packet* 9 (Series 1 1855): 262–9.

——. 'Likes and Dislikes'. *Monthly Packet* 11 (Series 1 1856): 417–38; 12 (Series 1 1856): 345–60.

——. 'School Sketches'. *Monthly Packet* 12 (Series 1 1856): 191–200.

——. 'Church of England Industrial Home'. *Monthly Packet* 14 (Series 1 1857): 657–9.

——. 'The Country Visit'. *Monthly Packet* 14 (Series 1 1857): 170–5.

——. 'An Object in Life'. *Monthly Packet* 15 (Series 1 1858): 36–50; 270–83; 486–506.

——. 'Autumn Wanderings'. *Monthly Packet* 18 (Series 1 1859): 102–5.

——. 'Life Among the Factories'. *Monthly Packet* 18 (Series 1 1859): 540–50.

——. 'Sandwell'. *Monthly Packet* 17 (Series 1 1859): 330–4.

——. 'Will No One Do Likewise? A Tale of East London Life'. *Monthly Packet* 17 (Series 1 1859): 289–302; 401–23; 505–24; 18 (Series 1 1859): 181–92; 290–304.

——. 'Grandmamma. "My Life, and What Shall I Do with It?"'. *Monthly Packet* 21 (Series 1 1861): 420–6.

——. 'Life Among the Factories'. *Monthly Packet* 21 (Series 1 1861): 105–11.

——. 'Shadow and Substance'. *Monthly Packet* 22 (Series 1 1861): 590–601.

——. 'Egotism'. *Monthly Packet* 4 (Series 2 1868): 517–18.

——. Review of *A System of Logic* by J.S. Mill. *Prospective Review* 6 (1871): 77–111.

——. The Revolution – in Logic. *The Month* 15 (1871): 385–401.

——. 'The Story of Thalaba'. *Spider Subjects*, March 1874, 4–8, separately paginated insert in *Monthly Packet* 17 (Series 2 1874).

——. 'The Novels of Miss Yonge'. *Edinburgh Review* 102 (1905): 375.

——. 'Children's Literature'. In *A Peculiar Gift: Nineteenth-Century Writings on Books for Children*, edited by Lance Salway, 299–331 (Harmondsworth: Kestrel, 1976).

Arnold, Matthew. *Complete Prose Works*. 10 vols (Ann Arbor: University of Michigan Press, 1960–1974).

——. 'Preface to Poems (1853)'. In *The Nostalgia for Classicism*, 1–15 (Ann Arbor: University of Michigan, 1960).

——. *Literature and Dogma*. In *Dissent and Dogma*. Edited by R.H. Soper (Ann Arbor: University of Michigan Press, 1968).

Artz, Johannes. 'Newman as a Philosopher'. *International Philosophical Quarterly* 16 (1976): 263–87.

Auden, W.H. 'The Quest'. In *Collected Poems*. Edited by Edward Mendelson (London: Faber, 1976): 224–31.

Auerbach, Nina. *Woman and the Demon: The Life of a Victorian Myth* (Cambridge, MA: Harvard University Press, 1982).

Author of 'Gentle Influences'. 'Gossip, or, The Domestic Demon'. *Monthly Packet* 17 (Series 1 1859): 75–82; 18 (Series 1 1859): 83–7.

B.L.K. 'Imagination'. *Monthly Packet* 1 (Series 2 1866): 469–74.

Baker, Joseph Ellis. *The Novel and the Oxford Movement* (New York: Russell and Russell, 1965).

Ballard, J.G. 'Introduction to the French Edition of *Crash*'. In *Crash* (London: Paladin, 1990): 5–9.

Barrett Browning, Elizabeth. *Poetical Works*. Edited by Frederic G. Kenyon (London: Smith, Elder and Co, 1897).

Barthes, Roland. *Mythologies*. Translated by Annette Lavers (London: Vintage, 1993).

Basham, Diana. *The Trial of Woman: Feminism and the Occult Sciences in Victorian Literature and Society* (Basingstoke: Macmillan, 1992).

Battiscombe, Georgina. *Charlotte Mary Yonge: The Story of an Uneventful Life* (London: Constable, 1944).

Baudelaire, Charles. 'Edgar Allan Poe: His Life and Works'. In *Selected Writings on Art and Literature*. Translated by P.E. Charvet (Harmondsworth: Penguin, 1992).

Beddoes, Thomas. *Hygeia, or Essays Moral and Medical on the Causes Affecting the Personal State of Our Middling and Affluent Classes*. 3 vols (Bristol: Phillips, 1802–1803).

Belsey, Catherine. *Critical Practice* (London and New York: Routledge, 1987).

Bewell, Alan. *Romanticism and Colonial Disease* (Baltimore and London: Johns Hopkins University Press, 1999.

Bloom, Harold. *Agon: Towards a Theory of Revisionism* (New York: Oxford University Press, 1982).

Borzello, Frances. 'Pictures for the People'. In *Victorian Artists and the City*. Edited by Ira Bruce Nadel and F.S. Schwarzbach (New York: Pergamon Press, 1980): 30–40.

Brontë, Charlotte. *Shirley*. Edited by Andrew Hook and Judith Hook (Harmondsworth: Penguin, 1974).

——. *Jane Eyre*. Edited by Margaret Smith (Oxford: Oxford University Press, 1993).

Brooke, Stopford. *Theology in the English Poets: Cowper, Coleridge, Wordsworth and Burns* (London and New York: Dent and Dutton, n.d.).

Brooks, Chris. *Signs for the Times: Symbolic Realism in the Mid-Victorian World* (London: George Allen and Unwin, 1984).

Brown, John. *The Works of Dr John Brown*. 3 vols. With an introduction by William Cullen Brown (London: Johnson and Symonds, 1804).

Brown, Marshall. *The Gothic Text* (Stanford, CA: Stanford University Press, 2005).

Brown, Thomas. *Inquiry into the Relation of Cause and Effect*. 3rd edn (Edinburgh: Constable, 1818).

——. *Lectures on the Philosophy of the Human Mind*. 4 vols (Edinburgh: Tait, 1824).

——. *Life and Collected Works*. 8 vols. With an introduction by Thomas Dixon (Bristol: Thoemmes Press, 2003).

Browning, Elizabeth Barrett. 'A Man's Requirements'. In *Poetical Works* (London: Smith, Elder, & Co, 1897): 304–5.

Browning, Robert. 'Porphyria's Lover'. In *The Poems*. 2 vols. Edited by John Pettigrew and Thomas J Collins (Harmondsworth: Penguin, 1981), 1: 380–1.

Budge, Gavin (ed.). *Aesthetics and Religion in Nineteenth-Century Britain*. 6 vols (Bristol: Thoemmes, 2003).

——. 'Poverty and the Picture Gallery: The Whitechapel Exhibitions and the Social Project of Ruskinian Aesthetics'. *Visual Culture in Britain* 1, no.2 (2000): 43–56.

——. 'Realism and Typology in Charlotte M. Yonge's *The Heir of Redclyffe*'. *Victorian Literature and Culture* 31 no.1 (2003): 193–223.

——. 'History and the New Historicism: Symbol and Allegory as Poetics of Criticism'. In *Critical Pasts: Writing Criticism, Writing History*. Edited by Philip Smallwood, 115–43 (Lewisburg, PA: Bucknell University Press, 2004).

——. 'Mesmerism and Medicine in Bulwer-Lytton's Novels of the Occult'. In *Victorian Literary Mesmerism*. Edited by Martin Willis and Catherine Wynne (Amsterdam and New York: Rodopi, 2006): 39–59.

Bullen, J.B (ed.). *The Sun is God* (Clarendon Press: Oxford, 1989).

Bulwer-Lytton, Edward. *Lucretia, or The Children of Night* (London: Routledge, n.d.).

——. *Night and Morning*. Knebworth edn (London: Routledge, n.d.).

——. 'On the Normal Clairvoyance of the Imagination'. In *Miscellaneous Prose Works*, 27–38 (London: Bentley, 1868).

——. *A Strange Story* (London: Routledge, 1897).

Burke, Edmund. 'Reflections on the Revolution in France'. In *The French Revolution 1790–1794*. Vol.8 of *The Writings and Speeches of Edmund Burke*. 9 vols. Edited by L.G. Mitchell and William B. Todd (Oxford: Clarendon Press, 1989).

Byatt, A.S. and Ignês Sodré. *Imaginary Characters: Six Conversations About Women Writers*. Edited by Rebecca Swift (London: Chatto and Windus, 1995).

Caldwell, Janis McLaren. *Literature and Medicine in Nineteenth-Century Britain: From Mary Shelley to George Eliot* (Cambridge: Cambridge University Press, 2004).

Caputo, John D. *The Prayers and Tears of Jacques Derrida: Religion Without Religion* (Bloomington, IN: Indiana University Press, 1997).

Carlyle, Thomas. 'Signs of the Times'. In *Critical and Miscellaneous Essays*. 7 vols (London: Chapman and Hall, 1872), 2: 230–52.

——. *Past and Present* (London: Oxford University Press, 1909).

Carroll, Lewis. 'The Hunting of the Snark'. In *Complete Works*. With an introduction by Alexander Woollcott, 677–99 (London: Nonesuch Press, 1939).

Carter, Angela. *Nights at the Circus* (London: Picador, 1985).

Chadwick, Owen. *The Mind of The Oxford Movement* (London: Adam and Charles Black, 1960).

Chalmers, Thomas. *On the Miraculous and Internal Evidences of the Christian Revelation*. 2 vols (Glasgow: Collins, n.d.).

——. 'Preface to Dr Brown's Lectures on Ethics'. In *Lectures on the Philosophy of the Human Mind*. 20th edn, xxxiv–xl (London: Tegg, 1860).

Chapman, Alison. 'Phantasies of Matriarchy in Victorian Children's Literature'. In *Victorian Women Writers and the Woman Question*. Edited by Nicola Thompson (Cambridge: Cambridge University Press, 1999): 60–79.

Coleridge, Christabel. *Charlotte Mary Yonge: Her Life and Letters* (London: Macmillan, 1903).

Coleridge, S.T. *The Friend*. 2 vols. Edited by Barbare E Rooke (Princeton: Princeton University Press, 1969).

——. *On the Constitution of the Church and State*. Edited by John Colmer (Princeton: Princeton University Press, 1976).

——. *Biographia Literaria*. 2 vols. Edited by James Engell and W. Jackson Bate (Princeton University Press, 1983).

——. *Confessions of an Inquiring Spirit*. Edited by Harold Bloom (New York: Chelsea House, 1983).

Collins, Anthony. *A Discourse of the Grounds and Reasons of the Christian Religion* (London [s.n.], 1724).

Colloms, Brenda. *Charles Kingsley: The Lion of Eversley* (London: Constable, 1975).

Cooper, Edward H. 'Charlotte Mary Yonge'. *Fortnightly Review* 69 (n.s. 1901): 852–8.

Courtney, Julia. 'Charlotte Mary Yonge: A Novelist and Her Readers'. Unpublished PhD thesis. London University, 1989.

Crichton, Alexander. *An Inquiry into the Nature and Origin of Mental Derangement.* 2 vols (London: Cadell and Davies, 1798).

Dallas, E.S. *The Gay Science.* 2 vols (London: Chapman and Hall, 1866).

Daly, Nicholas. 'Railway Novels: Sensation Fiction and the Modernization of the Senses'. *English Literary History* 66, no.2 (1999): 461–87.

Darwin, Erasmus. *Zoonomia.* Facs. edn of 1794–1796 edn, 2 vols (New York: AMS Press, 1974).

David, Deirdre. *Intellectual Women and Victorian Patriarchy: Harriet Martineau, Elizabeth Barrett Browning, George Eliot* (Ithaca, NY: Cornell University Press, 1987).

Dennis, Barbara. *Charlotte Yonge (1823–1901), Novelist of the Oxford Movement: A Literature of Victorian Culture and Society* (Lewiston, NY: Edwin Mellen, 1992).

Dickens, Charles. *American Notes and Pictures from Italy* (London: Oxford University Press, 1957).

Eagleton, Terry. *Ideology.* Longman Critical Reader (London: Longman, 1994).

Echolls, Alice. *Daring to be Bad: Radical Feminism in America 1967–1975* (Minneapolis: University of Minnesota Press, 1989).

Eco, Umberto. *The Open Work.* With an introduction by David Robey, translated by Anna Cancogni (Cambridge, MA: Harvard University Press, 1989).

Edgeworth, Maria. *The Parent's Assistant, or Stories for Children* (London: Macmillan, 1897).

Eigner, Edwin M. *The Metaphysical Novel in England and America: Dickens, Bulwer, Hawthorne, Melville* (Berkeley and Los Angeles: University of California Press, 1978).

Eliot, George. *Adam Bede.* Edited by Carol A. Martin (Oxford: Clarendon, 2001).

Eliot, T.S. 'Burnt Norton'. In *Complete Poems and Plays.* In *Poems and Plays,* 171–6 (London: Faber, 1969).

——. 'Hamlet'. In *Selected Prose.* Edited by Frank Kermode (London: Faber and Faber, 1975): 45–9.

Ellis, Sarah. *The Women of England: Their Social Duties and Domestic Habits* (London and New York, 1839).

Federico, Annette R. '"An 'Old-Fashioned' Young Woman": Marie Corelli and the New Woman'. In *Victorian Women Writers and the Woman Question.* Edited by Nicola Diane Thompson (Cambridge: Cambridge University Press, 1999): 241–59.

Flaubert, Gustave. *Madame Bovary*. Translated by Geoffrey Wall (Harmondsworth: Penguin, 1992).

Fletcher, Robert P. '"Convent Thoughts": Augusta Webster and the Body Politics of the Victorian Cloister'. *Victorian Literature and Culture* 31, no.1 (2003): 295–313.

Forster, E.M. *Aspects of the Novel* (Harmondsworth: Penguin, 1962).

Foster, John. *Essays, in a Series of Letters* 7th edn, revised (London: Holdsworth, 1823).

——. 'The Morality of Works of Fiction'. In *Critical Essays Contributed to the Eclectic Review*. 2 vols. Edited by J.F. Ryland (London: Bohn, 1856), 1: 417–28.

Fradin, J.I. 'The Novels of Edward Bulwer-Lytton'. University Microfilms (Ann Arbor, Michigan, facs. edn, 1973). Doctoral Dissertation Series, publication no.19,238 (Columbia University, 1956).

Franklin, Caroline (ed.). *The Wellesley Series: British Romantic Poets* (London and Bristol: Routledge/Thoemmes, 1998).

Friedan, Betty. *The Feminine Mystique* (Harmondsworth: Penguin, 1992).

Froude, Richard Hurrell. *Remains of the Late Reverend Richard Hurrell Froude MA, Fellow of Oriel College, Oxford*. 2 vols (London: Rivington, 1838).

Fuller, Margaret. *Woman in the Nineteenth Century* (Oxford: Oxford University Press, 1994).

Fuller Ossoli, Margaret. *Woman in the Nineteenth Century, and Kindred Papers Relating to the Sphere, Condition and Duties of Woman*. Facs. edn, orig pub 1855. Edited by Arthur B. Fuller. With an introduction by Horace Greeley (Freeport, NY: Books for Libraries Press, 1972).

Gaskell, Elizabeth. *North and South*. Edited by Dorothy Collin (Harmondsworth: Penguin, 1970).

Gaskell, Peter. *The Manufacturing Population of England, Its Moral, Social, and Physical Conditions, and the Changes Which Have Arisen from the Use of Steam Machinery* (London: Parker 1836). Facs. edn (London: Cass, 1968).

Gatty, Margaret. 'Rabbit Tails'. *Monthly Packet* 16 (Series 1 1858): 381–402.

Geertz, Clifford. 'Thick Description: Toward an Interpretive Theory of Culture'. In *The Interpretation of Cultures*, 3–30 (London: Hutchinson, 1975).

Goldsmith, Oliver. *The Vicar of Wakefield*. In *Miscellaneous Works*. With an introduction by David Masson (London: Macmillan, 1874).

Goleman, Daniel. *Emotional Intelligence: Why It Can Matter More Than IQ* (New York: Bantam Books, 1995).

Gramsci, Antonio. *Selections from Cultural Writings*. Edited by David Forgacs and Geoffrey Nowell-Smith. Translated by William Boelhaver (London: Lawrence and Wishart, 1985).

Grandmother. 'Correspondence'. *Monthly Packet* 24 (Series 1 1862): 440–4.

Green-Lewis, Jennifer. *Framing the Victorians: Photography and the Culture of Realism* (Ithaca: Cornell University Press, 1996).

Haley, Bruce. *The Healthy Body and Victorian Culture* (Cambridge, MA: Harvard University Press, 1978).

Hanson, Ellis. *Decadence and Catholicism* (Cambridge, MA: Harvard University Press, 1997).

Hardy, Barbara. *The Appropriate Form: An Essay on the Novel* (London: The Athlone Press, 1964).

Harrison, Antony H. *Victorian Poets and the Politics of Culture: Discourse and Ideology* (Charlottesville and London: University Press of Virginia, 1998).

Hayter, Alethea. *Charlotte Yonge* (Plymouth: Northcote House, 1996).

Helsinger, Elizabeth K., Robin Lauterbach Sheets and William Veeder. *The Woman Question: Society and Literature in Britain and America, 1837–1883*. 3 vols (New York: Garland, 1983).

Hilton, Boyd. *The Age of Atonement: The Influence of Evangelicalism on Social and Economic Thought, 1795–1865* (Oxford: Clarendon Press, 1988).

Hoffman, Michael J., and Patrick D. Murphy (eds). *Essentials of the Theory of Fiction* (London: Leicester University Press, 1996).

Holloway, John. *The Victorian Sage: Studies in Argument* (New York: Archon Books, 1953).

Hopkins, Gerard Manley. *Selected Prose*. Edited by Gerald Roberts (Oxford: Oxford University Press, 1980).

Horne, Thomas Hartwell. *An Introduction to the Critical Study and Knowledge of the Holy Scriptures*. 4th edn (London: Cadell, 1823).

Hughes, Thomas. *Tom Brown's Schooldays* (London: Gawthorn, n.d.).

——. *The Manliness of Christ* (London: Macmillan, 1894).

Hume, David. *Enquiries Concerning Human Understanding and Concerning the Principles of Morals*. Edited by P.H. Nidditch (Oxford: Clarendon Press, 1975).

——. *A Treatise of Human Nature*. 2nd edn. Edited by L.A. Selby-Bigge and P.H. Nidditch (Oxford: Clarendon Press, 1978).

Hutton, R.H. 'Ethical and Dogmatic Fiction: Miss Yonge'. *National Review* 12 (1861): 211–30.

Huysmans, J.-K. 'Préface Ecrite Vingt Ans Après le Roman'. In *À Rebours*, i–xxiv (Paris: Bibliothèque-Charpentier, 1925).

Irving, Edward. *The Doctrine of the Incarnation Opened*. In *Collected Writings*. Edited by G. Carlyle (London: Strahan, 1865).

James, Henry. 'Preface'. In *The Tragic Muse*, v–xxii (New York: Scribner's, 1936).

Jameson, Anna. *Legends of the Madonna, as Represented in the Fine Arts* (London: Longman, Brown, Green and Longmans, 1852).

Jay, Elisabeth. *Faith and Doubt in Victorian Britain* (London: Macmillan, 1986).

——. 'Charlotte Mary Yonge and Tractarian Aesthetics'. *Victorian Poetry* 44, no.1 (2006): 43–59.

Jay, Elizabeth. *The Religion of The Heart: Anglican Evangelicalism and The Nineteenth Century Novel* (Oxford: The Clarendon Press, 1979).

Jeffrey, Francis. 'Review of "Records of Woman" and "The Forest Sanctuary"'. *Edinburgh Review* 50 (October 1829).

Jennings, William. 'Tendencies of Modern Logic'. *Dublin Review* 36 (1854): 419–51.

Jessop, Ralph. *Carlyle and Scottish Thought* (Houndmills: Macmillan, 1997).

Kaplan, Fred. *Dickens and Mesmerism: The Hidden Springs of Fiction* (Princeton: Princeton University Press, 1975).

Keats, John. *The Letters of John Keats, 1814–1821*. 2 vols. Edited by Hyder Edward Rollins (Cambridge, MA: Harvard University Press, 1958).

Keble, John. *Sermons Academical and Occasional* (Oxford and London: Parker and Rivington, 1848).

——. *On the Mysticism Attributed to the Early Fathers of the Church* (Oxford and London: Parker, 1868).

——. *Keble's Lectures on Poetry, 1832–1841*. 2 vols. Translated by Edward Kershaw Francis (Oxford: Clarendon Press, 1912).

——. *The Christian Year*. With an introduction by J.C. Shairp (London and New York: Dent and Dutton, 1914).

Kettle, Arnold. *An Introduction to the English Novel: Volume One, to George Eliot* (London: Arrow, 1962).

Kingsley, Charles. *'What, Then, Does Dr Newman Mean?': A Reply to a Pamphlet Lately Published by Dr Newman* (London and Edinburgh: Macmillan, 1864).

——. *Two Years Ago* (London: Macmillan, 1886).

Korshin, Paul. *Typologies in England, 1650–1820* (Princeton: Princeton University Press, 1982).

Krueger, Christine L. *The Reader's Repentance: Women Preachers, Women Writers and Nineteenth-Century Social Discourse* (Chicago: University of Chicago Press, 1992).

Landow, George P. *Victorian Types, Victorian Shadows : Biblical Typology in Victorian Literature, Art and Thought* (London: Routledge and Kegan Paul, 1980).

LaPorte, Charles. 'George Eliot, the Poetess as Prophet'. *Victorian Literature and Culture* 31, no.1 (2003): 159–79.

Laqueur, Thomas. *Solitary Sex: A Cultural History of Masturbation* (New York: Zone Books, 2003).

Lawrence, D.H. *Selected Literary Criticism*. Edited by Anthony Beal (London: Heinemann, 1955).

Leavis, Q.D. *Fiction and the Reading Public* (London: Chatto and Windus, 1932).

——. 'Charlotte Yonge and Christian Discrimination'. *Scrutiny* 12 (1944): 153–59.

Levine, George. 'Determinism and Responsibility in the Works of George Eliot'. *Publications of the Modern Language Society of America* 77 (1962): 268–77.

——. *The Boundaries of Fiction: Carlyle, Macaulay, Newman* (Princeton: Princeton University Press, 1968).

——. *The Realistic Imagination: English Fiction from Frankenstein to Lady Chatterley* (Chicago: University of Chicago Press, 1981).

——. *Darwin Among the Novelists: Patterns of Science in Victorian Fiction* (Cambridge, MA and London: Harvard University Press, 1988).

Lewis, Sarah. *Woman's Mission* (London: John W. Parker, 1839).

Liebig, Justus. *Animal Chemistry, or Organic Chemistry in Its Applications to Physiology and Pathology.* Translated by William Gregory (London: Taylor and Walton, 1842).

Linton, Eliza Lynn. 'The Wild Women as Politicians'. *Nineteenth Century* 30 (1891): 79–88.

Littledale, Richard Frederick. *Innovations: A Lecture Delivered in the Assembly Rooms, Liverpool, April 23rd 1868* (Oxford and London: Mowbray and Simpkin, Marshall and Co, 1868).

Logan, Peter Melville. *Nerves and Narratives: A Cultural History of Hysteria in Nineteenth-Century British Prose* (Berkeley: University of California Press, 1997).

Low, Dennis. *The Literary Protégées of the Lake Poets* (Aldershot: Ashgate, 2006).

Mackay, Charles. *Extraordinary Popular Delusions and the Madness of Crowds* (1852) (Ware: Wordsworth Editions, 1995).

Magee, William. *Discourses and Dissertations on the Scriptural Doctrines of Atonement and Sacrifice.* London: Bohn, 1852.

Manns, James W. *Reid and His French Disciples* (Leiden: Brill, 1994).

Mansel, H.L. 'Sensation Novels'. *Quarterly Review* 113 (April 1863): 481–514.

Mansel, Henry Longueville. *The Limits of Religious Thought Examined in Eight Lectures* (London: Murray, 1859).

Mare, Margaret and Alicia C. Percival. *Victorian Best-Seller: The World of Charlotte M. Yonge* (London: Harrap, 1947).

Maynard, John. *Victorian Discourses on Sexuality and Religion* (Cambridge: Cambridge University Press, 1993).

Milbank, John. *Theology and Social Theory* (Oxford: Blackwell, 1990).

Mill, John Stuart. *Collected Writings.* 38 vols (Toronto: University of Toronto Press, 1969–1991).

——. *Autobiography and Literary Essays.* Edited by J.M. Johnson and Jack Stillinger (Toronto: University of Toronto Press, 1981).

Millingen, J.G. *The Passions: Or Mind and Matter* (London: Hurst, 1848).

Modiano, Raimonda. *Coleridge and the Concept of Nature* (London and Basingstoke: Macmillan, 1985).

Mossner, Ernest C. 'Beattie's "The Castle of Scepticism": An Unpublished Allegory Against Hume, Voltaire and Hobbes'. *Studies in English* 27 (1948): 108–45.

Musselman, Elizabeth Green. *Nervous Conditions: Science and the Body Politic in Early Industrial Britain* (Albany, NY: SUNY Press, 2006).

Newman, John Henry. *Parochial Sermons.* London and Oxford: Rivington and Parker, 1835.

——. *Loss and Gain* (London: Burns, 1848).

——. *Newman's University Sermons: Fifteen Sermons Preached Before the University of Oxford 1826–1843*. With an introduction by D.M. MacKinnon and J.D. Holmes (London: SPCK, 1970).

——. *An Essay on the Development of Christian Doctrine*. Edited by J.M. Cameron (Harmondsworth: Penguin, 1974).

Newsome, David. *Two Classes of Men: Platonism and English Romantic Thought* (London: Murray, 1974).

Nietzsche, Friedrich. 'On Truth and Falsehood in Their Extramoral Sense'. In *Early Greek Philosophy and Other Essays*. Translated by Maximilian A. Mügge (London and Edinburgh: Foulis, 1911).

Nockles, Peter Benedict. *The Oxford Movement in Context: Anglican High Churchmanship, 1760–1857* (Cambridge: Cambridge University Press, 1994).

Olson, Richard. *Scottish Philosophy and British Physics, 1750–1880* (Princeton: Princeton University Press, 1975).

Oppenheim, Janet. *'Shattered Nerves': Doctors; Patients and Depression in Victorian England* (New York: Oxford University Press, 1991).

Paley, William. *Works* (London: Allman, 1833).

Polidori, John. *The Vampyre, and Other Tales of the Macabre*. Edited by Robert Morrison and Chris Baldick (Oxford: Oxford University Press, 1997).

Porter, Roy. *Doctor of Society: Thomas Beddoes and the Sick Trade in Late-Enlightenment England* (London and New York: Routledge, 1992).

Prichard, James Cowles. *A Treatise on Insanity and Other Disorders Affecting the Mind* (London: Sherwood, Gilbert, and Piper, 1835).

Prickett, Stephen. *Romanticism and Religion: The Tradition of Coleridge and Wordsworth in the Victorian Church* (Cambridge: Cambridge University Press, 1976).

——. 'Keble's Creweian Oration of 1839: The Idea of a Christian University'. In *John Keble in Context*. Edited by Kirstie Blair (London: Anthem Press, 2003): 19–33.

Pugin, A.W. 'Contrasts; or, A Parallel Between the Noble Edifices of the Middle Ages and Corresponding Buildings of the Present Day'. In *Aesthetics and Religion in Nineteenth-Century Britain*, vol.4. Edited by Gavin Budge (Bristol: Thoemmes, 2003).

Pusey, E.B. *Parochial Sermons*. 3 vols (London: Walter Smith, 1883).

——. *Spiritual Letters*. Edited by Rev. J.O. Johnstone and Rev. W.C.E. Newbolt (London: Longmans, Green & Co, 1898).

Qualls, Barry. *The Secular Pilgrims of Victorian Fiction: The Novel as Book of Life* (New York: Cambridge University Press, 1982).

Reed, John R. *Victorian Will* (Athens: Ohio University Press, 1989).

Reed, John Shelton. *Glorious Battle: The Cultural Politics of Victorian Anglo-Catholicism* (Nashville and London: Vanderbilt University Press, 1996).

Reid, Thomas. *Works*. 7th edn. Edited by William Hamilton (Edinburgh: Maclachlan and Stewart, 1872).

Risse, Guenter B. 'Hysteria at the Edinburgh Infirmary: The Construction and Treatment of a Disease 1770–1800'. *Medical History* 31 (1988): 1–22.

———. 'Brunonian Therapeutics: New Wine in Old Bottles?' In *Brunonianism in Britain and Europe* (*Medical History*, Supplement no.8). Edited by W.Y. Bynum and Roy Porter, 46–62, 1988.

Roden, Frederick S. *Same-Sex Desire in Victorian Religious Culture* (Houndmills: Palgrave Macmillan, 2002).

Romanes, Ethel. *Charlotte Mary Yonge: An Appreciation* (London: Mowbray, 1908).

Rossetti, D.G. 'Jenny'. In W.M. Rossetti (ed.), *Poetical Works* (London: Ellis and Elvey, 1895): 83–94.

Rothfield, Lawrence. *Vital Signs: Medical Realism in Nineteenth-Century Fiction* (Princeton: Princeton University Press, 1992).

Rubin, Gayle. 'The Traffic in Women: Notes on the "Political Economy" of Sex'. In *Toward an Anthropology of Women*. Edited by R. Reiter (New York: Monthly Review Press, 1975).

Ruskin, John. *Works*. 39 vols. Edited by E.T. Cook and Alexander Wedderburn (London: Allen, 1903–1912).

R.W. 'A Discussion with Aunt Mena: Obedience'. *Monthly Packet* 4 (Series 1 1852): 1–7.

Sandbach-Dahlström, Catherine. *Be Good Sweet Maid: Charlotte Yonge's Domestic Fiction A Study in Dogmatic Purpose and Fictional Form* (Stockholm: Almqvist & Wicksel, 1984).

Schaffer, Talia. 'The Mysterious Magnum Bonum: Fighting to Read Charlotte Yonge'. *Nineteenth-Century Literature* 55, no.2 (2000): 244–75.

Schneewind, J.B. 'Moral Problems and Moral Philosophy in the Victorian Period'. *Victorian Studies* 9, no. Supplement (September 1965): 29–46.

Sedgwick, Eve Kosofsky. *Between Men: English Literature and Male Homosocial Desire* (New York: Columbia University Press, 1985).

Shelley, Percy Bysshe. 'A Defence of Poetry'. In *The Major Works*. Edited by Zachary Leader and Michael O'Neill (Oxford: Oxford University Press, 2003): 647–701.

Shuttleworth, Sally. *Charlotte Brontë and Victorian Psychology* (Cambridge: Cambridge University Press, 1996).

Shuttleworth, Sally, and Jenny Bourne Taylor (eds). *Embodied Selves: An Anthology of Psychological Texts 1830–1890* (Oxford: Clarendon Press, 1998).

Small, Helen. *Love's Madness: Medicine, the Novel and Female Insanity 1800–1865* (Oxford: Clarendon Press, 1996).

Smith, Adam. *Theory of Moral Sentiments*. Edited by D.D. Raphael and A.L. Macfie (Oxford: Oxford University Press, 1976).

Southey, Robert. Review of *Propositions for ameliorating the Condition of the Poor* etc by P. Colquhoun. *Quarterly Review* 8 (1812): 319–56.

Stephens, F.G. *William Holman Hunt and His Works: A Memoir of the Artist's Life with Description of His Pictures* (London: Nisbet, 1860).

Stewart, Dugald. *Collected Works*. Orig pub 1854, 11 vols. Edited by William Hamilton. With an introduction by Knud Haakonssen (Bristol: Thoemmes, 1994).

Stuart, Charles. *The West India Question* (London, 1832).

Sturrock, June. *'Heaven and Home': Charlotte M Yonge's Domestic Fiction and the Victorian Debate Over Women*. English Literary Studies (Victoria BC: University of Victoria, 1995).

Sussman, Herbert. *Fact Into Fiction: Typology in Carlyle, Ruskin, and the Pre-Raphaelite Brotherhood* (Columbus: Ohio State University Press, 1979).

Sutton-Ramspeck, Beth. 'Shot Out of the Canon: Mary Ward and the Claims of Conflicting Feminisms'. In *Victorian Women Writers and the Woman Question*, edited by Nicola Diane Thompson (Cambridge: Cambridge University Press, 1999): 204–22.

Taylor, Barbara. *Mary Wollstonecraft and the Feminist Imagination* (Cambridge: Cambridge University Press, 2003).

Taylor, Jenny Bourne. *In the Secret Theatre of Home: Wilkie Collins, Sensation Narrative and Nineteenth Century Psychology* (Routledge: London and New York, 1988).

Tennyson, Alfred. 'Maud'. In *Poems and Plays*. Edited by T. Herbert Warren, revised by Frederick Page (Oxford: Oxford University Press, 1965): 266–86.

Tennyson, G.B. *Victorian Devotional Poetry: The Tractarian Mode* (Cambridge, Mass: Harvard University Press, 1981).

——. '"So Careful of the Type?" – Victorian Biblical Typology: Sources and Applications'. *Essays and Studies* 37 (1984): 31–45.

Thackrah, C.T. *The Effects of Arts, Trades, and Professions, and of Civic States and Habits of Living: With Suggestions for the Removal of Many of the Agents Which Produce Disease, and Shorten the Duration of Life*. 2nd edn (London: Longman, 1832).

Thomas, Stephen. *Newman and Heresy: The Anglican Years* (Cambridge: Cambridge University Press, 1991).

Thompson, Nicola Diane. *Reviewing Sex: Gender and the Reception of Victorian Novels* (Houndmills: Macmillan, 1996).

——. 'Responding to the Woman Questions: Rereading Noncanonical Victorian Women Novelists'. In *Victorian Women Writers and the Woman Question*. Edited by Nicola Diane Thompson (Cambridge: Cambridge University Press, 1999): 1–23.

Toland, John. *Christianity not Mysterious* (Dublin: Lilliput Press, 1997).

Trench, Richard Chevenix. *On the Study of Words and English Past and Present* (London and Toronto: Dent and Dutton, n.d.).

Tromp, Marlene. 'Spirited Sexuality: Sex, Marriage and Victorian Spiritualism'. *Victorian Literature and Culture* 31, no.3 (2003): 67–81.

——. *Altered States: Sex, Nation, Drugs and Self-Transformation in Victorian Spiritualism* (Albany, NY: SUNY Press, 2006).

Vargish, Thomas. *The Providential Aesthetic in Victorian Fiction* (Charlottesville: Virginia University Press, 1985).

Verlaine, Paul. 'Langueur'. In *French Symbolist Poetry*, translated by C.F. Macintyre, 32 (Berkeley, CA: University of California Press, 1958).

Warburton, William. *Collected Works*. Facs. edn, 13 vols. With an introduction by Gavin Budge (Bristol: Thoemmes Press, 2005).

——. *The Divine Legation of Moses Demonstrated. Works* (London, 1811).

Ward, W.G. 'Review of *A System of Logic* by J.S. Mill'. *British Critic* 34 (1843): 349–427.

Waterman, A.M.C. *Revolution, Economics and Religion: Christian Political Economy, 1798–1833* (Cambridge: Cambridge University Press, 1991).

Watt, Ian. *The Rise of the Novel: Studies in Defoe, Richardson, and Fielding* (London: Chatto and Windus, 1957).

Weeks, Jeffrey. *Coming Out: Homosexual Politics in Britain from the Nineteenth Century to the Present* (London: Quartet Books, 1977).

Weinstein, Mark A. *William Edmondstoune Aytoun and the Spasmodic Controversy* (New Haven and London: Yale University Press, 1968).

Whately, Richard. *Elements of Rhetoric* (Oxford and London: Murray and Parker, 1830).

Wilde, Oscar. 'The Critic as Artist'. In *Complete Works*, with an introduction by Vyvyan Holland (London and Glasgow: Collins, 1966): 1009–59.

——. 'The Soul of Man Under Socialism'. In *Complete Works*, with an introduction by Vyvyan Holland (London and Glasgow: Collins, 1966): 1079–104.

Williams, Isaac. *The Gospel Narrative of Our Lord's Passion Harmonized: With Reflections* (London: Rivington, 1842).

——. 'On Reserve in Communicating Religious Knowledge'. Part One. *Tracts for the Times* (London and Oxford: Rivington and Parker 1842). Facs. edn in *Aesthetics and Religion in Nineteenth-Century Britain*. Edited by Gavin Budge, 6 vols (Bristol: Thoemmes 2003), vol 4, independently paginated..

——. 'On Reserve in Communicating Religious Knowledge'. Conclusion. *Tracts for the Times* (London and Oxford: Rivington and Parker 1843). Facs. edn in *Aesthetics and Religion in Nineteenth-Century Britain*. Edited by Gavin Budge, 6 vols (Bristol: Thoemmes 2003), vol 4, independently paginated.

Winter, Alison. *Mesmerized: Powers of Mind in Victorian Britain* (Chicago: University of Chicago, 1998).

Wolff, Robert Lee. *Gains and Losses: Novels of Faith and Doubt in Victorian England* (New York: Garland, 1977).

Wollstonecraft, Mary. *Vindication of the Rights of Woman*. Edited by Miriam Brody (Harmondsworth: Penguin, 1982).

Wordsworth, William. *Prose Works*. 3 vols. Edited by W.J.B. Owen and Jane Worthington Smyser (Oxford: Clarendon Press, 1974).

——. *The Prelude 1799, 1805, 1850*. Edited by Jonathan Wordsworth, M.H. Abrams, and Stephen Gill (New York and London: Norton, 1979).

———. *The Oxford Authors: William Wordsworth*, Stephen Gill (Oxford: Oxford University Press, 1984).

Yeo, Richard. *Defining Science: William Whewell, Natural Knowledge, and Public Debate in Early Victorian Britain* (Cambridge: Cambridge University Press, 1993).

Yonge, Charlotte M. *Abbeychurch, or Self Control and Self Conceit* (London and Derby: Burns and Mozley, 1844).

———. 'Introductory Letter'. *Monthly Packet* 1 (Series 1 1851): i–iv.

———. *The Castle Builders; or, The Deferred Confirmation* (London: Mozley, 1854).

———. 'Conversations on the Catechism: Conversation XXX. The First Commandment'. *Monthly Packet* 9 (Series 1 1855): 1–20.

———. 'Conversations on the Catechism: Conversation XXXI. The Second Commandment'. *Monthly Packet* 9 (Series 1 1855): 161–82.

———. 'Conversations on the Catechism. Conversation XXXIII. The Third Commandment. Reverence'. *Monthly Packet* 10 (Series 1 1855): 241–60.

———. 'Conversations on the Catechism'. *Monthly Packet* 14 (Series 1 1857): 225–41.

———. 'The Six Cushions'. *Monthly Packet* 1 (Series 2 1866): 205–14; 2 (Series 2 1866): 230–8; 409–1; 538–48.

———. 'Womankind'. *Monthly Packet* 17 (Series 2 1874): 24–9; 18 (Series 2 1874): 186–93.

———. *Magnum Bonum, or Mother Carey's Brood*. 3 vols (London: Macmillan, 1879).

———. *The Two Guardians, or Home in This World* (London: Masters, 1885).

———. *The Daisy Chain, or Aspirations* (London: Macmillan, 1886).

———. *Dynevor Terrace, or The Clue of Life* (London: Macmillan, 1888).

———. *Hopes and Fears, or Scenes from the Life of a Spinster* (London: Macmillan, 1889).

———. *The Young Stepmother, or A Chronicle of Mistakes* (London: Macmillan, 1889).

———. *Heartsease, or the Brother's Wife* (London: Macmillan, 1891).

———. *The Clever Woman of the Family* (London: Macmillan, 1892).

———. *Love and Life, An Old Story in Eighteenth Century Costume* (London: Macmillan, 1900).

———. *The Three Brides* (London: Macmillan, 1900).

———. *The Pillars of the House, or Under Wode, Under Rode*. 2 vols (London: Macmillan, 1901).

———. 'Authorship'. In *A Chaplet for Charlotte Yonge*. Edited by Georgina Battiscombe and Marghanita Laski (London: Cresset, 1965): 185–92.

———. *Abbeychurch / The Castle Builders*. Facs. edn (New York and London: Garland Publishing, 1976).

———. *The Heir of Redclyffe*. Edited by Barbara Dennis (Oxford: Oxford University Press, 1997).

———. Letter to Alethea Yonge, 30 September 1844 in *The Letters of Charlotte Mary Yonge (1823–1901)*. Edited by Charlotte Mitchell, Ellen Jordan and Helen Schinske, 2007. <http://hdl.handle.net/10065/337>.

316

Young, Edward. *The Harp of God: Twelve Letters on Liturgical Music: Its Import, History, Present State, and Reformation* (London: Nisbet, 1861).

Index

moral insanity 225–7
Morshead, Miss Anderson 65
muscular Christianity 59, 118
Musselman, Elizabeth Green 293
mysticism 132, 194
myth 198, 205

natural theology 62, 173, 295, 297
    and psychology, 301
naturalism 15, 28–9, 32, 39, 43, 62, 123, 139, 294
nervous irritability 17, 37, 40–1, 44, 51, 82–3, 100, 107–9, 118, 120, 162, 217, 228, 235, 252, 255–6, 269, 273–5, 279, 281–2, 293
    and gender 253, 258–9, 296, 298
    and mesmerism 259, 271, 285
    and moral power (female) 269, 292
    and women 249, 270
nervous subject 82, 111
    and masculinity 300
Newman, John Henry 24, 42, 53, 66, 241, 288
    and associationism 74, 88, 90, 95, 125, 199
    and character development 75, 100, 115
    and fiction (theory of) 198, 205
    and medical thought 74, 100
    and personal influence 76, 80, 154–5, 270
    and personal obedience 95, 97, 106
    and Personality of Christ 91, 93–4
    and providentialism 93, 209
    and rationalism (critique of) 79, 92, 94, 96
    and realist novel 167–8
    and Reid, Thomas 98
    and Roman Catholicism (conversion to) 85, 90, 114, 116, 192, 201
    and the unconscious 16, 112–13, 116, 209–10
    ideas

associationism 113
Atonement 94
calvinism (critique of) 100
Common Sense philosophy 97, 152
development 15, 89, 114, 168, 185, 199
heresy 16, 90, 101, 191
Incarnation 90
intuitionist philosophical position 153, 155
Mill, J.S. (critique of) 204
Paley, William (critique of) 93–4, 153
Personality of Christ 90, 92–3, 198
rationalism (critique of) 16, 97, 99–100, 103–6, 110, 124, 152–5
unreality, 99, 167
works
    Apologia pro Vita Sua 114–15
    Essay on the Development of Christian Doctrine 90, 101, 191
    Loss and Gain 15, 90, 101, 114–15, 167
    University Sermons 79, 90, 112, 152
Nietzsche, Friedrich 63, 179
novel
    and mesmerism 211
    and nervous irritability 210
    and self-consciousness 244
novel-reading 163

original sin 91, 179, 218

Paley, William 62, 69, 116, 296
poetry 262, 275
postmodernism 24, 61
poststructuralism 19, 31
preraphaelitism 69, 124, 127
Prichard, J.C. 225, 227
Prickett, Stephen 133–4